GCSE
Business Studies
for AQA

ALAIN ANDERTON

Causeway Press

Cover design by Tim Button
Cover image provided by Roy Wiemann/The Image Bank/2001
Graphics by Caroline Waring-Collins, Chris Collins, Rob Gittins and Alan Fraser
Cartoons by Alan Fraser
Photography by Andrew Allen, Alain Anderton and Dave Gray
Page design by Caroline Waring-Collins
Edited by Dave Gray
Reader - Mike Kidson

British Library Cataloguing in Publication Data
A catalogue record of this book is available from the British Library

ISBN 1-902796-29-2

Causeway Press Limited
PO Box 13, Ormskirk, Lancs, L39 5HP
© Alain Anderton
First impression 2001

Design and page origination by Caroline-Waring Collins and Rob Gittins (Waring Collins Limited)
Printed and bound by Butler and Tanner Limited, London and Froome

Acknowledgements
The publishers and the author would like to thank the following for the use of photographs and other material in this book.

AB Automotive Electronics p 128 (ta); Abbey National p 136 (tl); ALSTAM Transport p 122 (b); Arriva plc p 5 (bl,br); Barclays p 224 (tr); Big Yellow Group plc p 138; Billiton plc p 172 (ta); Blacks Leisure Group pp 106 (bac), 161 (ba, bb), 162 (tl, tr); BOC Group p 132 (ta); BT p 28 (t); Cadbury Schweppes p 100 (t); Chamberlin & Hill pp 156, 158; Charles Wait (process plant) Ltd p 58 (tl); Coca Cola p 73; Corel pp 10 (bbr), 17, 106 (tar), 151 (bb), 160 (b), 217; Coral Products plc pp 26 (tb, bl), 166 (lb); Cosmosair plc p 90 (br); CRH plc p 72 (b); Digital Stock pp 5 (t), 54 (b), 114 (t), 123 (ba), 172 (b), 173, 220 (ta); Digital Vision pp 6 (t), 12 (tl, tc), 24 (t), 30 (t), 110 (t), 118 (b), 120 (t), 122 (t), 123 (bb), 128 (ta), 176 (tr); Dti p 16 (tl, tr); Dixons p 132 (b); Equal Opportunities Commission p 16 (tc); Emap p 38 (tr); Europower p 144 (bb); Expro Group p 45; Express Dairies plc p 160 (tr); Express and Star p 133; First Technology p 132 (tb); Ford p 134; Games Workshop p 21 (ba, bb); GlaxoSmithKline pp 112 (t), 113 (bl, br); Halma plc p 23; Hand-Made Fish Co p 36 (tb); Hanson p 121 (l); Health and Safety Executive p 208 (t); Hewden Stuart plc p 170; HSBC pp 136 (tc), 224 (tc); Hurd Web Design p 33; IMI p 124 (ba, bb); IPC Connect p 38 (tl); Jarvis Porter Group p 166 (la); J.B. Broadley p 26 (bc); Johnson Matthey p 63 (tl, tr); KallKwik p 60 (b); Kingfisher plc pp 12 (lbl), p 38 (tl), 78 (bar), 216 (tl); Liverpool Football Club p 90 (bl); Lincat Group p 144 (ba); Loot Enterprises Ltd p 184 (l); Manganese Bronze Holdings plc p 139; MFI Furniture Group p 106 (bal); Millennium & Copthorne Hotels p 68; NatWest pp 136 (tr), 224 (tl); Nestlé pp 72 (t), 79 (ba), 86 (b), 98 (t); Network Photographers pp 18 (t) (Mike Goldwater), (b) (Jeremy Green), 19 (Nikolai Ignatiev), 22 (Mike Goldwater), 85 (Martin Meyer), 117 (Michael Abrahams), 143 (John Sturrock), 197 (Paul Lowe), 202 (John Sturrock), 207 (Peter Jordan), 212 (tl) (Mike Goldwater); Northern Recruitment Group plc p 168 (b); Oasis p 43 (ta, tb); Olivia Manduca p 74 (b); PA Photo Library/ The Press Association Ltd p 102; Peacocks plc 171 (ta); Personnel Publications Ltd p 184 (c); Pittards p 26 (ta); Photodisc pp 4 (ta, tb, b), 6 (bc), 8 (rc), 10 (tr, bal, bar), 11, 12 (lbr), 13 (tl), 16 (b), 20 (tl, tar, tbr), 24 (b), 27, 32 (b), 40 (tl, tr), 46 (t), 47, 48, 49 (ta, tb), 50 (t, b), 51, 53, 54 (t), 55 (t, b), 56 (tl, tr), 56 (ba, bb), 61, 66 (ta, tb), 67 (t, b), 74 (t), 76 (b), 80 (tl, tr, b), 89, 96 (t), 101, 104 (tbl, tbr), 105, 112 (ra, rb), 115, 120 (b), 124 (b), 125, 130 (t), p 136 (la, lb), 144, 146 (tl, tr), 150 (t), 151 (ba), 152, 153, 154 (t), 155, 157, 164, 168 (t), 174 (t), 176 (tl), 178, 179, 180 (ta, tb, b), 182 (ta, b), 186 (t), 188 (ta, tb), 190 (b), 191, 195 (tb), 192 (lf, t, f), 194 (tl, tr), 196 (b), 199, 200 (tb), 203, 208 (ba, bb), 209 (l, r), 212 (tr), 214 (ta), 216 (tr), 218 (b), 219, 220 (tb), 222 (tl, tr), 221 (l, c, r), 225; Plastics Engineering (Leamington) p 199 (ba, bb); Prontaprint p 60 (t); Renishaw plc p 128 (tb); Rex Features pp 6 (bl), 9, 10 (tl), 13 (tc, tr), 18 (tb), 41, 76 (t), 96 (bb), 114 (b), 124 (t), 128 (tc), 132 (tc), 135, 146 (ba, bb), 192 (ls), 196 (tl), 198 (ta, tb), 204, 206 (t), 215; Richer Sounds p 194 (b); Robinson Brothers Ltd p 185; Royal Bank of Scotland p 140 (b); Safeway p 88; Sainsbury's pp 104 (tal), 106 (tal); ScS Upholstery plc p 13 (b); SFI Group p 44; Silentnight Holdings plc 166 (r); Sky p 26 (br); SMG Magazines Ltd p 93 (tar); Sony pp 98 (lb), 102 (t); Spirit of Nature Ltd pp 36 (ta), 184 (r); Stagecoach plc pp 58 (tr), 99 (bb); Stephen Ramsay p 111; Stone Computers p 187; Tex Holdings plc pp 108 (bal), 167; Ghislain & Marie David de Lossy/The Image Bank/2001 p 149; Steve Niedorf/The Image Bank/2001 p 189; Steve McAlister Productions/The Image Bank/2001 p 205; Ghislain & Marie David de Lossy/The Image Bank/2001 p 216 (bl); Romilly Lockyer/The Image Bank/2001 p 216 (bc); Barros and Barros/The Image Bank/2001 p 216 (br); The Oriental Restaurant Group p 163; The Rank Group plc p 218 (tl); The Range Cooker Company p 159 (tl, tr); The Sunday Times p 37; TI Group pp 116 (tl, tr), 160 (tl); Tomkins plc p 172 (tb); Topham Picturepoint pp 6 (br), 8 (rb), 12 (la), 75, 81, 109 (bc), 138 (t), 142 (b), 154 (b), 182 (tb), 195 (ta), 196 (tr), 200 (ta), 206 (b), 211, 213; TT Group p 127 (ba, bb); Ultra Electronics p 59 (ba, bb); Umeco plc p 70 (tl, tr, b); Unilever p 93 (tbl); United Norwest Co-operatives Limited p 65; Wagon plc 129; Weldon Creamware p 14 (b); West Lancashire Economic Development Unit pp 30, 140 (t); Wolsely plc pp 62 (b), 104 (tar); WT Foods p 121 (r)

All other material is acknowledged at source.

PREFACE

GCSE Business Studies for AQA is based on the best selling **GCSE Business Studies** by Alain Anderton. It has been designed to be used as the core textbook for AQA Specification A. However, it is also suitable for use with other GCSE Business Studies specifications since the content of all specifications is broadly similar. In addition, the book will be useful for candidates being prepared for vocational GCSEs and standard and higher grade examinations. It has been designed in colour to give candidates a distinctive and unique resource for use in the classroom.

The book has a number of key features.

It is comprehensive The order of the book follows the order of content in AQA Specification A. Additional units have been included where appropriate to cover Specification A options. Enterprise and ICT activities can be found at key points throughout the book.

Unit structure The material has been organised into two page units. Each unit contains text, definitions of key terms, short answer questions and case studies. Data questions, enterprise activities and research exercises are also included in some units. The two page format is designed to help students focus and master a topic in Business Studies.

End of section case studies At the back of the book, there are six longer case studies designed to test a candidate's knowledge and understanding of one of the six key areas of Business Studies. These could be used as revision or as a test.

I would like to thank Dave Gray, who as usual has done a superb job editing the book. Mike Kidson proof read the work with great skill. The cartoons were drawn with great verve by Alan Fraser. The page origination of the book was sensitively accomplished by Caroline Waring-Collins. Not least I would like to thank my wife with all her help with the project.

The author and Causeway Press would welcome any comments you have to make about the book, whether critical or otherwise. We hope it greatly helps you in your teaching or learning of Business Studies.

CONTENTS

Wants and scarce resources

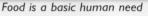

What is a business?

A BUSINESS is an organisation which produces **goods** or **services** (☞ unit 5). Different businesses produce different PRODUCTS. For instance:

- McDonald's produces fast food products, such as burgers;
- BT produces telecommunications services;
- the Post Office provides postal services;
- Volkswagen produces motor cars.

All businesses must organise different FACTORS OF PRODUCTION to make their products. Factors of production are the **inputs** into the production process. They are:

- LABOUR - workers, from machine operators to company executives to doctors and teachers;
- CAPITAL - machines, tools, offices, factories, shops and other physical assets which are used for a period of time, such as months or years;
- LAND - raw materials like crude oil or water, or land itself.

Take McDonald's as an example. It uses workers to cook and serve food in its restaurants. Each fast food restaurant is in a building and has cooking equipment and a seating area. These are examples of capital. The building is sited on land, a raw material.

Needs and wants

Consumers have basic human NEEDS. These are the things which people **must have** to survive. They are food and drink, shelter, warmth and clothes. In some countries

Food is a basic human need

today, people can't satisfy their basic human needs. Malnutrition may then occur or people might die from cold. In the UK, nearly everyone has enough income to buy essential products.

Needs are part of WANTS. Wants are people's desires to consume all goods and services, including essentials like shelter or food. Businesses SUPPLY products to satisfy those wants. For instance:

- McDonald's supplies fast food to satisfy consumers' hunger. The service is quick and people enjoy eating at a McDonald's restaurant;
- BT supplies telecommunication services to satisfy the desire of individuals and businesses to communicate;
- Volkswagen supplies cars to satisfy consumer desires to travel from one place to another for business or for pleasure.

Consumers seem to have no limit to their wants. However much they consume, they would always like to have more. For instance, once people own their home they often want a bigger house or one in a better area. They might also want to own a holiday home. If your income limits you to a one week holiday in Spain this year, you might have a two week holiday or visit more exotic places if you had more income. So wants are infinite. If incomes keep rising, so will people's wants. This will give greater opportunities for businesses to sell products.

You have organised yourself into a mini-company. EITHER answer the following questions for the business idea which you have chosen OR assume that you will bake and sell home made cakes as your mini-activity.

1. Make a list of all the resources your business will have to use to provide this service.
2. What choices might you have to make because you only have limited resources available? For instance, if you are making cakes, you might have to choose between ingredients which are cheap and those which are expensive.
3. (a) Explain what wants your products are designed to satisfy. (b) Why will customers demand your product rather than spend their money elsewhere?

Scarce resources

The world faces a situation of SCARCE RESOURCES. There are only 6 billion people alive who could be workers. The planet has only a fixed amount of land. Capital is scarce too. So only a certain number of goods and services can be produced by businesses. This means that customers are limited in what they can buy. They are forced to make CHOICES. With a limited income, a family might have to choose between buying a new car or going on holiday. A teenager might have to choose between buying a packet of crisps or a magazine.

Choices lead to DEMAND for a product. Demand for a product over a period of time is how much a customer will buy at any given price. For instance, demand each day for the *Sun* newspaper is

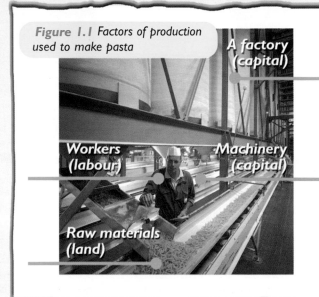

Figure 1.1 *Factors of production used to make pasta*

A factory (capital)

Workers (labour)

Machinery (capital)

Raw materials (land)

around 4 million copies. The demand during the winter season for a particular style of shoes might be 10 000 pairs. Over a week, 20 000 burgers might be demanded at a fast food restaurant.

Demand is not what customers would **like to buy** if they had unlimited incomes. It is what they **will buy** with scarce resources and limited incomes. The role of business is to satisfy this demand as efficiently as possible.

Arriva plc is a passenger services group. It operates in the UK and Europe.

1. What business activity of Arriva is shown in the photographs?
2. What resources are used by the business in providing its services?
3. Explain what consumer wants are being satisfied by Arriva's services.
4. (a) Suggest THREE ways in which Arriva could increase the demand for its services. (b) Explain how the use of resources might change for each of your suggestions.

Checklist

1. What is meant by 'a business'?
2. What products are made by:
   (a) Coca Cola Corporation;
   (b) Burger King; (c) Shell Corporation?
3. What resources do you think are needed to make a Volkswagen car?
4. What are the THREE factors of production?
5. What are a person's basic needs?
6. What is the difference between a need and a want?
7. Why are resources scarce?
8. Explain the link between scarce resources, choice and demand.
9. What is the difference between demand and supply?

UNIT 2
Specialisation and trade

Trade and exchange

In poorer countries around the world today, there are still examples of people who live and produce virtually everything they need for themselves. They grow their own food, build their own houses and make their own clothes. They are **self-sufficient**.

But most of the world's population don't live like this. They live in towns and cities and so can't grow the food they eat. Instead they rely on TRADE and EXCHANGE. In very simple societies, people make products and then BARTER or exchange them for other products. A farmer might swap a chicken for some wheat, or some eggs for a day's work. When goods or services are bartered, no money changes hands. One bundle of products is simply exchanged for another.

In a complex economy, people tend to work for businesses. In return for their time at work they are paid money. This money is then used to buy goods and services produced by other businesses. So a bus driver might work 38 hours a week for a bus company. In return, she would get paid wages. She may then spend these wages on products such as food, clothes and holidays.

Specialisation

Self-sufficiency is often a very inefficient way of producing goods and services. One reason is that it is almost impossible to be self-sufficient and make sophisticated products. Imagine a person trying to make a computer on his own. He would have to go to a mine and dig out iron ore for the metal. He would have build a factory to make microchips. He would have to be able to program software. He would have to generate electricity to run the factory and the computer.

SPECIALISATION allows computers to be produced without any single person having to make everything. Individual workers and businesses build up skills and knowledge in making **one part** of a finished product. They also own and use specialist capital equipment to help them. So a mining company extracts iron ore. A microchip manufacturer makes the chip. A plastics manufacturer makes the casings. A software company produces the programs. An electricity company provides the electricity.

Specialisation allows people to buy a much wider range of products than they could make on their own. Most products bought would be unavailable if we were still self-sufficient. British people wouldn't be able to consume bananas, holidays in Thailand or washing machines if specialisation didn't exist.

Specialisation also reduces the costs of products. Self-sufficient farmers hope to produce enough food for themselves and their family. A US farmer might grow enough wheat in one season to feed a thousand people. There are two reasons why specialisation reduces costs. First, specialisation allows resources to be used most efficiently. Instead of a Welsh farmer trying to grow wheat on poor soil, the wheat is produced on the most fertile wheat growing lands in the world. Second, specialisation allows physical capital (like tractors) and knowledge (like that used to create high-yield seeds) to be used. This allows far more to be made with the world's finite resources.

1. Explain what each business shown in the photographs specialises in producing.
2. How are the three businesses shown in the photographs interdependent?

Interdependence

Specialisation means that people and businesses are INTERDEPENDENT. Workers have to rely on others for the products they consume. Businesses buy products from other businesses and sell them to their customers. If one link in this chain is broken, production and consumption can come to a stop. For instance, if all petrol tanker drivers were to go on strike, it might take very little time for the UK economy to be on the verge of collapse. Workers wouldn't be able to get to work. Supplies of goods in the shops would start running out. Businesses would begin to run out of raw materials and wouldn't be able to move their finished products.

Interdependence is not just limited to the UK. GLOBALISATION means that people across the planet are dependent on other workers, businesses and consumers in different countries. A shirt may be made in India, a computer in Ireland, an orange in South Africa and a book printed in Italy.

Opportunity cost

Whether production is simple or complex, there is always an OPPORTUNITY COST in every decision. The opportunity cost is the benefit lost from the next best alternative. If you buy a magazine, the opportunity cost is the benefit you could have had by buying an ice cream. If a business buys a new machine costing £100 000, the opportunity cost might be the benefit from employing three workers for two years.

Businesses are constantly faced with decisions. To make the best decisions, they have to understand the opportunity costs of the decisions they take.

key terms

Barter - the direct exchange of products without the use of money.
Exchange - where one product is traded for another.
Globalisation - the process of ever increasing specialisation, trade and interdependence between different parts of the world economy.
Interdependence - where economies, businesses, consumers and workers are linked together through specialisation and trade and are reliant upon each other for their economic welfare.
Opportunity cost - the benefit lost from the next best alternative when making a choice.
Specialisation - system of production where economies, regions, businesses or people concentrate on producing certain products and trading them amongst themselves.
Trade - exchange of products either for money or through barter.

Reader Umbrellas makes and sells four million umbrellas a year. It has factories in the UK and in Thailand, but sells its products worldwide. It buys in many of the components to make umbrellas. For instance, the fabric to cover the umbrella is made by a company in France. The metal frame of the umbrella is made by a company in the UK. Reader designs the umbrellas, assembles them from bought in components and then sells them.

Its customers include shops and stores who sell the umbrellas on to consumers. However, it has also built up a market selling to businesses who put their messages and company name on the umbrellas. They are then used for advertising and promotion by employees or given away to customers.

1. What does Reader specialise in making?
2. Describe the activities of THREE other businesses which either buy from or sell to Reader.
3. Explain how the businesses mentioned in the case study are interdependent with each other.
4. (a) Suggest reasons why Reader has a factory in Thailand rather than making all its umbrellas in the UK.
   (b) What might be the opportunity cost of shutting its factory in the UK and moving all its manufacturing to Thailand?

Checklist

1. Explain the link between trade and barter.
2. Give TWO examples of barter from your own experience.
3. What is the difference between self-sufficiency and specialisation?
4. Explain the advantages of specialisation.
5. Explain the link between interdependence and specialisation.
6. A business spends £10 000 on photocopiers. What might be the opportunity cost of this decision for the business? In your answer, give THREE possible examples.

UNIT 3

Markets

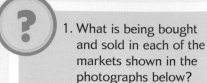

A market is where buyers and sellers exchange products

Markets

Businesses operate in the **market place**. When people hear the word MARKET, most think of a street market. Traders in the market have stalls where they sell or **supply** goods like food or clothes. Shoppers go from stall to stall to buy or **demand** the goods on offer. In Business Studies, the word 'market' is used more widely. A market exists wherever there are buyers and sellers exchanging products.

Different types of market

There are many different types of market. For instance, there is a **local market** for bread. Bakeries compete amongst each other to supply bread to consumers in a local area. There are **national markets**. For instance, there is a national market for cars. In the UK, car manufacturers compete to supply left hand drive cars to UK customers. There are also **international markets**. For instance, there is an international market in crude oil. Oil is produced in the Middle East and sold in Japan, the USA and Europe.

Markets can be defined by the product sold. For instance, there is an oil market. But within this market, there are also other markets. The market for unleaded petrol is distinct from the market for diesel or for heating fuel.

In some markets, like a street market, buyers and sellers meet face to face. But deals can be done and orders placed by letter or telephone, by fax or email, or over the internet.

Setting a price

A price is set whenever an exchange between buyer and seller takes place. In some markets, the price is set by the seller. For instance, if you buy fish and chips from a shop, the price is fixed. If the price of a good or service is too expensive, you won't buy. But in some markets, prices are negotiated between the buyer and seller. If you buy a second hand car, for instance, you may discuss the price with the car dealer. The result is that you may get a lower price than another customer for exactly the same car.

Another way to set prices is through auctions and tendering. In an auction, buyers compete amongst themselves, bidding up the price of the item for sale. The item is sold to the highest bidder. With tendering, the buyer invites suppliers to bid for a contract, like collecting rubbish from houses in an area over the next three years. The business which offers to do this for the least money wins the contract.

Market forces

Most goods and services are supplied through markets in the world today. The market is like a large voting machine. MARKET FORCES determine what is bought and what is produced. They also fix the price of products in a market.

Buyers Buyers have money to spend. They choose which products they want to buy from the millions on offer from sellers. For instance, a teenager might buy twenty different items in a week. Each time an item is bought, a spending vote is cast and demand is created.

Sellers Producers need spending votes in order to **supply** products

?
1. What is being bought and sold in each of the markets shown in the photographs below?
2. Who are the likely buyers and sellers in each market?
3. Explain how prices will be fixed in each of the markets.

★ Ford Focus

- **Ford Focus 1.4CL,** V reg, 1999, 5 door, 14,000 miles, 1 owner, full service history, aqua frost metallic, alloys, central locking, power front windows, climate pack, air conditioning, heated windscreen, heated washer jets, electrical heated door mirrors, twin air bags, CD player, fog lights, immaculate condition throughout, bargain £8,495 ono.
- **Ford Focus 1.8LX TDi,** V reg, 1999, rare car, tax, amparo blue, air conditioned, climate control pack, heated screens, electric windows and mirrors, central lock, immobiliser, radio cassette, clean condition inside and out, 50 plus mpg, 20,000 miles, first to see will buy, bargain at £9,750 ono.
- **Ford Focus,** T reg, 1999, metallic blue, usual electrics, 10 CD multichanger, immobiliser, excellent condition, £7,775 ono.

key terms

Market - where buyers and sellers meet to exchange goods and services.

Market forces - the forces of buying (or demand) and selling (or supply) which determine price and quantity bought and sold in a market.

Profit and loss - the difference between the money a business receives and its costs. A profit is made when costs are lower than receipts. A loss is made when costs are higher than receipts.

and survive in business. For instance, if a teenager buys the magazine *Just Seventeen* rather than *Sugar*, this gives money to the business which publishes *Just Seventeen*. It is then able to buy paper, employ staff and have the magazine printed. If a publisher launches a new teenage magazine which nobody buys, it will stop printing the magazine. It will not have the money to pay for the resources needed to keep the magazine going.

Profit

Profit acts as the most important signal for producers in a market. PROFIT is the difference between the money that the business receives and its costs, what it has to pay out. If the profit on a product is high, the business will tend to expand production and sales. If the business makes a LOSS, it will be forced in the long term to stop producing. A loss is the opposite of a profit. It occurs when the money paid out by a business is greater than the money it receives. Profits are a way for the market to tell producers that buyers value the product. Losses tell a business that buyers are not willing to pay what it costs to produce a product. If less money comes into a business than goes out, eventually it will have to close down.

Ron Brinston had been a pig farmer in Norfolk for the past thirty years. There were always hard times, but never this hard. Prices since 1980 had averaged at least 90 pence per kilogramme and in 1996 went as high as 135p. But since then, prices had collapsed. In 1998 they reached a low of 60p per kilogramme. In May 2000 the price was still only 75p.

The reason for the collapse was a sharp rise in the amount of pork brought in from abroad. The high value of the pound reduced the price of foreign pork to the British customer by 30p in the pound. At the same time, sales of British pork to foreign countries slumped because British pork was more expensive in foreign markets.

British pig farmers were also hit by higher costs. Over a two year period before the Millennium, farmers had to invest in new facilities. This was because the use of narrow stalls and tethers to keep pigs was banned on animal welfare grounds in January 2000. The BSE scandal had already led to higher slaughtering costs because of stricter inspection procedures.

The result was a sharp fall in the number of pigs on farms, down from 8.2 million in June 1998 to 6.5 million in June 2000. Ron Brinston had made a loss from his pigs for the past two years and he was thinking of getting rid of his herd.

Source: adapted from various sources, June 2000.

1. (a) 'Ron Brinston sells into the pig market.' Explain what this means.
   (b) Is this market for pork a local one in Norfolk, a national market for the UK or an international market? Give evidence from the passage to explain your answer.
2. Market forces drove down the price of British pork between 1998 and 2000. Explain TWO reasons for this fall in price.
3. In 1997, Ron Brinston made a £20 000 profit from his pig farming. In 1999, he made a loss of £10 000. (a) What is the difference between a 'profit' and a 'loss'? (b) Why did more losses in 2000 make Ron think about closing down his pig business?

Checklist

1. (a) Who are the two groups in any market? (b) What do they do in the market place?
2. The car market is a market. Give FIVE other examples of markets.
3. Give an example of a business which operates (a) in your local market selling bread; (b) in the national market selling cars; (c) in the international market selling crude oil.
4. Who decides what price is fixed (a) in a supermarket; (b) when a house is bought; (c) at a cattle auction; (d) when a car is serviced; (e) when a car is bought second hand?
5. How are producers rewarded in a market system when they sell products which customers want to buy?
6. Explain what happens to businesses which fail to supply goods that customers want to buy.

Planned, market and mixed economies

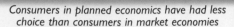

Markets

An ECONOMY is a system. This system sets the rules which influence:

- what is produced - for instance it might be 60 million cars and 1 million houses or 30 million cars and 2 million houses;
- how it will be produced - for instance, it might be produced in one huge factory with many machines and few workers, or in four small factories with few machines and lots of workers;
- who will receive the products - for instance, will the increase in the economy's production go mainly to the 'rich' or to pensioners?

In a MARKET ECONOMY, most production and distribution takes place through **markets** (☞ unit 3).

Businesses buy **factors of production** (☞ unit 1). Raw materials are bought in **product markets**. Workers are hired in LABOUR MARKETS. Buildings, machines and other equipment are bought or hired in **capital markets**. Businesses then sell what they have made either to other businesses in product markets or to consumers in **consumer markets**.

The role of profit

In a market economy, profits drive decision making by businesses. If a business can't make a profit on what it sells, it will be forced out of business. Businesses which sell products that customers want, at the right price, will earn high profits. For example, coal mining companies have closed mines in the UK because they have become unprofitable. In contrast, Starbucks, the US chain of coffee shops, has expanded in the UK. It has been able to increase profits by opening new outlets.

The state

For a market economy to work properly, the state has to provide some basic services. For instance, there has to be a set of laws which protect private property. People will not set up in business if they think that their production will be stolen by others. The state has to create a financial system, including the printing of notes and coins.

Also, markets are not always the best way to provide goods and services. Some services, like the army or prisons, would not be provided if left to markets. Others, like education or health care, would be bought mainly by higher income earners. The poor would struggle to afford them. Some services, like health care or the roads, would also cost more if provided purely by markets.

To pay for the services it creates, the state collects taxes from consumers, workers and businesses (☞ unit 7).

Market and mixed economies

There are two main types of market economy. The United States and Japan are examples of market economies (sometimes called FREE MARKET ECONOMIES). In these economies, more than 60 per cent of consumer goods and services is provided through markets in the PRIVATE SECTOR. Private sector

1. Which of the goods or services shown in the photographs are likely to be provided: (a) through the market or (b) by government in the UK?
2. 'The government should provide high quality free health care for all, paid for through taxes.' 'Health care should be provided entirely by the private sector.' Giving reasons, say which statement you agree with.

businesses are ones which are not owned by the state. Less than 40 per cent of products is provided by the state in the PUBLIC SECTOR.

Italy, France, Germany and the UK are examples of MIXED ECONOMIES. In a mixed economy, between 40 and 60 per cent of products is provided by the state. The rest is provided by the private sector.

Planned economies

A third type of economy is a PLANNED ECONOMY. In this type of economy, businesses are mostly owned by the state. Government planners decide what is going to be produced, how, where and when. They also decide who will receive the products. The role of businesses is to carry out the orders of the state.

For instance, Russia was a command economy from the 1920s to the 1980s. Avtogaz was the country's second largest car manufacturer. Like other Russian businesses, it was given production targets by government planners. It was told how many raw materials it could use and how many workers to employ to meet its targets. The business had no real competition because there were long waiting lists for new cars.

Today, Russia, like nearly all former planned economies, is being turned back to a mixed economy. This is because planned economies have not provided the benefits of mixed and free market economies. They restricted choice to consumers, goods were often of poor quality and standards of living didn't rise as fast as in market economies.

key terms

Economy - a system, a set of rules which influences what is produced, how it will be produced and who will receive the products.
Labour markets - markets in which workers supply and employers demand the services of labour.
Market or free market economy - an economy where over 60 per cent of consumer goods and services are produced by private sector businesses and sold through markets.
Mixed economy - an economy where over 40 per cent of consumer goods and services are produced by the state and not sold through markets.
Planned economy - economy where most consumer goods and services are produced by the state and state owned businesses.
Private sector - the part of the economy owned and controlled by private individuals and businesses.
Public sector - part of the economy owned and controlled by the state or government.

In 2001, the London Underground was one of the last major businesses owned by the government. But many people were unhappy with its performance. Londoners using the underground were faced with overcrowding at peak times, old trains, cancellations and badly maintained stations. Also, fares were some of the highest in the world.

One solution was for the government to invest large amounts to upgrade the system. Existing infrastructure (tunnels, track and trains) would be repaired or replaced. New lines would be opened. At the same time, fares would be brought down to encourage Londoners to use public transport. However, this would require large amounts of government and therefore taxpayers' money to fund. The investment would total billions of pounds. Also, cutting fares could mean that the underground ran at a loss.

An alternative was to sell the underground to private companies to own and run. The government would then not have to pay anything. But the fear was that private companies would fail to invest, fares would be even higher and the service would be even worse. After all, the private companies would need to make a profit.

A third idea was being pursued by government. It would still own and be responsible for running the underground. But private sector companies would improve the infrastructure. They would invest billions of pounds over a thirty year period and in return would be paid an annual fee by London Transport for use of the system. The fee and the work to be done would be agreed in advance. This would encourage the private sector firms to complete the work as efficiently as possible. It also meant that the government did not have to pay for investment. The money would come from the fares paid by Underground users.

1. Explain whether the London Underground was in the public or private sector in 2001.
2. Suggest why the government in 2001 did not want to modernise the London Underground system itself.
3. If government plans went ahead, work to modernise the Underground would be done by the private sector. Why might a private sector business want to invest billions of pounds in this project?
4. Discuss whether Londoners will benefit from a modernisation completed by the private sector.

✓Checklist

1. What is an economy?
2. 'A market economy is one where most consumer goods and services are produced by private sector businesses and are then sold to consumers.' Explain what this means.
3. What is the difference between a free market economy and a mixed economy?
4. What services are often provided by government in mixed economies?
5. What is the role of a state owned business in a planned economy?
6. Explain what has happened to the planned economies of Eastern Europe and Russia in recent years.

Primary, secondary and tertiary sectors

Industries in the primary, secondary and tertiary sectors

? 1. Draw and label a chain of production for the chocolate bar using the information in the photographs. Start with the primary sector and finish with the tertiary sector.

Sectors of industry

Businesses can be classified (i.e. grouped together) in different ways. One way is to group them by industry. So all shops selling food could be classified as retailers. All farms could be classified as part of agriculture. All schools and colleges could be classified under education. These industries are then often grouped into three sectors - the primary, secondary and tertiary sectors.

The primary sector

The PRIMARY SECTOR is that part of the economy where raw materials are extracted, grown or cut down. One industry in the primary sector is agriculture. Farmers grow crops like wheat and rear animals for slaughter like pigs or sheep. Fishing is another example of an industry in the primary sector. So is mining and quarrying. Coal mines produce fuel, whilst quarries produce stone for building or for road construction. Finally, very important to the UK, is oil and natural gas extraction, mainly from the North Sea.

Industries in the primary sector produce RAW MATERIALS which are needed to make other goods and services. Wheat, pork, fish, timber, coal, oil and gas are all examples of raw materials.

The secondary sector

The SECONDARY SECTOR is also called the MANUFACTURING SECTOR of industry. It is the sector where GOODS are produced. These range from steel bars to paper to motor vehicles to tins of food. A good is a physical product. It can be seen and touched. Goods are made from the raw materials produced by industries in the primary sector. Examples of industries in the secondary sector include energy and water supply, construction and all manufacturing industries.

The tertiary sector

The TERTIARY SECTOR is also called the SERVICE SECTOR of the economy. It is where SERVICES are produced. A service is a non-physical product like a haircut or a train journey. A service cannot be touched physically. Nor can services be stored for use in the future like a good. Services are used up immediately they are created. The main industries in the tertiary sector are:

- distribution of goods, including retailing;
- communication, such as telephone calls and postal services;
- hotels and restaurants;
- financial services, such as banks, building societies and insurance;
- transport and storage, such as road haulage, shipping, and rail and air travel;
- defence (army etc.) and public administration (e.g. the civil service);
- education, including schools and colleges;
- health and social work.

As Figure 5.1 shows, the tertiary sector has grown at a faster rate than the primary and secondary sectors over the past 40 years. As consumers' incomes grow, the proportion spent on services has grown. Today, about two thirds of all spending is on services.

The chain of production

Primary, secondary and tertiary industries are linked together in a CHAIN OF PRODUCTION. For example, wheat is grown on farms in the primary sector. Wheat is then turned into flour in a flour mill in the secondary sector. The flour is used

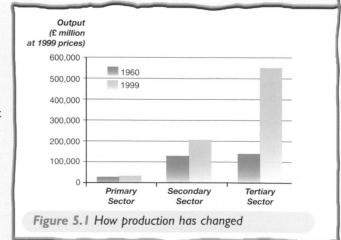

Output (£ million at 1999 prices)

- 1960
- 1999

Primary Sector / Secondary Sector / Tertiary Sector

Figure 5.1 *How production has changed*

to make bread in a bakery, also in the secondary sector. Finally, the bread is sold in shops and supermarkets in the tertiary sector. This chain of production is shown in Figure 5.2.

Businesses at different stages of the chain of production are customers and suppliers. A CUSTOMER is a business, individual or organisation which buys a good or service from a SUPPLIER. For instance, the bakery buys wheat from a farm. The bakery is the customer, whilst the farm is the supplier. Here, wheat is an example of a PRODUCER GOOD. This is a product which is bought by one business from another. It is used to make other products. Wheat is used to make bread which is sold to CONSUMERS. The bread is then a CONSUMER GOOD. The consumer is the individual who ultimately buys and uses the product. Consumer goods are products such as fish and chips, CDs or magazines which individuals buy from businesses.

Ingredients (Wheat)	Production (Bakery)	Sales to customers (Bread)

Figure 5.2 *Chain of production for a loaf of bread*

key terms

Chain of production - **the various production stages through which a product passes before being sold to a consumer.**
Consumer - **the person who ultimately uses (or consumes) a product.**
Consumer good - **a good or service which is sold to people (consumers) rather than other businesses.**
Customer - **a business or individual who buys products from a business.**
Goods - **physical products, like a car or a cabbage.**
Primary sector - **part of the economy where businesses mine, grow, collect or cut down raw material.**
Producer good - **a good which is sold by one business to another and which is then used to produce other goods and services.**
Raw materials - **natural resources, like copper or coffee beans, used to make products.**
Secondary or manufacturing sector - **part of the economy where primary products are transformed into manufactured goods.**
Services - **non-physical products, like a haircut or a train journey.**
Supplier - **a business or individual who sells products to a business.**
Tertiary or service sector - **part of the economy where services are created.**

✓Checklist

1. Explain the difference between primary, secondary and tertiary industry.
2. Are the following workers employed in primary, secondary or tertiary industry:
   (a) a farmer; (b) a worker in a carpet factory; (c) an insurance salesman; (d) a train driver; (e) a worker on a fishing boat; (f) the manager of a pub; (g) a secretary working for a bakery; (h) a worker in a soft drinks bottling plant; (i) a lawyer; (j) a teacher?
3. What is the chain of production?
4. What is the difference between a producer good and a consumer good?
5. What is the difference between a customer and a supplier?

ScS is an upholstery specialist. It sells furniture such as settees, chairs and sofa beds. It has 31 stores in the UK, from Newcastle in the North of England to Southampton in the South. It has a highly successful formula which allows it to keep costs down but sales high.

Stores carry only demonstration models of furniture. When a customer buys a product, ScS orders the item from a manufacturer. The customer then has to wait whilst the piece of furniture is made. The only items that ScS owns are the ones on display in the stores.

New stores are built in a special way. Display areas are organised vertically by using a series of mini-mezzanine floors. These are floors which each only cover a small part of the horizontal area of the building. Customers are pulled up the building as they go from mezzanine floor to floor. This reduces the amount of ground space for the building and makes its costs much cheaper than for a traditional furniture store all on one ground level.

ScS is expanding fast. In 2000 it opened 11 new store.

Source: adapted from the *Financial Times*, 8.5.1999 and *ScS Annual Report and Accounts*, 2000.

1. 'ScS is a retailer.' Explain what this means.
2. Draw a possible chain of production for a leather sofa which is sold by ScS, going back from the retailer to the farmer.
3. Discuss whether ScS is a successful business.

UNIT 6

Location of industry

Location

How do businesses decide where to locate? Some reasons are linked to production (☞ unit 55). Others are linked to the business environment, as explained in this unit.

Tradition

Tradition is one factor which influences the location of industry. Most businesses don't change premises once they have set up. If they do move, it tends to be within 10 miles of the old site. This reluctance to move is called INDUSTRIAL INERTIA.

There is a number of reasons for this. One is that it is costly to move. There are the costs of the move itself. Also, the business will lose production whilst the move is

taking place. The further away the move, the higher the costs. If a business moves further than 10 miles, it may find that it loses key staff who aren't prepared to move house. Having to recruit and train new staff is expensive.

Another reason is that a business may enjoy EXTERNAL ECONOMIES OF SCALE. These occur when businesses in the same industry locate near each other. Because they are close together, they all enjoy lower costs. For instance, the most important centre for UK pottery making is Stoke-on-Trent. Firms like Wedgewood can benefit from lower costs because there is a large pool of skilled pottery workers in the area. Staffordshire University in Stoke and colleges in the local area

Industrial estates may be built on brownfield or greenfield sites

provide courses for workers for which businesses do not have to pay. There is a large number of businesses in the area which specialise in supplying materials and services to pottery manufacturers. So businesses don't have to spend much time finding suppliers.

Demography

DEMOGRAPHY is the study of the size of the population and changes in population. Many businesses, particularly in the **service sector**, are influenced by demographic factors. For instance, Bournemouth on the south coast of England has the highest percentage of elderly people in its population in the UK. People are attracted to move to Bournemouth to retire because of its climate and the services it offers. As a result, there are many businesses specialising in providing goods and services for the elderly in the Bournemouth area, such as retirement homes.

Infrastructure

The INFRASTRUCTURE of an area will affect location. Infrastructure is the built environment, such as roads, railways, airports, schools, houses, offices and factories.

Businesses often buy or rent premises which already exist. A business thinking of setting up a shop may be attracted by a site with a customer car park. A US business aiming to set up in the UK and send over 100 staff may be attracted to an area with good housing, schools and leisure facilities.

A few businesses, however, prefer

Weldon Creamware is a pottery business based in Stoke-on-Trent. Peter Weldon, the owner, set up the business after being made redundant from a ceramic giftware company in June 1994. Before that, he was at Staffordshire University in Stoke, where he gained a first class degree in ceramic design.

His business has been through difficult times and a number of changes of direction. He started out making ceramic clocks. When these failed to sell he changed to making large creamware pieces such as urns and jugs. He was able to employ an assistant, also trained at Staffordshire University, to make his range of products as the business expanded.

Peter Weldon has benefited from the long tradition of pottery making in Stoke. He was able to borrow money from The Princes Youth Trust, which provides funds for small businesses. Materials and equipment were hired or bought from local businesses.

Source: adapted from the *Financial Times*, 18.7.1998.

1. Explain FOUR reasons why Weldon Creamware is located in Stoke-on-Trent.
2. It might be £500-£1000 a year cheaper to rent premises in many areas of rural Wales than in Stoke-on-Trent. Do you think that Peter Weldon should move his business to rural Wales? Give reasons for your decision.

to build on BROWNFIELD or GREENFIELD sites. A brownfield site is a site which has been cleared of previous industrial buildings or houses. A greenfield site is one which is currently agricultural or other undeveloped land. Greenfield sites have never been built on before.

A business setting up on a brownfield or greenfield site may find it costly because it has to pay to put in sewers, water and gas pipes, electricity and telephone connections. Brownfield sites may also have existing pollution problems from previous use by heavy industry. However, a business may prefer a brownfield or greenfield site because it is able to build the infrastructure to suit its own requirements. Existing sites may not have enough parking, the local road system may be too congested, or an existing building may be poorly laid out.

Labour

Availability of labour is important in location decisions. For instance, a business will need to check that it can hire suitable labour in its new location. This means that workers in the area must have the right mix of skills. The cost of labour is important too. Many manufacturing firms have relocated production to the Far East to take advantage of very low wages. US and Japanese firms have often preferred to locate new factories in the UK rather than in France or Germany because the total cost of hiring labour is lower. Also, the UK labour force is well educated and trained.

Other factors

Other factors affecting international location within Europe are whether a country is in the European Union or not (☞ unit 9) and whether it is part of the single currency area. Some businesses may be able to obtain government grants and other aid for locating in a particular area, which will also affect their decisions (☞ unit 66).

✓Checklist

1. Explain why businesses might be reluctant to move from their existing premises.
2. Give TWO reasons why external economies of scale might exist for a business.
3. A business manufactures sofas for sale throughout the UK, whilst another business in the same area sells sofas to customers. Explain how a 20 per cent fall in the population in the area might affect both businesses.
4. Why might a shop set up in a new shopping centre with plenty of customer parking?
5. Why might a business choose to locate on a greenfield site?
6. A business wants to employ workers who are as highly skilled and motivated as possible. It also wants to keep costs to a minimum. Wages are higher and unemployment lower in East Anglia than in Wales. Which region should prove the most attractive to businesses and why?

There is a shortage of suitable space and sites for large relocation projects in the West Midlands. This is the claim of Alan Knight of James & Lister Lea, the Birmingham based property consultants. 'There is a lack of good quality sites within the West Midlands area - with the largest sites only stretching to 20 acres' he said. 'To attract the major investors such as Philips or Siemens their needs are for sites up to 200 acres. Other areas of the UK have these sites available and inward investors will go elsewhere if we cannot bring sites of that size into development. The region has the skill base, the infrastructure and the expertise to rival any part of the UK but it is the space that is holding us back.'

Most sites in the West Midlands are brownfield sites - sites where there has been industry in the past but which have often been cleared to make way for new industry. In contrast, regions like Wales, Scotland or the North of England are more likely to be able to offer greenfield sites to major international investors, giving businesses much greater flexibility to design a site for their needs.

Source: adapted from the *Express & Star*, 6.7.1998.

1. What is stopping some businesses from locating in the West Midlands, according to Alan Knight?
2. Explain what the West Midlands can offer businesses locating in the area.
3. A German electronics company wants to build a plant to make micro-chips for use in mobile phones. Discuss whether it should go to the region of Europe which offers it the highest government grants for locating there.

UNIT 7

The impact of government

(?) Gaylene Jackson has always been fascinated by American diners and coffee shops. She grew up in the United States but moved to the UK to study. After working as an accountant for a time she decided on a career change. With the help of friends she set up the first New England Diner. She found the perfect location - an old hardware store on the edge of a high street in South London with plenty of parking. Gaylene had to get planning permission to convert it into a restaurant. The premises were inspected by the fire service before it could open on safety grounds.

Her friend, a catering manager, helped choose the kitchen equipment and set up local suppliers. She concentrated her time on designing the dining area and on the marketing for the opening night. Ten staff, including two chefs, were taken on. Gaylene had to decide on the terms and conditions she would offer staff, which would be in their contracts of employment.

The diner was an enormous success. Her accounting skills meant that she kept a tight control on costs. She kept the financial records, a legal requirement for VAT inspectors and for the Inland Revenue, herself. Food was always prepared and served to the highest standards and she never had any problems with health and safety inspectors who checked the premises.

1. Explain FOUR ways in which Gaylene was affected by government laws and regulations when she opened and ran New England Diner.

Laws and regulations

Businesses are affected by the actions of CENTRAL and LOCAL GOVERNMENT. Central government makes laws and regulations which can influence how businesses operate. Local government issues and enforces regulations which can restrict business activity.

Ownership of property

Some laws protect a business's **assets** - what they own (☞ unit 79). For instance, squatters can be evicted from land and buildings owned by a business. Business inventions can be protected by patent law. Trademarks, like the arches of a McDonald's sign or the Nike 'swoosh' logo cannot be copied by competitors.

Contracts

A contract is an agreement between two parties. The law forces businesses which enter into a contract to keep to its terms. For instance, if a business agrees to buy supplies at a fixed price, the seller cannot then raise the price. Contracts give businesses much greater certainty when trading.

Legal organisation

The law states how businesses must operate and how they must be organised (☞ units 23-31). For instance, it lays down how profits are to be distributed in a partnership or what happens if a business ceases trading.

Planning regulations

Planning regulations influence where businesses can locate their premises. They tend to keep industrial premises away from areas of housing, for instance.

Government laws affect business

Environmental controls

Businesses are forced to comply with laws and regulations about pollution and other environmental matters (☞ unit 1). Electricity power stations, for example, have limits put on their emissions of gases.

Employment law

There are laws about how a business must treat its workers. For instance, employees must have a contract, stating the hours they will work and their wages. Workers cannot be sacked without good reason (☞ unit 105). Businesses can not discriminate against certain workers (☞ unit 105).

Health and safety

Health and safety laws make businesses responsible for health and safety in the workplace (☞ unit 103). Businesses may be prosecuted if workers or customers suffer accidents on business premises.

Consumer protection

Businesses face a number of laws which protect consumers. For instance, it is illegal for businesses to sell goods which are underweight or are faulty (☞ unit 104). Businesses may be forced to change incorrect statements about what a product can do or its ingredients.

Many laws limit what a business can do to protect the interests of other businesses, workers or customers. However, laws also give businesses valuable protection, for instance from unfair competition or from their inventions being stolen.

Taxes and government spending

Decisions that government makes about its SPENDING and TAXES

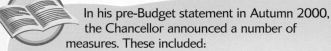

In his pre-Budget statement in Autumn 2000, the Chancellor announced a number of measures. These included:

- a cut in tax on low sulphur petrol and diesel of 3p a litre;
- a 50 per cent cut in the cost of a tax disk for lorries, averaging £715 per lorry;
- an increase in the state old age pension of £5 a week for single pensioners;
- a one year grant of between £4 000 and £30 000 for every school to spend on renovation and repairs;
- £23 million for a programme to get more single parents into a job.

1. Explain how each of the measures might benefit businesses.
2. Which industry do you think has particularly gained from these measures? Explain your answer.

Wordprocessing

3. You work in the public relations department of a large haulage company. Write a letter, preferably wordprocessed, to the Chancellor complaining that the measures announced in his pre-Budget statement did not go far enough in cutting taxes for haulage businesses. Explain why lower taxes for hauliers would benefit both consumers and businesses in the UK.

(called **fiscal policy**) affect all businesses.

The government might put up taxes paid by consumers. Raising income tax will reduce consumers' after-tax income. Raising VAT will increase the price of goods. The result will be that consumers will spend less, hitting sales by businesses.

The government could also put taxes on individual goods or services. For instance, it could put up taxes on cigarettes. This is likely to reduce the number of cigarettes bought because their price will rise. So cigarette manufacturers and other businesses

in the **chain of production** (☞ unit 5) for cigarettes will be affected.

Government is a major spender in the economy too. £4 out of every £10 in the UK is spent by government on everything from health care to education to roads. Increased government spending can lead to more orders for businesses. For instance, increased spending on drugs by the National Health Service (NHS) benefits pharmaceutical companies. A new road will lead to contracts for construction firms.

key terms

Central government - government run from the Houses of Parliament and the Civil Service in London. It is responsible for spending on programmes such as social security, health and defence. Its taxation and spending decisions can affect the performance of the economy.
Government spending - Expenditure on programmes such as social security, health, education and defence.
Local government - government responsible for spending on education, social services, roads, public libraries and refuse collection as well as enforcing law in areas such as trading standards. The UK is split up into areas, each run by a local authority.
Rate of interest - the percentage charged on a loan or given on savings as a reward for lending or saving money.
Taxation - a levy imposed by government on citizens and businesses to pay for its spending.

Interest rates

One important economic variable, controlled by government through the Bank of England, is the RATE OF INTEREST. This is the charge made for borrowing money. Most businesses borrow money. The higher the Bank of England sets interest rates, the more businesses will have to pay back in interest on loans. Falls in the rate of interest, on the other hand, will cut the costs of businesses and increase profits.

The rate of interest is also important for consumer spending. The lower the rate of interest, the more consumers are prepared to borrow to buy goods like cars, furniture or houses. So lower interest rates tend to mean more orders for businesses.

Interest rates can also affect the value of the pound against other currencies like the euro or the dollar. High interest rates tend to increase the value of the pound against other currencies. This raises the price of UK exports, making it more difficult for UK businesses to sell goods abroad. The price of goods bought from abroad tends to go down however.

Checklist

1. Heinz is a manufacturer of baked beans. How might the law protect it from another business which: (a) sells baked beans using identical packaging to Heinz including the Heinz name; (b) takes delivery of £10 000 worth of cans but fails to pay Heinz?
2. Explain whether a manufacturer could build a factory on any site in the UK.
3. Give TWO examples of how the law regulates the way a business treats its workers.
4. Explain how the following tax changes might benefit or harm business: (a) a rise in income tax; (b) a fall in VAT; (c) a rise in the tax on petrol and diesel.
5. Which businesses might benefit most from an increase in spending on road building?
6. 'Rocketing interest rates have hit my costs and my orders.' Explain why this could be true for a business.

Public ownership and privatisation

State owned businesses

Before 1980, many key industries in the UK were in the **public sector** (☞ unit 4). They were therefore owned by government. They included the rail, gas, electricity, coal, telecommunications and water industries. Companies such as British Airways (BA), British Telecom (BT), British Gas (now companies Centrica and Transco), British Rail (now Railtrack and other train companies) and British Petroleum (now BP Amoco) were fully or partly owned by government.

Many of these industries had been NATIONALISED between 1900 and 1980. Nationalisation means that companies were bought by the state from private sector owners, the shareholders. Today, the Post Office is the largest business still owned by the government. Other businesses still owned by the state are the BBC and the London Underground.

Privatisation

During the 1980s and 1990s, most PUBLIC SECTOR COMPANIES were PRIVATISED. This means they were sold off by the government to private buyers. So they are now PRIVATE SECTOR COMPANIES owned by private shareholders. There is a number of arguments in favour of privatisation.

Costs Most private sector companies aim to make profits. One way they can make more profit is by keeping their costs as low as possible. State owned businesses, on the other hand, have had little incentive to reduce costs because profits have only been one of the goals set by government. In practice, the companies and

industries which have been privatised, like gas and electricity, have seen costs fall. This means they are more **efficient** as producers.

Prices If costs fall after privatisation, this gives companies the opportunity to cut their prices to customers. So prices should be lower after privatisation.

The product The largest state owned businesses were usually **monopolists** (i.e. there was only one firm in the industry and so there was no competition). Without any competition, these businesses had little incentive to provide the goods and services that customers wanted. After privatisation,

Coal mining has been privatised but the London Underground is still owned by the state

businesses could increase their profits by taking into account what customers wanted. The quality of products and services therefore tended to improve.

Regulation

Some industries and companies which have been privatised operate

The Hatfield train crash shows why the railways should be renationalised. Railtrack, which is responsible for maintaining the track, knew that there was a problem with the rails at the scene of the accident months before. Yet Railtrack and Balfour Beatty, the private company responsible for repairing that section of track, did not do anything. With hundreds of different companies working on our rail system, what else can you expect?

If the railways were nationalised again, this sort of problem wouldn't occur. The railways would do its own repairs rather than relying on an outside contractor. Safety would not be put at risk in the way that it is today.

Of course, privatisation has led to some making large profits. But why should profits be made by a rail system which delivers overcrowding, late trains and a failure to cope with increasing passenger numbers? Even the investment programme to update the railway system over the next five years is going to be paid for mostly by the government. £30 billion of state cash is going to be pumped in. So why shouldn't the government simply own the system?

Source: adapted from *The Guardian*, 23.10.2000.

1. The article is arguing that the railways should be 'nationalised again'. What does this mean?
2. Explain THREE criticisms the article makes of the privatised rail system.
3. Discuss who might gain and who might lose out if the government were to nationalise the railways again.

in **competitive markets** (☞ unit 18). Competition often forces businesses to set lower prices. This is because, otherwise, they would lose customers and sales to other businesses. Telephone charges in the UK have fallen since privatisation, for instance, because BT has been forced to compete with businesses like NTL. Where there is no competition, as in the water industry, the government has set up **regulatory bodies**. These are:

- OFWAT for the water industry;
- OFGEM for the gas and electricity industries;
- ORR for the rail industry;
- OFTEL for the telephone industry;
- PostComm for the postal industry.

These regulatory bodies lay down rules for how businesses in the industry can compete. They also usually fix maximum prices that firms can charge. This ensures that the consumer is not charged too much. They may also lay down minimum standards of service that have to be provided.

Opportunities for business

Privatisation has created many opportunities for business.

Buying a former state owned business It is possible for businesses to buy companies which were previously owned by government. French and US companies now own and operate electricity and water companies in the UK, for instance.

Entering a market It is possible to expand into markets which before had been supplied by state owned monopolies. British Gas, also known as Centrica, used to have a monopoly on gas supplies. Today it faces competition from companies like Calor Gas which have entered the piped gas market. But Centrica has in turn entered the electricity and telecommunications markets. It now provides competition for local electricity companies and for BT, also a former nationalised

industry. In local markets, businesses can now **tender** (i.e. bid) for contracts to supply services like refuse collection and school cleaning. Before, these were always supplied by government departments.

Lower prices The prices of many products supplied by former nationalised industries have fallen. Gas, electricity and telephone charges, for example, have all come down. This gives British companies a competitive advantage over foreign companies in countries where these prices have not fallen as much.

Postal deliveries are to be thrown open to competition in towns and villages across the country. The Royal Mail, with its new company name of Consignia, will remain in public ownership. But it will lose its monopoly on the collection and delivery of letters in the UK. PostComm, the new regulator for the postal industry, plans to issue licences to rival companies from Autumn 2001.

There will be two types of licence issued. One will be for services in a local area. The other will be for deliveries over long distances such as between London and Birmingham, or between Manchester and Glasgow.

Licensed operators will be allowed to issue their own stamps and to install their own post boxes. To gain customers from the Royal Mail, they will have either to offer lower prices or a better service. For example, a local operator may choose to deliver three or four times a day, thus allowing same day delivery for letters.

The Royal Mail will be forced to retain its universal service obligation. This means it will have to deliver to every address in the country. It will also have to charge the same price whether the letter is going one mile or one hundred miles.

Source: adapted from *The Independent*, 19.2.2001.

1. 'The Royal Mail will remain in public ownership.' What does this mean?
2. What competition will the Royal Mail face from Autumn 2001?
3. Do you think that competition in the postal services market will benefit customers? Put at least one argument for and against in your answer.

Checklist

1. Explain the difference between the public sector and the private sector.
2. What is the difference between nationalisation and privatisation?
3. Give FIVE examples of industries which were privatised in the 1980s and 1990s.
4. Explain why privatisation might lead to lower costs for customers of the privatised industry.
5. (a) Which industries are regulated? (b) Why are these industries regulated?
6. Explain THREE ways in which privatisation might increase the opportunities for businesses to increase sales.

Trade between member countries of the EU, such as the UK, France and the Netherlands, should be as easy as trade within a country

A common market

The European Union or EU is a COMMON MARKET. This means that trade between member countries should be as easy as trade within a country. A business sited in Leeds, for instance, doesn't have to send its goods through customs control or pay taxes when it sends them from Leeds to London. Similarly, there are no taxes (taxes on imported goods are called TARIFFS or CUSTOMS DUTIES) or customs controls on trade between EU countries.

When the UK joined the EU in 1973, this was a great opportunity for UK businesses. Before 1973, some countries had imposed tariffs on products made in the UK. This raised their price, making them more difficult to sell. After it joined, UK businesses could compete on the same terms as other European companies and win orders throughout the EU. On the other hand, European businesses could also compete with UK businesses on the same terms in the United Kingdom. **Competition** (☞ unit 18) within the UK increased.

European Monetary Union

There are still barriers to trade between EU countries. One is that there are different currencies in the world.

The EXCHANGE RATE of one currency can change by the minute against another currency. So the pound constantly goes up and down in value against the US dollar and the Japanese yen. This means that UK businesses often do not know exactly how much they will receive in pounds for their sales sold abroad - their EXPORTS. Equally, they often don't know how much in pounds it will cost them to buy goods from abroad, which are IMPORTS for the UK.

What is more, businesses have to pay banks a commission to exchange foreign currency. Even if this is only 1 per cent, it still means a cost of £10 000 on a £1 million order.

There are ways in which businesses can minimise the risk of large changes in the value of the currency. For instance, they can agree a price at which to buy or sell currency for delivery later. This is known as **hedging**. However, it costs money to do this.

Monetary union To get around these problems, most countries in the EU entered into a **monetary union**. Individual currencies like the French franc, the German deutschmark and the Spanish peseta would disappear from 2002. They would be replaced by a single currency, the **euro**. This meant that the money used in Paris would be the same as the money used in Berlin, Madrid and Rome, just as £1 in England is the same as £1 in Wales.

The UK decided to stay out of the monetary union for two main reasons. One was that control over interest rates and exchange rates would be the responsibility of a European institution, the European Central Bank, rather than a UK institution, the Bank of England. The danger is that a European Central Bank could make decisions which might suit the majority of EU citizens and businesses. But these decicions may harm citizens and businesses in the UK. Something similar happens in the UK. The Bank of England might set interest rates to suit the needs of the South of England. But these may be the wrong ones for Northern Ireland.

The second reason was a political one. Power or **sovereignty** would shift from the UK to the EU. Some argue that only UK institutions and government should make decisions about what affects the UK.

Staying out of the euro-zone, though, is likely to make it difficult for UK businesses to compete. This is because firms in the euro-zone, like the French and the Germans, won't have the costs of changing their currencies when they trade with each other. UK businesses may have problems exporting to euro-zone countries as result.

Regulations

Membership of the EU affects UK businesses in other ways. The EU has its own laws and regulations which UK businesses and UK courts have to conform to. UK businesses, for instance, have to comply with EU health and safety regulations. UK workers have rights under European law on issues such as **equal opportunities** (☞ unit 105). UK production is affected by EU directives on the environment and pollution, such as the environmental management standard BS EN ISO 14001. UK businesses also have to meet product standards and **copyright** and **patent** (☞ unit 104) laws of the EU.

Barriers to trade

There are no tariffs or taxes on trade between EU countries. Many countries would have a single currency from 2002. Regulations might be the same. But barriers to trade between European countries could still exist.

Language is a problem. Selling to Germany means that UK businesses have to communicate in German with their customers, or customers have to speak English. Language barriers are coming down as more people speak two languages. However, continental companies are more likely to have English speakers than UK companies have, say, French or German speakers. This can make it more difficult for UK companies to compete.

There are **different market characteristics**. Some businesses, like chemical manufacturers, sell a standard product which can be sold to many countries. However, there may be problems when there are different tastes in each country. For instance, traditional UK manufacturers often find it hard to sell into some European countries because customers prefer styles of china from their own countries.

Distance can also be a problem. It is easier to communicate with a business half a mile away than one in another country. Transporting goods can also be very costly for low value, high bulk products like cement or bricks.

Games Workshop makes and sells model soldiers. People collect and paint figures as a hobby and use them for wargaming. The business is based in Nottingham, but there is an additional manufacturing facility in Baltimore in the USA.

Games Workshop has been expanding rapidly in Europe and the USA. It has opened its own stores in France, Italy and Germany. But it continues to sell widely through independent shops, mail order and through the internet.

It publishes a monthly magazine called *White Dwarf*. There are now separate editions in French, Spanish, Italian and Chinese. The magazine carries articles about the hobby, as well as acting as an important advertising medium for the business.

The increase in the value of the pound against the euro considerably reduced profits on sales into Europe in the late 1990s. If the UK had joined the transition to the single currency in 1996, Games Workshop would probably have earned more profits in the late 1990s and been better able to finance overseas expansion.

1. Explain why Games Workshop is (a) both a manufacturing company and a service sector company and (b) an exporter.
2. Games Workshop exports products both to the USA and to France. In what ways might exporting to France be easier for the company than exporting to the United States?
3. To what extent might the UK joining the single currency help Games Workshop?

Checklist

1. Explain THREE reasons why UK businesses found it easier to export to Europe after 1973.
2. Why was Britain joining the EU both an opportunity and a threat for UK businesses?
3. How might a UK business selling goods into Europe be helped if the UK adopted the single currency, the euro?
4. Why did the UK decide not to join the European single currency in 2002.
5. Explain why UK membership of the EU affects how businesses treat their workers.
6. (a) Why might you find several languages on the wrapping of a food packet?
   (b) Why do different European languages act as a barrier to trade between countries?

UNIT 10

The economy and business

Workers may find it easier to get a job in a boom, but more difficult in a recession

Growth, boom and recession

Economies tend to grow in size over time. Over the past forty years, for instance, production in the UK has more than doubled. So people can buy and consume more.

Some businesses have benefited more than others from this growth. Many service industries, such as health or catering, have grown faster than the average for the economy. Manufacturing industry and primary industry have not grown as fast.

Overall, growth in the economy is uneven. When the economy is in BOOM, it is growing very fast. Spending is high and unemployment falls. Businesses tend to do well in a boom because it is easier to sell products.

In a RECESSION, the economy doesn't grow or may even shrink. This happened in the UK between 1990 and 1992. Less is spent and produced than before and unemployment rises. Businesses tend to do badly because consumers are buying fewer of their products.

Unemployment

Unemployment is linked to booms and recessions. In a boom, unemployment is low and the numbers in work are high. People have higher incomes and so consumption levels tend to be high. Low unemployment also increases consumer confidence. Consumers are more willing to borrow money to spend on goods like cars or furniture. On the other hand, low unemployment means that businesses may find it difficult to recruit new staff. They may also have to offer higher wages to attract new staff or to prevent staff from leaving to take jobs with other businesses. All this could add to the costs of a business.

In a recession, unemployment is high. This reduces average incomes and consumer confidence. Consumer spending is therefore likely to be low. On the other hand, businesses should find it easier to recruit new staff and there will be less pressure to give wage increases to workers.

Inflation

INFLATION is a general rise in prices in the economy. Businesses lose and gain from inflation. They lose because their costs go up. For instance, a chocolate manufacturer will have to pay more for materials like sugar, aluminium foil for packaging and electricity. Workers will also demand pay increases.

Businesses can also gain because their sales revenues are likely to increase. If prices are rising, businesses are likely to be able to put up their prices to customers. Normally, higher prices should lead to fewer sales. But if all businesses are putting up prices, and workers are getting higher wages, then the number of sales for a business should stay the same. The same number of sales with higher prices means higher sales revenues.

Exchange rates

The **exchange rate** (☞ unit 9) is the value of one currency against another. For example, £1 may be

---

Massey Ferguson's plant in Coventry has been hit hard by the large rise in the pound against the euro over the past three years. The factory, which makes tractors, exports 70 per cent of its output. 1 800 workers are employed at the factory with thousands more in businesses which supply parts to Massey Ferguson. Only 14 000 tractors were made last year when the factory could make 25 000 a year. Massey Ferguson has been forced to cut its prices in pounds sterling to remain competitive in Europe. This means that the profits made from the Coventry plant have fallen sharply.

In an attempt to increase profitability, the company has increased imports of parts from suppliers in Europe. It has also forced its UK suppliers to accept cuts in the prices it pays them for components.

But in the long term, Massey Ferguson is threatening to shut the plant if the pound remains strong and it cannot cut its costs enough.

Source: adapted from *The Guardian*, 18.5.2000.

1. (a) How many tractors were made at Massey Ferguson's Coventry plant in 1999?
   (b) How many of these were exported?
2. (a) The value of the pound went up sharply against the euro between 1996 and 1999. Explain what might have happened to sales of Massey Ferguson UK manufactured tractors if the company had left the pound sterling price the same?
   (b) Explain why cutting the sterling price hit the company's profits.
3. How could buying more parts from Europe instead of the UK help the Coventry plant?
4. Put arguments for and against the suggestion that Massey Ferguson should shut its Coventry plant.

exchanged for 1.4 US dollars or 1.6 euros. Changes in exchange rates can affect businesses that sell and buy goods and services abroad.

Exports Some businesses sell goods and services to other countries. A rise or fall in exchange rates can affect these exports.

- Assume the exchange rate is £1 = $2. A shirt sold for £10 by a UK business will cost $20 in the USA (£10 x $2). If the exchange rate **falls** to £1 = $1, the shirt will only cost $10 in the USA (£10 x $1). The lower dollar price should mean that the UK exporter would sell more shirts in the USA.
- What if the exchange rate **rises** from £1 = $2 to £1 = $4? The price of a £10 shirt in the US would rise from $20 (£10 x $2) to $40 (£10 x $4). At this higher dollar price, the UK exporter should sell fewer shirts.

UK exporters might react to a change in the value in the pound in a different way. Assume the value of the pound rises from £1 = $2 to £1 = $4. A shirt is sold for £10 by a UK business. The UK business could try to maintain its US sales by keeping the US price at $20. With an exchange rate of £1 = $4 it would only receive £5 ($20 ÷ $4) for each shirt. So the profit on each shirt sold should fall. At this price the business would probably be making a loss on each shirt sold.

Imports Changes in exchange rates can also affect imports of goods and services.

- Cotton priced at $200 in the US would cost a UK business £100 ($200 ÷ $2) at an exchange rate of £1 = $2. If the exchange rate **fell** to £1 = $1, the cotton would cost £200 ($200 ÷ $1) in the UK. The higher price in pounds would mean increased costs for the UK

importer, which should buy less cotton.
- If the value of the pound **rises** from £1 = $2 to £1 = $4, the price of imports in pounds is less. The $200 cotton would fall in price from £100 ($200 ÷ $2) to £50 ($200 ÷ $4). The cost to the UK importer would be less and it should import more.

In general, a fall in the value of the currency is likely to benefit exporting businesses, but harm those which import goods. A rise in the value of the currency benefits businesses which import goods and services, but harms exporters.

The government

Government economic decisions also affect businesses. For instance, decisions about taxes, government spending and interest rates are all very important for businesses (☞ unit 7).

Halma is a UK based engineering company, although 65 per cent of its sales are overseas. It produces in a small number of specialist areas. These include fire, gas and water leak detection products, resistors, opthalmic optics and elevator electronics.

1. Look at Table 10.1. Give the output of the whole economy in (a) 1992, (b) 1996 and (c) 2000.
2. 'Between 1996 and 1998, the economy was in boom.' (a) What does this mean? (b) What would you expect to happen to the output of engineering companies in a boom? (c) What actually happened to engineering output between 1996 and 1998?
3. Between 1996 and 1998, there was a 20 per rise in the average value of the pound against other currencies. This meant that engineering companies like Halma would have had to increase their foreign currency prices to overseas customers by 20 per cent if they wanted to keep their prices in pounds the same. At the other extreme, they could have kept their foreign currency overseas prices the same but accept that this would reduce the pound sterling price by 20 per cent. Explain why this rise in the value of the pound could have hit the sales and output value in pounds sterling of engineering companies.

	at 1995 prices		
	Output of the whole economy	Output of the engineering industry	Output of Halma plc
	£bn	£bn	£m
1992	650.3	691.4	122.3
1993	665.4	795.1	150.2
1994	694.6	839.7	175.1
1995	714.0	860.2	198.9
1996	732.2	868.1	423.5
1997	757.9	837.0	387.4
1998	777.9	815.3	315.7
1999	794.7	884.3	357.6
2000	819.9	na	378.3

Table 10.1
Source: adapted from *Monthly Digest of Statistics*, Office for National Statistics; Halma, *Annual Report and Accounts*, 2000.

Checklist

1. What is the difference between a boom and a recession?
2. What are the likely effects of a recession on a business?
3. What will happen to unemployment in a boom and how might this affect businesses?
4. How does inflation affect a business?
5. Explain whether a fall in the value of the pound would be good for: (a) a UK businesses exporting cars to France; (b) a French business exporting clothes to the UK; (c) a UK engineering business buying steel from Germany.

Businesses in the UK have to pay a landfill tax to dump waste

Society

Businesses have to operate within the **laws** (☞ unit 7) of a country. But they are also affected by the wider **rules** and **conventions** of society. There are many examples.

- A UK exporter is not likely to include pork ingredients in food sold to Saudi Arabia. Most people in the country are Muslims, who will not eat pork.
- Wedding dresses sold in the UK are mainly white, cream or ivory because this is the custom. So a wedding dress business will tend to stock these colours.
- Many goods in the UK are imported from abroad. Some are made by children or in factories with poor working conditions. Businesses which import these goods

may find that consumers will not buy their products. This is because society in the UK does not approve of the exploitation of workers or the use of child labour.

- At Christmas, some companies give workers a Christmas party or a Christmas bonus. This increases the costs for these businesses. But they hope that it will make staff more motivated and loyal to the business.

Society is constantly changing. Businesses have to keep up with these changes. For instance, fifty years ago, it was mainly men who bought cars. Today, increasingly, cars are bought by women. So car dealers have aimed their advertising and promotion far more at women. More people are vegetarians today than fifty years ago. As a result, food manufacturers have produced meals to suit the needs of those who don't eat meat.

Population

Another factor that can affect businesses is changes in population. Between 2000 and 2030 it is forecast that in the UK there will be:

- an increase in the number of old age pensioners, particularly those over 75;
- a fall in the number of workers;
- a fall in the number of children.

This creates opportunities for businesses which sell to old age pensioners. Building companies which specialise in building houses for the elderly should do well. On the other hand, clothes shops aimed at the teenage market may face problems as the number of customers shrinks.

Changes in the places people live also affect businesses. The population of the South East of England is forecast to grow in future. So businesses such as house builders, restaurants or estate agents should benefit. Other areas in the North of England may see a fall in their population. This will lower spending power and make trading conditions more difficult for many service companies in the area.

The environment

Many businesses now take into account the environmental impact of their activities. They might be forced to do this by government. For instance, building companies which want to dump their rubbish

? 1. What, according to the data, is projected will happen between 2001 and 2021 to the number of people aged:
  (a) 65-74;
  (b) 75-84;
  (c) 85 and over?
2. Name THREE opportunities for selling products which these trends will create for businesses.
3. The number of people aged 0-44 is forecast to fall between 2001 and 2021. So there will be more old people, but fewer young people in the population in 2021. Discuss how businesses might be affected by this change.

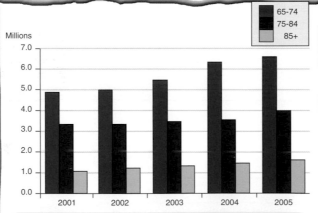

Figure 11.1 *Projected changes in the population aged 65 and over in the UK*
Source: adapted from *Annual Abstract of Statistics*, 2000, Office for National Statistics.

now have to pay a landfill tax when they get rid of the waste. But many businesses are doing more than what the law or the government requires. For instance, they might send their waste paper to be recycled rather than putting it into their waste collection. They might deliberately buy equipment which is energy saving, even though it doesn't make any more profit for the business.

In general, though, when making decisions, businesses tend only to consider the costs and benefits to themselves. The costs which a business pays are called PRIVATE COSTS. The benefits which a business receives are called PRIVATE BENEFITS.

Other costs and benefits which the business doesn't pay or receive are known as EXTERNALITIES. For instance, a business may send its goods by road to its customers. The lorry creates both noise and air pollution. People living near motorways suffer from this noise, but don't receive any compensation. Equally, air pollution may cause illness in some people. Greenhouse gases caused by burning petrol and diesel are leading to global warming. For the UK, this is likely to create more frequent storms, floods and droughts than before. On the other hand, a business may build a beautiful office block which people who pass by enjoy looking at. Their enjoyment is a benefit for which the business receives no money. Noise pollution, air pollution, global warming are examples of **negative** externalities. The beauty of a building is an example of a **positive** externality.

The full cost to society of an activity is equal to the cost to the business, the private cost, plus any other costs, the externalities. These two added together equal the SOCIAL COST of an activity.

Businesses are under more and more pressure to pay the full social cost of anything they do. Environmental groups, for instance, campaign against large companies which create pollution. Residents protest against local factories which harm their local environment. These protests can lead to bad publicity and lower sales. Some companies, like The Body Shop, have gained customers by convincing them that their activities are environmentally friendly.

Wolverhampton Council plans to crack down on litter louts like a ton of bricks - using every means legally available to get and keep Wolverhampton clean and sparkling. Draconian measures will be enforced to crack down on city litter, fly tipping and fly posting.

'Council departments will work together over this', said environmental chief Counsellor Pat Byrne. 'For example those whose clubs are advertised by means of fly posting and who say it is nothing to do with them will get a shock next time they apply for a licence. And I fully expect litter wardens to be appointed in the near future.'

Among the recommendations is power to crack down on commercial premises which create litter like fish and chip shops; fixed penalty fines or a visit to court for people dropping litter; cleansing of yards and passageways recovering the costs from those who own these areas or who create the waste; removal of waste likely to attract vermin and recovering the cost from the owners of the property; and the use of statutory nuisance provisions for those who persist in dumping litter and waste.

Source: adapted from the *Wolverhampton AdNews*, 26.4.2001.

1. (a) What are the private benefits to (i) a business which tips its waste onto waste ground it does not own by the side of a road; (ii) a night club which pastes posters onto street lights; (iii) a homeowner who dumps his 15 year old unwanted car onto waste ground?
   (b) Why does each of these examples create an externality?
   (c) For each example, explain one measure which Wolverhampton Council is proposing to use to reduce the problem.
2. In 1999, the government introduced a landfill tax which has considerably increased the cost to businesses of taking their waste to an official landfill disposal site. Discuss whether this is likely to increase the problem of fly tipping (illegally dumping waste on ground which does not belong to the business or individuals dumping the waste).

key terms

Externalities - the costs or benefits of an activity which are not paid for or received by the individual, business or government engaged in that activity.
Private costs and benefits - the costs and benefits to individuals, businesses or government of an economic or business activity.
Social costs and benefits - the costs and benefits to society as a whole of the activities of individuals, businesses and governments. Social costs and benefits = private costs and benefits plus externalities.

Checklist

1. Give TWO examples of how businesses can be affected by the conventions of society.
2. How have businesses been forced to change because of changes in how people eat?
3. The number of single parent households has grown over the past twenty years. Explain what businesses might have benefited from this trend.
4. Explain FOUR social costs created by a local coal mine.
5. Suggest THREE examples of industries where negative externalities might be quite large.

UNIT 12

Technology and business

Technology and change

Businesses face constant and rapid changes in technology. In the past, new technologies such as steam power or electricity greatly changed the way in which businesses operated. Today, the pace of technological change is even greater. Businesses are unlikely to survive unless they adapt to changes in technology.

The product

One way in which technology affects business is through new products. Technological advances allow businesses to create new products. Here are three examples.

- Thirty years ago, mobile phones did not exist. Today, over half the UK population has a mobile phone.
- One hundred years ago, the motor vehicle had only just been invented. Today, it is the most important form of transport in the world.
- Two hundred years ago, people's diets were limited because it was difficult to keep food fresh. Today, through refrigeration, everyone in Britain is offered a variety of foods from all over the world in shops and supermarkets.

Businesses have to decide how to respond to such changes. Some try to develop new products. In biotechnology, companies carry out **research and development** (☞ unit 5) to find new products that will fill a gap in the market, such as a new drug. Many businesses, however, develop and improve their existing products. In the mobile phone market, for example, companies like Nokia and Motorola constantly introduce new models. The mobile phones may be smaller and lighter, they may have longer battery life, or they could have additional functions like internet access.

Businesses that don't change their

New technology has affected design and production

products are likely to see their sales fall. Looking back, there are very few examples of products sold today which are exactly the same as they were 100 years ago. Even food products like milk have changed. Today, almost all milk sold to consumers is pasteurised. Consumers can also buy semi-skimmed and skimmed milk. Change which incorporates new technology is therefore vital for survival.

Internet

1. Find out using books or the internet what changes in technology allowed the invention of THREE of the following: (a) pasteurised milk; (b) the television set; (c) the telephone; (d) the printed book; (e) compact discs; (f) satellite television; (g) waterproof clothing; (h) the Dyson vacuum cleaner; (i) GM foods.

2. Explain TWO ways in which the invention of these products has affected businesses.

The pace of work is increasing. Workers can now do more work in less time thanks to new technology. Take, for instance, the mobile phone. Before, when workers caught a train to go to a meeting, they could sit back, relax and read a newspaper. Today, they are available 100 per cent of the time to receive incoming calls. They can also make calls they didn't have time for in the office or read and reply to e-mails on their wap phone. Or take the example of a delivery van. An office can phone the delivery driver and change the route to make a drop off for a last minute order. The driver could also be called back to the depot to pick up an urgent delivery. The office can check where the driver is to make sure there are no unauthorised breaks. Even building workers benefit. They can order urgent supplies immediately, instead of waiting for site supervisors to visit the site but only place the order when they return to the office.

Greater productivity (output per worker) has come at a price, though. As more and more time in a worker's day is filled with work, so stress has increased. Gone are the 'good old days' when workers could sit around doing nothing, waiting for everything to be in place for them to start. Life today is lived in the fast lane. Not everyone can cope with that.

Source: adapted from the *Financial Times*, 28.11.2000.

1. Explain how the mobile phone has forced many workers to work harder.
2. Why do you think this has helped to increase the levels of stress at work?
3. Discuss whether or not mobile phones have benefited businesses when they are used by their employees for work.

Production methods

Technological change has also revolutionised the way in which most goods and services are produced. Nearly all processes today, for instance, use electricity at some point in production. Yet 100 years ago, few businesses had electricity supplies. Today, supplies can be bought from all over the world because modern transport allows goods to be delivered to customers in any country. One hundred years ago, transport was often too slow or unsuitable for this. Goods can be mass produced quickly using **computer technology** (☞ unit 63), even when the processes are complicated and require great accuracy.

Improvements in technology have led to production being ever more CAPITAL INTENSIVE. This means that more machines, buildings, equipment and less labour is being used. This is true even of LABOUR INTENSIVE industries like the restaurant trade. Kitchens in restaurants today have more equipment than they did one hundred years ago. What is more, many areas of the restaurant trade have been transformed with the use of frozen food and microwave ovens. Large batches of food products can be produced in factories. They are then sold to restaurants that defrost and serve meals on the premises.

One hundred years ago, some believed that machines would completely replace human workers. It is unlikely that this will ever happen. Human beings are still needed to make decisions about what to produce and how to organise production. However, the introduction of new technology like ICT (information and communications technologies) (☞ unit 13) will see more being produced with even fewer workers. Businesses which make the best use of new technology will be the ones which survive and grow. Businesses which fail to adapt will be forced to close.

key terms

Capital intensive production - in capital intensive industries, large amounts of capital are used relative to the amount produced.
Labour intensive production - in labour intensive industries, relatively large amounts of labour are used.

Checklist

1. Name TWO technologies which have changed the way in which businesses operate.
2. Describe TWO new products that have been sold in UK markets recently which include new technology.
3. 'The manufacturer of cars is highly capital intensive.' Explain what this means.
4. Explain how the introduction of new technologies has changed the restaurant trade.

The internet and e-commerce

BTinternet

For reliable surfing,
get online with BTinternet

Excellent quality

Great value for money

Comprehensive communication services

Great customer support

Install>>

Businesses give away disks to consumers to get online

Mothercare, the mother-to-be and baby products retailer, said yesterday that the internet was vitally important for the future of the company. It has spent £7.4 million over the past year launching its web site, Mothercare.com. The web site is part of the Mothercare Direct strategy. Customers can order goods from its mail order catalogue or from the web site. Customers who prefer to use the phone to place orders ring up a call centre. Sales from Mothercare Direct rose 28 per cent in the 28 weeks to October 14. In contrast, Mothercare has closed 82 unprofitable high street shops over the past year and now has 257 UK stores left.

Source: adapted from the *Financial Times*, 24.11.2000.

1. How much did Mothercare spend on setting up its e-commerce operation?
2. What might be (a) the similarities and (b) the differences between shopping with the Mothercare mail order catalogue and the Mothercare.com web site?
3. Suggest why the internet might be 'vitally important for the future' of Mothercare.

The internet

The 1990s saw the start of an electronic revolution which has changed the way in which firms do business. The INTERNET was developed in the 1960s by the US government as an alternative form of communication in case of war. The internet is a system which allows computers to communicate with each other.

Email

The internet allows messages to be sent from one computer to others. This is EMAIL. The messages are like letters, but sent electronically. There are advantages of using email rather than letters.

- The email can be sent and received immediately. It doesn't take 24 hours for messages to be delivered, like a letter. It is also possible to have a conversation 'online', with questions and replies being written and sent.
- The message can be written on computer and sent without having to transfer it to paper. So it is easier and quicker to send.
- It is cheaper than passing round a written memo (a message) within a business or sending a letter.

One disadvantage of email is that both the sender and the receiver must have access to a computer. This may be more of a problem when sending messages from home than in business, as many houses do not have computers. However, an increasing number of appliances have email facilities. Some mobile phones and televisions can receive and send email messages. Internet cafes also allow people to communicate by e-mail.

Email has become a standard means of communication between businesses. It allows workers within the business to pass messages more easily. It also allows businesses to communicate with each other. Improved communication means that work may be carried out more efficiently. It also helps sell products to other businesses.

The world wide web

The WORLD WIDE WEB is a system which allows information to be offered and accessed through the internet. Businesses can set up their own web sites. A web site is like a page or several pages in a book. Anyone can visit the web site and look at the information. Businesses, for instance, can describe what they do and the products they sell. They can give financial statistics to investors. They can tell visitors how to contact the business by giving addresses, telephone numbers or email addresses.

E-commerce

A web site can also be used to sell the products of a business. The web site acts like a mail order catalogue. Buyers can order an item and pay for it by giving their credit card details. Consumers can order books from amazon.com or buy groceries from Tesco or Iceland, for instance. Businesses can also order supplies from other businesses.

It was predicted that E-COMMERCE would grow rapidly after the year 2000. Some suggest that soon most goods will be ordered over the net. Others point out that mail order catalogue

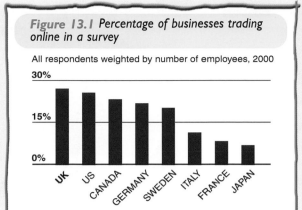

Figure 13.1 *Percentage of businesses trading online in a survey*

All respondents weighted by number of employees, 2000

Source: adapted from *Business in the Information Age 2000*.

shopping accounts for only 5 per cent of total consumer sales in the UK.

One problem with catalogues and e-commerce is that consumers can't feel, smell or try on the goods immediately. For instance, there are many catalogues and web sites offering clothes for sale, but most people prefer to try on goods when they are buying. Equally, someone spending £1 000 on a sofa is likely to want to sit on it before buying.

Another problem is that goods have to be delivered to the customer. Many consumer goods today are collected by customers from shops when they are bought. With e-commerce, goods have to be delivered to homes or businesses. This drives up the cost of each transaction. For instance, a £10 shirt might cost an extra £3 to deliver.

Another limit on e-commerce may be that shopping has become a leisure experience. People enjoy going to shops to select goods. New shopping malls have been designed with this in mind. E-commerce does not allow this activity.

Business sales

E-commerce could become very important in areas where businesses trade with each other. A business selling standard parts or components, for instance, can put its catalogue onto a web site and get customers to place electronic orders rather than using paper orders. This will cut down costs.

Large businesses, like car manufacturers, may also be able to set up auctions for supplies. A car manufacturer, for instance, may want to buy ten million parts of a particular size. Through its web site, it can invite suppliers to offer the lowest price for the contract. This will help it to lower costs.

Advertising

The World Wide Web offers businesses a medium for advertising. At the moment, most advertising on the web is placed by web-based businesses. Amazon.com, the web book seller, advertises and sells books on the world wide web, for instance. However, web advertising is likely to become more important as more consumers and businesses use the World Wide Web.

GroupTrade is a UK-based web site aimed at small and medium-sized enterprises. It offers office supplies, equipment and services at prices normally only enjoyed by larger companies. The site includes a car-leasing service provided by BCH Vehicle Management. The catalogue contains promotions, buyers' ratings and reviews. GroupTrade's inquiry service finds products for businesses and negotiates group deals.

CTRLP.com offers printing services, from stationery to company reports. Customers can request instant estimates or put a job out to tender. Site features include competitive quotes within four hours, an online print expert, free downloadable software to compress digital artwork and online tracing of orders. Customers can choose between a 'soft' proof sent to their computer or a traditional 'hard' proof that is printed out. All work is guaranteed.

Source: adapted from *Connectis*, December 2000.

1. What could a small to medium sized business buy on the GroupTrade and CTRLP web sites?
2. Explain TWO reasons why a business might prefer to order from one of these two online companies rather than a traditional local supplier.
3. Do you think that in ten years time businesses will order all their supplies using the internet? Give reasons for your answer.

Checklist

1. How might a business use email?
2. What might a business put onto its web site?
3. What might be (a) the advantages and (b) the disadvantages to a shopper ordering a pair of shoes from the internet?
4. How might a business use e-commerce to reduce the costs of the supplies it buys from other businesses?
5. Explain which type of business is most likely to advertise over the internet.

Business support and advisory services

Businesses are supported by local, national and international organisations

Support and advisory services

Businesses can get support and advice from a wide variety of sources. This unit considers how government and various associations of businesses can help. In units 15 and 16 other sources of support and advice for businesses are outlined.

Trade associations

In some industries there are TRADE ASSOCIATIONS which represent the interests of members. Examples include the Wool Marketing Board, the Association of British Travel Agents and the Booksellers Association. Businesses have to pay a membership fee to the trade association. In return, they get a variety of services. These can include the following.

- The association may act as a PRESSURE GROUP for the industry. A pressure group is any group which attempts to influence others. Environmental groups like Friends of the Earth are pressure groups because they attempt to influence individuals, businesses and government to act in a more environmentally friendly way. Trade associations often attempt to LOBBY government to get it to make decisions in favour of their industry. For instance, the Brewers and Licensed Retailers Association, the pressure group for brewing companies, puts pressure on government to cut taxes on alcohol.

- The association may provide help and advice. For example, some trade associations provide advice about employment law or product standards. The trade association may also have a research department which looks at future trends in the industry. For example, it may predict what demand for the industry's products may be like in six months' time. This helps businesses to plan production and investment. The Association of British Travel Agents (ABTA) provides an insurance scheme for members. If one of them is forced to close down, ABTA will get tourists home and provide compensation for any holiday maker who has booked a future holiday.

Chambers of commerce

Every local region in the UK has a chamber of commerce. This is an organisation which represents all businesses in the local region. Like a trade association, a chamber of commerce charges its members a fee and provides a variety of services. It is also a pressure group. It acts particularly to influence decisions which will affect the local area. For instance, it might lobby local government about planning issues. Or it may try to get a government department to give funds for business development in an area.

Some chambers of commerce obtain grants from government or the European Union to offer services, such as training or programmes to promote exports. Local businesses can take advantage of these.

Business Links

Like the Chambers of Commerce, Business Links work at a local level. In most areas there is a Business Link organisation. The National Federation of Business Links helps individual local organisations to provide services. Business Links

---

In 2001, Business Link Walsall offered business representatives in the town a helping hand to explore overseas markets. It organised a visit to Norway where representatives would be provided with relevant market information and introduced to named contacts in the overseas market.

Companies that took part were allocated an international trade advisor to provide valuable advice and guidance before, during and after the visit.

Allen Matty, head of international trade at Business Link Walsall, said: ' 'Norway is an ideal market for companies wanting to take their first export step. The UK already has 10 per cent of Norway's import market and we hope that companies in Walsall will take the opportunity to increase their market share'.

Ian Bourne, company secretary of Walsall-based Bourne Tools, took part in a previous scheme and the company then went on to discover fresh avenues and new markets. 'The Explorer scheme was definitely the key that opened the door to the export market for us', he said.

Source: adapted from the *Express & Star*, 4.12.2000.

1. Why might a company want to send a representative on the visit to Norway organised by Business Link Walsall?
2. What services were included in the visit to Norway?

key terms

Lobbying - putting pressure on government to change the law or its policies.
Pressure group - a group which attempts to influence business, government and individuals.
Trade associations - organisations which represent the interests of the businesses which are its members. Individual industries often have a trade association.

Checklist

1. What services does a trade association offer to its members?
2. Explain the difference between a trade association and a Chamber of Commerce.
3. Why might a business use the services of a local Business Link?
4. How can the government help and advise businesses?
5. How might a UK business benefit from EU funding?

have been very successful at attracting government and European Union funds for a range of business support services. These include giving training, advice and support for new businesses and help with writing business plans, selling abroad, improving quality and meeting regulations.

National associations

There are associations which represent all businesses in the UK. One is the Confederation of British Industry (CBI). The CBI acts as a pressure group for business interests. It lobbies government to introduce laws and policies which will help business. It has an economic research department which looks at future trends for the economy and how individual measures, like the minimum wage, will affect businesses.

The Institute of Directors (IoD) also claims to represent the interests of business in the UK. Like the CBI it is a pressure group and provides support services for its members.

Small firms are represented by bodies such as the Federation of Small Businesses. This lobbys

government to improve the position of small firms in areas such as employment law and taxes. It also gives free legal advice and insurance.

Government organisations

Government offers help and advice to businesses in a number of ways. It works with independent organisations like Chambers of Commerce and Business Links. It also provides more direct help. For instance, it funds the Learning and Skills Council. This promotes training in local areas and provides funding for further education. The government also funds the Small Business Support Scheme. This is a Department of Trade and Industry agency which gives help and advice to small businesses. It also runs the Loan Guarantee Scheme and gives smart grants for the introduction of new technology.

Other sources

Young people who want to set up in business can get grants from the Princes Youth Business Trust. This is a trust set up by the Prince of Wales. It aims to help the unemployed and those who might find it difficult to get a job or to set up in business on their own. It doesn't just give grants. It also supports those setting up in business by running courses and arranging for successful business people to act as advisors.

Shell Livewire, sponsored by the oil company Shell, also works with disadvantaged young people. Again, help with setting up in business is offered.

The European Union

The European Union also gives funds to help businesses. Its help is concentrated on areas where income is well below the average for the European Union. These funds can be passed through organisations like Business Links to help the training of workers or the setting up of new business.

Employers from the Dudley area were offered a free breakfast in return for hearing about the benefits of a diverse workforce. The organisers were Dudley Training & Enterprise Council. The TEC network was replaced by the Learning and Skills Council in 2001. Dudley TEC said that many local businesses were losing production and potential profits by leaving staff vacancies unfilled. There was, however, a wider pool of potential employees who could be both available and keen to take the opportunities on offer.

It was organising the event in partnership with Dudley Racial Equality Council. The aim was to launch a new good practice guide on race, gender and disability entitled *Equal Opportunities is Your Business too*. The document was designed to help small and medium-sized enterprises put equal opportunity issues at the top of their agenda.

John Woodall, chief executive at the time, said: 'This seminar will provide an excellent opportunity for local employers to get together to hear about the wide range of assistance available and participate in the discussion.'

Source: adapted from the *Express & Star*, 3.7.2000.

1. What help and advice would businesses get at the event?
2. You run a business in Dudley making weighing equipment for businesses. You employ 15 people. What might be the (a) benefits and (b) costs to you of attending the seminar? Do you think you should go to it?

Private sector business support services

Support from the private sector

There is a large number of **private sector** (☞ unit 4) businesses which provide support services to other businesses. Unlike government funded bodies or trade associations, these support businesses aim to sell a service and make a profit. They are no different from a **supplier** to a business, which might be selling raw materials, for example.

Accountants

Most businesses employ accountants. An accountant is someone who will help to keep a record of the financial transactions of the business. This is important for a number of reasons.

- A business needs to know how it is performing financially. Is the flow of money into the business greater than the amount going out? Is the business making a profit? Every business has to survive, and keeping track of the money coming in and going out of the business is essential.
- Businesses must keep financial records so tax authorities can assess the amount of tax they owe. If a business sells more than £50 000 of products each year, it must charge value added tax (VAT) to customers. VAT is collected by Customs and Excise. The business may also pay taxes such as corporation tax on profits and National Insurance contributions on employees' earnings. These are collected by the Inland Revenue.
- If the business is a **company** (☞ unit 27) or a limited liability partnership (☞ unit 25) it has to produce a set of accounts. The accounts must, by law, be certified by an accountant.

Solicitors

Businesses may need the help and advice of **solicitors**. Solicitors are trained lawyers. They may be used, for instance, to draw up a **Deed of Partnership** if people decide to go into business together as partners. A business may also require advice on employment law or help to collect money from clients who have not paid their bills on time (**debtors**).

Computer services

Some businesses employ specialists

Solicitors provide legal advice for businesses

to help them with their computer requirements. There are many examples of services that might be needed. A business may employ a specialist computer company to:

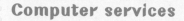

Geena and Tony Radcliffe set up the Bristol based consultancy, Radcliffe Partners, to help firms through the minefield of employment and the latest health and safety legislation. The business was founded in 1995. Both had been practising lawyers. They felt that there was a market for a legal service aimed at small and medium sized firms. Radcliffe Partners offers a full range of services, from documentation to representation at employment tribunals.

Small and medium sized businesses often seemed unaware about changes in employment legislation. Since 1999, for example, employees only needed to have worked for a company for 12 months to qualify for a claim for unfair dismissal. The compensation limit in such cases had also risen to £50 000. These were matters on which smaller businesses often needed guidance.

The business also recognised that there was a demand from large companies which employ their own personnel and human resources managers. From time to time they often needed additional help.

1. What services does Radcliffe Partners offer (a) small and medium sized businesses and (b) larger businesses?
2. The owner of a local Bristol business has threatened one of its workers with dismissal because he keeps arriving late for work. What might be (a) the advantages and (b) the disadvantages to the owner of seeking advice from Radcliffe Partners about the issue?

- install new computers and give training to staff on how to use the software;
- design and run a **web site** (☞ unit 13) on the internet. The site may be regularly updated to include changes in products and prices;
- write a software program specifically to meet the needs of the business, such as a database of all its customers;
- set up a company **intranet** (which allows internet communication only between members of the business);
- write a CD Rom to show customers how its product works. This often takes place when the product is very technical;
- provide videoconferencing services to communicate with other businesses or customers;
- carry out tasks that the business might otherwise do itself. This is known as OUTSOURCING. For instance, a business might use computer specialists to repair its computers instead of its own staff. Employees of the computer specialist may even work alongside employees of a large company in the same building.

Communication services

All businesses buy in a variety of communication services apart from those which are computer related. Businesses use standard methods of communication, such as the telephone and the post. Their telephone line will also enable them to send faxes. A telephone line is also needed if the business wants to use email or other internet services. Many businesses use companies other than the Post Office or British Telecom (BT) as suppliers of these services. For example, to send parcels a business may use a company like TNT or Omega.

Most businesses buy in services from specialists if they want to communicate with customers via brochures, flyers or catalogues. Design companies will produce the design for these whilst printing companies will print the copies. Large businesses may use outside companies to produce internal communications like company newsletters.

Larger businesses may employ a marketing or **advertising agency** (☞ unit 45). These provide a wide range of services, such as researching a market or developing an advertising campaign. Large businesses may also hire a **public relations** (☞ unit 46) company to handle its communication with the media and with customers. Large businesses need, for example, to ensure that newspapers write about them in a favourable way.

key terms

Outsourcing - buying in goods or services which would otherwise have been produced within the business.

Selling and buying products over the internet is becoming more and more popular. But getting started can be the hardest part. One solution is to use Hurd Web Design of Cannock. It specialises in e-commerce and prides itself on helping anyone to get going on the internet. It deals with every aspect of trading, from designing a web page to sorting out credit card arrangements with banks.

Mr Hurd, the managing director, said that people can come to the business with an idea and it can set up a web site for them and help them start trading online. It includes full training with the package.

Hurd Web Design also offers a range of reasonable priced PCs for sale. And by building its own computers, it is able to meet specific customer demands.

In future Hurd Web Design is planning to transform the ground floor of its office into three conference rooms. Here companies can take part in online conferencing with other businesses around the world.

Source: adapted from the *Express & Star*, 17.7.2000.

1. Explain TWO services that Hurd Web Design offers businesses.
2. Gough's is an antiques dealer specialising in selling clocks nationwide and internationally from a base in Birmingham. Suggest what might be the advantages to this business of (a) having a web site and (b) getting Hurd Web Design to set up and maintain the web site rather than trying to do it itself.

Payments can be made in different ways

Money transmission services

All businesses handle money. Money can be transferred in a variety of ways.

Cash Customers might pay for products using notes and coins. Or a business might buy supplies using cash. To prevent cash being kept on the premises, businesses tend to pay their cash into a bank each working day. Equally, if they need cash or change, they will go to their bank and withdraw it from their account.

Cheques A cheque is an order to withdraw funds from a bank account. Nearly all cheques today only allow payment to be made into another bank account to prevent fraud. So a business might receive a cheque from a customer. The cheque is paid into the bank account of the business and the funds are transferred from the customer's bank account.

Direct debits and standing orders Money can be transferred regularly. A standing order is an order by a customer to a bank to make a regular payment to another bank account. A direct debit allows a business to fix how much it collects from a customer on a regular basis. For instance, a customer might set up a standing order to pay £200 a month to a landlord to pay for rent on premises. Or a customer might pay its telephone bills by direct debit, allowing the telephone company to withdraw money from its account every three months.

Debit card and credit card transactions Many customers pay for products by using debit cards or credit cards. A debit card allows customers to pay for goods by withdrawing money from their bank accounts and transferring the money automatically into the account of the business. A credit card allows a customer to pay for goods by borrowing money from a credit card company. The credit card company transfers money into the account of the business to pay for the item.

Banks offer all these ways of transferring money between individuals and businesses. But businesses can also use Post Offices, for instance to deposit daily takings. Some building societies also allow the transfer of money by businesses.

Being able to transfer money is essential for a business. However, banks and other financial providers charge for their services. Credit card companies, for instance, may take 3 per cent of every credit card transaction as a charge. Banks may charge for every cheque they process. So this is a cost to businesses.

Transferring money abroad

Businesses which export and import may need to transfer money abroad. Often they will need to change pounds into a foreign currency. Banks and the Post Office offer this type of service, usually for

---

Whether you are starting a new business or switching your existing business account from another bank to NatWest, opening a NatWest business account is simple. Call in at your local branch, or phone them and arrange a meeting with a NatWest Small Business Adviser.

Your NatWest business account offers you:

 chequebooks, paying-in books and regular statements;

 the option to pay by standing order and direct debit;

 access to one of the largest banking networks in the UK, with over 1,700 branches nationwide;

 a NatWest Servicecard;

the ability to do your business banking over the phone or by PC. This service is available 24 hours a day, 365 days a year (see page 14); and

a NatWest Business Card (see page 16).

The cost
As a new business start-up customer, we will give you 12 months' free banking whether you are in credit or go overdrawn, as long as you do not pay more than £1,000,000 from your account during your first year.
If you complete a NatWest accredited training course we will extend this free banking period to 18 months.
When your free terms have ended, we will work out charges at a reduced rate for two years with no charge for automated payments into or out of your account.
Free banking means you won't be charged for paying amounts into and out of your account and running your account.
If we agree an overdraft, you will have to pay an arrangement fee. If you go overdrawn by more than the agreed amount, or if you go overdrawn without our agreement, you will have to pay a further fee. You will find information on these charges, and charges for other services, in our brochure 'Itemised account charges for businesses'.

Source: *Starting and Developing a Business*, NatWest.

1. Gary Philpott has just opened a business account with NatWest. He runs a small newsagent. This week, he has received 10 cheques from customers. (a) What is a cheque? (b) How much will it cost him to pay these cheques into his account?
2. Suggest why Gary might find it an advantage to do business banking 'by PC' (i.e. using his computer and the internet).
3. Gary has transferred his account from another bank to NatWest to take advantage of the free banking offer. Discuss whether it is in NatWest's best commercial interests to make this offer.

a fee or a commission. If the UK joined the euro, the costs of this would go down greatly because around 60 per cent of the UK's trade is with other euro countries.

Insurance

Businesses need INSURANCE. With insurance, a large number of customers each year pay small amounts to an insurance company. A few customers suffer losses because of risks such as fire, theft or accident. The insurance company then pays these customers to cover their losses.

For instance, a pub might pay £2 000 a year in PREMIUMS (payments) and receive cover which includes risk of flooding. Due to bad weather, the pub may be flooded, causing £100 000 worth of damage. The insurance company would then pay the £100 000 to have the pub repaired. The money comes from all the customers which have paid premiums in that year, but haven't suffered any losses.

Businesses need to take out insurance against a variety of risks. There are risks to premises, such as from fire or flooding. There are risks to people from accidents. This includes both workers and customers who are on business premises. A business may also want to insure against production being disrupted. For instance, if a factory is burnt down, production may not be able to restart for 6 months. But workers may have to be paid to stop them leaving and getting a job elsewhere. Insurance could cover these costs.

Other services

Financial institutions are very important to businesses because they offer various ways of obtaining funds. For instance, banks **lend money** to businesses. Banks and other financial institutions organise issues of new **shares** for companies. They can also help businesses collect debts from customers through **factoring** services. These are discussed in more detail in units 67-69.

Protect your
assets

Our commercial insurance specialists can help you decide what level of protection is sensible for your type and size of business.

The costs of insuring against the impact of various unforeseen events is one more overhead for a small business.

Some insurance is compulsory. This includes employers' liability insurance, motor insurance and - for some businesses - specialist inspection contracts for engineering plant.

Other cover remains your choice. Our insurance specialists can advise you how to protect your business against damage to your assets and disruption to your trading operations from fire, flood, theft, subsidence and other events. They can ensure you are covered against claims from people using your products or services or - if you offer a professional service - acting on your advice.

You may also insure against loss of cash or goods in transit, and the death or illness of yourself or a key member of your team. You name the area of concern and our specialists will help you find a cost-effective solution for your particular protection needs.

Source: adapted from *Starting and Running a Business*, Barclays.

1. Kim Lawton owns a restaurant next to the River Severn. In 2000, the restaurant was flooded out twice by the rising river. What insurance should she have taken out as protection?
2. In 2001, the cook in the restaurant failed to maintain proper hygiene. The result was that four customers and two members of staff who ate some fish developed food poisoning. They threatened to sue. What insurance should Kim have taken out to cover this problem?
3. Many small businesses don't take out insurance against all the risks which they face. Discuss whether this is the right thing for them to do.

The moral and ethical dimension

Advertisements for ethical businesses

The ethical business

Businesses, like people, have to make ETHICAL choices. They have to decide whether an activity is morally correct or not. There is a number of business areas where ethics can be important.

Customers A business must decide whether or not it is 'right' to sell a product. For example, a department store might let floor space to a business selling fur coats. Should it stop this? An international bank might have a branch in a country which abuses human rights. Should it pull out? An engineering business might own a company which sells guns. Should it sell this business?

Suppliers Businesses buy supplies from other businesses. Some do not think that they are responsible for the actions of suppliers. The important thing is that the supplier provides quality goods, on time, at the best price. Others argue that businesses should not buy from suppliers which exploit workers, for example. This includes those that use child labour. Nor should they buy from suppliers which damage the environment. In the food industry, there are many ethical issues. Some businesses will not buy from farms where animals are badly treated or which grow GM foods.

Competitors Businesses have to decide how far they will go to win customers from their rivals. Is giving a bribe acceptable, for example? Should businesses hire detectives to find out what their competitors are planning? Should they drive a company out of business? Should they push down

---

McDonald's has come in for criticism from a variety of groups over the past ten years. Environmentalists accuse it of creating unnecessary waste through packaging. They also argue that the farming practices used to supply beef to McDonald's destroy local environments. Animal rights groups say that McDonald's buys its animal products from farms which abuse animals. Left wing groups say that McDonald's exploits its workers. It pays low wages and conditions of work are so poor that most workers leave within three months of starting. Anti-globalisation groups accuse McDonald's of destroying local eating traditions and imposing its American cultural values on the world.

Unlike other companies, so far the concerns have had little impact on McDonald's sales. Recently, however, the company has been more willing to listen. For instance, it has held meetings with Compassion in World Farming. This is an animal welfare organisation which lobbied McDonald's on its choice of egg and meat suppliers. As a result, the group claims, 90 per cent of the eggs used by McDonald's in the UK are now free range.

Source: adapted from the *Financial Times*, 3.5.2000.

1. Explain THREE of the criticisms made of McDonald's.
2. How has McDonald's responded to such criticism?
3. Do you think that, in the long run, McDonald's can afford to ignore its critics? In your answer, put forward arguments both for and against.

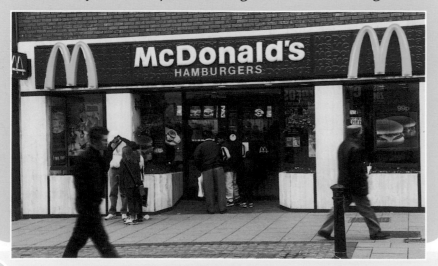

their prices so low that a company loses all of its customers?

Workers Businesses that act ethically often consider the needs of workers. For example, they may pay workers much more than the minimum amount. They may try to improve workers' skills through training, even if this costs money. They may allow workers to take time off to look after sick children.

The environment All businesses have an impact on the environment. Some, like coal mines, change the local landscape. Others, like asbestos manufacturers, create products which can be dangerous to human health. Some cause pollution by their use of energy and the disposal of waste. Ethical businesses try to reduce their effect on the environment. But should a business recycle materials if it adds to its own costs?

The local community Many businesses have little to do with their local communities. They may simply sell goods in the area. Some argue, however, that they should do more than this. For instance, they have a responsibility to employ unemployed workers in the local area. They should support local environmental work. They should contribute to local charities.

Can businesses be ethical?

Some argue that businesses exist purely to make a profit. So long as an activity is legal, then the business has no further responsibilities. Others say that businesses have wider obligations. They should act ethically even if this reduces their profit.

But it could be argued that acting in an ethical way will lead to higher profits in the long run. Customers will buy from a business which they know trades in a fair way. Workers will work harder for a business which treats them well. A business that acts in an ethical way will also gain a good reputation in the community.

Checklist

1. Explain whether you think a business should make and sell: (a) products which have first been tested on animals; (b) toy guns; (c) cigarettes; (d) landmines.
2. Explain whether you think a business should buy products made by children as young as five in the Third World.
3. Give THREE examples of unfair actions by one business against another.
4. Why might treating workers well benefit a business even though it might seem more costly?
5. Explain what responsibility a business might have to the local environment in which it operates.

Botanicus opened its first shop in the UK in 2000. The business is the result of the vision of Dr Malcolm Stuart. In 1992, with just £500, he started the business in Ostra, a village in the Czech Republic. There are now 26 shops in the Czech Republic. The move to go global starts in London.

All the goods in the shops are produced in Ostra from organic ingredients. It includes foodstuffs, home fragrances, wines and beeswax candles, as well as a few cosmetics. The ingredients come from a 25 acre farm. The farm employs local people to do everything, from growing the crops to weaving and packing products. The farm and village itself has also become a tourist attraction. Despite its remoteness, the village attracted 1 000 visitors in its first month of opening.

Malcolm Stuart is determined that Botanicus should put something back into the Ostra community. The company trains local people in a variety of skills, including languages. There are opportunities for other local businesses to sell their products, as Botanicus is a success. Profit is also put back into the village. For instance, the local school and sewage system were rebuilt with money from Botanicus.

Source: adapted from *The Sunday Times*, 12.11.2000.

1. Botanicus could claim to put ethics at the top of the list of its business aims. Explain why the business could argue that it is:
(a) putting the needs of its customers first;
(b) producing in an environmentally sound way;
(c) putting its workers before its profit;
(d) serving the local community.
2. Botanicus would like to establish an organic farm somewhere in the UK to provide food for its shops. Discuss whether the business could compete nationally against large chains of shops like Boots.

UNIT 18

Competition in the market

Competition in the market for teenage magazines

Competition

Nearly all businesses in the UK face COMPETITION from other businesses. For example, in the market for ice creams, consumers can choose from Birds Eye Wall's, Mars and Hagen Daaz. In the market for magazines, consumers can choose between *J-17*, *Sugar*, *Bliss* and *Mizz*. In the market for televisions, consumers can choose between JVC, Hitachi, Sony, Panasonic and Toshiba.

Price takers

Some **markets** (☞ unit 3) are highly competitive. Businesses have no control over the price they receive for their products. They are **price takers**. Farming is an example. When a farmer takes sheep to market, he has to accept whatever price is arrived at in the **auction** (☞ unit 3).

The same is true for businesses which produce commodities like oil, iron ore, coal or gold. If they want to sell today, they have to accept the market price.

This price is set by the forces of **supply** and **demand** (☞ unit 1). The greater the supply or the less the demand, the lower will be the price. For example, farmers may have a good year and produce a bumper crop of potatoes. This is likely to lead to a fall in the price of potatoes. Demand for potatoes has not changed, but the supply has increased because of the good harvest. So the price goes down. If demand for potatoes falls, price will also go down.

In markets where firms are price takers, they tend to produce **generic products** (☞ unit 48). These are products which are identical. A

potato of one variety from one farm is the same as a potato from another farm. Gold from an Australian mine is the same as gold from a South African mine.

In these highly competitive markets, the main decision which firms have to make is how much to produce. The farmer, for instance, must decide how many acres of potatoes to grow. The gold mining company has to decide how much gold to mine this year.

Branded products

In many markets, though, firms can choose the price at which they sell. This is because products tend to be

---

Early in 2001, Sega announced that it would end production of its Dreamcast games console. The Japanese company had been making games consoles since 1983 and writing software for arcade games since the 1960s. The reason for Sega's decision was that it had been losing money on consoles. It lost an estimated 32 billion Yen (nearly £200 million) in the six months to September 2000. This was one fifth of the value of its total sales.

The launch of PlayStation by Sony in 1995 pushed it into third place in the international market. Its Dreamcast console was technologically the most advanced of its time when it was launched in 1998. But it failed to capture the public's imagination. This was despite the popularity of some of Sega's software, which included Sonic the Hedgehog. By 2001, it was in fourth place for sales, behind the original PlayStation, PlayStation 2 and Nintendo's Game Cube. Competition could only get worse when Microsoft

launched its own games console, the Microsoft X-Box in 2001-2002.

Sega's failure in the hardware market can, to some extent, be put down to its actions in the software market. Software companies were not able to develop games for Sega's machines. Instead, Sega restricted access to the source code for its games consoles to selected software partners. The benefit to Sega was that it sold more of its own software and collected higher royalties from the partners. The downside was that there was less software available for the Dreamcast than, say, PlayStation 2. With less software, consumers tended to buy PlayStation or the Nintendo Game Cube.

Sega is now going to concentrate on producing software games for other machines, including PlayStation.

Source: adapted from the *Financial Times*, 25.1.2001, *The Independent*, 5.2.2001.

1. How do businesses in the market for games machines and games software compete against each other?
2. Suggest why Sega decided to leave the games consoles market after 18 years.
3. Microsoft's new X-Box might be so popular that it pushes both Sony's PlayStation and Nintendo's Game Cube out of the market. Would this be good for consumers? Justify your answer.

branded (☞ unit 48) i.e. they are slightly different from each other. In these markets, businesses can choose to compete on price. But they often compete in other ways. For instance, they might develop new products. Or they might use advertising to give them an advantage over rivals. They might open up new markets by selling abroad or into a new area of the UK.

Where there are only a few competitors in the market, it is important for a business to respond to changes in the behaviour of other businesses. For instance, one toothpaste manufacturer might produce a new brand with a special ingredient. The new brand may be popular with consumers, who may switch to buying this product. Other toothpaste manufacturers are likely to bring out their own versions of the product. This will help them regain some of the sales they have lost.

Monopoly

In some markets there is no competition. One firm produces everything. This is known as a MONOPOLY. In the UK, for instance, the Post Office has a monopoly on the delivery of letters under the value of £1. Railtrack has a monopoly on the railway lines over which companies like Virgin or GNER run trains. Transco has a monopoly on gas pipelines used to take gas from terminals to homes and businesses.

Monopolists have considerable market power. They try to raise prices to the point where profits are maximised (☞ unit 20). For this reason, governments often control how monopolists behave. In the UK, the gas, electricity, water, telecommunications and rail industries are all controlled by a **regulator** (☞ unit 8). The regulator prevents monopolists exploiting consumers.

Businesses with large market shares and few rivals may also be known as monopolists. For example, Microsoft has 90 per cent of the world market for personal computer operating systems. It spends large amounts improving its products over time. This is because it risks losing its monopoly power to a business which produces a better product.

In 2000-2001, BT (British Telecom) came under attack from rival telephone companies. BT owns the telephone lines which go from the main trunk lines that connect different parts of the UK to individual houses and businesses. These local lines are known as the 'local loop'. Since the late 1990s, rival companies have been able to lease space on the local loop from BT. The price for this has been fixed by the regulator for the industry. This prevented BT charging such high prices that no other company could compete in the market.

However, the government and the industry believe that broad band access to homes and offices is the future for the industry. Broad band access would allow much faster transmission of internet services. It would also allow services such as video-on-demand. This is where a household could watch a video downloaded on the telephone line, rather than renting it from a shop.

To get broad band access, special equipment needs to be installed at local telephone exchanges. Each telephone company would install its own equipment rather than use that of BT. However, BT has been dragging its feet on this. It said that many of its telephone exchanges are now so full with equipment that there is no space for any more. This is particularly true in cities, where the majority of potential customers live or work. It has allowed some equipment to be installed, but only in telephone exchanges serving relatively few customers.

BT claims that it wants to allow competitors to offer broadband services. But it could be years before building work is finished to extend many of its telephone exchanges. Competitors argue that BT is using this as an excuse to keep them out of the market. BT's actions give it a head start in signing up customers for the new services.

Source: adapted from the *Financial Times*, 20.9.2000.

1. How, according to its competitors, has BT been acting as a monopolist on the 'local loop'?
2. Suggest why BT might want to maintain its monopoly on broad band services.
3. Discuss whether consumers would be better off if the regulator were abolished in the telecommunications industry, allowing BT to act in whatever way it wanted.

Checklist

1. Name THREE firms which compete in the petrol market.
2. 'Farmers are price takers.' What does this mean?
3. What is a generic product?
4. How might businesses compete in a market where they produce branded products?
5. Why is there no competition in a market with a monopolist?
6. Why might government want to regulate monopolists?

key terms

Competition - where more than one business makes products for a market. Businesses have to adopt strategies to prevent other businesses from forcing them out of the market.
Monopoly - an industry where one business produces all the output or has a very large share of the output.

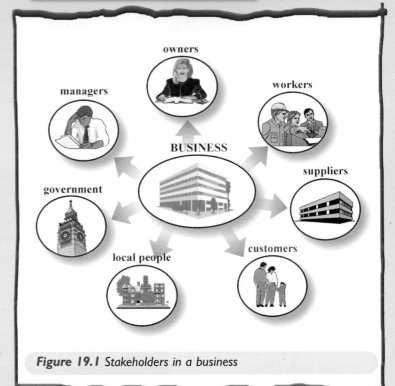

Stakeholders are people outside and within the business

Stakeholders

The STAKEHOLDERS of a business are those individuals or groups which are affected by the activities of the business. A business can have a number of different stakeholders, as shown in Figure 19.1.

Owners

One group of stakeholders is the owners of the business. In small and medium sized businesses, they are likely to be the people who run the business on a day to day basis. Owners of small businesses will be interested in how much money they can earn from the business. This might include the wage they pay themselves or the profit the business makes which is paid out to the owners. There may be two or three owners of a small business, who will then have to share out the profit that is made.

In large companies, the owners, called **shareholders** (☞ unit 27), are unlikely to be involved in the day to day running of the business. They will probably have bought **shares** (☞ unit 68) in the company through a stock exchange. They will be interested in the profit that is paid out to them as a reward for holding shares, the **dividend** (☞ unit 21). But they will also be interested in the price of the shares. The higher the price, the more they could gain if they sold their shares.

Managers

In a large company, the day to day running of the business is left to managers. They want the company to succeed for three main reasons.
- If the company does badly, they could lose their jobs.
- A successful company is likely to offer them more chance of promotion.

- A company may reward its managers for success by paying them higher salaries or giving them a bonus. Successful companies may also pay benefits on top of salaries, such as free private health care insurance.

Workers

The workers of a business have a stake in its success too. Like

Figure 19.1 Stakeholders in a business

In May 2000, Boo.com announced that it was going out of business. The failure was spectacular because the company had managed to spend £91 million invested in it by shareholders, which included members of the Benetton family, Bernard Arnault who owns the LVMH luxury goods group, and members of the Saudi Arabian royal family.

Boo.com was an internet company. It sold up-market sportswear at high prices to consumers in 18 countries including the USA and the UK. It failed mainly because it could not control its costs. It spent large amounts of money creating a state-of-the-art web site. It also spent heavily on advertising to gain consumer recognition. However, running costs were also high. When it failed, it was still spending £500 000 a month taking 3D photographs of its products to put on its web site. But it was only selling £300 000 worth of goods a month.

Many of the managers amongst the 450 workers made redundant had been promised large bonuses to attract them to the company. These would have been paid in the future if the company had been a success. Not only did they lose their jobs, they also lost these bonuses.

Source: adapted from the *Financial Times* 20.5.2000, 19.5.2000 and *The Guardian* 19.5.2000.

1. Explain how (a) owners and (b) managers as stakeholders in Boo.com were affected when it went out of business.

✓Checklist

1. A business is making a loss. How might this affect the owners of a business?
2. A business is expanding in size due to increased sales. How might this affect the managers of a business?
3. 'Workers are stakeholders in the business in which they work.' Explain why this is the case.
4. A business is about to launch a new drug. How might this affect the customer and suppliers who are stakeholders in the business?
5. A chemicals company is about to close a chemicals plant in Scotland employing 500 workers. Which stakeholders might be affected by this and how?

key terms

Stakeholder - an individual or group which is affected by a business and so has an interest in its success or failure.

managers, a failing company will threaten the jobs of workers. Management might also ask workers to take a pay freeze or even a cut in wages. In a successful business, workers are more likely to get pay rises. There will be more money available to provide workers with benefits, like a staff canteen or a pension scheme. If the business is growing in size, there will be chances for promotion within the business.

Suppliers

Businesses buy goods and services from suppliers (☞ unit 5). For instance, a car manufacturer will buy components from engineering suppliers. Suppliers have a stake in the business. The more successful a business, the more likely it is that its orders for supplies will increase. A failing business could see falling orders for supplies, leading possibly to lower profits and job losses.

Customers

Customers have a stake in any business from which they could buy goods or services. Customers want low prices, with the best quality available at that price. They also want good service and are looking for innovative products. If a business is to be successful in the long term, it has to provide customers with the products they want to buy.

The local area

Businesses have an impact on any

area where they are located. For instance, they create jobs for workers living locally. They will often buy from local suppliers. They might provide a service to local people or businesses. They might also have an impact on the local environment. So the local area has a stake in any business located there. For instance, the local area will suffer if a firm closes a factory with the loss of 500 jobs. Local people

might welcome the opening of a new supermarket. They might oppose the opening of a tyre recycling plant because of fears of pollution.

Government

Government too is a stakeholder. A business pays taxes. When businesses are doing well, government will collect more in taxes. It can then either spend more or choose to cut taxes on households. If businesses fail and workers are made unemployed, the government will have to pay unemployment benefits. Pollution is also something for which the government is responsible.

In November 2000, a train came off the tracks at Hatfield. The problem was a cracked rail. The company which owns the rail system, Railtrack, immediately ordered a complete inspection of all the track in the UK and the replacement of any cracked rails. Until work was completed on any stretch of track, speed restrictions were imposed.

The result was chaos. Many trains were cancelled. Others suffered delays. A half an hour journey could now take one hour, with overcrowding common. Passengers were furious. Some commuters decided to go to work by car instead, increasing traffic congestion, especially in London. Other passengers simply didn't travel.

The railway train operators, which ran trains across the tracks owned by Railtrack, suffered sharp falls in their revenues. Not only did they lose passengers, but they had to pay out compensation to them because of late trains. Their profits were down even though Railtrack paid them more than £200 million in compensation.

The only happy ones were the rail contractors fixing the rail lines. These companies, employed by Railtrack, were likely to record higher profits from all the work they were suddenly given to do by Railtrack.

Source: adapted from various articles after November 2000.

1. List the possible stakeholders in Railtrack.
2. How do you think each of the stakeholders in Railtrack were affected by the problems in 2000?

UNIT 20

The aims and objectives of business

Survival is important when trading conditions are difficult

Survival

One important objective of most businesses is survival. This is particularly true when a business first starts up. It is also true for a business which gets into trading difficulties, for instance in a **recession** (☞ unit 10). To **survive**, a business has at least to **break even** (☞ unit 73) over time. This means that it makes neither a profit nor a loss. If it continually makes a loss, it will almost certainly go out of business.

Profit maximisation

Most businesses want to do more than survive over time. They want to make a profit. So another objective of a business may be to MAXIMISE PROFITS.

The main stakeholders who benefit from profit maximisation are the owners. For a small business, the owner is likely to be the person running and working in the business. A painter and decorator, working on his own, would obviously prefer to make £20 000 a year rather than £2 000 a year.

In a large business the owners will be the shareholders, who may not work for the business. They hold these shares to make a financial gain. If a business maximises its profits, two things often happen. First, the amount of money paid out to shareholders each year as their share of the profits, the **dividend** (☞ unit 21), is likely to be high. Second, the value of the shares on the stock market is likely to be high too. So shareholders may be able to sell their shares at a higher price than they paid for them. They will then make a **capital gain**.

Maximising dividends, together with a rise in share in price, will maximise SHAREHOLDER VALUE. The owners, then, have a strong incentive for the business they own to make as much profit as possible.

Sales objectives

Some businesses choose to maximise sales rather than profits. One reason is that it is difficult to know the maximum amount of profit a business could make. So it might be easier to aim for sales growth. Usually, higher sales lead to higher profits anyway.

In large businesses there may be another reason for maximising sales. Shareholders delegate the 'day to day' running of businesses to directors and managers. If a business grows, directors and managers can benefit. Large companies often pay higher salaries and bonuses to top managers. So it might be in managers' interests to have higher sales and smaller profits in order to gain high earnings. Managers, however, must always make sure that the business is able to PROFIT SATISFICE. This is where it makes enough profit to keep shareholders happy.

Other objectives

Owners and managers may have other objectives. Owners of small businesses, for instance, often value their freedom and independence. They might not be willing to take on contracts which tie them down to working long hours. Equally, they might want to remain small and not take on extra workers. They might take on work which they enjoy most rather than work which is most profitable.

Managers of large businesses might prefer a job with less responsibility to one which is stressful but has a higher salary. Some managers like variety and choice. They may enjoy visiting clients to being in the office all day.

Peter Fowler opened his first fitness club twelve months ago. He had high hopes for it, but it turned into a nightmare. £750 000 was spent on the building and buying equipment for the new club, as well as marketing before it opened. After one year of operation he still only had 800 members compared to the 3 000 he hoped for. Just to break even, he needed 1 900 members.

Peter Fowler put £300 000 into the club himself and is the sole owner. He borrowed another £600 000 from his bank. £500 000 of that was a second mortgage on his house. He now feels he badly needs some business advice.

1. What problem does Peter Fowler now face?
2. What do you think Peter Fowler's objective for his business should be (a) now, in the short term and (b) over the longer term of the next five years?
3. Discuss ONE way in which the business could be turned around. Write down the possible advantages and disadvantages of your business idea.

Oasis Stores plc is a design led retail company that originates and procures the production of all its merchandise which is then sold exclusively through its own Oasis stores and concessions targeted at the womenswear market in the 18-35 year age bracket.

The Company has a second brand trading under the name 'Coast' aimed at a slightly more mature market. It also designs and sells its products exclusively through its own outlets which are separate to those of Oasis.

Management's short term priority is to focus on profit growth. Through better management of our sources of supply and tighter management of markdowns, our aim is to increase gross margins. With greater operational efficiency and close control of costs, operating margins will be further improved.

At Coast our immediate priority is to grow profitability. We remain convinced that there is a gap in the market for the older, more discerning customer who requires the appropriate fashion interpretation.

I am confident that we have the skills at Oasis to make sure we further increase our market share profitably. Above all to be in the forefront of developing our product and store environment to make sure our customers enjoy and are excited by the Oasis shopping experience. We will also be alert to the opportunities of new methods of bringing our goods to market as well as developing new markets for our offer.

Source: Oasis, *Annual Report and Accounts*, 1999-2000.

1. 'The main objective of Oasis is to provide customers with a shopping experience that they enjoy and are excited by.' Discuss whether you think this is true. Use evidence from the extracts to support your argument.

Owners and managers are not the only **stakeholders** (☞ unit 19) in a business. Other stakeholders will have their own objectives.
• Workers are interested in how much they earn, their conditions of work, etc. Better pay and conditions of work mean increased costs for a business. This could lead to a lowering of profit.
• Customers want better quality products at lower prices.
• Local groups might want to see jobs preserved in the local economy or pollution restricted.

So there could be a conflict of objectives between different groups within a business and outside it. Whose objectives become the most important in any situation will depend upon the relative power of each group. For instance, environmentalists might be able to force a change in the policy of a business by organising a boycott of its products. Workers might be able to earn higher wages at the expense of lower profits by going on strike. Customers might force a business to spend more on research and development by buying more innovative products from rivals. In the long term, however, a business must always at least break even to survive.

1. Most businesses aim at least to break even. Why is this true?
2. Why might the aim of a business be to maximise its profits?
3. (a) What is meant by sales maximisation? (b) Why might a business want to maximise its sales?
4. What conflict of objectives might there be between different groups in a large company?

Judging the success of a business (1)

Newspaper headlines from 2001. Increases in sales and profits may indicate successful companies

The stakeholders' perspective

How can the success or a failure of a business be judged? There is a number of different **criteria** (or ways) which can be used. These are discussed in this unit and the next.

Different **stakeholders** (☞ unit 19) in a business will have different views. For workers, a successful business might be one which pays above average wages and a good range of benefits. For shareholders, it might be one which cuts costs, including wages, to achieve a high profit. For the local economy, it might be a business which creates jobs. So what one group of stakeholders might see as success, another might see as unimportant. They might even argue that the business is failing.

Profit

One way to judge success is to look at profit. The more successful the business, the more profit it makes. But in practice, comparing profit is often difficult. BT (British Telecom) is not necessarily more successful because it makes £500 million profit a year than a small engineering business which makes £100 000 profit. There are different factors which must be taken into account.

Capital employed The size of the business needs to be taken into account. One common way of doing this is to compare the **rate of return on capital employed** (☞ unit 84). This divides the amount of profit made by the value of the capital in the business. For instance, a large business might have £1 billion (i.e 1 000 million) of assets like offices, factories, equipment and cash. If it makes £100 million profit, its rate

of return is 10 per cent (100 per cent × £100 million ÷ £1 000 million). A small business might have £20 000 worth of assets and make £10 000 profit. Its rate of return is 50 per cent (100 % × £10 000 ÷ £20 000). So the smaller business would be more successful using this measure.

The dividend paid For the owners of the business, the profits made might be less important than the share of the profit paid out to them. In a company, this share of profit is called the DIVIDEND. The **dividend per share** is the amount paid out on each share held. It is equal to the total dividend divided by the number of shares in the business. Businesses often don't pay out all the profits made because they want to

retain some of them (☞ unit 67). They do this to keep cash reserves in case of emergencies. Or they might be used to pay for investment in the business. For owners, a successful business might be one which pays out large amounts of profits to them. A sign of failure might be when a business has to cut the profits paid out.

A highly profitable business might not necessarily be one which benefits most of its stakeholders. The owners might do well because they receive a

	1996	1997	1998	1999	2000
Profit (£million)	12.6	16.4	29.8	41.0	61.8
Assets (£million)	22.2	36.6	49.5	70.0	108.5
Dividend per share (pence)	0.56	0.71	1.20	1.80	2.15

Table 21.1 *SFI Group plc, financial statistics*
Source: adaopted from SFI plc, *Annual Report and Accounts*, 2000.

The SFI Group is a company which runs pubs and coffee and sandwich bars. Its businesses have brand names such as 'The Slug and Lettuce', 'The Litten Tree', 'Bar Med' and 'Cafe Litten'. Between 1996 and 2000, the company saw strong growth.

(a) Describe what happened between 1996 and 2000 to (a) profits, (b) the assets owned by the SFI Group and (c) dividends paid out.
(b) Discuss whether the figures suggest that the SFI Group has been successful between 1996 and 2000.

The Expro Group is a company which provides services and products to other companies engaged in oil and gas exploration and production. In 1999-2000, the Expro Group experienced some difficulties because the price of oil fell sharply. This led to its business customers cutting back on their spending on exploration.

1. Describe what happened to (a) sales turnover, (b) profit and (c) dividends paid between 1996 and 2000.
2. Discuss how successful the Expro Group has been between 1996 and 2000.

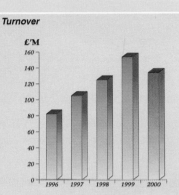

Turnover

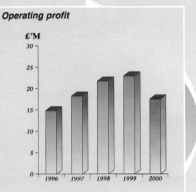

Operating profit

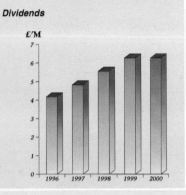

Dividends

Figure 21.1 The Expro Group, financial statistics
Source: adapted from The Expro Group, *Annual Report and Accounts*, 2000.

share of the profits. But the business may pay low wages or pollute the environment. It may force its suppliers to sell at very low prices, whilst it charges high prices to its customers. On the other hand, some highly profitable businesses might give benefits to all stakeholders. Profits can only be one measure of success from a stakeholder's viewpoint.

Sales growth

Another common way to measure success is to look at the growth in sales. A business which sees sales grow by 50 per cent in one year is likely to be more successful than one which has no growth.

But other factors need to be taken into account. Sales growth without growth in profit is not necessarily good for a business. At worst, sales could grow fast, but the business may be forced to close down

because the extra sales are unprofitable.

Also, it is often important to compare businesses within an industry. If sales in an industry, like textiles, are falling over time, then a textile business which keeps its sales constant is being successful.

The same is true for industry as a whole. In 1990-92, the UK economy went into a deep recession (☞ unit 10). Many businesses saw

their sales fall. Businesses which grew even quite slowly at the time might have been said to be successful.

As with profits, high sales growth might benefit some stakeholders more than others. For instance, jobs might be created but the growth in sales may have a negative effect on the environment. Also, directors might pay themselves an extra 30 per cent when wages only go up by 2 per cent.

key terms

Dividend - a share of the profits of a company received by those who own shares in it.

✓Checklist

1. A business awards a five per cent pay rise to its workers. Why might workers judge that the business is being a success when the owners might see it as a sign of failure?
2. Business A makes £2 million profit with assets of £10 million. Business B, in the same industry, makes profits of £10 million with assets of £100 million. Explain which company is most successful.
3. One year, a company makes £10 million profit and distributes £5 million in dividend to shareholders. The next year it makes £8 million profit and distributes £6 million to shareholders. The following year, it makes a loss of £2 million but still distributes £6 million in dividends. Explain, from the shareholders' viewpoint, in which year or years the company was most successful.
4. Explain why growth in sales might be seen as a sign of success for a business.

Judging the success of a business (2)

In Unit 21, two measures of the success of a business were considered - profit and sales growth. This unit explains four other measures.

Market share

The MARKET SHARE of a business can be measured as the sales by one business in a market compared to the total sales in the market. This is then shown as a percentage. The formula is:

$$\text{Market share} = \frac{\text{Sales by the business}}{\text{Total sales in the market}} \times 100\%$$

For instance, a business might sell £100 million worth of goods in a market. If total sales in the market were £200 million, then it would have a market share of 50 per cent (100 × £100 million ÷ £200 million). So it would have half the sales in that market. Figure 22.1 shows the market share of UK mobile phone companies.

A business might be considered successful if it gains market share from its competitors. This would suggest that it is doing better than its rivals. Perhaps it has been able to cut its costs more and pass this on to customers as lower prices. Or it might have introduced new products which attracted customers. Either would benefit customers, who are stakeholders in the business.

An increased market share is likely to be linked to increased sales. This should benefit the owners and workers, as well as the local economy where the business is based. However, sales could fall despite increased market share if the sales in the whole market are in decline.

Job creation

Growing businesses are likely to need more workers. They create jobs. Owners of a business might not judge the success of a business by how many employees it has. But other stakeholders, like the workers of a business, the government and people living in the area where jobs are created will see job creation as an important measure of success. Job creation brings new wealth to an area and more opportunities for workers.

When a business has to make workers redundant, this is often taken

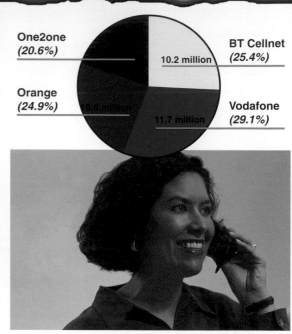

One2one (20.6%)   BT Cellnet (25.4%)
10.2 million
Orange (24.9%)   Vodafone (29.1%)
10.0 million   11.7 million

Figure 22.1 *Market share of mobile phone companies, UK Q4, 2000, subscriber numbers*
Source: adapted from the *Financial Times*, 1.2.2001.

as a sign of failure. Workers who lose their jobs can be badly affected if they don't get another job quickly. Income in the local area is likely to go down, which could affect other businesses including suppliers. The government might have to pay out more in benefits.

More than 2 000 workers at the Goodyear tyre plant in Wolverhampton were told that 550 jobs would have to go in 2001. Goodyear, whose headquarters is in the USA, has been hit by tough trading conditions which have led to falls in demand for its tyres. Cutting the jobs in Wolverhampton would help reduce its costs. A spokesperson for the company said: 'We regret the impact that these redundancies will have on the associates (the workers), their families and the community of Wolverhampton'.
Source: adapted from the *Express & Star*, 8.1.2001.

1. Explain which of Goodyear's stakeholders is (a) likely to benefit and (b) lose out from the announced job cuts in Wolverhampton.
2. Do you think that the redundancy programme shows that Goodyear as a business is doing well or badly? Give reasons to support your judgment.

key terms

Market share - the proportion of sales by one business in a market compared to the total size of the market.

Wealth creation

Some argue that a successful business is one which creates wealth. The term 'wealth' has different meanings.

- Wealth might be the assets of a business - factories, offices, shops, machines or land. The more assets held by a business, the more it should be able to produce. So a business which is creating wealth should be increasing its production and therefore its sales. This should benefit most of its stakeholders.
- Wealth might be the workers in a business. A business which is creating wealth might be one which is increasing the skills of its workers and making them more productive. This tends to benefit society as a whole because those workers can now produce more. It should benefit shareholders because profits could rise. Also, the workers themselves might be able

to earn higher wages if they are more productive.
- Wealth might be all the production associated with a business. This includes the production of suppliers to the business. It also includes production that results from increased spending by workers of a business. A successful business would then be one which created wealth in society as a whole, not just in the business itself.

✔Checklist

1. Business A has sixty per cent market share, whilst business B has 15 per cent market share of the same market. (a) Explain the difference between the two businesses. (b) A year ago, Business A had 70 per cent market share and business B had 5 per cent. Suggest, with reasons, which has been the most successful firm over the past year.
2. A car manufacturer which employs 2 000 workers at a site in Birmingham announces that it will build a new model at the plant and will need to employ another 1000 workers. Why might this suggest that the firm is successful?
3. A microchip manufacturer announces that it will set up a new £500 million plant in South Wales. Explain how this (a) will lead to wealth creation and (b) could be an indicator that the business is successful.
4. Between 1870 and 1970, Cadbury, the chocolate manufacturer, was famous for treating its workers well. For instance, it built Bourneville Village to provide workers with decent housing. Why might this be an indicator that the company was successful?

Social benefits

Some businesses are judged as successful because they benefit stakeholders other than owners. The John Lewis Partnership, for instance, passes the profits made on to its workers. The Body Shop makes a point of being environmentally friendly, by not using animals to test its cosmetics (☞ unit 17). Some businesses create new roads or remove waste ground in local areas where they build factories.

Powers had been the only butchers in the village of Castleton for 50 years. Thirty years ago, the local Co-operative Society had opened a small supermarket opposite the shop selling some pre-packed fresh and frozen meat. But it provided little competition for Powers.

Castleton had grown over time and become very attractive for those on above average incomes. Last year, a new butchers, Bennetts, had set up next to the Co-op. It announced that it was a seller of 'Fine Meats'. It stocked up-market goods from local farms and produced its own prize-winning range of sausages and burgers. Prices were higher than at Powers, but so too was the quality.

For Powers, the entry of Bennetts into the local market was disastrous. The butchers lost about a quarter of its customers almost overnight. Worse still, they tended to be the highest spending customers. The result was that sales were cut in half.

To survive, the owner of Powers sacked three out of the four workers employed at the time. Even then, the profit, out of which the owner was paid a wage, fell from £30 000 a year to £10 000.

1. Compare the two businesses, Powers and Bennetts. Which is the more successful business? In your answer, consider 'success' from the viewpoint of all the stakeholders in each business.
2. Discuss whether Powers should stay in business.

Sole traders

Andy Garner is a painter and decorator. For years, he had worked for Pete Spencer with another couple of workers. But 12 months ago he decided to go it alone and establish his own business. To promote the business, he bought a second hand van and had his name put on the side. Andy had no savings, so he borrowed the £5 000 needed to pay for the van.

Unfortunately, business was a lot tougher than he expected. He wasn't very convincing when meeting potential customers. As a result, few of the quotes he gave were taken up. He found himself doing a lot of sub-contracting work. Some of it was for Pete, but at lower rates of pay than he was on before. Then he started to get behind with the repayments on the van. The loan company began to send him threatening letters. It said that he would be taken to court if he didn't catch up with the repayments.

1. 'Andy Garner is a sole trader.' What does this mean?
2. What does his business sell?
3. Andy Garner has unlimited liability. What does this mean for him as he has problems making repayments on his van?
4. Suggest TWO ways in which Andy could deal with the problems he is facing. Explain the advantages and disadvantages to him of taking up each of your suggestions.

Sole proprietorships

Most businesses in the UK are SOLE PROPRIETORSHIPS. This type of business is owned by just one person, the SOLE TRADER (or SOLE PROPRIETOR). Some sole traders employ other workers to work for them. Many, though, work on their own. Because sole traders are not employed by a business they are also called the SELF-EMPLOYED. There are about 3 million self-employed in the UK today. Nearly all are sole traders.

Sole proprietorships tend to be small businesses. They are often found in service rather than manufacturing industries. They are common in agriculture and retailing, as well as building services like plumbing, decorating and roofing.

Liability

In law, there is no difference between the private money and the business funds of a sole trader. This is important when it comes to paying debts. For instance, a sole trader might borrow £20 000 to set up in business. She might not earn enough from the business to repay the loan. But the sole trader is still liable for the repayments. She would have to use her private money to meet the debt. If necessary, she might be forced to sell her own car or house to raise the money. This is known as having UNLIMITED LIABILITY. There is no limit to the amount that an individual is liable for when paying the debts of the business.

Funding

Sole proprietorships tend to be small businesses. So they can often be started with little money. For instance, a decorator would need almost no money to change from being employed by

Small businesses offering roofing services tend to be sole proprietorships

someone else to setting up on his own as a sole trader. Setting up in the retail trade is more costly. Even so, a small shop might be started for less than £50 000. This is less than half the average price of a house in the UK.

The money used to set up in business often comes from two sources. First, sole traders put in their own savings. Second, they may borrow money from a bank or from family and friends. They would then repay the money with interest over time.

If the business is a success, the sole trader is likely to use the profit it makes for extra investment. For instance, a shop may increase the amount of stock it holds for sale over time. The extra stock is a cost to the business, which could be paid for from **retained profits** (☞ unit 67).

Tax

The personal and business finances of sole traders are also treated the same by the tax authorities. So the profit of the business is the income of the individual. As such, sole traders have to pay **income tax** on their profits. They also have to pay National Insurance contributions (NICs). Rates of NIC are different for sole traders compared to workers employed by someone else. Sole traders also have to charge VAT if their sales are more than around £50 000 a year.

Aims and objectives

Most sole traders aim to make as much profit as possible from their business. Self-employed people often work longer hours than workers in

Gloria Valdez runs her own business which organises weddings. For a 10 per cent fee, she will do everything - book the wedding venue and reception, arrange wedding insurance, lay on a creche and buy the wedding invitations.

She started the business with her own savings, from the spare room in her home. She still works from home, although it has now been extended so that a part-time secretary can work there. She uses her own car and her telephone. The only other expense is printing some stationery. She has changed little, although she now drives a BMW and wears designer clothes to impress her customers.

Much of her time is spent visiting clients and discussing with them every detail of their wedding day. Over the years she has built up a large number of contacts in the wedding industry. These include hotels, caterers and vicars in Surrey and London where she operates.

The money she earns is not the only part of her job which motivates her. She enjoys meeting people and finds great satisfaction in organising the 'big day' for the bride and groom. In summer, especially, she may work long hours, but life is less hectic in the winter.

Wordprocessing

1. Gloria has been interviewed by a reporter from a local newspaper. The reporter is running a feature on small businesses. Write a short article which should include:
(a) a description of Gloria's business;
(b) how she obtained the funds to set up and run her business;
(c) what motivates Gloria to work as a sole trader.

a business. This might suggest that they prefer more money to more leisure time. So most are **profit maximisers** (☞ unit 20).

However, some workers become self-employed because they can work fewer hours than if they were employed by someone else. They may also like the freedom to take time off when they want. For instance, a self-employed electrician could just work three days a week, or work over Christmas and take holidays in January if he wished.

In the first few years of setting up, a sole trader might just aim to survive. This might also be true if sole traders were hit by factors outside their control. For instance, a local hardware store might find that sales fall because a B&Q DIY warehouse opens nearby. Or a recession might cause sales to fall sharply.

Checklist

1. Who owns a sole proprietorship?
2. Who keeps the profits of a sole proprietorship?
3. 'Meena had unlimited liability.' What does this mean?
4. How do sole traders tend to raise the money to start their businesses or make new investments?
5. What taxes do sole traders have to pay?
6. What are likely to be the aims of a sole trader?

key terms

Self-employed - individuals who work for themselves and are not employed by someone else.
Sole proprietorship - a business owned by a single person who has unlimited liability.
Sole trader or sole proprietor - the owner of a sole proprietorship business.
Unlimited liability - a legal obligation on the owners of a business to settle (pay off) all debts of the business. In law, there is no distinction between the assets and debts of the business and the personal assets and debts of the owner.

Why become a sole trader?

Sole proprietorships give decorators freedom and flexibility

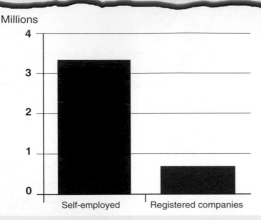

```
Millions
4

3

2

1

0
      Self-employed    Registered companies
```

Figure 24.1 Most self-employed are sole traders. The rest are partners in partnerships. The number of self-employed people outweighs the number of companies in the UK
Source: adapted from *Monthly Digest of Statistics*, ONS; *Business Monitor PA P003*.

The advantages of being a sole trader

As Figure 24.1 shows, many businesses in the UK are sole proprietorships. There must therefore be some major advantages to setting up this type of business.

Easy to set up It is easy to set up as a sole trader. A person can set up in business immediately. There are few, if any, forms to fill in or procedures needed to set up. Sole traders do have to fill in an income tax form each year. And they have to keep accounts to show how much they have earned. They may also have to register with Customs and Excise, which collects Value Added Tax (VAT). If sales are approximately over £50 000, sole traders have to charge VAT on their sales and keep records of payments. This can take a great deal of time.

Easy to run Any business is difficult to operate successfully. But a sole proprietorship is easier to run than other types of business. Owners are in sole charge. They do not need to get others to agree before making changes. Lawyers and accountants don't need to be hired to set up the business. Many sole traders do use an accountant to help keep the accounts needed by the Inland Revenue and Customs and Excise.

Tax advantages A sole trader is taxed in a different way to people in other types of business. For instance, National Insurance contributions are lower for a self-employed person than if they were working for a **company** (☞ unit 27). Sole traders also have more scope for reducing their income tax bills. This is because they can often claim money back against tax for work expenses, such as computer equipment and books.

Control The owner is in sole charge. She can make whatever changes she wants. For instance, sole traders don't have to call partnership meetings or shareholders' meetings to agree changes.

Capital A business nearly always needs capital to start trading. However, the amount needed to set

---

Kerry James wants to set up in business. She has trained as a draughtsperson. She has asked a friend who knows about business for advice. One of the things her friend talked about was tax and fees for setting up and running a company rather than being a sole trader. This advice is summarised in Table 24.1. Kerry hopes to earn £10, 000 from the business in the first year.

1. Look at Table 24.1. Would she be better off from a tax and fee viewpoint becoming a sole trader or setting up a limited company?

	Sole trader	Limited company
Legal fee to set up business	None	At least £100
Annual accounts fees for audit	None	At least £200
Income tax	Payable twice yearly	Payable monthly, immediately after the money has been earned
National Insurance contributions	*Class 2 contributions* £104.00 per year **plus** *Class 4 contributions* 7% on income earned between £4,385 and £27,820 a year	*Class 1 contributions* Employees' contributions of 0% on earnings up to £76 a week and 10% on earnings between £76 and £535 a week **plus** Employers' contributions 11.9% of income in excess of £76 a week

Table 24.1

up in business as a sole trader is usually low.

Profits All the profits of the business are kept by the sole trader. They don't have to be split up amongst other owners or shareholders. So there is a link between the effort and rewards of a sole trader. The harder a sole trader works, and the more successful the business, the more can be earned.

Privacy Only the Inland Revenue and Customs and Excise need to know about the finances of a sole trader. A sole trader doesn't have to publish any information which could be seen by the public or by rivals.

Labour relations The larger a business, the more scope there is for misunderstanding and problems. Many sole traders work on their own, although some hire extra workers. Because the number of workers is so small, relations between the workers and the employer are likely to be good.

Flexibility Many sole traders have some choice about when they work. They don't have to ask permission, for instance, to have an hour off.

The disadvantages of being a sole trader

Being a sole trader also has some disadvantages.

Unlimited liability Sole traders have **unlimited liability** (☞ unit 23)

for any business debts. If the business does badly, they could be forced to sell possessions like their car or house to pay for these debts.

Lack of continuity Because the sole trader **is** the business, it may not survive if the sole trader stops work. If the business is a shop, it might be possible to sell it on to someone else. But if it is a decorating business, it may cease trading if the sole trader decides to retire.

Illness Sole traders can have problems if they become ill. This is because their businesses may stop if they don't work. They will lose income. At worst, the businesses could collapse if they are ill for a long time.

Long hours Many sole traders work long hours to keep their businesses afloat. They often work longer than workers who are employed by someone else.

Difficulty of raising capital Sole traders often get the money to start and expand their businesses from their savings or from bank loans. Larger types of business tend to have more choice about how to raise capital (☞ unit 67). So they may find it easier to expand if the opportunity is there.

Limited specialisation Sole traders carry out many jobs in a business. They develop a wide range of skills needed to survive. For instance, they may learn how to

market their products and keep their own accounts. Large businesses often buy in specialist workers to do these jobs. Specialist workers are likely to be quicker and more effective. Sole traders may not gain these advantages of **specialisation** (☞ unit 2).

Limited economies of scale Sole traders may have higher average costs than larger businesses. They are often unable to gain **economies of scale** (☞ unit 34). For instance, a small grocer can't buy in the bulk that a large supermarket chain can. So they don't get the same discounts. Sole traders often work in industries where economies of scale are not particularly large, such as plumbing or farming. This means that they can compete on cost grounds against large businesses.

✓ Checklist

1. Why are sole proprietorships easy to (a) set up and (b) run?
2. What tax advantages do sole traders have?
3. What happens to a sole proprietorship if the owner falls ill or dies?
4. Why do sole traders often find it difficult to raise the money to start a business?
5. 'A lack of specialisation can often hinder the success of a sole proprietorship.' Explain why.

Mike Haggett has just sold up his bike shop. He is a disillusioned man. He started 15 years ago when his grandmother left him £4 000. The money was used to rent a bike shop on the edge of the town centre of Leeds and to buy stock. At the time, the economy was booming. He had no trouble establishing the business and making it profitable. He bought a second shop three years later in Headingly, Leeds, just as the economy was beginning to go into recession. Sales slumped and instead of having one shop that was unprofitable, he now had two. What's more, he found that hiring and motivating staff took a lot of time and effort. Then there were also the books to keep for the business.

A turning point came in 1991 when his second shop was burgled twice in two months. His insurance premiums became so high that he couldn't afford to keep the shop open. He lost £10 000 closing down the shop. This was more than he ever made in profit from it. During the 1990s, his original shop went through ups and downs, but never made the sort of money that Mike hoped for. He was working seven days a week, six days in the shop and Sundays doing the books and ordering stock. In 1998 he suffered a robbery when some of his bikes were stolen. Competition from big retailers like Halfords seemed to get worse.

He finally sold the business in 2001 for £20 000, including stock, after suffering serious back problems.

1. Explain THREE problems that Mike faced as a sole trader.
2. Discuss whether his business would have been more successful if he had continued to open branches and developed a chain of bike shops in Yorkshire.

UNIT 25

Partnerships

Accountancy businesses are often partnerships

Partnerships

PARTNERS are the joint owners of a business. The law says that an ORDINARY PARTNERSHIP can have between 2 and 20 partners. Partners in an ordinary partnership have **unlimited liability** (☞ unit 23). This means that they have to pay any debts of the business, even if they have to sell their personal possessions.

In a partnership, all partners are liable for debts even if they have been caused by another partner. For instance, one partner might take out a loan to buy an expensive company car without asking permission from the others. The loan agreement will be signed in the name of the partnership. All partners then become responsible for repaying the loan.

Many partnerships are ordinary partnerships. But there are two other types of partnership. Both can have more than 20 partners.

- In LIMITED PARTNERSHIPS, some partners can own part of the business but have no active role in its running. They are then called SLEEPING PARTNERS. In law, sleeping partners in limited partnerships can have **limited liability** (☞ unit 27) There must be at least one partner, however, that is involved in running the business and has unlimited liability.
- In LIMITED LIABILITY PARTNERSHIPS, all partners have limited liability.

Deed of partnership

When a partnership is set up, the law states that every partner is equal. However much partners work or put into the business, each partner must get the same share of the profits. They must also take equal responsibility for debts.

But in many partnerships, partners put in unequal amounts of money and work different hours. So partners often get a solicitor to draw up a DEED OF PARTNERSHIP. This is a legal contract between the partners which sets out:

- who are the partners;
- how much money (or capital) each partner has put into the partnership;
- how profits should be shared out;
- how many votes each partner has in any partnership meeting;
- what happens if any of the partners want to withdraw from the business, or new partners are brought in. Figure 25.1 shows a deed of partnership for a business that runs an antique store in East Anglia.

Funding

Like sole proprietorships, partnerships often get the funds to start or expand the business from two sources. First, partners put their savings into the business. As time goes on, they may keep back part of the profits made to invest in the business. Second, partnerships borrow money, mainly from banks.

Partnerships may require more finance than a sole proprietorship. One of the reasons why partners join together is that the cost of setting up a business is more than

---

EITHER draw up a deed of partnership for your mini-company using the questions OR carry out the following activity. Four students have decided to set up in a partnership to sell stationery, such as pens, pencils, note paper, plastic wallets etc. They each have different views about the partnership and are prepared to put in different amounts of money. Draw up a deed of partnership for the business. You will need to take into account factors such as:

- who will own the business;
- how the profits will be distributed;
- how much capital (money) will be needed;
- who will put up the money to buy stock for the business;
- the roles of people in the business;
- what will happen if some people are more active in the running of the business. You could carry out this activity as a role play exercise.

Faisal - hardworking, a natural leader, has two part time jobs, willing to put £20 into the business to start it off.

Claire - not very reliable, gets excited about work to start with, often stands up for 'her rights', never had a job, thinks her mum will put some money in.

Wayne - not very interested, only in the group because he's got to be, sometimes doesn't get on with others in the group.

Susan - meticulous, likes everything organised properly, always on time and well prepared, doesn't like people who don't pull their weight, has £300 in the building society.

> **This deed of partnership is made, the 1st day of January 2001**
> **BETWEEN**
> 1. James Driscoll of 255 Easter Road, Norwich (Mr Driscoll); and
> 2. Heather Driscoll of 255 Easter Road, Norwich (Mrs Driscoll); and
> 3. Mughal Shahid of 56 Diss Road, Attleborough (Mr Shahid); and
> 4. Jenny Leyland, The Manors, Old Road, Banham (Ms Leyland)
> **WHEREAS**
> (1) Mr Driscoll, Mrs Driscoll, Mr Shahid and Ms Leyland have agreed to enter into partnership together to practise as buyers and sellers of antiques.

Figure 25.1 *Part of a deed of partnership*

one person can afford. However, some partnerships are formed with very little capital.

In limited partnerships, **sleeping partners** may provide vitally needed money to help set up or expand the partnership.

Tax

Like a sole trader, partners have to pay income tax on the profits they earn from the business. Partnerships with sales in excess of around £50 000 also have to charge VAT to customers. They then pay this to Customs and Excise.

Partnerships in business

Most partnerships are relatively small businesses. Shops, farms and catering businesses account for half of all partnerships in the UK. Many are family partnerships, particularly in farming. This is where a husband and wife, or parents and children, for instance, own the business jointly.

In some professions, like medicine, accountancy and law, it is normal for businesses to be partnerships. Doctors, dentists, accountants and other professionals like to keep their business affairs private. However, partnerships allow them to offer the range of services their customers expect.

The very largest partnerships today may become limited liability partnerships. This is because limited liability protects the personal assets of partners if the partnership fails and large debts are left to be paid. However, limited liability partnerships have to have their accounts audited independently, which is costly. Many

partnerships don't want to deal with all the regulations associated with being a limited liability partnership. So they stay as ordinary partnerships.

Aims and objectives

Most partners take a full and active role in the business. So they are both owners and workers. Making as much profit as possible, **profit maximising**, is an important objective for many partners. However, many also place value on being able to organise work in the way they want. Having a pleasant job may be more important than making more money. For some, like doctors, being of service to the community is an important objective.

key terms

Deed of partnership - **the legal contract which governs how a partnership will be owned and organised.**
Limited liability partnership - **a business organisation where at least two partners own the business and have limited liability.**
Limited partnership - **a business organisation where some partners play no role in the running of the business. These sleeping partners just provide financial capital for the business. They are entitled to limited liability.**
Ordinary partnership - **a business organisation which has between 2 and 20 owners, all of whom have unlimited liability.**
Partners - **the owners of a partnership.**

Caroline Chesney set up her publishing business three years ago. She specialises in producing children's books. The business, a sole proprietorship, has had some success. Last year, for the first time, it was profitable enough for her to draw £15 000 from the business. However, she is having to turn down manuscripts from authors who want to have their work published even though she thinks she could publish them profitably.

The immediate problem is lack of finance. She doesn't have enough capital to fund all the books she would like to publish. There is also a question of time. She is now working full time in the business and can't increase the number of books published per year.

So she has decided to look for a partner. That person would put money into the business to allow it to publish more books. The partner would also concentrate on the aspects of the business Caroline least enjoys - dealing with the printing and distribution of the book, as well as the marketing.

1. What would be the advantages to Caroline of having a partner?
2. Caroline has approached you as a solicitor to draw up a deed of partnership.
   (a) What are the essential points which must be covered in the deed of partnership?
   (b) What terms would you advise Caroline to offer her new partner in the partnership agreement? (For example, how should the profits be distributed? Who will control the business?)
   Wordprocessing
   (c) Draw up a simple partnership agreement. You could use a wordprocessing package to present the agreement.

Checklist

1. Who owns a partnership?
2. 'Partners have unlimited liability.' What does this mean?
3. What is the difference between an unlimited partnership and a limited liability partnership?
4. If there is no partnership agreement, how are profits distributed in a partnership?
5. What might be written in a deed of partnership?
6. What is a 'sleeping partner'?
7. Why are partnerships likely to be profit maximisers?

Why set up a partnership?

Two or more people can set up in partnership

The advantages of a partnership

A partnership has many of the advantages of a sole proprietorship.

Easy to set up Partnerships are easy to set up. Two or more people can start in business as partners with few legal documents. Many partnerships draw up a deed of partnership first (☞ unit 24).

Easy to run **Ordinary partnerships** are easy to run. Accountants and solicitors don't have to be employed. In practice, partnerships may use an accountant to keep their books for tax purposes. A solicitor may also be needed to draw up a deed of partnership. This is not true of **limited liability partnerships** (☞ unit 25). These partnerships may be as complex to run as a company (☞ unit 27). For instance, accounts have to be audited (checked) by an independent accounting firm and sent to the Registrar of Companies.

Tax advantages Partners pay lower National Insurance contributions than they would if they set up a company and paid themselves a salary.

Control The partners share control of the business. In many businesses, each partner has an equal say in how the business should be run. However, some partners may be given more responsibility and control. This would be shown in the deed of partnership. Because partners usually work in the business, they have a good knowledge of how it works. This allows them to make more informed decisions.

Capital All partnerships have the advantage over sole proprietorships that two or more people are likely to raise more money than one. This usually allows more money to be invested in the business. Limited liability partnerships have the added advantage that limited liability can attract individuals to invest in a business (☞ unit 28).

Expertise Another advantage over a sole proprietorship is that partners can have different areas of expertise. The partnership can then benefit from **specialisation** (☞ unit 2). Each partner is doing what he or she is best at. This is likely to strengthen the business.

Profits All the profits of the business are kept by the partners. There is a clear link between effort, success and money earned. So there is a strong incentive to make the business work. The partners may share profits equally or not. This will be shown in the deed of partnership.

Privacy Except for the few limited liability partnerships, the accounts of the business are private. Only the Inland Revenue and Customs and Excise have the right to see the accounts.

Labour relations Partnerships tend to be larger than sole proprietorships. More people are usually employed. Even so, many partnerships

Business is really motoring for a Portsmouth firm after winning a major contract with a London-based transport company. FHR Conversions boasts of being able to take even the most basic of vehicles and turn it into a luxury minibus. It can work to whatever specifications the customer may have. The company's latest contract was to supply ten fully-fitted 16-seater minibuses in just eight weeks for Coaches of London.

The firm started life as a joinery business a number of years ago. Two friends, Mark and Suresh, set up an ordinary partnership. By chance, they were asked to fit out a builder's van with trays to hold components. They realised there was a market for van conversions. They quickly began to specialise in this line of business. The business now has six full-time staff, with a variety of specialist skills. It means they can tackle everything from the mechanical side of a job to painting the finished article.

1. Suresh is a partner, whilst Pete is one of the full-time staff who work for the business. How might the order for the ten vans have affected how much each receives or gets paid by the business?
2. Who is likely to know how much the partners, Mark and Suresh, make from the business?
3. Mark's young son had an accident a year ago. He has been in and out of hospital as a result. Why might being a partner rather than being an employee have helped Mark with the situation?
4. Mark and Suresh are introduced to Liam. He his impressed with the business. But, he argues, they have only scratched the surface of a large national market for conversions. What they need is a marketing consultant to win new orders and he has just the right experience. If they made him an equal partner, he would transform their business. Discuss whether they should take up his offer.

remain small. So relations between employees and partners are likely to be good.

Flexibility Like sole traders, partners often have more flexibility about when and how they work than employees. They may have to liaise with their partners, though, if they want to take a day off to take care of children, for instance.

Professionalism Partnerships are the accepted form of organisation in businesses like doctors, accountants and lawyers. In these professions, there is a great deal of expertise about how to run the business successfully.

Disadvantages of partnerships

Liability Partners in ordinary partnerships have unlimited liability. This is a risk for the partners. One partner may run up a large bill without the knowledge of others. This can be a problem because all the partners are then liable for the debt. So people in partnership have to trust each other. But they also need to keep a check on the activities of their partners. In limited liability partnerships, there is no such risk because partners have limited liability.

Long hours Partners, like sole traders, tend to work longer hours than employees.

Disagreements between partners Partnerships mean that people have to work together. There are likely to be disagreements. For instance, one partner may feel that another partner is not working hard enough. Or partners may think that one partner is not earning enough money for the business. Partnerships can easily break up because of this. Family partnerships tend to be more stable. This may be because family members are more used to having disagreements and resolving them.

Lack of a deed of partnership Some partnerships are not set up with a deed of partnership. When disagreements arise, partners may

have very different views of how the business should be run. This can lead to the partnership splitting up.

Lack of continuity When one partner leaves, the partnership or a company automatically ends. If the business is to be kept going, a new partnership (or a company) must be formed. This can create uncertainty. It might even lead to the break up of the business because the remaining partners disagree about the future. If the partner leaving has a vital skill, the business may not be as successful as before. On the other hand, the weakest partner may leave. This could allow the business to attract a better partner. A problem in family partnerships is that parents

may run a successful business, but their children do not want to take it over. They may be forced to close the business when they retire.

Checklist

1. Why is a partnership easy to set up and run?
2. Why is it usually easier for a partnership to get funds to start up than a sole proprietorship?
3. Why is unlimited liability a risk for a partner?
4. What are the possible problems if a partnership is set up without a deed of partnership?
5. What happens to a partnership if one partner leaves?

Rebecca Johnson taught dance to children and adults for ten years before she met Mai Ling Tsui. Like most dance teachers, she found herself buying and selling clothes and equipment to her pupils. Mai Ling was the mother of one her pupils. She had previously worked in the local library. But she also had a flair for designing and making dance costumes, which she discovered the first year her daughter was in a show. She volunteered to be in charge of all costumes for Rebecca's shows and then for buying and selling clothes and shoes.

That was when they decided to set up a shop and dance room. Mai Ling would run a shop, selling everything for the dancer. Rebecca would use the first floor of the premises to run classes. The dance room was also let out to other teachers. They both put in £20 000 to start the business, which was an ordinary partnership. They assumed they were equal partners, but no deed of partnership was signed. The premises were rented. The business was a success from the first day. But it soon became clear that the shop was more profitable than the dance room. Rebecca worked in the shop when she wasn't teaching and her pupils were its main customers.

Mai Ling also began to design and make innovative dance costumes. At first she sold these through the shop. Then word got around. Other dance shops would ring up asking if they could place orders.

Mai Ling felt increasingly that most of the success of the business was due to her. Rebecca worked hard, but Mai Ling thought she do better on her own.

1. Suggest why Mai Ling felt that 'most of the success of the business was due to her'.
2. Mai Ling has told Rebecca that she wants to break up the partnership. She has offered Rebecca £40 000 for her share of the business. Mai Ling would pay the rent on the premises, but would sublet the dance rooms to Rebecca. Rebecca feels unhappy about this. She wants £60 000 for her share and would move her dancing classes elsewhere. (a) How does this show some of the drawbacks of partnerships? (b) Discuss whether Mai Ling should accept Rebecca's terms for the break up.

Companies

A COMPANY is a different form of business organisation than a sole proprietorship or an ordinary partnership. One difference is that a company has a separate identity in law from its owners, its SHAREHOLDERS. The company can own property, be sued in court and remain in existence if its owners die. In a sole proprietorship or partnership, there is no legal distinction between the owners and the business.

A second difference is that the owners, the shareholders, have LIMITED LIABILITY. If the company runs into debt, shareholders cannot be forced to pay the money owed. All they can lose is the value of their

In a small company shareholders, directors and managers may be the same people; in a limited company, directors are elected by shareholders

SHARES in the company. When a company ceases trading it becomes **insolvent**. Any assets the business has left are used to pay those who are owed money by the company. Some will receive a little of what is owed to them. Others will get nothing.

The Registrar General

The Registrar General (or Registrar of Companies) keeps records on all UK limited companies. Two documents have to be sent to the Registrar of Companies to set up a limited company.

- The MEMORANDUM OF ASSOCIATION gives details about the name of the company, the address of its registered office, a statement that the shareholders will have limited liability, the type and amount of share capital and a description of the activities of the company.

- The ARTICLES OF ASSOCIATION give details about the voting rights of shareholders, how profits will be distributed, what are the duties of the directors and what procedures will be followed at the **annual general meeting** (the AGM).

The Registrar of Companies has to issue a **certificate of incorporation** before a company can start trading, i.e. start up in business. Every year, a limited company has to send audited accounts and other documents to the Registrar of Companies at Companies House. These can be seen by anyone who is interested. The affairs of the business, therefore, can't be kept private like

You have decided with three friends to set up a company. You may already have a business idea. If you don't have an idea, assume that you will set up a company selling headed letter paper and similar printed stationery products in your school or college.

1. Draw up a Memorandum of Association for the company as follows.

> The Companies Act 1985
> Company Limited by Shares
> Memorandum of Association of _____ (name of your company)
> The Company's name is _____ .
> The Company's registered office is _____
> (unless you have decided otherwise, put the home address of one of the shareholders).
> The Company's objectives are _____
> (description of your trading activity).
> The liability of the Members is limited.
> The Share Capital of the Company is £ _____ (figure for your starting share capital) divided into _____ shares of £1 each.

2. Now draw up the Articles of Association. Use the following heading.

> The Companies Act 1985
> Company Limited by Shares
> Articles of Association of_____ (name of your company)

Write one sentence about each of the following under your heading: (a) which of the shareholders has a vote and how many votes each shareholder has; (b) what proportion of the profit will go to each shareholder; (c) the duties of the company directors (e.g. they have the right to authorise the company to borrow money); (d) who will act as chairperson for the AGM and where it will be held.

a sole proprietorship or a partnership. Anybody can find out the sales and profits of the company from the last set of its accounts sent to Companies House.

Control

In theory, shareholders control limited companies. Each year they elect DIRECTORS to represent the interests of shareholders at an annual general meeting,. The board of directors then appoints MANAGERS to run the company. The most important manager is the managing director. He or she is automatically a director of the company. Some other managers will also sit on the board of directors. Managers who are also directors are called EXECUTIVE DIRECTORS. This is because they 'execute' or carry out policies decided at board level.

In a small company, the shareholders, the directors and the managers will all be the same people. For instance, a husband and wife might set up a company for their business, which is running a shop. In law, they are both shareholders and directors. In practice, they are also the managers because they manage the day to day running of the business.

At the opposite extreme are large companies like BT or BP Amoco. Directors and managers may own a few shares, but almost all the shares are owned by separate shareholders. The policy of the business is decided at board level by executive directors and NON-EXECUTIVE DIRECTORS. These are directors who only work part-time for the company and are not managers. Policy is carried out by managers, most of whom are not directors. In this situation, shareholders have almost no power to control the day to day running of the business. If they don't like the way the company is being run, they tend to sell their shares. It takes a crisis for shareholders to vote directors off the board at the annual general meeting.

Johnson Sandford Ltd is a specialist pharmaceuticals manufacturer. It makes drugs on contract from other larger companies. These companies then sell them to hospitals and pharmacies in the UK. There has been a growing trend for large drugs companies to contract out manufacturing to small specialist businesses. Such specialist companies are often able to produce pharmaceuticals at lower cost.

Johnson Sandford Ltd was set up as a limited company five years ago. Claire Johnson and Marvin Sandford were the two shareholders. Claire and Marvin left their jobs at an international pharmaceuticals company to exploit this growing market. They sank all their savings into the start up.

Today, the business employs ten workers. The company has struggled to make a profit, but a turning point came three years ago with a large contract which now amounts to half of all sales. But this contract is due to end in six months time and the customer has stated that unless Johnson Sandford cuts its price by 25 per cent, it will not be renewed.

A cut in price of one quarter would mean taking losses on the contract. This would be unacceptable for the business. Worse still, the company invested heavily in equipment to cope with the contract. The loans raised to make the investment still have two years of repayments to be made. Without the contract, the business could not generate enough cash to continue making those payments. Johnson Sandford Ltd would be facing insolvency.

1. What does it mean to say that Johnson Sandford Ltd was a 'limited company'?
2. Explain why the company faces financial problems in six months time.
3. If the company becomes insolvent, who is responsible for the debts of the firm?
4. Discuss TWO ways in which the company could deal with the crisis. In your answer, put the possible advantages and drawbacks of your suggestions.

Checklist

1. What does 'limited' mean if it refers to a company?
2. A company goes out of business leaving debts of £2 million. How much will the shareholders of the company have to pay as a result?
3. Who owns a company?
4. What documents does a company have to give to the Registrar of Companies before it can begin trading?
5. What is the role of (i.e. what is the job of) (a) a director and (b) a manager of a company?
6. What is the difference between an executive director and a non-executive director?

Private and public limited companies

A Ltd company and a plc

Ltd and plc

There are two types of limited company - PRIVATE LIMITED COMPANIES and PUBLIC LIMITED COMPANIES. Private limited companies add Ltd after their names. For instance, MGA Developments Ltd is a private limited company that designs and makes bodies and models for the motor industry. Public limited companies add plc after their name. For instance, Marks & Spencer plc is a public limited company in the retail industry.

Differences between private and public limited companies

There are important differences between private limited companies and public limited companies.

Sale of shares The shares of a plc are traded on a stock exchange. Marks & Spencer plc, for example, is **listed** on the London Stock Exchange. New, smaller plcs in the UK tend to get a listing on AIM (the Alternative Investment Market). A listing means that the stock exchange is prepared to allow the shares of the company to be bought and sold through the exchange. In contrast, there is no open market for the shares of private limited companies. Anyone wanting to sell shares in a private limited company has to have the permission of the majority of shareholders. This can make it difficult to sell shares to people outside the business.

Share capital In law, a plc must have at least £50 000 in share capital to start up. A private limited company can start up with just £2 in share capital. In practice, stock exchanges in the UK will not accept new plcs unless their share capital is worth millions of pounds. In contrast, many private limited companies are started with just £2 in share capital on the Memorandum of Association. But it is likely that the shareholders will invest more over time.

Size and number of shareholders The number of shareholders is likely to be far greater in a plc than in a private limited company. This is because plcs tend to be much bigger companies.

Control In theory, shareholders control both types of limited company. However, the larger the company, the more likely it is that managers, rather than shareholders, will influence how the company is run (☞ unit 27).

Advantages and disadvantages of limited companies

The main advantage of being a limited company is that it is easier to attract extra shareholders to invest money in the business. This is

---

Lakot Ali and Chloe Howdle are at a crossroads. By day, Lakot works in a foundry. At night and at weekends, he restores and makes traditional Black Country ranges from outbuildings in his backyard. Chloe buys the kitchen ranges from builders who are knocking down old houses or from salvage yards. She also handles the administration and accounts in the partnership.

The customers of the business often learn of the business from others. Local builders and kitchen outfitters know of the work and recommend the business to clients who want to install a range alongside more modern kitchen fittings. There has also been a steady trickle of enquiries from people who have ranges which no longer work and who want them repaired. Last year, Lakot and Chloe decided to have a go at building a new range. This was very successful and four have been sold to date.

Lakot now wants to give up his job in the foundry to work full time on the ranges. Lakot and Chloe feel there is a much bigger market out there if only they could tap into it. Expanding the business would mean moving into industrial premises and for the first time paying rent. To survive three years, they think the business needs £100 000. That money could be borrowed from their bank. Alternatively, they have thought of raising the money by turning the business into a private limited company and selling shares in it.

1. What are the differences between a partnership and a private limited company?
2. Why would limited liability be attractive to any possible shareholders in the business?
3. Lakot and Chloe hope that somebody with marketing expertise would be prepared to buy shares in the company. Realistically, though, they know that the share capital is most likely to come from friends or relatives. (a) Why would it be useful to have an investor who would also be prepared to spend time marketing the ranges?
(b) Why would it be far more likely that a relative or friend of Lakot and Chloe would put up money to invest in the company rather than a complete stranger?

because shareholders have limited liability (☞ unit 27). Greater investment means that the business has a better chance of growing.

One disadvantage is that information about the company has to be given to the general public. More information has to be given if the company is a plc than if it is a private limited company. Giving information is also costly. For instance it can cost over £100 000 to produce the annual report and accounts of a public limited company.

Another disadvantage of being a plc is the cost of complying with stock exchange rules. The London Stock Exchange imposes a variety of rules on companies seeking a listing. These are meant to protect future shareholders, by giving them more information about the business. Some companies prefer to trade

shares on the Alternative Investment Market (AIM). Regulations are less strict on the AIM, so it is cheaper for a company to get a listing. On the other hand, the shares are seen as higher risk. So it might be more difficult to raise money through new share issues.

It is sometimes claimed that shareholders in a plc are only interested in making short term profits. They are not interested in taking the long term view. So the company is discouraged from investing money in projects which will be profitable in the long term but not in the short term.

Aims and objectives

Most private limited companies are relatively small. Owners control the business and are also likely to run it

as managers. Owners want to maximise the return on their work and investment in the company. So they are likely to want to maximise profits over the long term.

In a large plc, the owners are usually different people from the managers who control the day to day running of the business. So there is a separation or **divorce of ownership and control**. Managers have to keep shareholders happy by making some profit or by **profit satisficing** (☞ unit 20). But they may then pursue other objectives, like maximising sales. They might do this because they may be able to increase their salaries if sales increase. So in a large company, the danger is that the managers run the company to suit their own objectives.

Number of shares owned	Number of shareholders	% of shareholders	Number of shares (millions)	% of shares
1-1,000	959	67	0.3	-
1001-50,000	353	25	2.1	3
50,001-100,000	26	2	2.1	3
100,001 and over	80	6	60.8	94

Table 28.1 *Ultra Electronics Holdings plc - number of shareholders at 30 December 1999*

Source: adapted from Ultra Electronics plc, *Company Report and Accounts*, 1999.

Ultra Electronics is a group of specialist businesses designing, manufacturing and supporting electronic and electromechanical products and sub systems for the international defence and aerospace markets.

1. How many shareholders did the company have on 30 December 1999?
2. How many shareholders owned (a) between 1 and 50 000 shares and (b) more than 50 000 shares?
3. How many shares in total did (a) small shareholders owning 1-50 000 shares hold and (b) large shareholders each owning more than 100 000 shares hold?
4. 'Although Ultra Electronics is owned by over 1 400 shareholders, it is mainly owned by a fraction of that number.' Do you agree with this statement? Give evidence from the table.
5. The directors of the company owned approximately 1.4 million shares. (a) What proportion of the total number of shares in the company is owned by the directors? (b) To what extent do you think there might be a 'divorce of ownership from control' in this company?

Checklist

1. If a company has 'Ltd' after its name, what does this mean?
2. What are the differences between a private limited company and a public limited company?
3. What is the difference in cost of having accounts audited and reports published between a private limited company and a public limited company?
4. Why is it easier to attract new shareholders to a plc than to a private limited company?
5. What is meant by the 'divorce of ownership and control' for a large company?

key terms

Private limited company (Ltd) - a company whose shares are not openly traded on a stock exchange.
Public limited company (plc) - a company whose shares are openly traded on a stock exchange.

Franchising

Franchisors and franchisees

Two thirds of new businesses stop trading within five years. One way someone setting up a new business can reduce the risk of failing is to take on a FRANCHISE. A FRANCHISOR is a business which gives others the right to use a business idea and its name. A FRANCHISEE is a business which buys into this franchise and sells goods and services to customers. There are many examples of businesses which have franchise operations. These include Body Shop, Prontaprint, Benetton, Kentucky Fried Chicken and Dyno-Rod.

What the franchisor provides

The franchisor provides its franchisees with a range of services which helps the franchisees to be successful. These can include:
- a recognised brand name, like Benetton or Kentucky Fried Chicken;
- advertising which covers all franchisees in an area;

A franchiser gives franchisees the right to use its business idea and its name

- training to start the business;
- equipment, such as shop fittings or specialist machinery;
- goods to sell directly to customers;
- materials to use in the production of a good or service. This might help the franchisee maintain the quality of the product or make sure that the finished product is the same for all franchisees. It might also allow the franchisee to enjoy lower prices because the materials are bought in larger bulk;
- finding customers. Advertising will help this, but the franchisor might also have lists of existing customers who could be contacted for further sales;
- an exclusive area in which to sell products;
- a range of back up services, like advice, cheap loans and insurance cover.

With around 180 Centres nationwide, Kall Kwik is the market leader in print, copy and design services to businesses. Kall Kwik is highly regarded for quality, speed, reliability and product knowledge. The average annual Centre sales turnover is in excess of £400 000. So Kall Kwik Centre owners enjoy very high potential earnings with a number generating net profits in excess of £120 000 per annum.

We are looking for highly motivated ambitious people who are willing to work hard to achieve financial success and a quality lifestyle. A background in management with experience in sales and the ability to follow a successful system is required.

Source: adapted from *The Franchise Magazine*, March 2001

1. What does Kall Kwik sell?
2. What might be the benefits to an individual of buying a Kall Kwik franchise?
3. Jon Kenyon has just inherited a house worth £100 000 from his mother. He has been the manager of a branch of Next for the past ten years. He is interested in buying a Kall Kwik franchise. (a) What assets and skills might he have which would help him to make the franchise a success? (b) Discuss whether Kall Kwick should accept an application from him to become a franchisee.

The cost to the franchisee

The franchisee doesn't provide all its services for free. Franchisors often charge a fixed sum at the start of the franchise agreement to cover the costs of starting a new operation. Then they charge a **fee**, usually a proportion of the value of everything sold. Or they might charge higher prices for the products bought by the franchisee than if they were bought on the open market.

Advantages and disadvantages for the franchisee

For the franchisee, franchising is a relatively safe way to start a business. Only 6-7 per cent of franchisees fail. This is much smaller than the national average for all businesses. The difference in failure rate comes about for many reasons.

- The franchisor carefully chooses people from those who want to buy a franchise. This tends to eliminate people who are unsuitable for the business.
- The franchisor sets out at the start how much money the franchisee needs to put into the business. Many new businesses fail because the owners badly underestimate the amount of money they will need to survive in business.
- The franchise formula has already been tried out and tested and has been successful. The franchisee only has to repeat the success of other franchisees.
- The franchisor provides on-going support and can help the franchisee sort out any problems, such as quality control or tax problems.

On the other hand, the franchisee doesn't have the freedom to operate that an ordinary business would have because of the franchise agreement. In particular, the franchisee can't sell the business without the franchisor's permission. In some franchises, the franchisor can end the franchise without any compensation. The franchisee is also tied to making payments to the franchisor. Successful franchisees often feel that they are being overcharged by the franchisor.

Advantages for the franchisor

For the franchisor, there are two main advantages.

- The franchisee puts up money at the start and during the running of the business. This means that the franchisor doesn't have to find that money to run its business. It can

therefore expand at a faster rate than it would otherwise.
- The franchisee is as keen and motivated to make a success of the business as the franchisor. This might make the whole business more successful than if the franchisor simply employed staff to run branches of the business.

Does a franchise always work?

Not all franchises work. The franchisor might have a poor business idea and mislead people into buying a franchise. Both the franchisor and the franchisees might then go out of business.

Equally, franchisees might not provide a good product or service because they run the business badly. In a well run franchise, the franchisor monitors quality and could tell the franchisee to improve or risk losing the franchise. However, poor quality could be a problem. It could drag down both the business of the local franchisee and the national business of the franchisor.

✓Checklist

1. What is the difference between a franchisor and a franchisee?
2. What may the franchisor provide for the franchisee?
3. How does the franchisor make a profit?
4. What are the advantages of a franchise for the franchisee?
5. Why are businesses willing to franchise their valuable business ideas to other businesses?

Kerry Chen wants to go into business. In the past she has been a successful Avon cosmetics representative, selling cosmetics door to door in her local area. This time she wants to run something more substantial. But she doesn't want the risk of setting up on her own. So she has decided to look at buying a franchise.

One franchise she has noticed was The Nail and Beauty Factory. This is a franchise which sets individuals up in business running salons that provide manicures and beauty treatment. Specific experience of running a salon is unnecessary. The franchisor trains franchisees. It also provides them with stock, shop fittings and staff. The cost is £10 000 for the training on top of £20 000 for the start up package. The franchisor also takes 10 per cent of turnover. It takes an estimated 2 years for franchisees to earn the money to cover the cost of the start up, according to the franchisor.

1. What would be the cost to Kerry of buying the franchise?
2. Suggest what would be the advantages to Kerry of buying into the franchise.
3. Discuss what skills Kerry would need to make the franchise a success.

UNIT 30

Multinational companies

The oil industry is dominated by multinationals

Multinational companies

A MULTINATIONAL COMPANY is a company which operates in several countries. It will own factories, sites and even businesses in more than one country. Production will be sold in the countries where it is located and also in other countries. Examples of multinational companies include McDonald's, Ford and BP Amoco.

A UK multinational will almost certainly be a plc (☞ unit 30). All major industrialised countries have their own multinational companies. They are owned by shareholders in their own countries, but operate internationally. Some multinationals have shareholders in more than one country. For instance, Unilever is both a UK and a Dutch company. The same is true of Shell.

Company structure

Multinational companies often have complex structures. Many are split up into a PARENT COMPANY with a number of SUBSIDIARY COMPANIES. The parent company owns all the subsidiaries. There is a number of reasons for adopting this structure.

- A multinational may pay less tax than if it operated as just one company.
- Subsidiaries have **limited liability** (☞ unit 27). If a subsidiary becomes insolvent, the parent company will not be forced to pay off its debts. It will only lose the value of its shareholding in the subsidiary.
- A country's laws may make it easier to set up a subsidiary company than to own assets like factories or offices.
- Setting up a subsidiary allows accountability. The subsidiary will often manage its own finances. It will then be clear whether the company is performing well or badly.

Benefits of larger size

Companies often become multinationals because size can help them compete against other businesses. Size can lead to lower costs of production, as a business can gain **economies of scale** (☞ unit 34). A company may also be able to locate production more cost effectively (☞ unit 66). For instance, it may be able to shift production from a high labour cost country to a low labour cost country. Size may also give a business an advantage in product design. In some industries, a manufacturer can gain a competitive edge if it has research, development and design facilities across the world. This helps the business to cope with the demands of local markets into which it sells. The same may be true of promotion and distribution. Having local people in charge who understand the local market can help increase sales.

Problems facing multinationals

A multinational must have strategies to cope with a number of different problems.

Size A large business, with operations in several companies, can

Wolseley plc is one of the world's largest specialist trade distributors of heating and plumbing products, as well as building materials, lumber products, industrial pipes, valves and fittings. It owns subsidiary companies in France, Austria, Denmark, Ireland, Italy, Luxembourg, Sweden, Switzerland, Germany, Belgium and the USA.

According to its Annual Report and Accounts, its size has helped the company achieve 'benefits of scale in sourcing, distribution and operating efficiency'. Subsidiary businesses have been 'increasingly sharing best practice and ideas for the benefit of the group as a whole'. Examples include 'e-business experience and warehouse management systems in our distribution centres'.

At the same time, the company allows each of its subsidiaries to remain 'customer-facing businesses in ways tailored to match local markets'.

Source: adapted from Wolseley plc, *Annual Report and Accounts*, 2000.

1. What makes Wolseley plc a multinational company?
2. In how many countries does Wolseley own subsidiary companies?
3. Explain TWO advantages to Wolseley in being a large company.
4. Suggest why 'sharing best practice and ideas' might help overcome some of the problems it might face by operating in so many countries.

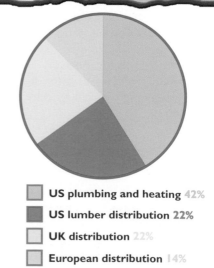

- US plumbing and heating 42%
- US lumber distribution 22%
- UK distribution 22%
- European distribution 14%

Figure 30.1 *Wolseley: sales turnover by region, 2000*

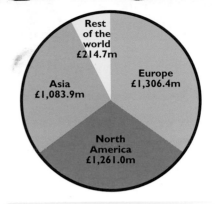

Johnson Matthey is a UK based company. It also has operations in the US, European countries such as Spain and Italy, China, India and Australia. It is organised into three divisions - catalysts and chemicals, precious metals and colours and coatings. The catalysts and chemicals division is the world's leading manufacturer of catalysts for control of vehicle exhaust emissions. The precious metals division refines and markets platinum, gold and silver. The colours and coatings division is ranked among the world's top three suppliers of decorative products and associated raw materials for ceramics and glass.

Johnson Matthey's operations involve many industrial processes which could be extremely damaging to the environment. An example is the processing of precious metals. To prevent any such damage, Johnson Matthey has set up an Environment, Health and Safety (EHS) Committee. It is directly responsible to the main Board of Directors. It sets out policies and standards. It also organises internal audits (inspections) of sites.

The value in pounds sterling of Johnson Matthey's sales and profits is affected by exchange rate fluctuations. In 1999-2000, for instance, Johnson Matthey gained £0.2 million in extra profit from its US operations compared to 1998-1999 because the value of the pound fell against the US dollar.

Source: adapted from Johnson Matthey, *Annual Report and Accounts*, 2000.

1. Giving evidence from the data, explain why Johnson Matthey is a 'multinational company'.
2. (a) How does Johnson Matthey check that it is operating in an environmentally friendly way? (b) Suggest why it is important for Johnson Matthey to set the same environmental standards across all its world operations.
3. Explain why exchange rate fluctuations can affect the value of Johnson Matthey's profits when measured in pounds sterling.

Figure 30.2 *Sales turnover by region, 2000*

Rest of the world £214.7m
Europe £1,306.4m
Asia £1,083.9m
North America £1,261.0m

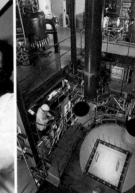

lose direction. Individual parts of the business may work against each other as they struggle to achieve power within the company. So a multinational must establish clear **objectives** (☞ unit 20). Then it must find ways of making everyone work together to achieve these goals. The size and geographical spread of a multinational means that good **communication** is essential (☞ unit 106).

Law and politics A multinational must understand and work within the different legal and political systems of the countries in which it operates. It must deal with governments, both at a local level and a national level. For instance, it might need permission to operate factories, open offices or employ workers. It must pay taxes to the local government. Permission might have to be obtained to import and export products, and to send profits from one country to another. It might also have to deal with environmental issues, especially if it is a mining or oil extraction business.

Exchange rate fluctuations
Multinationals may sell products and earn profits in a number of different currencies (☞ unit 9). However, the values of currencies are constantly changing against each other. For a UK multinational, a change in the value of the pound against other currencies can have an important effect on its profits and the value of overseas sales. For instance, assume a UK multinational earns $3 million profit in the USA. At an exchange rate of £1 = $1.00, this is worth £3 million. But if the exchange rate were £1=$1.50, it would only be worth £2 million. Multinationals may see their overseas production and sales grow strongly. As a result, profits in foreign currency may rise. But when they convert the profit back into pounds, profit may fall if the value of the pound has increased.

key terms

Multinational company - a business which operates in at least two countries, usually both selling products and producing them in these countries.
Parent company - a company which owns and controls other companies called subsidiary companies.
Subsidiary company - company owned by another company rather than individual shareholders or owners.

Checklist

1. Name FOUR multinational companies.
2. What is the difference between a parent company and a subsidiary company?
3. Why might companies become multinational companies?
4. (a) What problems do multinational companies face and (b) how can they overcome these?

Co-operatives

Co-ops are important in the holiday market

Worker co-operatives

A WORKER CO-OPERATIVE is a business which is owned by its workers, the **producers** in the business. Worker co-operatives are uncommon in the UK. Most tend to be small businesses.

The workers are the owners of the business. So they have to make decisions about how it should be run. Normally there are more meetings in a worker co-operative than in a limited company because of this. In many worker co-operatives, each worker has one vote when it comes to making a decision. This is the case even if workers own different numbers of shares in the business. In other businesses, like a limited company, the number of shares owned determines how many votes a worker can use. The workers/shareholders in a worker co-operative enjoy limited liability.

Advantages and disadvantages

Worker co-operatives have advantages over other businesses. These are all linked to the fact that the workers own the business.

- There is less likely to be a conflict of interest between owners and workers. Profits made by the business either go to the workers or are invested back in the business to ensure its long term success.
- The business is likely to be conscious of its place in the community. For instance, some worker co-operatives use manufacturing methods which reduce damage to the environment. Co-operatives may give a proportion of their profits to charity.

However, there can be problems with worker co-operatives.

- It is often difficult to persuade other workers to establish a worker co-operative because it may be easier to set up a partnership.
- New workers usually have to become owners of the business. They might find it difficult to raise money to buy a share in the business.
- Successful worker co-operatives often end up being sold to other limited companies. The workers/owners are happy to take the money from the sale of their shares.

- If the worker co-operative needs extra money to expand, it can't look to new shareholders to finance this expansion. This means that worker co-operatives often find it difficult to grow. They are forced to rely on **overdrafts** and **loans**, as well as **retained profit** (☞ unit 67), for finance.
- Worker co-operatives often set limits on the amount that top workers can be paid. Workers who start the co-operative may believe that all workers should be paid

PaperCall is a worker co-operative with 15 members. It collects a variety of recyclable waste products, including paper from businesses in London. It was set up in the mid-1990s. The workers/owners wanted to do something practical to improve the environment.

The rules of the co-operative state that each member has an equal say in how the company is run. It also states that all members are equal shareholders in the business and must be paid the same wage. Liz and Daniel Dagnall are managers of the business. The other 13 members do a variety of jobs, from picking up the waste to dealing with the paperwork in the office.

Today, the co-operative will hold one of its regular monthly meetings. There are two important issues on the agenda.

First, Liz Dagnall wants to stop working for the co-operative for a while. She feels that it has become too commercial. She wants to explore setting up another business in the environmental field. It has been suggested that she is replaced with an employee who would not be a member of the co-operative. But the new employee would have to be paid the going rate in London for a manager. This is double what each member of the co-operative is currently being paid.

Second, the company is making a loss. It has been squeezed by falling prices for recycling products and by competition from new companies setting up in the industry.

1. Explain (a) who owns PaperCall and (b) how decisions are made in the business.
2. What would (a) the advantages and (b) the disadvantages to members of the co-operative be to employ a manager who is not a co-operative member to replace Liz?
3. At the monthly meeting, it is disclosed that there has been an offer from another company to buy the co-operative for £60 000. It would be conditional on all 15 members agreeing to continue to work for PaperCall, or at least not to take another job, for at least another 24 months. Discuss whether the members should agree to the sale.

key terms

Consumer (or retail) co-operative - a business organisation owned by customer shareholders, which aims to maximise benefits for its customers.
Worker co-operative - a business organisation owned by its workers who run the business and share the profits among themselves.

roughly the same wage for the same amount of work. It can then be difficult to recruit managers, for example. They are likely to get higher salaries working for a business that is not a co-operative. This can pose problems for worker co-operatives because they may not be able to get the best workers for the job.

Consumer co-operatives

CONSUMER or RETAIL CO-OPERATIVES, like worker co-operatives, are fairly rare in the UK. However, although few in number, they tend to be large. The result is that consumer co-operatives are important businesses in certain markets.

- Retailing. The combined sales of supermarket Co-ops give them about 5 per cent of the total grocery market in the UK.
- Travel agents. Co-ops are important retailers in the holiday market.
- Funeral directors. Co-ops organise more funerals than any single business in the UK.
- Wholesaling. The Co-operative Wholesale Society, which supplies retail co-operatives, is the largest wholesaler in the UK.
- Banking. The Co-operative Bank, although smaller than the main UK banks such as Lloyds TSB and HSBC, is still a major bank in the UK.
- Insurance. The Co-operative Insurance Society (CIS) is a major insurance company in the UK.

Consumer co-operatives are owned by customers. Traditionally, customers have received a share of the profits made (the **dividend**). They have also had limited liability.

Consumer co-operatives were originally set up in the 19th century to protect consumers from shops and other businesses which charged high prices and gave poor quality goods or services. This aim, of working for the benefit of customers and the wider community, remains the most important for Co-operative societies.

Checklist

1. Who owns a worker co-operative?
2. How are decisions made in a worker co-operative?
3. What are the advantages of worker co-operatives?
4. What are the problems of worker co-operatives as a form of business organisation?
5. What is the aim of a consumer co-operative?
6. Name THREE markets in which consumer co-operatives operate.

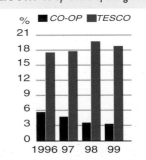

The Co-operative movement announced plans for major changes yesterday. It has been in steady decline in its main grocery market for the past 50 years.

Co-op stores have been out-competed by the main supermarket chains which have delivered lower prices, more choice and an ever growing number of outlets.

In contrast, other parts of the Co-operative movement have performed better. The Co-operative Bank is highly regarded. Co-operative travel agents have been successful. The Co-operative funeral business has enjoyed steady trade.

The changes announced include:
- setting a minimum dividend level of 10 per cent of profits to be distributed to individual and local community Co-ops;
- a new national brand for all grocery stores;
- setting a minimum performance target of 10 per cent on profitability. This would be measured by the amount of profit earned divided by the value of the assets in the Co-operative business (called the rate of return on capital employed);
- a move into new sectors, such as long-term care for the elderly and childcare, where the Co-op's community values would be appropriate;
- cross-selling between the Co-operative Bank and the grocery stores;
- putting greater emphasis on ethical issues like organic farming or cruelty to animals in retailing. This would copy the success that the Co-operative Bank has had with its ethical policies.

Source: adapted from *The Independent*, 9.2.2001.

1. What are the main problems for the Co-operative movement today?
2. Improving the profitability of Co-ops would give them the money to reinvest in the business. (a) State TWO ways in which this money could be used for the benefit of customers or the wider community. (b) Discuss whether either of these two ways is likely to make any difference to most people in the UK.

Figure 31.1 Co-op share of the grocery trade

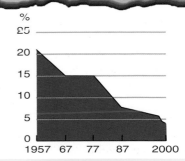

Figure 31.2 Return on capital employed

UNIT 32

Growth and objectives

A large construction company may gain more economies of scale than a small building business

Growth of businesses

Businesses can grow in size. For instance, their sales may increase. They may take on more workers. The **assets** (☞ unit 79) of the business may increase. Their **market share** (☞ unit 22) may rise.

Growth may help a business to achieve its **aims and objectives** (☞ unit 20). These are the goals of the different **stakeholders** (☞ unit 19) in the business such as the owners, the managers and the workers.

Why do businesses grow?

Larger returns for the owners Making profit is an important objective for the owners of a business. The larger the business, the more likely it is that owners will earn large profits and own more assets. For instance, a sole trader with sales of £100 000 a year is likely to make more profit than if sales were £40 000 a year. In public limited companies, higher profits are likely to increase the **dividends** (the share of the profits) paid to owners, the shareholders. But they may also lead to the shares becoming more attractive to investors. This will raise the price of the shares. Higher dividends and higher share prices will increase the overall returns to shareholders.

More rewards for the directors and managers In a large company, shareholders are likely to be different people from managers and directors. However, the managers and directors also have an interest in seeing the business grow. The larger the company, the larger are likely to be the salaries paid to directors and senior managers.

Survival Growth of the business may be the only way to ensure its survival. Small businesses may be at a competitive disadvantage against larger businesses because they can't gain **economies of scale** (☞ unit 34). This means they can't compete because their average costs are higher than those of larger firms. If their costs per unit are too high, a solution is to increase production, i.e. grow in size. Some small companies may be at risk from being bought by larger companies. Growing in size may reduce this risk.

Investment opportunities A business may find a good investment opportunity. It may only be able to take advantage of this if it expanded. Growth will then raise profits and sales.

Spreading risk A risk of markets collapsing can be an incentive for businesses to diversify. DIVERSIFICATION occurs when a business enters a new market. For instance, a shop selling bread and cakes may diversify into the cafe market. It could open a cafe where customers can enjoy coffee, cakes and sandwiches. The business then becomes less dependent on the shop for its success. Growing through diversification reduces the risk of being in one single market.

Reasons for staying small

Not all businesses want to grow.
- For a sole trader or a partnership, a larger business could mean more work and more responsibility.
- A bigger business is likely to mean taking on more workers. But some sole traders may want to work on their own.

In 1998, LVD took over Strippit. The two companies are both machine tool producers. They make equipment for metal manufacturers. LVD is one of Europe's biggest makers of machines for bending and punching pieces of metal. Before taking over Strippit, its US sales accounted for only 10 per cent of its total sales turnover. The other 90 per cent came mainly from Europe. By taking over Strippit, it acquired the second largest US company selling punching machines. As a result, sales turnover was expected to rise by half.

Since 1998, LVD has integrated Strippit into the company. In the United States, the company is known as Strippit/LVD. Putting the old US name first was a deliberate choice to emphasise a well known brand name in the American market. It hopes soon to start producing a relatively new family of laser-cutting systems in the USA that would sell for about £300 000, three times more than its conventional press tools.

Source: adapted from the *Financial Times*, 11.6.2000.

1. What does LVD and Strippit make?
2. Suggest why LVD bought Strippit.
3. Discuss how LVD could use the purchase of Strippit to expand sales into Asia.

- Some owners don't want to lose control of the business they have created. So they won't sell out or merge with another business.
- Some owners are happy to sell their businesses and retire once it has reached a certain size. Going on holiday may be more important to them than working and running a business.
- The business may only sell to a small or local market.

Sometimes businesses become smaller because they think it will make them more profitable. For instance, some large public limited companies DEMERGE, i.e. split up into two or more smaller, independent companies. One objective of this is to raise the share price. The stock market might put a higher value on two smaller companies than on one larger company. Also, it might allow each company to concentrate on what it is best at doing. This could raise profits.

key terms

Demerge - when a business splits itself up into two or more legally separate businesses.
Diversification - a business entering a new market, increasing the number of markets into which it sells its products.

Checklist

1. Why might the growth of a business benefit its owners?
2. What incentive is there for the directors and managers of a large business to aim for growth in size?
3. How might the growth of a business ensure its survival?
4. Why might growth and diversification of a business lead to the spreading of risk?
5. Explain why some businesses choose not to grow.

A business making cakes may remain small for many reasons

Paul O'Brien is a boat builder and repairer. Working on a river in Scotland, he opened his business five years ago. By trade a joiner, he learnt his skills during an apprenticeship. Following that, he had a job working for a furniture manufacturer. But his first love was always boats.

When he was made redundant, he used the redundancy money to set himself up in business on the riverside. Initially, work was slow coming in because no one knew him. But as word of his high quality workmanship and reasonable prices spread, trade picked up. Today, he has a sales turnover of £30 000 a year, out of which he has to pay for his raw materials and the rent on his premises.

He has thought about expanding. Work from businesses on the river, like hotels and farmers who own fishing rights, is unlikely to increase. So he would have to look further afield. This would mean visiting trade fairs up and down the country. But he would be taken away from what he loves best, which is working with wood. Since he is working full time now, it would also mean taking on an extra worker. It would be satisfying to take on an apprentice to pass his skills on to. But on present turnover he could not afford the wages. Anyway, he doesn't want to deal with the paperwork involved in having an employee. He also hasn't had much luck at the few trade fairs he has attended in the past. His stand, with a couple of new boats on it, has attracted a lot of attention. But this hasn't led to many orders. He is also concerned that as he gets older he may become less productive.

1. How could Paul O'Brien expand his business?
2. (a) Suggest what are his business objectives today. (b) Discuss whether he is likely to expand his business given these business objectives.

UNIT 33

Types of business growth

Ways in which businesses grow

Many businesses increase in size through INTERNAL GROWTH. This means that they produce more without joining with another business. This growth can be shown by an increase in sales turnover. It may also involve hiring of more workers, buying more equipment and perhaps moving to larger premises.

However, businesses can also increase in size through EXTERNAL GROWTH. This is where businesses join together to form a larger business. It can occur in a number of ways.

Mergers When businesses agree to join together, it is usually called a MERGER. Mergers tend to be between businesses of similar size.

Takeovers When one business buys another business, it is usually called a TAKEOVER. The takeover may be an **agreed takeover**. This is where the business being bought is happy with the terms of the offer. However, takeovers may be **contested**. This

occurs when the business being taken over doesn't want to be bought out or there is another bidder. Takeovers tend to be of smaller businesses by larger businesses. This is because larger businesses can afford to buy smaller businesses.

Acquisitions Some acquisitions are takeovers. However, others occur when one business buys a part of another business. For instance, a pet food manufacturer may buy the pet food operations of a larger food company. Businesses sell (or **divest** themselves of) parts of their operations for a number of reasons. They may need the cash to pay off debts. They may want to buy a company which they feel will be more profitable. Equally, they may be offered a price which is far greater than what they expect to earn in profits in the future. Finally, part of their operations may be making little or no profit, or even be making a loss. Selling the operations may be the best way to get rid of this problem.

Joint ventures A business may join with other businesses to sell a product together. They might, for instance, set up a **subsidiary company** (☞ unit 30) in which each owns a proportion of the shares.

Types of integration

There are different types of integration.

Vertical integration VERTICAL INTEGRATION occurs when one business joins with another business in its **chain of production** (☞ unit 5). For instance, a bakery may buy a manufacturer of flour. This is an example of BACKWARD VERTICAL INTEGRATION. The bakery business has joined with a business further back in its supply chain. FORWARD VERTICAL INTEGRATION occurs when a business buys another business which is further down in its chain of production. For instance, a bakery buying a chain of bakers shops would be an example of forward vertical integration.

Source: adapted from Millennium & Copthorne Hotels, *Annual Report and Accounts*, 1999.

1. Explain how Millennium & Copthorne Hotels has grown, giving examples of both (a) internal growth and (b) external growth.

Sales turnover of existing hotels increased from £221.9 million in 1998 to £236.8 million in 1999. The acquisitions in 1999 contributed another £106.3 million to sales turnover.

Millennium & Copthorne Hotels plc operates 117 hotels with 31 000 rooms located in 13 countries.

During 1999 our focus was concentrated on two main areas, namely, continuing to ensure the operational growth of existing properties and, at the same time, developing the Group by significant acquisitions.

Three acquisitions were made in 1999. The first was 43 hotels in Asia and Australasia purchased from CDL hotels. The second was the 673 bedroom Hilton in Seoul, South Korea, from the Daewoo Corporation of Korea. The third was Regal Hotels USA, bought from Regal Hotels International of Hong Kong.

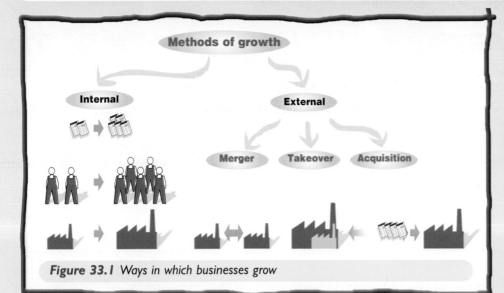

Figure 33.1 Ways in which businesses grow

Methods of growth
Internal
External
Merger   Takeover   Acquisition

Horizontal integration

HORIZONTAL INTEGRATION occurs when two businesses making broadly the same products join together or integrate. One bakery merging with another bakery would be an example.

A conglomerate merger

A conglomerate company is one which produces widely different goods or services. A CONGLOMERATE MERGER occurs when two businesses merge which are in completely different industries. For instance, a bakery being taken over by a steel company or a cigarette manufacturer taking over a clothes manufacturer would be conglomerate mergers.

Conglomerate mergers are examples of **diversification** (☞ unit 32). By diversifying (i.e. getting into another market), a business can reduce risk.

Tetley is the world's second largest brand of tea. In March 2000 it was taken over by an Indian conglomerate, Tata, for £271 million. The logic behind the deal was that Tata owns an important subsidiary, Tata Tea. This company is India's largest producer of tea.

Tata Tea wants to exploit Tetley's skills in tea buying, blending and packaging. It also wants to learn from its flair for product development and brand promotion. 75 per cent of Tata Tea's sales come from packeted tea, but it only has 26 per cent of the Indian market. This is behind the 44 per cent market share enjoyed by another company, Hindustan Lever. So Tata Tea has considerable room to increase its market share if it could bring new products to the Indian market.

But Tata Tea is also looking at the global market. Tetley is a familiar brand name in many countries worldwide. Tata Tea wants to use the Tetley brand to expand sales in these markets, particularly in Eastern Europe, Russia and the Middle East.

At the same time, Tetley will obtain more of its tea from plantations owned by Tata Tea in India and Sri Lanka. Tata is now actively changing its tea plantations to grow more tea which is suitable for Tetley blends. Tea plantations in African countries like Malawi will lose out as a result.

Source: adapted from the *Financial Times*, 19.10.2000.

1. What is meant by (a) a conglomerate and (b) market share?
2. Suggest why Tata Tea bought Tetley.
3. Discuss which companies stand to lose most in the future from strong internal growth of Tata Tea.

✓Checklist

1. What is the difference between external and internal growth.
2. 'Harding and Jones agreed a merger.' What does this mean?
3. What happens when one company 'takes over' another company?
4. What is a joint venture?
5. What type of integration would the following be: (a) Tesco buying a breakfast cereal manufacturer; (b) BT buying a bank; (c) Ford Motor Company buying a steel works; (d) the merger of LloydsTSB Bank with HSBC Bank?

The effects of growth

Growth can affect the employment and capital of a business

Effects of growth

Growth can have various effects on a business.

Sales revenue Sales revenue is likely to increase. Over time, the value of sales (the number of sales × price) will go up.

Profit The larger the business, the higher is likely to be the level of total profit. This is because sales are likely to rise as the business grows. Each sale should earn profit for the business. So more sales are likely to lead to more profit.

Employment The number of workers is likely to increase. More workers are needed to produce more goods and services. This would increase wage costs. There is also likely to be greater **specialisation** (☞ unit 2). A larger output will mean that workers can concentrate on what they are best at doing. The larger the business, the more managers there will be. Personnel departments may also be set up to cope with the larger workforce.

Capital employed The capital employed in the business, such as premises, machines and equipment, will increase. A business would need to invest in more machines to increase output.

Value of the business Growth should lead to an increase in the value of the business. This could be measured by the value of capital employed (☞ unit 80). Or it could be measured by its sale value to another business. For a plc, the share price acts as a measure of the value of the business. For instance, if there were 1 million shares each worth 200p, then the MARKET CAPITALISATION of the business would be £2 million.

Market share Another effect of growth could be an increase in **market share** (☞ unit 22). A growing firm will take sales away from its competitors. So its share of market increases. On the other hand, the market as a whole might be growing. This could allow the business to grow, but its market share may remain the same. The business might also grow by expanding into different markets.

Economies and diseconomies of scale

Growth of a business can change the average costs of production. A small car manufacturer may produce 1 000 cars at £6 000 each. The same car might cost only £5 000 a year to produce if production could be raised to 200 000 per year.

Falls in average costs of production when production increases are known as ECONOMIES OF SCALE. There are various reasons why economies of scale occur.

Purchasing economies Larger businesses are likely to buy in greater bulk than smaller firms. Suppliers often give discounts if large orders are placed. So bulk buying leads to lower purchasing prices for materials.

Marketing economies Marketing costs are the costs of selling the product, like advertising or employing a sales team. The average cost of marketing may fall if more is sold. For instance, it costs the same to place an advert for a product in a magazine whether sales are 100 or 1 000. However, the marketing cost per item will fall as sales rise. If the advert cost £1 000 to place and 100 items were sold, the average marketing cost is £10 (£1 000÷100). But if 1 000 are sold, the average marketing cost is £1 (£1 000÷1 000).

Managerial economies It may cost less per item produced in administration and managerial costs to run a large business than a small business. For instance, in a large company accountants and lawyers can

Umeco plc is a company which specialises in providing distribution services mainly to the aerospace industry. For instance, it buys and distributes aerospace components, composite materials and chemicals.

1. From Table 34.1, explain how the company grew in size in 1999-2000.
2. 'Umeco's market share grew in 1999-2000.' Explain what this means.

	1999	2000
Sales turnover £ million 1 April 1999-31 March 2000	53.5	96.1
Number of workers at 31 March	289	518
Capital employed £ million at 31 March	14.8	33.0
Market capitalisation £ million at 31 March	45.2	118.7

Table 34.1 *Umeco plc, financial statistics*
Source: adapted from Umeco plc, *Annual Report and Accounts*, 2000.

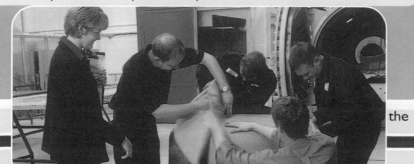

be employed full time. This allows the business to exploit **specialisation** . A small business may have to hire specialists with these skills, at a higher cost per hour worked.

Financial economies A large company might be seen as less of a credit risk than a small business. Hence, banks are likely to lend to a larger business at a lower rate of interest than to a small business. This will reduce its average costs. Large businesses will also have greater access to new **equity** (☞ unit 67). It may be cheaper to gain extra finance by issuing shares than borrowing money.

Technical economies Large businesses are more likely be use equipment efficiently. For instance, a builder working on his own may own a truck. This could sit on the building site for most of the day unused. A large building firm may own a truck which it uses all day, supplying various building sites. The average cost of the truck for the small builder per job will be much higher than for the large builder.

✓Checklist

1. Explain FOUR ways in which a business is likely to be affected if it is growing.
2. A company has 1 million issued shares. The stock market price per share today is 63p. What is its market capitalisation?
3. What is the difference between the capital employed and the market capitalisation of a company?
4. There are large economies of scale in the manufacture of motor cars. Suggest THREE reasons why building 10 cars a year is likely to be far more expensive per car than building 10 million cars a year of the same design.
5. Why might costs per unit of production be lower in a small business than in a large business?

Larger businesses, however, may experience DISECONOMIES OF SCALE. This is when average costs rise as production increases. Diseconomies of scale often occur because it is more difficult to manage a large business than a small business.

- The managing director of a business with 10 000 workers cannot speak directly to each worker. Orders passed down through managers may become distorted. In a business with 5 workers, the owner can tell each worker exactly what she wants.
- In a large business, the goals of workers may be different from

those of the shareholders, who are its owners. Some workers may want to work as little as possible. In a business with 1 000 workers, it may be easier for them to get away with this. In a business with 5 workers, the owner should know if workers are slacking.

key terms

Economies of scale - the fall in cost of production per unit as output increases.
Diseconomies of scale - a rise in cost of production per unit as output increases.
Market capitalisation - a measure of the value of a company, defined as the share price x the number of shares issued.

The Ford Motor Company has made hardly any profit in Europe over the last ten years. Its market share has also been falling. To change this situation, it started a restructuring and cost-cutting programme. Several car manufacturing plants are to close. These include Ford's plant at Dagenham in the UK. As Figure 34.1 shows, in 1999 Ford only made 71 cars for every 100 that it was possible to make in its existing plants. Assembly utilisation (the number of cars made divided by the possible number of cars that could be made in the plant) was well below the average for European car plants. By cutting the number of plants and switching production to the factories that remain open, Ford will save money.

The manufacture of car transmission components is to be moved from Ford to a new company. This will be half owned by Ford and half owned by Getrag of Germany, a major independent transmission manufacturer. Combining the two operations should allow costs to fall. There will also be changes in distribution. Single regional centres will be created from several smaller units. These will organise services to Ford dealers, the marketing of cars and finance. By increasing the size of these operations, it is hoped that costs can be cut.

Source: adapted from the *Financial Times*, 23.6.2000.

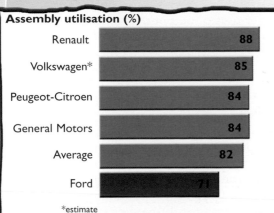

Assembly utilisation (%)

Renault	88
Volkswagen*	85
Peugeot-Citroen	84
General Motors	84
Average	82
Ford	71

*estimate

Figure 34.1 Assembly utilisation
Source: adapted from company information.

1. (a) In 1999, for every 100 cars that could have been made in their European car plants, how many did the following make: (i) Renault; (ii) General Motors; (iii) Ford? (b) Assume there was enough production capacity in European car plants to make 100 million cars in 1999. How many cars were actually made?
2. The Ford Motor Company is the world's second largest motor manufacturer. It should be able to exploit economies of scale. Explain TWO different types of economies of scale described in the data.
3. It could be argued that Ford in Europe was suffering from diseconomies of scale. (a) What is meant by diseconomies of scale? (b) Suggest why British Ford car workers might be against Ford reducing these diseconomies of scale.
4. Ford would like to regain market share and see a strong increase in sales. (a) Why might this improve its profitability? (b) Discuss ONE way in which it could achieve this.

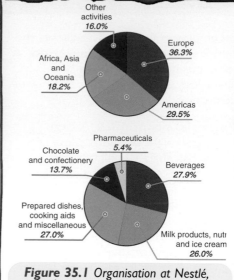

Organisation

Businesses must be organised. This organisation should allow the business to work efficiently. It should also allow it to achieve its **aims and objectives** (☞ unit 20). The larger the business, the more complicated is likely to be the organisation.

By product

A business can be organised on a **product basis**. This is where it divides itself into areas that produce different goods or services. For instance, a company may run a chain of hotels and a catering business. It may separate the businesses into two **divisions** - the hotel division and the catering division.

It could also make the businesses into SUBSIDIARY COMPANIES.

These are companies which it, the PARENT COMPANY, owns.

Organising on a product basis allows each division to **specialise** at what it is good at doing. This should lead to greater efficiency.

This type of organisation also improves **accountability** (showing who is responsible for what). Divisions are often **cost centres**, which must account for their own costs of production. They are also likely to report on sales revenues, so the profit earned from each division can be calculated. If a subsidiary company is set up, a set of accounts must be produced. These will show how the subsidiary is performing. Accountability gives management and workers an incentive to perform better. It also helps directors of the parent company to identify parts of

Figure 35.1 *Organisation at Nestlé, sales by region and product*
Source: adapted from Nestlé, *Management Report*, 2000.

the business that are doing well and those doing badly. They can then make decisions based on this information.

By function

Larger businesses tend to be organised by **function**, i.e. into a number of departments. These might include production, marketing and personnel. Production would look after the making of the product. Marketing would specialise in selling the product. Personnel would be responsible for the workers, including paying wages and recruitment.

This type of organisation has two advantages.
- It allows **specialisation**.
- The structure of the organisation is **clear**. Workers know 'who does what' in the business.

However, there are drawbacks, which can lead to **diseconomies of scale** (☞ unit 34). This is where large businesses have higher costs per unit of output than smaller businesses.
- The organisation may become too large to manage effectively. Management may find it difficult to control what is happening lower down the organisation.
- Individual departments may become more interested in promoting their own interests rather than those of the business.
- The whole organisation may become too **bureaucratic**. Large

---

CRH plc has its headquarters in Ireland and operates in 18 countries. It is a major supplier to the construction industry. CRH has 37 000 employees at more than 1 100 locations worldwide. The Group is organised on a product and geographical basis, with four divisions in Europe and the Americas:
- Materials: Europe
- Products and distribution: Europe
- Materials: the Americas
- Products and distribution: the Americas.

Materials include cement, aggregates, ready mixed concrete and asphalt. These are used in the building and the making of roads. Products and distribution include the manufacture of bricks, glass and precast concrete products, as well as builders' merchants and do-it-yourself stores.

Organisation on a product basis brings focus to business development and sharing of best practice. Organisation on a regional basis tailors the product organisation to suit country, market and cultural needs.

CRH operates on a decentralised basis. It has strong, experienced management teams in each division, a high degree of individual responsibility and local autonomy. A small corporate centre provides support and overall co-ordination.

Source: adapted from CRH plc, *Annual Report and Accounts*.

1. What does CRH plc make?
2. (a) Explain the ways in which the company is organised.
   (b) Discuss the possible advantages and disadvantages for CRH of organising itself in these ways.

numbers of forms may have to be filled in before a department will carry out a task.

Forming divisions or subsidiary companies helps to avoid these problems. This is because it splits the business into smaller units, which are easier to control and hold accountable.

By region

Some large companies are organised on a **regional** basis. For instance, a company might be organised into a North American division and a UK division. Companies which organise themselves on a geographical basis may sell a narrow range of products. It then makes sense for operations in a region to co-operate with each other. They can, for instance, share their knowledge about the market in the region, its economic environment and government regulations.

By market

Some businesses are organised on a **market basis**. For instance, a publisher might have a number of divisions, such as education and technical. Books will be produced by one division. However, the same book might be included in sales catalogues of other divisions. It might even be sold under a different title by another division if it thinks this will improve sales.

Centralisation

Large businesses can be CENTRALISED. This is where many decisions about the business are made by managers and directors at the head office of the company. They decide upon the objectives for the whole businesses and work out strategies to achieve them. Common systems and procedures are laid down, so that economies of scale can be maximised.

The main problem with centralised organisations is that they can be slow to make decisions and to respond to the needs of the market. DECENTRALISED organisations may be better at this. In a decentralised organisation, the power to make decisions is devolved (or given) to smaller parts of the business. For instance, the decision about what price to charge might be left to a subsidiary company rather than being taken by head office. Decentralisation encourages workers to change as the business environment changes. It gives power to those who are closest to customers, suppliers and the market. Any large business needs to achieve the right balance between centralisation and decentralisation.

Sometimes you have to stumble before you realise you have wandered off the right path. That is what happened to our company in 1999. After 15 years of consistent success, we suffered a year of dramatic setbacks. Those events provided us with a clear wake-up call. During the 1970s and 1980s, we generally moved towards consolidation and centralised control. There was geographical expansion into nearly 200 countries. We had to centralise control to manage that expansion and make sure that our local businesses operated together as one.

But in the late 1990s the world had changed. The world was demanding greater flexibility, responsiveness and local sensitivity. Nimbleness, speed and transparency were needed to cope with changing local conditions. Instead, we were operating as a big, slow, sometimes even insensitive 'global' company.

This is why I have decided we need to change. We need to think local and act local. We are placing responsibility and accountability in the hands of our colleagues who are closest to the billions of individual sales we make. We will not abandon the benefits of being global. But if our local colleagues develop an idea or strategy that is the right thing to do locally, then they have the authority and responsibility to make it happen. Just as important, we will hold them accountable for the outcomes of that idea or strategy.

Source: adapted from an article by the Chairman and Chief Executive of Coca-Cola in the *Financial Times*, 27.3.2000.

1. 'Coca-Cola is a global business.' What does this mean?
2. What were the possible advantages of centralisation for Coca-Cola in the 1970s and 1980s?
3. (a) What were the problems facing the old centralised organisation in 1999? (b) How would it become more decentralised according to Coca-Cola's Chairman?
4. A local manager for Coca-Cola in the UK might consider launching a Coca-Cola flavoured ice cream bar with the Coca-Cola name on it. (a) Discuss whether this is likely to be successful. (b) Suggest what might happen to the manager if the product was a disastrous failure, according to the article.

Checklist

1. What is meant by a product based organisation?
2. What are the advantages and disadvantages of functional organisation?
3. What is the difference between functional and market based organisation structures?
4. What does 'bureaucratic' mean?
5. What is the difference between a centralised and a decentralised organisation?

key terms

Centralisation - a type of business organisation where decisions are made at the centre or core of the organisation and then passed down the chain of command.
Decentralisation - a type of business organisation where decision making is pushed down the hierarchy and away from the centre of organisation.
Parent company - a company which owns and controls other companies called subsidiary companies.
Subsidiary company - a company which is owned and controlled by another company, the parent company.

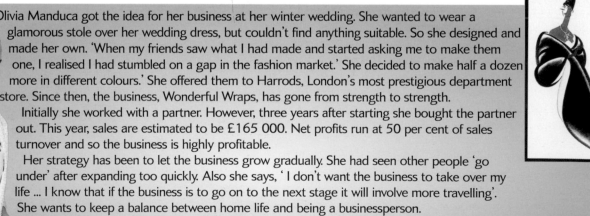
Small businesses are able to survive in certain circumstances

Size and profit

The larger the business, the more profit it is likely to make. Burger King, with thousands of outlets around the world, is likely to make more profit in a year than a one person hot dog business.

However, in some industries small businesses dominate production. They may be able to make just as high a **rate** of profit as large firms. The rate of profit might be measured as profit divided by the value of sales (the **profit margin** ☞ unit 83) or profit divided by the capital invested in the business (the **return on capital employed** ☞ unit 84). There is a number of reasons why small firms may be able to compete successfully in a market.

Lack of economies of scale In some industries, small businesses can produce at the same average cost as larger firms. **Economies of scale** are, therefore, very limited. In the taxi industry, for instance, a

national firm with 10 000 taxis could not reduce average costs below those of a local firm with 15 taxis. The larger business may even face **diseconomies of scale**, where average costs rise with size. A firm operating 10 000 taxis across the country would have high costs coordinating the business.

Capital employed In some industries, little capital is needed to start up and run a business. In the window cleaning business, for instance, anyone with a ladder, a bucket and some sponges can run a business. Small firms are less likely to be found in industries where millions of pounds of equipment are needed to set up.

Size of the market Some markets are very small. The market for cricket balls is an example. Large firms may not be interested in producing for these markets. But small firms may be able to survive and be highly profitable.

Flexibility Large firms can be

inflexible. They may fail to spot changes in the market. They may not be willing to sell into markets that require effort and skill. Small firms, in contrast, may prosper because they can see new opportunities and exploit them. They may also be prepared to sell to customers who have special needs.

Production methods In some industries, the method of production dictates small scale production. For instance, a high class restaurant can only serve a small number of customers if it is to maintain the quality of food and service. In contrast, the fast food market, where products are standardised, is suited to large firms like McDonald's or Burger King.

Entrepreneurs An ENTREPRENEUR is a business person who runs and owns a business. There are many people who

Olivia Manduca got the idea for her business at her winter wedding. She wanted to wear a glamorous stole over her wedding dress, but couldn't find anything suitable. So she designed and made her own. 'When my friends saw what I had made and started asking me to make them one, I realised I had stumbled on a gap in the fashion market.' She decided to make half a dozen more in different colours.' She offered them to Harrods, London's most prestigious department store. Since then, the business, Wonderful Wraps, has gone from strength to strength.

Initially she worked with a partner. However, three years after starting she bought the partner out. This year, sales are estimated to be £165 000. Net profits run at 50 per cent of sales turnover and so the business is highly profitable.

Her strategy has been to let the business grow gradually. She had seen other people 'go under' after expanding too quickly. Also she says, ' I don't want the business to take over my life ... I know that if the business is to go on to the next stage it will involve more travelling'. She wants to keep a balance between home life and being a businessperson.

Source: adapted from the *Financial Times*, 17.10.1998.

1. Suggest what has happened to profit as the size of Wonderful Wraps has increased.
2. The market for wedding garments is dominated by small firms. Suggest why small firms can successfully compete against larger firms in this industry.
3. (a) If Wonderful Wraps were to grow much larger in size, how do you think this would change the business? (b) Discuss what objectives Olivia Manduca might have in running the business.

Pret a Manger is a highly successful chain of sandwich bars in the UK. Outlets are sited in city centre areas where office workers are looking for somewhere to buy coffee and sandwiches. Its success is the result of keen pricing, good service and high quality food.

In 2000, the chain opened its first outlet in the United States in New York. Traditionally, British food chains have performed badly when they attempted to set up a successful UK formula to the United States. Partly this is because there are many well established US chains like Starbucks, Dunkin Donuts and McDonald's with which to compete. So Pret a Manger was taking a big risk in attempting to break into the US market. If successful, however, the chain would compete in a market six times the size of the UK.

To improve the chance of success, Sinclair Beecham, a co-founder of the company, moved to New York to oversee operations. Pret a Manger also brought over staff from the UK rather than use local New Yorkers who were unfamiliar with the format. After two and a half months, the first store was serving 5 000-6 000 customers a week. Its sales revenues were close to the average for a UK store.

Source: adapted from *The Guardian*, 3.10.2000.

1. What, according to the article, is the secret of success for Pret a Manger in the UK?
2. Why is it difficult to take a format like Pret a Manger from the UK to the United States?
3. How has Pret a Manger attempted to reduce the risk of failure when opening its first store in New York?
4. Discuss why Pret a Manger is prepared to take the risk of operating in the United States.

would like to own and run their own business. They can often see gaps in the market and can respond more flexibly to this than large businesses. Entrepreneurs are also often prepared to work for longer hours and earn less money per hour than if they were someone else's employee. This helps reduce their costs and means that they can compete successfully against large businesses.

Size and risk

There does not have to be a link between the size of the business and the risks it faces. For example, both small and large firms face risk when an economy goes into **recession** (☞ unit 10).

But small firms can be more vulnerable to risk for a number of reasons.

- Most business start ups are small businesses. Starting up a business is risky. The new business has to attract customers. It has to pay the costs of starting up. It has to produce a product which it can sell at a profit. Most new businesses do not survive the first five years of trading.

- Small businesses have less access to funds when they get into trouble. Often the only source of money for a small business is a bank loan. If the bank refuses a loan, the business may be forced to close. In a large business, there are many sources of funds (☞ units 68 and 69). The business may also decide to sell of some of its assets to raise money to keep it afloat.

- Small businesses may rely on one particular market or group of customers. If there is a downturn in that market, or customers stop buying, the business may be forced to close. A larger business may sell into a number of markets and

have a large number of customers. A downturn in one market or the loss of a customer may be damaging. But it won't necessarily force it out of business.

Risk and profit

No business likes taking risks. If things go wrong, the business may not survive. So businesses often want to earn higher profits if they think a business activity is likely to be risky. Take, for example, the pharmaceuticals industry. Nearly all medicines and drugs developed by companies fail to make it to the market. Either they don't work, or they have side effects which outweigh the possible benefits. The few new drugs that pass all the tests are highly profitable. A pill which costs pence to produce will be sold for pounds. To compensate them for the risks they take, pharmaceutical companies tend to earn above average profits. In contrast, water companies face very little risk. They have an established product and a known market. So in the long term water companies should earn lower profits.

✔Checklist

1. 'Brown's profit is much smaller than Smith's which is one hundred times its size. But its rate of profit is the same.' Explain what this means.
2. In the taxi industry, there are few economies of scale. Explain why not.
3. The market for taxi rides is very small in the village of Peynton. Why might this explain why Sandy Garratt runs her own taxi business with just one car from her home in the village?
4. Bill Gates made Microsoft big by spotting that all personal computers would need an operating system. Explain why Bill Gates is often described as an 'entrepreneur'.
5. Why do businesses tend to want higher profits if they take on more risk?
6. Why might taking on a very large repeat order for a company increase risk for the supplier?

key terms

Entrepreneurs - people who run and own their own businesses.

UNIT 37

Stakeholders and business size

Stakeholders

The **stakeholders** (☞ unit 19) of a business are those individuals or groups which are affected by its actions. As a business grows in size, its relationship with its stakeholders will change in a number of ways.

The owners

The most common type of business is the sole proprietorship. There are over 2 million self-employed workers in the UK who own and run their own business.

As the business gets larger, the number of owners is likely to increase. For instance, a sole trader changing to a **partnership** (☞ unit 25) or a **private limited company** (☞ unit 28) will need another partner or shareholder.

There are reasons why a sole trader may want to bring another person into the business.

- The sole trader may need extra funds to expand.
- The new owner may bring skills needed to help the business grow.
- The owner may want **limited liability** (☞ unit 27) by becoming a private limited company. This reduces risk for the owners. It also changes the way in which the business is taxed, which might benefit the owners.

Plcs usually have large numbers of shareholders, but few attend the AGM

There are also reasons why a private limited company might want to become a public limited company.

- The company may need the extra funds that 'going public' is likely to bring.
- The shareholders may want to sell some or all of their shares. It is easier for shareholders of a plc than those of a private limited company to sell their stake in the business. This is because they can offer their shares for sale to the public.

Increasing the number of owners means that existing owners have to accept a smaller share of any profits paid out. Hopefully, though, the total profit made will rise and so they could still receive more. Their ability to influence the business will also fall. For instance, a shareholder in a private limited company many own 75 per cent of the shares. If it 'goes public', and his shareholding falls to 30 per cent, he will lose overall control of the company.

Suppliers

Growth of a business should increase the number of orders placed with its suppliers. A decorator, for instance, will need to order more paint and wallpaper if her business expands. If a business grows very fast, it may change its suppliers. A small supermarket may buy its stock from a **wholesaler** (☞ unit 51). If it grows to a chain of 100 stores, it may cut out the wholesaler and buy directly from food manufacturers. Larger businesses should also be able to gain **purchasing economies of scale** (☞ unit 34). This means the larger the orders it places, the larger should be the discounts it can get from suppliers.

Customers

Customers can benefit from the

Minorplanet Systems plc is a company which provides satellite-based tracking systems for fleets of lorries. The exact position of a vehicle can be pinpointed on computer. It prevents lorry drivers from cheating on their employers, for instance by taking longer routes than necessary. It also allows transport managers to be kept up to date on where their lorries are at any time.

The company which makes the system was founded in 1996 by a Leeds entrepreneur, Jeff Morris. He put up £2 million and, with other investors, launched this hi-tech venture. In 1997, the private limited company was turned into a public limited company when it was launched on the Alternative Investment Market (AIM). There were two reasons for the float. The first was to raise further cash for future investment. The second was to raise the profile of the company. Being a plc gave the company status and a feeling that it would not disappear from business tomorrow. This was important for any company buying Minorplanet Systems products.

Today, the company is working with a number of other businesses to develop a range of services. For instance, it is working with Aon Risk Services, the UK branch of a multinational insurance corporation.

Source: adapted from the *Financial Times*, 8.1.2000.

1. Explain why Minorplanet Systems decided to float on a stock exchange in 1997.
2. What effect did this float have on the control of the company?
3. Minorplanet Systems plc is working with other companies to develop services. Some of these have bought shares in Minorplanet Systems. Discuss the possible advantages to Minorplanet Systems of this.

growth of a business. In some industries, prices may fall because of **economies of scale**. Service may improve and the quality of work done may be better. In other industries, customers may be better off using small local businesses. They may be more flexible than larger businesses. They may also offer lower prices because they don't have the **overhead costs** (☞ unit 72) of a large business.

Competitors

A growing business may be taking a growing share of the market. This would result in competitors facing increased competition. If the market as a whole was growing, all businesses could increase in size. Some businesses, though, would be growing faster than others.

Management

A growing business is likely to require more complex management. Running a company with 10 000 employees in 5 countries is different from running a sole proprietorship with no employees. The **organisation** of the business (☞ unit 35) will have to change. For a large public limited company a board of directors will be needed to decide on strategy. The board will expect management to carry out this strategy in the day to day running of the company. Growth will give managers the chance to improve their careers But it could give them less contact with the owners of the business. This might lead to a **divorce of ownership and control** (☞ unit 28).

Workers

A growing business will mean that there are more jobs available and opportunities for promotion. There are also likely to be better opportunities for training and getting qualifications. Benefits are likely to be better too. For instance, a small business is unlikely to run a pension scheme. Most large companies offer this benefit to their workers. Some workers prefer to work for a small business, whilst others prefer the security and opportunities that a large business might bring.

The local area

A growing business is likely to bring benefits to the local area in which it is located. New job opportunities may be created. Local suppliers could gain extra orders. Local customers may get a better service if products are sold locally. Other businesses not directly linked to the business could also benefit. They may gain greater sales as a result of higher income and spending in the local economy.

✓Checklist

1. Why might the owners of a partnership turn their business into a private limited company?
2. Suggest why a business selling £1 billion worth of products a year and employing 5 000 workers is most likely to be a public limited company.
3. How might the growth of a business affect (a) suppliers and (b) customers?
4. What opportunities might there be for workers if their business grows rapidly in size?
5. Why might the local area in which a business is sited welcome the growth of the business?

Jordans is a specialist cereal producer. It makes breakfast cereals like Jordans' Original Crunchy cereal and cereal bars such as Jordans' Frusli. In 2000, it had annual sales of £50 million and a workforce of 340.

However, it faces enormous challenges from changes in retailing. Supermarkets want to cut their costs, especially now that the world's largest supermarket chain, Wal-Mart, is selling in the UK market, having bought Asda. So they are putting pressure on suppliers like Jordans to lower their prices. This is affecting Jordan's revenues and profits, particularly the 20 per cent of its business accounted for by supplying 'own label 'cereals to supermarkets.

Jordans would like the business to grow. It needs to spend more on marketing its brands. Higher sales would spread the increased marketing costs across more sales. Stronger branding would also help Jordans to resist pressure for price cuts. Consumers are prepared to pay higher prices for brands, which they see as 'quality products'.

If the business grew, Jordans could also expand further into Europe. There are large markets to be gained if Jordans could sell into a country like Germany, with its population of 90 million.

Source: adapted from *The Sunday Times*, 12.3.2000.

1. Who are Jordans' main customers?
2. Discuss what would be the main effects on (a) Jordans and (b) its main customers if Jordans could substantially increase sales.
3. Discuss the possible effects on Jordans' stakeholders if it could expand successfully into large European markets like Germany.

Sales and objectives

Businesses need to sell products if they are to achieve their **objectives** (☞ unit 20). For instance, no business can survive in the long term without receiving enough money from sales to cover its costs. If the **objective** is to make a profit, then sales revenues must be greater than costs. Businesses that try to maximise sales revenues make selling their main priority.

Marketing

MARKETING is about sales. It is the process of identifying products that might be profitable and then selling them to customers. It involves:

- researching the market to find out what customers want to buy (☞ units 39-41);
- developing and designing a **product** that satisfies customers' needs and wants (☞ units 42 and 50);

- producing the right amount and to the right quality specification (☞ unit 42);
- getting the **price** right, so that the product is affordable to customers, but at a price which allows a business to make a profit (☞ unit 43);
- making sure that the customer knows about the product through **promotion** (☞ units 45-46);
- ensuring that the product is on sale in **places** convenient for the customer to buy it (☞ unit 47).

Sometimes, this list is known as the MARKETING MIX or 'the 4 Ps'. These 4 Ps are product, price, promotion and place.

The need for marketing

Each year, millions of new products are launched. Most are unsuccessful and are withdrawn from sale after a period of time. Market research (☞ units 39-41) is one way of

PLACE PRICE PRODUCT PROMOTION

Suthers (Star Garage) Ltd

ESSO

PRICE WATCH
79.9
81.9
84.9

Figure 38.1 The marketing mix

1. Why do you think these products need to be marketed?
2. (a) What is meant by the 'marketing mix'?
   (b) How do you think these products could be marketed? To answer this question, you need to comment on each of 'the 4 Ps'.

reducing the risk of failure because it helps to identify what customers want to buy.

In some markets, suppliers of products work directly with customers. In the car industry, for instance, there is often co-operation between car manufacturers and car component makers. For suppliers, this partnership is a form of marketing. It allows them to be able to meet the needs of their customers.

Good products, which satisfy consumer needs, can be failures without careful marketing. Price is a key factor. If a product is too expensive, it will not sell. Businesses must identify what price customers will pay so that sales will be high enough to make a profit.

Place is also important. Coca-Cola, for example, wants its products to be 'at arms reach of its consumers'. It distributes and sells products worldwide. Coca-Cola is available within a few hundred yards of a customer in any town or city. Rival soft drinks manufacturers find it hard to compete against this successful marketing.

Finally, products need to be known by customers. This is the role of promotion. Methods of promotion range from advertising, to brochures, to displays in shops. Promotion can affect customers' views about a product. For instance, advertising may be used to stress the quality of a product.

Buyers' and sellers' markets

Marketing is important because there is so much choice in the market. There are many different ways in which customers can spend their money. A business would like to be in a **sellers' market**. This is where customers have little choice but to buy from them. Where a business has a **monopoly** (☞ unit 18), for instance, marketing is not so important.

In a **buyers' market**, though, businesses have to compete against each other for sales. The greater the **competition**, the more businesses have to be **market orientated** (☞ unit 55) and the greater is the need for effective marketing.

key terms

Marketing - the process which is responsible for identifying potentially profitable products and then selling them to customers.
The marketing mix - the combination of factors which help the business sell a product - usually summarised as the 4 Ps, which are price, product, promotion and place.

Checklist

1. Why do businesses need to market their products if they are to achieve their objectives?
2. List FOUR different aspects of marketing a product.
3. A product has a very high price and is hardly known by potential customers. Why is it likely to be a failure?
4. What is the difference between a buyers' market and a sellers' market?

Nescafé was first produced in 1938, the result of research by the Swiss food company, Nestlé. It was the first company to make powdered coffee. The Second World War in 1939-1945 devastated Nestlé sales worldwide. However, during the War Nestlé's US branch was asked to provide Nescafé for soldiers' rations. This proved a marketing dream. The US armed forces were a huge market. US soldiers also distributed Nescafé from their rations to civilians wherever they were stationed. This created a future demand for the product.

In 1966, Nestlé launched Nescafé Gold Blend. This was the first variant on the original product. Later it launched other brands such as Blend 37 and Cap Colombi.

Nestlé estimates that, on average, 3 000 cups of Nescafé are drunk every second around the world. It suggests an overall consumption of not fewer than 100 billion cups a year worldwide. More than 40 million cups of Nescafé are drunk every day in Britain. Instant coffee is drunk in 93 per cent of British homes.

Source: adapted from *The Guardian*, 24.7.1999.

1. (a) How many cups of Nescafé are drunk a day in Britain?
   (b) Nestlé estimates that 3 000 cups of Nescafé are drunk every second around the world. Using this information, calculate how many cups are drunk every day around the world.
2. With so many cups being drunk, why does Nestlé need to market Nescafé?
3. In future, Nestlé may consider launching a new brand of instant coffee. Discuss how this launch might help it to achieve its business objectives.

Market research - market segments

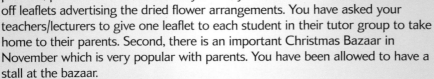
Market segments - by age and gender

Market research

Businesses sell their products into **markets** (☞ unit 3). Over time, they build up a knowledge of these markets. Businesses can use this knowledge to market their products more effectively. One way of gaining knowledge is through MARKET RESEARCH. This is where a business finds out information about customers' needs, market trends and competition.

Markets and market segments

Markets can often be split up into MARKET SEGMENTS. A market segment is a part of a market which contains a group of buyers with similar characteristics. For instance, in a fast food outlet the main groups of buyers might be single people aged 14-20 and young children with an adult. In the market for razors, there is a male market and a female market.

Some businesses are able to sell their products to the whole market. Others offer different products to different market segments.

Segmenting the market

Markets can be segmented according to the characteristics of buyers.

Age Very young children, teenagers and old age pensioners have different wants and needs. So markets can be segmented according to the age of the buyers. For instance, products to help mobility are sold mainly to older people.

Gender Men and women may have different needs and tastes. For instance, in the perfume market, females are sold 'perfumes' and 'fragrances', whilst males are sold 'after shave'. Products might also be advertised in different ways to males and females.

Income Those on low incomes have different spending patterns to those on high incomes. So markets can often be segmented by the incomes of consumers. For instance, a retailer might target low income consumers by stocking cheap goods. A retailer like Harrods may target high income earners.

Area Consumers in the South East spend more on recreation than those in other areas of the UK. People in the North West spend more on clothes than those in the North East. Customers in France may like different fragrance smells in their washing powder to those in Italy. So there are differences in buying patterns between areas within the UK and within the world economy. Businesses have to take these into account in their marketing.

Ethnic, cultural and religious groups Different ethnic, cultural and religious groups can have different buying patterns. For instance, orthodox Jews will only eat 'kosher' food, which does not contain pork products. So there is a market segment for food which does not contain pork. Other products are also targeted at these groups. Digital television shows programmes such as Asian TV and the GOD Channel aimed at ethnic minorities and at people with religious beliefs.

EITHER answer questions 1 and 2 for your mini-company OR answer all the questions based on the company below.

Your business idea has been to make dried flower arrangements. One member of the company has a parent who is a well known local expert on dried flower arrangements. She has shown you how to make them and has promised help if you run into any problems. She has also talked to you about where to get all the dried flowers from and the baskets needed to make the arrangements. It is the Autumn term. You have decided to sell your product, priced at £4.99, in two ways. First, you have run off leaflets advertising the dried flower arrangements. You have asked your teachers/lecturers to give one leaflet to each student in their tutor group to take home to their parents. Second, there is an important Christmas Bazaar in November which is very popular with parents. You have been allowed to have a stall at the bazaar.

1. What is the products that you are selling?
2. Who are your customers likely to be? For instance, are they likely to be men or women, older people or younger people, people with a high income or people with a low income?
3. Which method do you think is most likely to result in sales from your targeted customers - the leaflet or the Christmas Bazaar? Explain your answer.
4. You have decided that you want a second product to sell alongside your existing product.
   (a) How could you adopt your existing product to make it appeal to a different segment of the market?
   (b) Explain why it might appeal to a different market segment.

Socio-economic groupings One of the most important ways of dividing up the market is to split consumers into SOCIO-ECONOMIC GROUPS. This divides people up according to their occupation (i.e. job) or the occupation of the head of the household (such as the mother or father in a family). Table 39.1 shows that households can be split into five categories from A to E. The C category is divided into C1, lower middle class, and C2, skilled manual workers. Businesses may then target particular socio-economic groups as market segments.

Other ways of segmenting the market

Businesses can analyse their markets in different ways, other than just by type of consumer. One way is whether customers are **repeat customers** or **one-time customers**. Repeat customers are those who keep on buying the product. They have brand loyalty. A one-time customer is one who buys the product once, but is unlikely to do so again.

Another way of analysing the market is to find out whether customers buy the product on impulse or whether the purchase was planned. For instance, buying an ice cream from a newsagents is likely to be an impulse buy. Purchasing a pack of ice creams from a supermarket is more likely to be a planned purchase. Products bought on impulse need to be easily available to consumers. So the ice cream manufacturer must ensure that its products are sold in a large number of locations.

Social grade	Social status	Head of household's occupation
A	Upper middle class	Higher managerial, administrative or professional such as doctors, lawyers and company directors
B	Middle	Intermediate managerial, administrative or professional such as teachers, nurses and managers
C1	Lower middle class	Supervisory or clerical and junior managerial, administrative or professional such as shop assistants, clerks and police constables
C2	Skilled working class	Skilled manual workers such as carpenters, cooks and train drivers
D	Working class	Semi-skilled and unskilled manual workers such as fitters and store keepers
E	The poorest in society	State pensioners or widows, casual or lower grade workers, or long term unemployed

Table 39.1 Socio-economic groups

key terms

Market research - the process of gaining information about customers, rivals and market trends by collecting primary and secondary data.
Market segment - part of a market which contains a group of buyers with similar characteristics, such as age or income.
Socio-economic groupings - the division of people according to common characteristics.

Checklist

1. Why is it important for a business to know at which segment of the market to aim its products?
2. Explain what type of person by (i) age, (ii) gender and (iii) income you think is likely to buy: (a) clothes from Top Shop; (b) a pair of ladies shoes from Marks & Spencer; (c) a pint of beer in a pub; (d) a copy of the *Financial Times*; (e) a £5.99 spaceman Lego set; (f) a Porsche car; (g) a month's holiday in Spain in February.
3. What is the difference between an A and C1 in terms of socio-economic grouping?
4. Socio-economic group E is not usually a sales target for businesses. Why not?
5. A person in socio-economic group B might go touring in France in the summer. A person in socio-economic group C or D might go to Benidorm on a package tour. Why do you think there is a difference in the holiday destinations of the two groups?
6. What is the difference between a repeat customer and a one-time customer?
7. What is an impulse purchase?

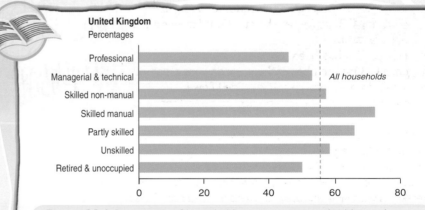

United Kingdom
Percentages

Figure 39.1 Percentage of households participating in the National Lottery: by social class of head of household, 1998-99
Source: adapted from *Social Trends*, Office for National Statistics.

The National Lottery is studying its market.
1. Using the data, explain what is meant by 'socio-economic groupings'.
2. Which TWO socio-economic groups are (a) likely to have the highest incomes and (b) most likely to participate in the National Lottery?
3. If the National Lottery was concerned that the numbers playing its games were declining, discuss which socio-economic groups it might target in its advertising campaigns. In your answer refer to the data and your answer to question 2.

Market research (1)

Stages of market research

Figure 40.1 shows the process or stages of market research. Market research attempts to find answers to questions that a business might have about its market. For example, a manufacturer of soap powder might want to find out how to increase the market share of its product.

The business must decide what information might help answer this question. For example, it might try to find out the existing pattern of sales in the market and how the market is changing. It might want to identify **market segments** (☞ unit 39) within the soap powder market to target. It may want to know the views of consumers about the existing product and how it could be changed to increase sales.

The market researcher must then decide how to collect this information. There are two ways of doing this - **desk research** and **field research**.

The information will then be collected and analysed. Finally, the business has to make a decision about what to do in the light of the information it has found.

Desk research

DESK RESEARCH involves the use of SECONDARY DATA. This is information which is already available, both within and outside the business. Figure 40.2 shows some of these sources.

- **Information within the business.** A business collects information routinely. Invoices, for instance, will tell it how much it has sold and who it is selling to. Accounts will give information about the value of sales and costs of production. A soap powder manufacturer, for example, will know sales figures for its brands of soap powder. It can see trends in sales over time.
- **Information from outside the business.** Businesses can also collect information which is available from sources outside the business.

Field research

FIELD RESEARCH involves the collection of PRIMARY DATA. This is information which no one has yet collected. It is collected specially for the particular piece of research. Primary data is collected through direct investigation, usually in one of three ways - observation, experiments and surveys (☞ unit 41).

A magazine company is thinking of branching out into other markets. It is considering setting up a new national newspaper.

1. 'Table 40.1 is secondary data.' Explain what this means.
2. Does the data suggest that the newspaper market is expanding or contracting?
3. The magazine company is wondering (a) whether to publish a quality newspaper like *The Times*, *The Guardian*, *The Independent* or the *Financial Times*, or a tabloid newspaper like *The Sun* or the *Daily Mail* and (b) whether to aim it more at males or females. How might it use the data in Table 40.1 to help make these decisions?

	Males			Females		
	1981	1991	1998-99	1981	1991	1998-99
The Sun	31	25	24	23	19	17
The Mirror	27	20	15	22	15	12
Daily Mail	13	10	12	11	9	12
Daily Express	16	8	6	13	8	5
The Daily Telegraph	9	6	6	7	5	5
Daily Star	13	8	5	8	4	2
The Times	3	3	5	2	2	3
The Guardian	4	3	3	2	2	2
The Independent	-	3	2	-	2	1
Financial Times	2	2	2	1	1	1
Any national newspaper	76	66	60	68	57	51

Percentages

Table 40.1 *Percentage aged 15 and over reading a national daily newspaper*
Source: adapted from *Social Trends*, Office for National Statistics.

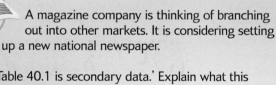

Figure 40.1 *The stages of market research*

What is the question which the business wants to find an answer to?

What information is needed to answer this question?

What method of market research will be used?

Collect the data

Analyse the data, draw conclusions and make recommendations

- **Internal sources** - such as sales invoices, reports and accounts.
- **Government** - published statistics, such as consumer spending figures; reports such as Competition Commission reports
- **The media** - reports in newspapers, magazines, on radio and on television.
- **Trade associations** - statistics or reports published by national organisations such as the TUC, the CBI or chambers of commerce, or industry associations such as the Engineering Employers Federation or the National Farmers Union.
- **Research organisations** - reports prepared by specialist market research organisations such as Mintel or Mori; articles published in academic journals such as university journals.

Figure 40.2 Sources of secondary data

Observation

Looking at and recording what people do and how they behave can be important. For instance, a supermarket may find that sales in one aisle in the store are poor. By observing people, it may be possible to see whether the problem is that shoppers are avoiding the aisle. Or it could be that there are plenty of shoppers in the aisle, but they aren't buying. However, observation can't tell the supermarket anything about **why** shoppers are behaving in this way.

Experiments

Market researchers can use experimental techniques. To launch a new product is often costly. So manufacturers **test** products as they are being developed to check that they are likely to succeed.

For instance, a new soap powder could be tested in a number of ways.

- It could be tested in washes many times by the manufacturer to check its ability to wash.
- **Home placement tests** could be used. This is where a small number of households are asked to use the product for a period of time, like one month. They are then interviewed to find out what they think about it.
- It might be **test marketed**. This is where it is sold in an area before being launched nationally or internationally. Launching a product in, say, the North East of England is much cheaper than launching it nationally. Fewer products need to be manufactured and much less needs to be spent on advertising and promotion. If the product has poor sales, it can be withdrawn. The manufacturer will have lost less money than if there was a national launch. If it is a success, it can be launched. The test market launch may also provide evidence about how to market the product. For instance, consumers may prefer one set of advertisements compared to another.

Paul Reagon's marketing consultancy was hired by Features, a department store in London. The management at Features asked the consultancy to conduct a one month in-depth observational study into the sales areas of the four storey building.

One outcome of the study concerned the tie department. Researchers looked at video tapes of people buying ties. They noticed that shoppers became edgy and nervous when there were groups of people immediately behind them. They often left the area without making a purchase to avoid the crush. The tie racks were unfortunately situated next to a busy walk-through aisle which connected an outside door to the escalators.

As a result of this observation, the store moved the tie racks away from the aisle by a few metres. This allowed shoppers looking at the ties to stand without being in the way of people who were moving from one area of the store to the next. Giving shoppers this 'personal space' led to an average 50 per cent increase in tie sales. When the store was busy, for instance at sale time or in the run up to Christmas, tie sales doubled.

1. Giving examples from the data, explain what is meant by an 'observational study'.
2. How did the observational study help Features to increase its sales?
3. Moving the tie racks away from the busy aisle meant that the luggage department, sited next to the ties, lost a few metres of space. The luggage department staff responded by pushing their displays closer together. The result was that the walkways between the luggage displays were slightly narrower than before. Discuss whether this is likely to have any effect on sales of luggage.

Checklist

1. List the stages of market research.
2. What sources of information are available to someone undertaking desk research?
3. Distinguish between field research and desk research.
4. A shopping centre wants to find out how many shoppers visit the centre. How could it gather this information?
5. What is meant by (a) 'home placement tests' and (b) 'test marketing'?

Surveys allow respondents to answer questions

Surveys

A SURVEY involves asking questions of RESPONDENTS. These are people or organisations who reply to the questions asked. For example, a car hire company may survey customers who have hired vehicles. It may ask questions about the quality of service they received when collecting the vehicle and about the vehicle itself.

There are different ways of conducting surveys. **Postal surveys** are where QUESTIONNAIRES are sent through the post. **Newspaper surveys** are where people are asked to fill in and return a questionnaire in a newspaper. These are relatively cheap ways of gaining information.

Telephone surveys, personal **interviews** and **consumers' panels** are more expensive because an interviewer has to be employed to interview customers. Only a fraction of customers tend to respond to a postal survey. A much larger proportion of those asked will take part in telephone and personal interviews. The interviewer can also help respondents understand what questions mean and how they should be answered.

Some surveys allow consumers' reactions to products to be recorded. A **consumer panel** is where a group of people meet together. It allows researchers to see how consumers react in a group situation to a product or idea. **Home placement** tests may also be used. This is where consumers are asked to use the product in their homes over a period of time. Their actions and opinions are monitored and recorded.

The results of surveys might be used to calculate whether consumers would buy the product again (a **repeat purchase**). They may also be used to find out how often consumers would buy the product **(the purchase frequency)**.

Open and closed questions

Surveys can only be useful for market research purposes if the questions asked are appropriate. For instance, sometimes it is important to ask **closed questions**. These are questions which have a definite answer. An example would be: 'How many packets of crisps did you buy last week?'. At other times, the market researcher might want to find out about opinions and allow the respondent to develop an answer. It is best then to ask **open questions**. Open questions have many possible answers. For instance, 'Do you like the packaging of Persil?' is an open question.

Sampling

A survey cannot ask every customer for their opinion. Only a fraction or SAMPLE of customers can be surveyed. To be useful, the sample chosen must be representative of all consumers (the **population**).

Random sample In a random sample every potential respondent has an equal chance of being chosen. Random numbers can be used to do

Database and wordprocessing

Conduct a survey about biscuits.

1. Before you start asking questions, you need to do two things. (a) Draw up your questionnaire. This should cover: (i) how many biscuits people eat; (ii) what are their favourite styles and brands; (iii) where they buy biscuits from; (iv) what influences them to buy a particular style and brand; (v) whether they think biscuits are a healthy part of their diet. You could write your questionnaire using a word processing package. (b) Decide what type of sample you will use. You are likely to want to get responses from people of different ages and of different genders.
2. Conduct your survey.
3. You now need to analyse your findings. You could enter your results on a computer database and the program would then do much of the work for you.
4. Write a short report. You could use a wordprocessing package for this. (a) The report should outline briefly the questionnaire and the sample you chose to use. Were there any problems you found with the survey? (b) Briefly present the main findings of the survey. (c) A small but growing chain of supermarkets is thinking of launching own brand biscuits. What does your survey suggest is important if sales are to be high?

this. Or it can be done by 'picking people out of a hat'. It is often quite complicated to construct a truly random sample.

Systematic sample A cheaper and quicker method is to use a systematic sample. This is where, say, every 100th or 1 000th person on a list like a telephone directory or the electoral register is chosen. A systematic sample is not truly random though, so the results may be less reliable.

Quota sample In a quota sample, the sample is broken down (or **stratified**). For instance, a food manufacturer might want to target 16-24 year olds with a new chocolate bar. It might know that 3 out of 10 people who bought chocolate bars are be aged 0-15. 6 out of 10 might be aged 16-24 and the rest might be over 24. So out of a sample of 100 it would ask 60 people (6 out of 10) aged 16-24 to complete a survey.

One problem with a quota sample is that any people who fit the description can be asked to complete the survey. So a business that wanted to find 60 people aged 16-24 to complete a survey could ask the first sixty 16-24 year olds it met in Leicester Square in London. The problem is that they may not be representative of 16-24 year olds nationally.

Stratified random sample A stratified random sample may get around this problem. It is a quota sample where all the respondents must be chosen at random. For the chocolate bar sample to be random, the business would have to find some way of choosing 60 people aged 16-24 by pure chance.

Decisions

The purpose of market research is to help a business come to a decision. For example, it may help a business to find out what the customer wants from a new product. The product will then be developed. Consumer trials will show whether the product is likely to be a success. Finally, the product will be launched. At every stage, the business can change or adapt the product. Or it may decide to stop developing the product altogether. A product which does not sell is less costly to stop at the development stage than if it is launched nationally. So market research reduces the risk of any product launch and minimises costs of development.

Women are more likely to be frequent buyers of flowers than men. The most likely occasion for buying flowers is as a gift for someone who is not well or is in hospital. 40 per cent of those buying flowers tend to buy them from supermarkets, compared to 30 per cent who used specialist florists and 15 per cent from a market stall. These were the findings of a survey of the flower market by the NOP Research Group. A nationally representative sample of 1 000 adults age 15+ were interviewed.

Not surprisingly, socio-economic groups A and B had the highest rates of purchase. They made up the largest proportion of people who bought flowers at least once a month. On average, 6 out of 10 respondents said they would buy flowers more often if they were less expensive. This rose to 7 out of 10 for respondents from socio-economic groups D and E. People aged 55 and over make up 47 per cent of frequent buyers, compared to 35 per cent for 35-54 year olds and 16 per cent for 15-34 year olds.

Supermarkets are likely to increase their dominance of this market. Half of all frequent and regular flower purchasers buy from supermarkets. Given that more women than men do the supermarket shopping, supermarkets are in a good position to push sales further. Already, they typically put flowers at the entrance to attract customers before they start their shop.

Source: adapted from *Marketing Week* 22.3.2001.

1. Give THREE findings of the NOP Research Group survey.
2. (a) Suggest what is meant by a 'nationally representative sample'.
   (b) Suggest why the NOP Research Group made their sample 'representative'.
3. A marketing expert for a supermarket chain writes a report suggesting that it should make greater efforts to market flowers to men, to those aged under 55 and to socio-economic groups D and E. Discuss whether this would be a better strategy than marketing to women, those over 55 and to socio-economic groups A and B.

✓Checklist

1. What differences are there between a postal survey and personal interviews in surveys?
2. Consumers are far more likely to make repeat purchases of a brand of crisps than a brand of bed. Explain why.
3. Give TWO examples each of (a) a closed question and (b) an open question.
4. A business wants to take a random sample of people in the London area. How could it do this?
5. A chocolate bar manufacturer wants to find out if a new bar of chocolate is going to sell well in the UK. How could it find this out without having to go to the expense of launching the product nationally?

---

key terms

Questionnaire - a list of questions to be answered by respondents, designed to give information about consumers' tastes.
Respondent - person or organisation answering questions in a survey.
Sample - small group out of a total population which is selected to take part in a survey.
Survey - research involving asking questions of people or organisations.

A Dyson cleaner - a product with an original design and formulation

The product and the marketing mix

The **marketing mix** (☞ unit 38) is the combination of factors which helps a business to sell its products. One of the '4 Ps' of the marketing mix is the **product** (☞ unit 1) which a business makes. A product may be a **good** or a **service** (☞ unit 5), or a combination of both. A television set, a railway journey or a sofa that is delivered to your home are all examples of products sold by businesses.

The product range

Businesses may offer a RANGE of products for sale. For example, The Coca-Cola company sells Coca-Cola, variations on the original drink like Diet Coke and other soft drinks like Lilt. For larger businesses, the product range is likely to be part of its total PRODUCT MIX. For example, Unilever, a multinational company, has many ranges of products. These include washing powders, cosmetics and ice creams. These products all form part of Unilever's product mix.

Product differentiation

Selling a range of goods or services allows a business to DIFFERENTIATE its products. Different consumers want different products. By producing a range, the business can sell more and make more profit by satisfying different consumers' **wants** (☞ unit 1). For example, not everyone likes Coca-Cola. Lilt is an alternative soft drink that these customers might buy.

Smaller businesses may be able to differentiate their products from others by making something that is new or unusual.

Ways of differentiating the product

There is a number of ways in which a business can make its products different from others.

Design and formulation Every soft drink produced by Coca-Cola has a different formula. For instance, some contain sugar, whilst others contain sugar substitutes. Some contain caffeine, whilst others are caffeine free. Similarly, car manufacturers produce a range of cars. Each car model may have hundreds of different features, from the colour of the car to the engine size to whether it has a fitted sunroof or not. McDonald's sells a variety of foods, from Big Macs to Chicken Nuggets to coffee. More expensive UP-MARKET PRODUCTS are likely to be better quality than a better selling but cheaper MASS MARKET PRODUCT.

New or small businesses may be able to produce novel products. The Dyson vacuum cleaner became popular because it did not need a bag to collect dust and dirt. A small business may be able to offer a more personal service, such as alterations to clothes.

Name Different products have different names. The name of the product is important if it is to sell. For example, calling a chocolate bar 'Sickbar' is likely to result in few sales. New products often have short names which are easy to pronounce and remember. The name should say something positive about the product. Polo, the mint sweet produced by Nestlé, has

1. 'The products shown are part of the product range of Nestlé.' Explain what this means.
2. Why does Nestlé produce such a range of chocolate products instead of producing just one chocolate bar?
3. The range of Nestlé chocolate products on sale varies from country to country. Why do you think this is the case?

Every hour of the day, 1 million packets of crisps are eaten in the UK. 8.9 billion packets are sold each year. 90 per cent of the market is taken by brands such as Walkers and Golden Wonder. However, 10 per cent of the market is taken by speciality up-market crisps. The most important of these is Pringles.

Pringles are a hi-tech crisp made by the most advanced methods of crisp making. Potato flakes are dehydrated and then moulded into an exact shape before frying. Then they are packed into cardboard cans to ensure no breakages. The result is a perfectly uniform crisp every time, which arrives unbroken to the consumer.

In contrast, some up-market crisp makers have taken a different route. Gourmet crisps, like Kettle Chips and Benson Organic crisps, have reverted to the original techniques of crisp making. Gone are techniques like double washing the sliced potato to get rid of extra starch, and putting in large amounts of artificial flavours and additives. Crisps are fried in batches. Dashes of natural flavouring like balsamic vinegar are included. The result is a less uniform but more natural crisp. The crisp itself changes from month to month depending on the season of the year.

Source: adapted from *The Guardian*, 14.1.2000.

1. How do the manufacturers of (a) Pringles and (b) Kettle Chips differentiate their products from a mass market product like Walker's crisps?
2. How does the distinctive packaging of Pringles help sell the product?
3. Benson Organic crisps are made using only organic products. Discuss the possible advantages and disadvantages to its manufacturers of producing an organic product using traditional techniques of cooking.

two 'o's in the name. This links it with the hole in the product. Müller Fruit Corners reminds the customer that the product comes in two separate compartments. One contains yoghurt and the other a fruit mix.

However, the name is only a small part of the marketing mix of the product. No marketing company would have advised a UK baked bean manufacturer to brand its product 'Heinz'. However, Heinz baked beans is the most successful brand name for baked beans in the UK today.

Packaging Packaging is used to deliver products safely to the consumer. For instance, putting tin foil around a KitKat, a Nestlé product, keeps the bar fresher and prevents deterioration. Instant coffee tends to be sold in jars to prevent spillage and because glass is a strong material.

Packaging should also help businesses and consumers store the product. Bottles need flat bottoms for stability, for instance. Packaging gives information to the customer about the product. Frozen food products, for example, usually give cooking instructions. Packaging has other uses though. It is a way of **promoting** the product (☞ unit 45). Colours, designs and letters attract the customers' attention. M&M packets, for instance, are brightly coloured because they are sold mainly to children.

key terms

Mass market product - a product which sells in large quantities to a large proportion of the market.
Product differentiation - making one product different from another, for instance through the quality of a product, its design, packaging or advertising.
Product mix - the combination of products that a business sells, like soap powders, cosmetics and medicines.
Product range - a group of similar products made by a business, like a number of different soap powders.
Up-market product - a product which is typically of better quality and higher price than a mass market product, but sells in smaller quantities.

Checklist

1. Give THREE examples each of products in (a) the Cadbury Schweppes' range of chocolate and (b) the Ford car range.
2. Why do businesses usually sell ranges of products rather than just one single product?
3. How do the following businesses differentiate their products: (a) a multi-screen cinema; (b) a record company; (c) a manufacturer of crisps?
4. Why do you think the following brand names help sell their product: (a) Cadbury's Flake; (b) Kellogg's Corn Flakes; (c) Bold, manufactured by Procter & Gamble?
5. Why do manufacturers use packaging?

Discounts and special offers are often used by supermarkets

Pricing and the marketing mix

Pricing is one of the '4 Ps' of the marketing mix (☞ unit 38). Businesses have to decide what price they will charge for their products.

They know that the higher the price, the lower will be the **demand** for the product. So the higher the price they set, the less will be demanded and sold. But there are many other factors which they need to take into account when setting prices.

Competition based pricing

One strategy for deciding on a price is to look at the prices of competitors. This is known as COMPETITION BASED PRICING. For instance, a supermarket might find that a rival charges 9p a can for its budget baked beans. So it might also charge 9p for its own product. A manufacturer of vacuum cleaners might charge £250 for its top of the range model because its main competitor charges £250 for its model.

Setting the price at the average for the market avoids price competition. It is also a safe strategy for a business for two reasons.

- If it charges a higher price than other businesses, customers might buy rivals' products.
- If it charges a lower price than other businesses, it takes the risk that its rivals might reduce their prices. It would then not have gained any competitive advantage. Even worse, sales revenues and profits would be lower than if it had charged a higher price.

Market orientated pricing

An alternative to competition based pricing is MARKET ORIENTATED PRICING. This is where prices are set based on an analysis of the market and its characteristics.

Discounts, special offers and sales

Businesses would prefer to sell all their products at their 'full price'. But they may offer discounts or run special offers and sales to increase the quantity bought. For instance, a retailer like Miss Selfridge or Oasis will hope to sell its clothes at full price between September and Christmas. But they often hold sales after Christmas when the price of clothes is reduced. A record company may give retailers a special discount for a period on certain CDs to increase their sales. Retailers may put 'special offer' on the packaging to show that this is a bargain.

They also offer LOSS LEADERS. These are products which are priced so cheaply that the retailer makes no profit or even a loss on every sale. But they attract customers into the store, who then buy other full price products.

Price discrimination

Designer clothes manufacturers like Calvin Klein or Gucci sell their clothes at different prices in different areas of the world. Selling the same product at different prices to different **segments of the market** (☞ unit 39) is known as PRICE DISCRIMINATION. Businesses use price discrimination to maximise profit in each different market. They charge what the market will 'bear'. For instance, designer clothes are more expensive in the UK than in the US because British buyers are prepared to pay higher prices than American buyers.

Penetration pricing

In some markets, it is common for a business to discount prices when a product first goes on sale. This is known as PENETRATION PRICING. Businesses hope to gain **market share** (☞ unit 22) more quickly and easily than if they had launched the product at full price. One problem with this strategy is that consumers may refuse to buy at the higher long term price. They

key terms

Competition based pricing - setting a price based on the prices charged by competitors for similar products.
Cost plus pricing - fixing a price by adding a percentage profit margin to the cost of production of the good or service.
Creaming or skimming - selling a product at a high price, sacrificing high sales in order to earn high profits.
Loss leader - a product which is sold at a loss to attract customers to buy other full price products sold by the business.
Market orientated pricing - setting a price based on an analysis of the market.
Mark-up or profit margin - the percentage added to the cost of production which equals the profit on the product.
Penetration pricing - setting an initial low price for a new product so that it is attractive to customers. The price is likely to be raised later as the product gains market share.
Price discrimination - setting a different price for the same product in different segments of the market.
Profit margin - the extra which is added to the cost of a product to cover the profit to be made.

might see the initial price as 'fair' and the more expensive price as not being 'value for money'.

Creaming CREAMING (or SKIMMING) is the opposite of penetration pricing. It is charging a high price for a product at first and lowering it later. It is often used with electronic products. For instance, when CD players were first launched in the 1980s they were typically priced between £200-£300. Today, despite **inflation** (☞ unit 10), a CD player with better features is priced at £100-£200 on average. In the early days, enthusiasts were prepared to pay a high price to get a new product. However, to create a mass market for CD players, manufacturers had to lower their prices even though they put more features onto machines.

Prestige pricing Prestige pricing is where a business deliberately sets a high price for a product. It does this to convince consumers

that it really is a luxury, up-market product. Manufacturers of luxury perfume brands use this pricing strategy. The luxury nature of the product is then reinforced in advertising and promotion. The product may also be sold in up-market shops. High prices are likely to lead to lower sales. But selling less at a high price may be more profitable than selling more at a low price.

Cost based pricing

Businesses need to make a profit to survive in the long term. Charging a price similar to those of competitors is one way to set prices, but might lead to losses. Another way could be to base price on costs of production. This is known as COST PLUS PRICING. A business might calculate that it costs £1 to make a product. It could then add a MARK-UP or PROFIT MARGIN. The price of the product would then be the cost of production plus profit for the

business.

The cost is the average cost and is made up of:

- the variable cost - like the cost of potatoes in making crisps;
- the fixed cost - such as the wages of staff, the cost of equipment and buildings, and heating and lighting.

When the price covers both the average fixed and variable cost of the product, the business is said to be **full-cost pricing**.

Sometimes, it is difficult to get orders. For instance, a business may find that other crisp makers are offering lower prices. So it might have to cut its price to below the full-cost price to get orders. So long as the new price more than covers the variable cost, it will at least make some **contribution** towards paying the fixed costs of the business. In the long term, the crisp manufacturer has to cover all its costs to survive. Otherwise it won't be able to buy new machinery, for instance. In the short term, though, it can set any price above its variable cost.

SP Wear is a sports shop located opposite a large school and on a parade of shops in South London. Wilson Parker has agreed to buy the shop from its present owners and is due to take possession in one month's time. He feels that the present owners have not exploited the potential of the sports shop. Wilson wants to double sales in the next two years.

Wilson's main pricing strategy is simple. He will roughly double the cost of an item bought from a manufacturer. He aims to have two sales a year, one in January and one in June-July. There is potential for direct links with the school. If it orders any item in bulk, it will be offered a 20 per cent discount from what he would otherwise have charged.

Wilson is still uncertain about what pricing strategy to use when the shop comes under his 'new management'. He has considered offering a 20 per cent discount on all items for the opening week. Alternatively, he could offer a 50 per cent discount on ten of his potential best selling products. Another idea is to distribute leaflets in the local area, possibly through the local free paper. He would offer a 20 per cent discount to anyone bringing in the leaflet.

1. Identify and explain the pricing strategies mentioned in the passage.
2. Discuss which of the pricing strategies Wilson should use in the opening week. In your answer, you will need to weigh up the advantages and disadvantages of each.

Checklist

1. Using sports products as an example, explain what is meant by 'competitive pricing'.
2. Why do shops have sales?
3. How might a hairdresser price discriminate?
4. Why might penetration pricing be a good price strategy to use when launching a new brand of yogurts?
5. 'Mobile phone companies have used price creaming strategies when setting prices.' Explain what this means.
6. Calculate the price of a product if its cost of production is: (a) £10 and the mark up is 50 per cent; (b) £100 and the mark up is 10 per cent; (c) £5 and the mark up is 100 per cent.
7. What is meant by a 'contribution' in pricing?

To what extent would lower prices lead to more goods being bought?

Price and demand

There is a link between price of a product and the quantity bought. For instance, the price of a Mars Bar might be 30p. If the price went up to 50p, but nothing else changed, some consumers would stop buying Mars Bars. They would spend their money on something else, like another chocolate bar. So a rise in the price of a product will lead to a fall in the quantity demanded.

This is shown in Figure 44.1. The curve shows the relationship between the amount bought (the quantity demanded) and the price of a chocolate bar. The higher the price, the less will be bought. So if the price rises from 30p to 50p the amount bought falls from 10 million to 5 million bars per year. The curve is called a DEMAND CURVE.

Price elasticity

When a business changes the price of a product, the effect on the amount bought could be large or small.

Inelastic demand Most motorists would buy the same amount of petrol if oil companies put up the price. Only a few motorists would cut back their demand for petrol. This is shown in Figure 44.2. If there is little change in quantity demanded when price changes, demand is INELASTIC. It is like an elastic band. You may use force to pull the band (the change in price). But it may not stretch very much (the change in quantity demanded). So the band is not very elastic, i.e it is inelastic.

Elastic demand A market trader sells 20 kilos of bananas an hour at 80p a kilo. At 2pm on a Saturday afternoon he still has 60 kilos left to sell before going home at 3pm. He needs to get rid of them before they go rotten. So he cuts his price to 40p a kilo and sells the 60 kilos in an hour. By halving his price (80p to 40p), he trebles the amount sold (20 kilos to 60 kilos). This is an example of ELASTIC demand. A change in price brings about a larger percentage change in quantity bought. It is like an elastic band. You may use force to pull the band (the change in price). If it stretches a lot (the change in quantity demanded) the band is elastic. Elastic demand is shown in Figure 44.3.

?
1. Do you think there would be a small or a large fall in quantity demanded if the price of:
(a) a Twix chocolate bar rose from 32p to 40p;
(b) the price of a season ticket rose from £365 to £400.
(c) a holiday for one adult to Gran Canaria on 23 July rose from £829 to £1 036?
2. Using your answer to 1, explain whether demand for each of the three products is likely to be elastic or inelastic.

Proportions and percentages

There are precise definitions for elastic or inelastic demand.

Inelastic demand Demand is inelastic when a percentage (or proportional) change in price leads to a smaller percentage (or proportional) change in quantity demanded. For instance, a business might reduce its price by 10 per cent (or one tenth). If quantity demanded only rises by 5 per cent (or one twentieth), then demand is inelastic.

Elastic demand Demand is elastic when a percentage (or proportional) change in price leads to a greater percentage (or proportional) change

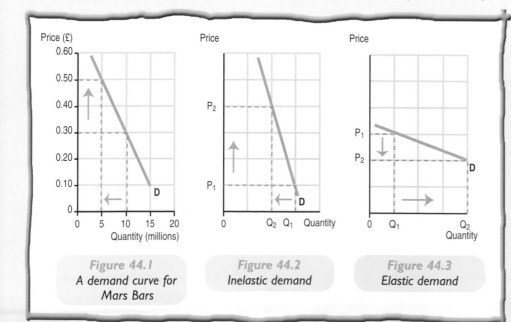

Figure 44.1
A demand curve for Mars Bars

Figure 44.2
Inelastic demand

Figure 44.3
Elastic demand

Soumaia, Sean, Louise and Peter have set up The Fabulous Tuck Company. It is a mini company operating as part of their GCSE Business Studies course.

The Fabulous Tuck Company buys mainly sweets and crisps and sells them at break times in the Year 10 area of the school. They have been surprised at how easy it is to make a profit from the enterprise. Stock is bought each Saturday from a local cash and carry by Peter's father who runs his own business. The Fabulous Tuck Company then adds a profit mark up and sells it. Any line which fails in a week to sell at least half of what was bought the previous Saturday is discontinued.

Next week, The Fabulous Tuck Company is going to introduce a new line - Mars Bars. The cost price for Mars Bars from the cash and carry is 20p each and they are sold in local shops for between 32p and 35p.

Soumaia and Sean think they ought to sell them for 27p. They argue that this would undercut the price in the local shops. It would also make the line more affordable to Year 10 students. Louise and Peter think they should be sold for 30p. This would still be cheaper than in the local shops. They also think that the potential customers for Mars Bars will not be influenced by price when deciding whether to buy or not.

1. In the first week of sales, The Fabulous Tuck Company sets the price of Mars Bars at the higher price of 30p and sells 20. In the second week, it decides to cut the price to 27p and sells 30. Is the demand for Mars Bars elastic or inelastic? Explain your answer carefully.
2. Did The Fabulous Tuck Company earn more in revenue in the second week compared to the first week? Explain your answer.
3. Soumaia and Sean think they should push the price down still further to 25p. Discuss whether this would benefit the company.

in quantity demanded. For instance, a business might reduce its price by 10 per cent (or one tenth). If the quantity demanded increases by 20 per cent (two tenths), demand is elastic.

A formula

Price elasticity of demand can be calculated and given a numerical value by using the formula:

$$\text{Price elasticity of demand} = \frac{\text{\% change in quantity demanded}}{\text{\% change in price}}$$

If demand is inelastic, the percentage change in price will lead to a smaller percentage change in quantity demanded. Using the formula,

inelastic demand will have a value of less than 1.

If demand is elastic, the percentage change in price will lead to a larger percentage change in quantity demanded. Using the formula, elastic demand will have a value of greater than 1.

The importance of elasticity to business

Price elasticity of demand is important to businesses. If they change their prices, they want to know how this will affect sales. For instance, if demand is elastic, a rise in price of 2 per cent could lead to a fall in sales of 15 per cent. This would see a fall in sales revenue (quantity sold x price) of 13 per

cent. In general, if demand is elastic, a rise in price will see a fall in total sales revenue. But if prices fall, then total sales revenue will go up.

If demand is inelastic, a business may put up its prices by 10 per cent and see sales fall by 3 per cent. This will lead to a rise in sales revenue of 7 per cent. In general, if demand is inelastic, a rise in price will see a rise in total sales revenue. But if prices fall, then total sales revenue will also fall.

UNIT 45

Promotion and advertising

Billboards are examples of advertising media

Communication

Businesses need to communicate with their customers. PROMOTION is about:

- making customers aware that the product is for sale;
- telling or explaining to them what the product is;
- making customers aware of how the product will serve their needs;
- persuading them to buy it for the first time or to buy it again.

Promotion is the most direct form of communication in the **marketing mix** (☞ unit 38).

There is a number of techniques of promotion. Advertising is explained in this unit. Direct mailing, personal selling, public relations, sales promotion, and branding are explained in unit 46.

Advertising agencies

ADVERTISING AGENCIES are businesses which specialise in organising the advertising of other businesses. An example is Cordiant, which includes the Saatchi & Saatchi, Zenith and Bates Dorland agencies.

Within the advertising agency, an **account executive** will be appointed to run a particular campaign. In a traditional large advertising business there are four main areas, as shown in Figure 45.1.

- The **market research** department organises market research (☞ units 39-41) into the product. The information collected is then used to plan the advertising campaign.
- The **creative department** devises the advertisement, from the words to be used (the **copy**) to the pictures to the sound.
- The **art buying department** organises the making of film advertisements, the taking of photographs, etc.
- The **media buying department** buys slots on television, on radio, in newspapers and magazines, etc.

The advertising agency is crucial to the success of any advertising campaign. Adverts must attract the attention of potential customers. They might do this by being highly informative, funny or even

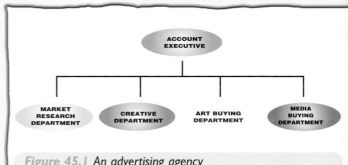

Figure 45.1 An advertising agency

---

1. Look at Figure 45.2. How much in 1999 was spent on advertising (a) in national newspapers; (b) on radio; (c) through directories?
2. Between 1985 and 1999 the share of total advertising spending on cinema, radio, directories and television rose. At the same time the share of total advertising spending on national and regional newspapers and consumer magazines fell. Suggest reasons why this occurred.
3. (a) What has happened to total advertising spending between 1985 and 1999? (b) Why do you think there has been this change?

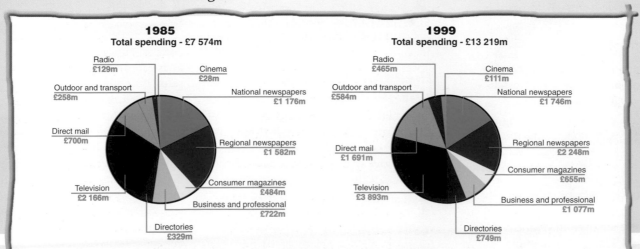

Figure 45.2 Advertising expenditure (£ million at constant 1995 prices)
Source: adapted from *Advertising Statistics Yearbook*, 2000.

key terms

Advertising agency - a business which specialises in organising the promotion for other businesses.
Promotion - communication between businesses and customers, making customers aware that the product is for sale, telling or explaining to them what is the product, making customers aware of how the product will service their needs and persuading them to buy the product for the first time or again.

Checklist

1. What is meant by 'media advertising'?
2. How can an advertising agency help a business?
3. What might be the role of each of the departments within an advertising agency?
4. What media can be used for advertising?
5. (a) What is a 'directory'. (b) Give TWO examples of sales directories used by businesses.
6. What might be the advantages and disadvantages to a large food manufacturer wanting to advertise a brand of dog food to consumers of using (a) television; (b) trade journals; (c) billboards?

Each of the photographs above shows a different form of advertising medium.
1. Name each of these.
2. The following want to advertise their products. Explain which of the advertising media shown in the photographs would be suitable. In your answer, consider (i) the cost of advertising; (ii) the target audience; (iii) the impact of the advertisement on the potential customer.
   (a) An internet recruitment agency, a business which advertises jobs on behalf of employers seeking workers, wants to advertise its services to workers looking for a change of job.
   (b) A small business repairing washing machines wants to advertise its services.
   (c) A sports clothing manufacturer wants to advertise a new range.
   (d) Cadbury Schweppes wants to advertise a new chocolate bar.
   (e) A holiday company wants to advertise short climbing holidays.

provocative. Successful adverts tend to be memorable and capture people's imagination.

Media advertising

Businesses advertise through the **media**. These include:

- television, radio and cinema;
- magazines;
- national and local newspapers;
- trade newspapers and journals - these are specialist publications aimed at businesses or workers in a particular industry;
- directories - including the telephone directories *Yellow Pages* and *Thomson Directory*;
- posters and transport - such as billboards on the side of the road and advertisements on buses and vans;
- the internet (☞ unit 13).

Each medium has its advantages and disadvantages.

Cost Television advertising and advertising in national newspapers may be expensive. Advertising campaigns on television tend to be conducted only by large companies. Advertising in local newspapers, magazines and directories is less expensive and can be afforded by small firms. So might advertising on the internet.

Target audience Different media have different audiences. For instance, television advertising or a national newspaper advert is usually aimed at consumers. Adverts in trade papers are aimed either at workers or businesses.

Size of audience Television advertising is likely to have the widest audience of any type of media. A trade journal will tend to have a low audience. However, the total size of the audience is not always important. The key measure is the size relative to the target audience. For instance, an advert for an accountancy job may be advertised in *Accountancy Age*, a journal read by accountants. The circulation of *Accountancy Age* is not large. But it is read by a high proportion of accountants, particularly if they are looking for a new job. Hence, job adverts in *Accountancy Age* often reach a large proportion of those at which they are aimed. Many advertisers use the internet. But adverts on the internet do not always reach the target audience.

Delivering the message Different media are able to deliver messages in different ways. For instance, television and the internet allows the use of colour and moving pictures, unlike a small ad in a local newspaper. Adverts in newspapers, magazines and directories can be cut out and referred to again, unlike television and radio advertising. Television is good at delivering advertisements aimed at changing the audience's perception of a product. The small ads in a newspaper are much better at giving information.

Other methods of promotion

Direct mail is a form of sales promotion

It would be easier if you did this survey as part of a group. You need to collect information about promotions currently on offer. You could do this by:

- looking through local newspapers, including free newspapers;
- noting down any promotions offered on television or radio commercials;
- checking through food, particularly tins and packets, which you have at home;
- visiting local shops, such as your nearest supermarket, and noting down products and promotions on offer;
- using the internet.

1. Give TEN examples of different promotions you have found.
2. (a) For each one, explain why you think it could increase sales of the product.
   (b) Which do you think will be the most effective promotion and why?

Above and below the line promotion

Using the media for advertising, discussed in unit 45, is called ABOVE THE LINE PROMOTION. Other methods of promotion, discussed in this unit, are called BELOW THE LINE PROMOTION.

Direct mail

DIRECT MAIL involves a business sending advertising leaflets directly to a household or business through the post. To keep costs down, the advertiser needs a list of potential customers. For instance, it may target households in a particular area, getting names and addresses from the electoral register. Or it may have a list of clients who have bought products in the past. This is often used by financial services businesses like banks and insurance companies, and by mail order firms. Businesses can also buy lists of names and addresses of people who

have bought a related product. For instance, a mail order company selling camping equipment might buy a mailing list from a business that sells hiking shoes and boots by mail order. Direct mail is often called 'junk mail' by customers because most of it is unwanted.

The internet provides great opportunities for direct mailing. Customers can be targeted through their e-mail addresses. E-mail messages can then be sent directly to internet users.

Packaging

Packaging is important for many products. It needs to be instantly recognisable so that shoppers identify the product on the shelves and don't buy another brand by mistake. The colour and design of the packaging need to reflect the image of the product. It also needs to give any information required by law.

For example, the wrapper on a Heinz baked bean tin is a distinctive

'blue' colour and the name 'Heinz' is clearly displayed. KitKat has a distinctive red colour wrapping which helps it to stand out from competing products.

Personal selling

Some products are sold door-to-door. A double glazing or insurance salesperson might arrange to call at a house. A sales representative (a 'sales rep') might tour local businesses trying to sell a product. These are examples of **personal selling**. The advantage is that the value of the product can be explained to the customer directly. On the other hand, many people don't like feeling pressurised into buying a product. They may also resent the time wasted by sales reps knocking on their door.

Public relations

PUBLIC RELATIONS (PR) is another way in which businesses try to communicate with their customers. The public relations department of a business deals with letters which come in from customers about the product. It also tries to get good news about the product into the media. For instance, it might issue a press release about the launch of a new product.

Public relations departments may also have to deal with bad publicity. Some manufacturers have been criticised for making products in the Far East, where factory conditions and wages are poor. The public relations department would try to defuse such criticism and show the business in a more positive light.

Sales promotion

Sales promotion attempts to give a

Paul Cardinal can trace his family back six generations. Each has been involved in some aspect of the brewing trade. This is perhaps why he is so good at starting up pub chains which go on to be highly successful. His latest idea is Hopmaster. It will stock a large range of real ales. Each week, one ale will be singled out for promotion. There will be a small price discount. But the main factor pushing sales will be blanket point of sale advertising. This will include everything from the beer mats in the pub to posters in the window, to banners across the bar. Popular mass market beers and other drinks will be stocked of course. But the idea is to increase sales of higher profit margin real ales, as well as making the pub a distinctive venue. The pubs will be aimed at 18-30 year olds. and the decor will reflect the fun element which attracts this target market.

Paul Cardinal also aims to use the internet to raise customer awareness. Customers will be encouraged to sign an on-line address book, at home, at work or in the pub. They will then be sent regular details of offers and special events at their local Hopmaster pub. To add a personal touch, a birthday card will sent with a voucher for a free drink to celebrate. Paul wants to experiment with sending different types of 'cool' and 'crazy' messages or setting weird competitions. Their main aim is to get customers talking to others about Hopmaster.

1. Explain FOUR ways in which Paul Cardinal intends to promote Hopmaster and get people spending money in the pubs.
2. Discuss which of these is most likely to appeal to:
    (a) a male aged 20 with a relatively high income who likes to go out drinking regularly with other males;
    (b) a female aged 25 who only goes out occasionally for a fun night out;
    (c) a female college student aged 18 who goes out regularly with her friends but isn't a loyal customer of any pub.

short term boost to sales. A number of methods can be used.

Money off Businesses can offer discounts on their products. For instance, mobile phone companies like Orange use retailers to sell their services to customers. These retailers are paid a commission for each new customer they sign up by Orange and other mobile phone companies. The retailers often use part of the commission to give 'money off' deals to customers. For instance, they might offer a mobile phone at a price below its cost to the retailer if the customer signs up.

Better value offers Businesses often give 'offers' to customers. For instance, when Orange first started, it offered free local telephone calls to subscribers. This was designed to attract large numbers of customers to a new network.

Competitions Some customers are attracted to buy a product through competitions. For instance, a breakfast cereal manufacturer like Kelloggs may run a competition which it puts on the back of a brand of cereals. Prizes can range from holidays to hi-fi equipment to toys.

Free gifts Giving something away with a product can make the purchase seem better value. For instance, you may get a free carrying case if you buy a mobile telephone.

Discount vouchers These usually give money off the next purchase of a product or off another product in a manufacturer's range.

PR promotions For instance, sometimes products are sold with the manufacturer promising to donate money to a charity for each item sold.

Point of sale material Another way to give a short term boost to sales is through the use of POINT-OF-SALE MATERIAL. This promotion takes place **where** the product is sold. For example, retailers selling a new brand of biscuit may be supplied with posters and leaflets by the biscuit manufacturer. It may also give three dimensional cardboard displays to put in the shop window. In a supermarket, the product might be put into special **dump bins**. These are containers which are often situated at the end of aisles. They aim to attract customer attention. Supermarket trolleys may even carry advertisements for the product.

key terms

Above the line promotion - the use of the media to advertise a product.
Below the line promotion - media other than advertising which is used to promote a product, such as direct mail or point-of-sale materials.
Direct mail - advertising promotions sent to potential customers' homes.
Point-of-sale material - promotion of a product where it is sold. Examples include special displays or distribution of leaflets in shops.
Public relations - promotion of a positive image about a product or business through giving information about the product to the general public, other businesses or to the press.

Checklist

1. How can direct mail increase sales of a product?
2. What can packaging tell customers about a product?
3. Give ONE advantage and ONE disadvantage of personal selling for a business.
4. Why are public relations important for a business?
5. What point of sale material might there be in a large supermarket?

Place

A food outlet needs to be convenient for customers

Place and the marketing mix

For a product to sell, it must be in the right place at the right time for customers to buy. Place is therefore one of the '4 P's' of the marketing mix (☞ unit 38).

The right place

Being in the right place is essential for a business. For service businesses, place or **location** (☞ unit 6) is crucial. For example, a hypermarket needs to be situated near a centre of population. It also needs good road links and a large car park. A fast food outlet needs to be convenient for car users to visit. Or it must be on a busy street where it is easy for shoppers to step inside. For a village shop to survive, there has to be a large enough population in the village and local area to provide customers.

Place is also important to manufacturing businesses. Many manufacturers make consumer goods. They must ensure that these goods are on display in shops and are easily available to consumers. This means choosing a suitable **channel of distribution** (☞ unit 51).

Place is important too for a business which sells to other businesses. Being local can give a business an advantage over rivals because deliveries can be made quickly. Local businesses also often form networks. This helps them to know what is on offer in the local area and to buy from each other.

The right time

Timing is an essential part of any marketing. For instance, a new toy which is launched in January will have missed the all important Christmas selling period. Clothing which was in fashion yesterday

Cadbury's chocolate has been sold from vending machines on the London Underground for more than 50 years. But today that is under threat. The London Underground has put up the contract to supply vending machines, worth £3 million, for renegotiation. London Underground wants to expand the range of products sold in vending machines to include soft drinks and snacks. More than three million people use the Tube every day. But each passenger only spends an average £1 a year in the vending machines. A source close to the talks said: 'Cadbury has not done much to advance the vending business in the last 20 years. It has great potential for selling all kinds of confectionery and drinks.'

This dissatisfaction could allow another company to take over the contract. One of those bidding is Coca-Cola, in partnership with local UK vending machine companies. Coca-Cola and Cadbury Schweppes are locked in competition in the world's soft drinks markets.

Source: adapted from *The Times*, 15.2.2001.

1. What is a 'vending machine'?
2. Suggest why vending machines might be important in the marketing mix for a soft drinks and confectionery business. Use the example of the London Underground to explain your answer.

may not sell today. So timing can be closely linked to the **product** (☞ unit 42) in the marketing mix. A business has to have a product that customers want to buy at that point in time.

Timing is also linked to **stock control** (☞ unit 56). Many businesses carry stocks of goods, waiting for sale. A supermarket, for example, will have pizzas for sale in its freezers. A car manufacturer will have finished cars waiting to go out to car dealers. Carrying stock is important for a business. A customer may want to buy a product now. If it isn't in stock,

the customer may buy from another business. On the other hand, holding stock can be risky. For instance, dolls in the form of characters from a new film may be popular today, but unsalable in sixth months.

Some businesses solve this problem of stock by changing to **just-in-time** production (☞ unit 62). This means they only make goods 'to order'. They buy materials and make goods only when the customer wants the product. Just-in-time production then becomes a key part of the marketing strategy of a business.

✔Checklist

1. What is meant by 'place' in the marketing mix?
2. Explain why place is important in the marketing mix for (a) a shoe shop; (b) a manufacturer of shoes; (c) a manufacturer of leather.
3. Why is time an important element of 'place' in the marketing mix?
4. How does just-time-production affect marketing?

In June 2000, Iceland, the frozen food chain of stores, announced that its own label vegetables would be organically grown in future. Management at Iceland thought they had come up with a great idea to win market share. After all, in independent national surveys around three quarters of customers said they would prefer to eat organic food. These surveys also found the reason why consumers were not buying more organic food. It was too expensive compared to non-organic food. Iceland announced that it would be selling frozen own label organic vegetables at the same price as its existing non-organic vegetables.

During the autumn of 2000, the new strategy came unstuck. First, Iceland was forced to put up the price of its own label frozen vegetables to make a profit. This was because organic vegetables cost more to buy from the farm. The higher prices hit sales. Second, Iceland found it could not buy enough organic vegetables to keep its own label packs in its freezers. Iceland is a large company. Its new policy meant that it had to buy 40 per cent of the world's supply of organic vegetables. Organic farmers simply could not deliver reliably enough.

The combination of stock-outs (no stock available to sell of certain products) and higher prices led to a fall in sales. Worse for Iceland, it took place during the Christmas period. At this time sales were highest during the year.

Source: adapted from *The Times*, 23.1.2001 and the *Financial Times*, 23.1.2001.

1. 'Iceland is a frozen food retailer.' Explain what this means.
2. Explain why its introduction of organic vegetables was a problem because of (a) pricing and (b) place in its marketing mix.
3. Suggest how Iceland could have changed its strategy on organic foods after the trading problems of Autumn 2000. Justify your answer.

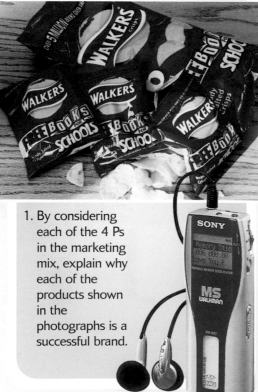

1. By considering each of the 4 Ps in the marketing mix, explain why each of the products shown in the photographs is a successful brand.

Nestlé brands

Brands

Every business would like its products to be strong BRANDS. A brand is a product which is different from other, often similar, products in the eyes of consumers. For instance, Heinz baked beans are seen as different from Asda own label baked beans. A Yorkie bar is seen as different from an Aero bar. Persil is seen as different from Bold. Brands are created through the **marketing mix** - product, price, promotion and place.

Product Successful brands are ones which tend to have a different FORMULATION to other products. For instance, Coca-Cola is made with different ingredients to Pepsi-Cola or Virgin Cola. The result is that it has a unique taste which many consumers prefer. A Kit-Kat has a different shape and taste to a Mars Bar, although both are chocolate bars. Businesses hope that their brand will appear to be superior to those of rival businesses. This will help them to gain a greater market share than other products.

To compete against rivals, some businesses continually improve their products. For instance, soap powder manufacturers often change their washing powders to improve their ability to clean. Sony has improved the technology of its best-selling Walkman since its launch in 1979.

The formulation of some products, though, has remained the same over time. The Coca-Cola formula has been the same for the past 50 years. The company changed the formula in the 1980s, hoping to make it more appealing. But many consumers didn't like the new taste and sales dropped. So Coca-Cola brought back the original formula.

It is important to the success of a brand that products should be as **uniform** as possible. Consumers buying Coca-Cola expect one bottle to taste the same as the next. It is difficult to create a brand when quality differs. For instance, branding in wine tends to be weak. This is because the quality of wines from one vineyard differs so much from year to year.

Price If customers think that a branded product is superior in quality, they may pay a PREMIUM PRICE. This is a higher price than those of similar products. A business might need to charge a higher price because it is more costly to produce a brand than rival products. High prices might also be needed to fund research and development, to improve the product in future. However, a higher price is also a signal to customers that the brand is a superior product. So a high price becomes part of the product's promotion.

Higher prices are also an incentive for businesses to develop and maintain brands. They enable businesses to earn much higher profits than rival businesses.

Promotion Branded products tend to be promoted more than non-branded products. Customers need to be kept aware that the brand is superior to rival products. They need to be told about its qualities. They must also be 'persuaded' to buy it. Promotion is a central part of keeping a brand alive. Brands which are not promoted often lose *sales*. Businesses find it more difficult to charge premium prices for them. Profitability of the brand therefore declines.

Place Branded products must be easily available to customers. Customers are more likely to pay a premium price for a product that is available in the right place, at the right time.

key terms

Brand - a named product which customers see as being different from other products.
Formulation - the recipe or design used for a product.
Generic product - a product made by a number of different businesses in which customers see no difference in the product of one business compared to the product of another business.
Own brand - a product which is sold under the brand name of a supermarket chain or other retailer rather than under the name of the business which manufactures the product.
Premium price - a price which is above the average for products of a particular type.

✓Checklist

1. Name a leading brand in the following markets: (a) washing powders; (b) trainers; (c) breakfast cereals; (d) instant coffee; (e) luxury cars.
2. Why is it important for a brand to maintain consistent quality between each product sold?
3. 'Brands are sold at premium prices.' Explain what this means.
4. What is the difference between a branded product and a generic product?
5. Why do own brands compete successfully against branded products?

Generic products

The opposite of a branded product is a GENERIC PRODUCT. Potatoes are generic products. Consumers often don't see any difference between the same type of potatoes produced on different farms. Coal, steel, milk and bananas are other examples of generic products.

Businesses producing generic products find it difficult to influence the market. They are not able to fix a price. Instead, they have to accept the price that the market will offer. It is not possible to get customers to see that the product is superior to others.

Own brands

Promoting and improving the product is essential if the brand is to survive. Today, many brands face strong competition from OWN BRANDS. These are products which carry the brand labels of retailers such as Sainsbury's, Dixons or Woolworths. Own brands are usually cheaper than branded products from manufacturers.

A danger for a business producing a branded product is that customers might **see** own brands as being of just as high quality. If this happens, customers could choose the own brands simply because they are cheaper.

A brand is a valuable commodity. Coca-Cola has been around since 1886, Heinz Tomato Ketchup since 1876, Kellogg's Corn Flakes since 1906 and Colgate toothpaste since 1896. But manufacturers are finding it difficult to create new brands. Procter & Gamble, which makes products such as Bold and Daz, spends billions of dollars each year on research and development. But its last major successful launch was Pampers disposable nappies decades ago.

As a result, businesses have increasingly been 'stretching' their brands. A leader in this has been Virgin. The Virgin brand name has been put on record stores, cinemas, trains, airlines, soft drinks, mobile phones and financial products. When customers buy a Virgin product, they are not just buying the product. They are also buying the brand image of the fun, 'we're on your side' approach of the founder, Richard Branson.

There are dangers to this approach, however. Virgin Trains has faced problems in operating a train company with outdated trains and run down tracks. If the bad publicity associated with Virgin Trains spread to other Virgin companies, it could tarnish their products with this image. Also, putting Virgin on a product has not guaranteed success. Soft drinks, clothing and make up are all areas where Virgin has found it difficult to gain any real market share.

Source: adapted from the *Financial Times*, 22.3.2000 and 26.5.2000.

1. Explain, using the example of Heinz Tomato Ketchup, what is meant by a 'brand'.
2. Why can a brand like Pampers or Colgate Toothpaste be a 'valuable commodity' to its owners?
3. What might be the advantages and disadvantages to the owner of a brand like Virgin of extending the brand name across a variety of products?
4. A consultant suggests that Nestlé, the maker of Nescafé, should produce a 'Nescafé washing powder'. Discuss whether or not you think this would be a success for Nestlé.

Marketing: the international dimension

Reasons for international marketing

Globalisation (☞ unit 2) is shrinking the world. The wardrobes of consumers in the UK are likely to be full of clothes made in the Third World. Consumers living in India or Thailand are likely to drink Coca Cola. If they own a computer, it is likely to use Microsoft's Windows operating system. Both Coca Cola and Microsoft are US companies. International trade is increasing at a much faster rate than the incomes of individual consumers as businesses exploit **specialisation** in the world economy.

There is a number of reasons why businesses might trade internationally.

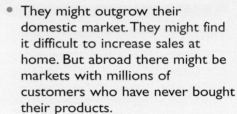

Cadbury Schweppes brands sell in many countries

- They might outgrow their domestic market. They might find it difficult to increase sales at home. But abroad there might be markets with millions of customers who have never bought their products.
- Profits in overseas markets might be higher than from extra sales in domestic markets. Overseas customers might be prepared to pay higher prices for a product.
- By selling into a number of different countries, a business can spread its risks. If the UK market suffers a downturn this might be offset by strong sales growth in the Far East for example.
- Barriers to trade may come down. Since the UK joined the European Union 30 years ago, barriers to trade between the UK and other EU countries have fallen. Today, for example, there are no tariffs (taxes) on UK goods exported to EU countries. For EU countries that have adopted the single currency, the euro, even money is now the same in different countries.

Differences in overseas markets

Marketing products to overseas customers is not always easy, however. There are many differences between countries.

Britain is one of the great chocolate eating nations of the world. But British consumers are notoriously conservative. Nearly all the brands of chocolate eaten were launched at least 30 years ago. Some, like Cadbury's Dairy Milk, go back to the 19th century.

So launching a new brand successfully is very difficult. It is even more difficult if the chocolates are liqueur chocolates for which there is only a niche market. But this is what Chocolates Turin, a Mexican company, is attempting. It wants British consumers to eat tequila liqueurs. Tequila is a spirit like brandy or vodka which is increasingly popular with young consumers.

The Mexican company appointed an agent, David Shaer, to handle sales in the UK. He has signed up deals with Waitrose and Asda, the supermarket chains, to sell the product. He has persuaded a number of restaurants and small shops to stock the liqueurs. They are also being marketed to orthodox Jews, on the grounds that they don't contain any ingredients which offend their food laws. They would therefore be suitable for celebrations like weddings or barmitzvahs.

This year, sales should total £80 000, out of a total market for liqueur chocolates of £10 million. But Chocolates Turin and David Shaer hope that their product will make eating liqueur chocolates more fashionable amongst the young and so the market will grow.

Source: adapted from the *Financial Times*, 17.12.1999.

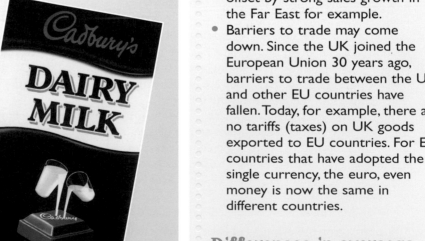

1. 'Chocolates Turin are exporting to the UK.' What does this mean?
2. The company is using an agent. How will David Shaer help Chocolates Turin sell into the UK?
3. What market segments are Chocolate Turin targeting in the UK?
4. Discuss whether the company could, within five years, see its sales grow to £1 million per year.

There are differences in customer preferences. Some of these are cultural. For example, baked beans are very popular in the UK. But there is little tradition of eating them elsewhere in Europe. So exporting baked beans to Spain is likely to be difficult. Some differences are religious. Fast food chains like McDonald's have to be careful not to include any beef ingredients in food sold in India. This is because Hindus are not allowed to eat beef.

Politics can be a barrier to trade. Exporting to North Korea, for example, may not possible because the government of the country refuses to trade with certain countries. Setting up a factory in some parts of Africa may be risky because of war.

No two countries have exactly the same laws. For example, a UK toy manufacturer may find it difficult to sell toys in Sweden because advertising products aimed at children is not allowed. Also, safety specifications for farm tractors are different in the USA than in Italy. So a US exporter may have to change its product to sell in Italy.

The cost of selling differs between countries. For example, there are differences in the fees that banks charge for dealing in different currencies or providing insurance for trade contracts. Transport costs are different for goods sold to a French customer compared to an Australian customer. There may be a risk that payment for a contract will not be received if a new customer is a company from a Third World country.

How to sell overseas

Businesses can adopt a variety of strategies to sell into overseas markets.

Most businesses make a product and then **export** it overseas directly to their customers. Some overseas customers will send buyers to place orders. Equally, many exporting businesses will have sales representatives who will visit their customers overseas to secure orders. Some businesses use an **agent** (☞ unit 51) to sell their products overseas. An exporter may also secure orders through the internet, although internet trading is still very small.

A company may decide to sell **franchises** (☞ unit 29) overseas. The franchisor will then collect fees and royalties from its franchisees abroad rather than selling directly to overseas customers.

A company may **licence** a foreign company to produce goods or services for which it has a **patent** or **copyright**. The company would then receive payments from the overseas company rather than making the product itself and exporting it.

A **multinational company** (☞ unit 30) may establish production facilities abroad. For example, Cadbury Schweppes has bottling plants for its drinks in many countries.

✓Checklist

1. Why do businesses trade internationally?
2. State FIVE differences that exist between markets in different countries.
3. What strategies might a company use to sell overseas?

Stentor is a UK company which sells violins and other instruments. It has a 100 year long history of importing instruments from Europe and selling them in the UK. But in recent years, rival companies have been adopting the same strategy, cutting into Stentor's UK market.

The company realised it had to change its strategy to cope with this challenge. It decided to become a global player. The future would lie in selling its violins worldwide instead of just in the UK. To meet the challenge of competition, it would also have to buy instruments at a cheaper price. So it decided to set up a factory in China to manufacture instruments. It could now control both costs and quality, important to any buyer. The Chinese factory might also be a springboard in the future to sell into the huge Chinese market, with a population over three times that of the USA or the EU.

Source: adapted from *The Sunday Times*, 9.1.2000.

1. Explain why Stentor wants to increase sales outside the UK.
2. What are the advantages to it of buying a Chinese factory to make instruments?
3. Discuss how Stentor might sell instruments to a country where it has not sold to before.

The product life cycle

The product life cycle

The PRODUCT LIFE CYCLE shows the stages through which, it is argued, a product passes over time. Figure 50.1 shows the product life cycle which is usual for most products.

Development

Products start life at the development stage. A new good or service may be created. This may involve R&D (**research and development** (☞ unit 55). For example, a chocolate manufacturer may produce 100 versions of a possible new chocolate bar. Experiments may be conducted to discover the best way in which it could be mass produced. **Market research** (☞ units 40 and 41) may be carried out to see whether consumers like the new product.

After launch, the sales of successful products will grow

Launching the product

In the next stage, the product is launched. Most products coming on the market will be backed up by **advertising** and other forms of **promotion** (☞ units 45 and 46). Sales of the product will hopefully begin to take off.

The growth stage

In the growth stage of the cycle, sales and profits will be rising. Again, a business may want to support these sales with various forms of promotion.

Product maturity

In the maturity stage, the product reaches a peak in terms of sales. Research and development costs are likely to have been paid off. The product is profitable enough to finance the development of new products.

Saturation

Towards the end of the maturity stage, the market becomes saturated. Competitors bring out rival products which reduce the sales of the product. For example, chocolate manufacturers might bring out rival chocolate bars in response to a successful launch from another chocolate manufacturer. Sales of durable products like mobile phones, cars, colour televisions or microwave ovens may also flatten out because customers have bought the original product and are not prepared to change it yet.

Decline

Eventually, a product is likely to go

In January 2000, the US toy company Hasbro announced that it was withdrawing Subbuteo from the market. The football game, played with miniature figures being flicked against a ball on a miniature football pitch, had been around for 53 years. In its heyday, most boys wanted to own the game. Keen players would own a number of different teams painted in the colours of real football teams.

In 1999, only 50 000 kits were sold in the UK. This was not enough for Hasbro to continue marketing the product. It said that the number of football related products that were for sale, particularly computer football games, had reduced the commercial viability of Subbuteo. Children were increasingly turning away from traditional toys in favour of electronic games.

Robert Nathan, manager of the British Toymakers Guild, however, said that the popularity of electronic toys was not crippling the market for traditional toys like rocking horses, board games and dolls' houses. Children under the age of 7 were still keen on such toys. They were also being bought them by nostalgic twenty and thirtysomethings keen to give their children, nephews, nieces and god-children the same experience that they had enjoyed as children.

Source: adapted from the *Financial Times*, 22.1.2000.

1. Explain, using a diagram, where in its product life cycle Subbuteo was in (a) 2000 and (b) 1947.
2. What explanation did Hasbro give for the decline of the product?
3. Following the January 2000 announcement, there was an outcry by Subbuteo fans about Hasbro's decision. As a result, Hasbro decided to carry on producing and selling the game. Discuss TWO extension strategies Hasbro could use to increase sales.

into decline. Sales begin to fall as customers buy other products which they prefer. Eventually, sales will fall so low that the product will be unprofitable. It will then be withdrawn from sale.

Extension strategies

Producers are likely to try to extend the maturity stage of the product for as long as possible. Producing a completely new product would involve all the start up costs again.

It may be possible to raise sales in the maturity stage by using EXTENSION STRATEGIES. This involves slightly changing the product to give it fresh appeal to its target market. For example, car manufacturers tend to bring out a 'new model' of an existing car each year. The new model is often the same as the old one. But the style of the car body may be slightly different or the specification of the interior may differ.

Extension strategies can also help a product appeal to a new **segment** (☞ unit 39) of the market. For example, a car manufacturer may produce a special 'sports' edition of a car to make it appeal to young women and men.

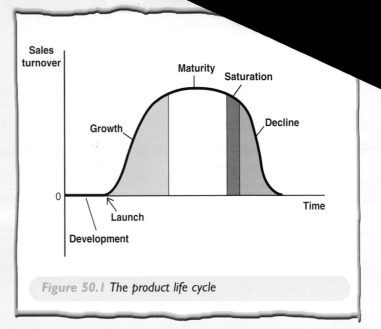

Figure 50.1 The product life cycle

Checklist

1. What happens during the development stage of a product's life?
2. Why is a product likely to need advertising and promotion when it is launched?
3. Profits for a product which is a market leader in its maturity stage tend to be very high. Why is this?
4. What happens to a product in the decline stage of its life cycle?
5. What is an extension strategy?

How can you persuade someone to pay £3 000 for a return flight to the United States when you are offering the same journey on the same plane for £300? The answer is to differentiate the product and sell it to a segment of the market which can afford £3 000.

Over the years, airlines have come up with a variety of ways of persuading businesses to pay large amounts for the flights of their company executives. Caviar and champagne were once important. In today's weight and alcohol conscious age, though, this isn't the draw it once was. Exclusive booking in facilities and luxury lounges at airports are common. The amount of leg room and the width of the seat has long been important too. Executives don't want to be too near their fellow passengers and they want to stretch their legs.

The latest gimmick in the battle for the highly profitable executive air traveller is the bed in the sky. British Airways is converting its transatlantic planes to give top paying passengers the privilege of sleeping through the journey on a bed. Having someone lying horizontal on a plane means you can't pack in as many passengers as you could if they were sitting upright. But if they are paying ten times the price, it may still make good business sense.

Source: adapted from various sources 2000, 2001.

1. What is the basic service that British airways offers all its transatlantic passengers?
2. Suggest THREE ways in which British Airways has extended the basic service for its executive passengers.
3. Virgin Atlantic is one of British Airways main competitors on transatlantic flights.
   (a) Suggest how it might respond to British Airways introduction of beds.
   (b) Discuss the costs and benefits to British Airways of extending its product by providing beds.

Supermarkets are retailers

Builders buy products from wholesalers

distribution

Farmers may sell direct to customers

Car dealers are agents for motor manufacturers

The ... ... of DISTR... ... ...een the manufactu... ... ...oduct and the customer. Th... ...he path taken to get products from producers to customers. There are different channels of distribution which can be used.

Through retailers A manufacturer can reach consumers through RETAILERS. A retailer is a business which sells goods to consumers, like Tesco, The Body Shop, HMV or Miss Selfridge (☞unit 52). Large retailers like Marks & Spencer may have a team of buyers. They choose the goods that the retailer will sell. A manufacturer will negotiate with these buyers for the sale of goods. Manufacturers may reach smaller retailers with a SALES FORCE or SALES TEAM. The sales force will visit retailers and sell them products. Some businesses use **telesales**. They will ring retailers and try to persuade them to buy over the phone. Businesses often produce leaflets and catalogues to back up the work of the sales force. Another way to contact retailers is for the manufacturer to exhibit at a TRADE FAIR. This is like a street market, except the sellers tends to be manufacturers and the buyers are

retailers. Exhibition centres, like the National Exhibition Centre near Birmingham, often hold large trade fairs.

Through wholesalers A WHOLESALER is a type of business which specialises in selling to smaller shops and other traders. The wholesaler buys in bulk from manufacturers. Many shops can't buy directly from the manufacturer because their orders are too small. Kellogg's, for instance, is not prepared to pay the cost of delivering a few packets of Cornflakes to a small shop. Instead, these small shops buy from a wholesaler. So the wholesaler acts as an **intermediary** or link between the retailer and the manufacturer.

Through agents An AGENT is a business which is given the rights to sell a product by the manufacturer. Like a wholesaler, agents act as intermediaries. Agents are often appointed for overseas markets. A UK business might, for instance, allow an agent to sell its products in France. The advantage to the manufacturer is that the costs of marketing the product in France are paid by the agent. If it didn't have an agent, its marketing budget might not be large enough to sell in France. Agents are often paid a percentage of

the value of every sale they make. This is known as a COMMISSION.

Some agents sell directly to the consumer. They may visit houses or hold parties to collect orders. In the UK, for example, Avon sells cosmetics and Betterware sells household goods through agents. They go from door to door collecting orders.

Directly to the consumer A business may sell directly to the consumer, without going through retailers, wholesalers or agents. For instance, a farm may have its own farm shop. An insurance company may have sales representatives (often called **sales reps**). They will visit customers in their own homes to sell them financial products. A manufacturer may produce a catalogue and sell by **mail order**. Or it may have a **website** on the internet which allows consumers to buy directly. A drinks or confectionery manufacturer may sell through **vending machines**.

Choosing the channel of distribution

How does a business choose which channel of distribution to use?

The product Different products tend to be distributed in different ways. For instance, perishable products, like lettuces or oranges, need to be taken to the consumer quickly. So their channels of distribution need to be fast and efficient. They also tend to produced and consumed in different areas or different countries. So perishable products tend to be sold via

Ruffles is a mini-company whose business idea is to make and sell soft toys. It makes three designs - an owl, a lion and a squirrel. It will sell the owl for £7, the lion for £5 and the squirrel for £3. EITHER write a report about the channels of distribution for your mini-enterprise OR answer the following questions.
1. State THREE different channels of distribution it could attempt to use to get its products to the consumer.
2. (a) What are the advantages and disadvantages of each of these channels of distribution for the mini-company?
   (b) Which is the best channel of distribution for it to use and why?

wholesalers, retailers and markets which have the expertise in this type of distribution. Complex products are often sold directly because the manufacturer needs to be able to deal with any installation and running problems. Products which are very heavy or are odd sizes also tend to be sold directly because producers provide specialist transport delivery. Low price, high volume products like

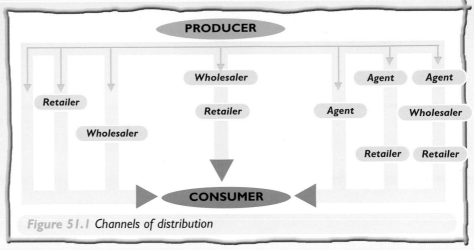

Figure 51.1 Channels of distribution

baked beans or soft drinks will be supplied in bulk either to large retailers or to wholesalers.

The market Mass market products tend to be sold to wholesalers or large retailers, who can buy in bulk. Niche market products can be sold through wholesalers. But they are often sold directly to retailers, for instance through trade fairs. Alternatively, they may be sold directly to consumers through a shop owned by the manufacturer, through mail order or on the internet .

Effectiveness Many businesses have little choice about the channels of distribution they use. They are fixed by existing patterns of selling and buying. For instance, a manufacturer

of a new brand of margarine may use the same channels of distribution as other brands. This is because they are likely to be the most effective way of getting products to the consumer. Sometimes, new technology allows businesses to change their distribution patterns. But they are not likely to change very fast. Also, they may not be effective for all products. For instance, Amazon.com has been able to compete with wholesalers and retailers by selling books via the internet. But e-commerce clothes retailers have found it difficult to persuade consumers to buy from them.

Fleeceline is a textile company based in Leicestershire. Some time ago, it decided that to survive it needed to become a niche player supplying luxury fabrics. It exports 60 per cent of its sales.

To get such large overseas sales, it maintains sales agents across most of the world. It also has the advantage that it is not overdependent on any one market, like the Japanese market or the US market. If sales in one market fall sharply, as they did in the Far East in the late 1990s, overall sales are likely to fall too. But this is not sufficient to put the survival of the company at risk.

The disadvantage of maintaining such a large network of agents is that it is extremely costly. The agents gain the orders. But Fleeceline also invests heavily in sending staff to its main customers. It argues that it is important to keep in regular contact with customers, even in lean years when they are not buying.

1. How has Fleeceline specialised in its market?
2. (a) Explain how it gains overseas sales. (b) What are (i) the advantages of using this channel of distribution and what are (ii) its disadvantages for Fleeceline?
3. An outside consultant has suggested that Fleeceline should move towards a strategy of gaining most of its overseas sales through its website. Do you think this is good advice? Justify your answer.

Checklist

1. What is the difference between a wholesaler and a retailer?
2. Why might sales reps be important for a business?
3. How can agents help distribute products?
4. Why are new ships and aircraft sold directly to customers rather than through other channels of distribution?
5. Why do businesses like Kellogg's choose to distribute their products through wholesalers and retailers rather than direct to the customer?

key terms

Agent - an individual or business which sells a product on behalf of another business and receives a commission or payment for doing so.
Commission - payment made to an agent in return for the sale of products.
Channel of distribution - the route by which a product gets from the manufacturer or service provider to the customer.
Retailer - a business which specialises in selling goods in small quantities to the consumer.
Sales force or sales team - a group of workers in a business which specialises in selling its goods or services.
Trade fair - a type of market where manufacturers have stands and sell to retailers who visit the fair to buy stock for sale to consumers.
Wholesaler - a business which buys in bulk from a manufacturer and then sells the stock on in smaller quantities to retailers.

Supermarket retailing and wholesalers of cycle parts

Retailing

Towns and cities are full of **retailers**. These shops buy goods from suppliers and then sell them to consumers. Examples of retailers include Woolworths, Marks & Spencer, Tesco, Sainsbury's, Top Shop and New Look. Retailers charge a higher price for the goods they sell than they pay for the goods they buy from manufacturers. Clothes, for instance, they are often sold by retailers at twice the price they pay for them. So why do consumers buy from retailers rather than straight from the manufacturer?

Breaking-of-bulk One **function** (i.e. service) of a retailer is to **break bulk**. Manufacturers want to sell products in large, bulk quantities. For instance, Heinz would like an order for thousands of cans of baked beans, not thousands of orders for just one can. But a customer will not want to buy such a large amount. Retailers buy in bulk and then sell in much smaller quantities to customers.

Convenience Another function of a retailer is to sell goods at a convenient place and time. A consumer in London doesn't want to travel to Glasgow to buy a pair of shoes just because they are made in Glasgow. Retailers can bring in goods from around the world and sell them in places near to the consumer. These might be a city centre shop or an out of town supermarket. The retailer can also buy in a variety of goods from different manufacturers. This gives consumers choice in what they buy.

Other services The level of service offered is another important aspect of retailing. For example, some retailers allow customers to take back goods they do not want. Some retailers will deliver goods to your home. Some retailers provide a better, more luxurious shopping environment than others.

Retailers provide an important service both to manufacturers and consumers. They are part of the supply chain from manufacturer to consumer. Running a retail outlet is costly though. There is rent to pay on the premises or the cost of buying property. Staff wages must be paid. Electricity, gas and telephone bills are other costs. This explains why shops sell their goods at a higher price than they pay to the manufacturer.

Wholesalers

Some shops may be too small to buy directly from a manufacturer. They cannot buy in the quantities that the manufacturer wants to sell. So instead they buy from a **wholesaler** (☞ unit 51). This is a business which buys from manufacturers and sells to retailers. It performs many of the same functions as retailers. It breaks bulk and offers a range of goods for sale in a local area. Many wholesalers

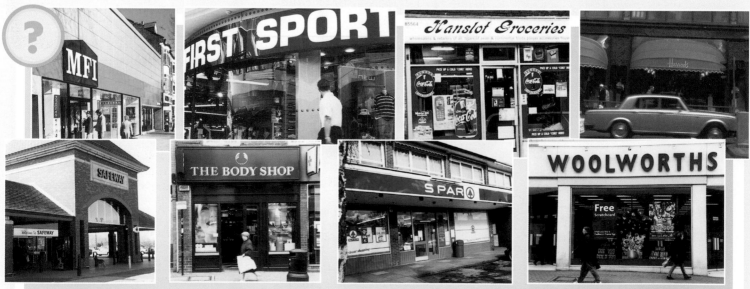

1. Which retailers shown above would be classified as: (a) a supermarket chain; (b) a variety chain store; (c) a specialist multiple; (d) an independent; (e) a franchise; (f) a department store; (g) a voluntary chain?
2. Suggest why customers might buy from these shops rather than using either mail order or ordering over the internet.

advertise themselves as CASH AND CARRY WAREHOUSES. They are **warehouses** because they hold stocks of goods. Businesses come to the warehouse to buy and can **carry** goods away immediately. Goods are paid for in **cash**, either using notes and coins, cheque or debit card. However, some customers may have an account with the warehouse and be invoiced (i.e. billed) later. They will therefore be given **credit**.

Types of retailer

The most common type of retailer is the INDEPENDENT. The shop will be run by the owner. It will almost certainly be a small shop. It may be found in a small village or a local parade of shops. The owner is likely to own just that one shop.

One hundred years ago, nearly all shops were independents. However, there has been an enormous growth in MULTIPLES. These are **chains** of shops like Top Shop, HMV, WH Smith or Tesco owned by a single company. Today, multiples sell far more than independents. Multiples can be split up into various types.

Supermarket chains like Asda, Morrisons, Sainsbury's or Tesco sell mainly groceries. **Specialist multiples** are chains which sell limited ranges of products. Examples are Comet, which sells electrical equipment and Miss Selfridge which sells clothes. **Variety chain stores** are chains which sell a wide variety of products. Boots the Chemist sells goods from medicines to cosmetics to kitchen equipment. Woolworths sells CDs, toys, sweets and clothes.

Many large towns and cities have a **department store**. Such a store may be an independent, owned perhaps by a family. Most department stores, however, are multiples. House of Fraser is a chain of department stores. Like variety chain stores, department stores sell a wide variety of goods from clothes to washing machines. They offer one-stop shopping in up-market surroundings.

To try to remain competitive with large supermarket chains, some independent grocery stores have joined voluntary chains, like Spar or Mace. The chain is able to buy in bulk and provides support services like advertising. **Voluntary chains** share some of the same characteristics as **franchise operations** (☞ unit 29).

Finally, large **mail order** companies, like Littlewoods or Great Universal Stores, act as retailers. E-commerce retailers like Amazon.com are similar to mail order companies. However, goods can be viewed and ordered online rather than through a mail order catalogue (☞ unit 13). Supermarket chains, such as Asda, specialist chains such as Dixons, and variety chains such as Boots also allow consumers to buy through the internet.

Checklist

1. Explain THREE important functions of a retailer.
2. Why does a retailer provide a service to manufacturers of goods?
3. What is the difference between a retailer and a wholesaler?
4. What is the difference between (a) an independent and a multiple retailer and (b) a specialist multiple and a variety chain store?

1. What services are available from the retailer, wholesaler and mail order catalogue companies shown in the photographs?
2. How do the services differ between them?
3. The large mail order catalogues have been struggling in recent years to increase their sales, whilst supermarkets have seen their sales grow by up to 10 per cent a year. Do you think that mail order catalogues will survive in retailing in the future? Give arguments for and against.

Changes in retailing

Shopping malls have had a major effect on retailing

Change

Retailing has changed enormously over the past 50 years. Many different factors have affected the ways in which consumers buy goods.

Choice

Rising income has altered the face of retailing. Over 50 years ago, most of the week's wages for a family went on basics - rent, heating and food. People had little equipment in their houses. Large increases in spending power mean that, today, consumers can buy a much wider range of goods. Consumers also want choice in **where** and **when** they buy. For example, they may want to buy from home, in the city centre or outside a town. They may want to buy late at night or on Sundays.

Sometimes customers want shops which offer the lowest prices. But sometimes they are looking for other factors, such as convenience, quality of service or after sales care.

Costs

One result of increases in spending power is that multiple retailers can take advantage of **economies of scale** (☞ unit 34). Tesco, for instance, can buy baked beans in far greater bulk than a local independent shop. This means that it might negotiate lower prices from, say, Heinz than a smaller chain. Local independent grocers have the extra cost of buying from a wholesaler which takes a profit from the sale. Independents have found it difficult to survive in many areas of retailing because large multiple retailers have such low costs.

Branding

Successful multiples have another important advantage over independents. Shops like Boots the Chemists guarantee a certain **quality of service**. Shoppers know what they can expect to find in a Boots store. They know, for instance, that goods will be exchanged without any fuss if they prove unsuitable. They know that they can get advice at the pharmaceutical counter. Multiples have, in fact, managed to establish a **brand** identity (☞ unit 48) for the service they give. Independents don't have this national brand image. Consumers increasingly shop at branded multiple stores, This has driven many independents out of business.

Investment

Linked to this quality of service has been **investment** by successful multiples. They have continually changed their ways of operating to cut costs and meet consumer needs. For example, the major supermarket chains like Tesco and Sainsbury's continually open new stores and refurbish existing stores. They have also invested in new services like internet home delivery services.

The clothing market in the UK could soon be radically changed by one company. Fast Retailing has grown from 4 to 487 stores in just four years in Japan. Annual sales total £3 billion. In 2001 it will open its first overseas store in London. It is then planning to open 10 new stores every six months throughout the UK.

It has been compared to Gap, which aims to offer quality merchandise at affordable prices. The difference is that Fast Retailing offers the same type of product for around one third of the price charged by Gap. The founder of Fast Retailing, Tadashi Yanai, denies that Uniqlo, the brand name for the stores, is a Gap look-a-like. Gap sells an American lifestyle. Uniqlo sells individual, essential items which can be put together with more expensive designer clothes.

Low costs have been achieved by buying products from large factories in China. The large orders placed have allowed the Chinese manufacturer and Fast Retailing to achieve significant economies of scale without compromising on quality.

If Uniqlo takes off in the UK, Gap is the obvious company which could suffer. But companies like Next and Marks & Spencer are also vulnerable. They are in the same market niche as Uniqlo. Supermarkets like Asda and Tesco which sell clothes could also suffer because of Uniqlo's low prices.

In 2000, Uniqlo sold 300 million items of clothing in Japan, an average of nearly 3 per person. If it could achieve that in the UK, it would sell 180 million items. That would be an astonishing retail story.

Source: adapted from *The Sunday Times*, 4.2.2001.

1. Explain why Fast Retailing has been so successful in Japan.
2. Some analysts argue that in future British clothes shops will be split into two types. There would be retailers selling small quantities of designer labelled goods at high prices and others selling large quantities of more standardised products at very low prices. Companies like Marks & Spencer, Gap and Next are caught in the middle ground. They sell mainly mid-priced non-designer clothes. (a) If this is true, do you think Uniqlo will be a success in the UK? (b) Suggest THREE ways in which companies like Marks & Spencer could change to survive in the clothes retailing market. (c) Discuss whether these three strategies would prevent companies like Uniqlo from gaining market share.

key terms

Market niche - a small segment of a much larger market.

Location

The location of shops has changed too. Over 50 years ago, shoppers either went to the local shop or went into town to the high street. Today, the local shops and the high street are still busy. But a lot of businesses have also gone to new out-of-town shopping developments. These are designed for people with cars. A few are **shopping malls** which have a wide range of shops. Examples are the Merry Hill Centre in Dudley, the Brent Cross shopping centre in London or the MetroCentre on Tyneside. Others are more specialised **retail parks** where there might be a few large stores. For instance, amongst them there might be a Comet (electrical retailing), an MFI (furniture) and a Halfords (bicycles, car parts and

Checklist

1. Why are there more shops today than 50 years ago?
2. 'Successful multiples are those which sell at lowest prices.' Explain whether you think this is true.
3. Why do successful retailers have to invest in their businesses if they are to survive?
4. How has the location of shops changed over the past 50 years?
5. A CD shop opens which carries large stocks of CDs aimed at people who like jazz. It is located a few hundred yards away from a HMV and a Virgin store. Explain why this shop is in a niche market.
6. How is e-commerce changing the retailing market?

accessories). The great advantage to the retailer of out-of-town development is that the cost of land is much cheaper than in the high street. Shoppers can also park their cars more easily to wheel out their trolleys full of goods.

Location is also the main reason why small independents are likely to survive. Shoppers are prepared to pay higher prices for the convenience of being able to buy a few items locally. They don't want to

have to travel miles to the nearest supermarket or shopping centre just to buy a pint of milk or a loaf of bread.

Market niches

High streets are likely to carry on being important shopping centres. The high street can offer a large variety of shops from which customers can buy. Independents are having increasingly to offer services which the multiples don't give. Independent grocery stores, for instance, frequently open long hours and they are sited near the customer. They will increasingly have to become NICHE retailers, providing a unique service and taking a small share of the market.

Use of technology

Technology is slowly changing buying habits. Mail order, which uses transport services, the post and the telephone to get goods to people's doorstep, is over one hundred years old. Today, though, mail order doesn't just mean replying to adverts in newspapers or buying from a paper catalogue. Sky Broadcasting runs a shopping channel where goods are sold by television and telephone. More importantly, the internet is providing shopping opportunities (☞ unit 13). Using the computer to order products which can be viewed on screen is unlikely ever to replace shopping in the high street. But it may become a major method of shopping in future.

Look at the photographs. The photograph in the centre shows retailing in 1903. The others show modern retailing.
1. (a) What changes in retailing are shown over time in the photographs?
   (b) Explain THREE factors which might have caused these changes.
2. Shopping on the internet is a new trend in UK retailing. Do you think that shopping using your computer linked to the internet will eventually lead to the closing down of most shops in the high street? In your answer, you need to write about the advantages and disadvantages of shopping from home or the office compared to shopping in your local high street.

Warehouses store products before they are distributed to customers

Channels of distribution

Businesses have to get their products to customers. Sometimes, the **channel** or **chain of distribution**, the link between the supplier and customer (☞ unit 51), is short and simple. For instance, coal may be dug out of a coal mine, put on a train and taken straight to an electricity power station. Other times, the channel of distribution can be complex, using different types of transport, warehousing, wholesalers and retailers.

Transport

Nearly all goods have to be transported to customers. There are different types of transport that may be used.

Road Road transport is the most important type of transport today for deliveries within the UK. It is relatively cheap. Partly this is because it is flexible. Deliveries can be made 'door to door' without having to transfer the **cargo** (the goods or materials that are being carried). The motorway system also means that road transport is fairly quick and reliable.

Rail Only a few per cent of all cargo is now transported by rail within the UK. Rail transport is suited to long journeys. For instance, rail is often used to transport goods from Scotland to the south of England or from the UK to Germany through the Channel Tunnel. Journeys over distance can reduce the cost of rail transport per mile. This is because the cost of loading and unloading cargo from the train is a smaller proportion of total cost. It is also suited to delivering bulk loads, such as new cars or chemicals. However, unless two business sites are linked by rail terminals, transport by rail can be expensive. Cargo has to be moved by road to a rail terminal, loaded onto a train, unloaded at the end of the journey and then moved by road again. Rail transport also tends to be slow.

Sea For cargo which has to go overseas, sea transport is much cheaper than the alternative, air travel. It is often much slower though. Most cargo could not go by plane anyway because it is too bulky. Crude oil, coal, cars and television sets are just some of the cargoes which are sent by sea for this reason.

Air Shipping cargo by air is very expensive. However, it is much quicker to send goods by plane over long distances than by any other form of transport. So air transport tends to be used to send high value goods where speed is essential. For instance, a company might have parts sent by air for a broken down machine. It is cheaper to use air transport than to wait and lose production.

Pipelines A few goods, like water, oil or gas, can be transported through pipelines. This form of transport has a very high initial cost, including the building of the pipeline. But the running costs are much lower than sending a product by road or sea tanker.

The type of transport used, therefore, depends upon a variety of factors. In many cases there is little or no choice. For instance, road transport may be the only way to get goods from one point to another because there is no suitable rail link. Cost is important where there is a choice of transport. So too

---

Poundland was created from nothing in 1989 by Steve Smith to become a £100 million a year national business today. The idea was simple - set up a shop where all the items were priced at £1. Shoppers loved it right from the start. The company has plans to increase turnover to £250 million a year by 2001 and increase the number of shops from 50 to 86.

The company has two warehouses. One is based at its Wolverhampton headquarters. The 130 000 square foot site operates 24 hours a day. The other is at Coventry. Plans are also being drawn up for a third warehouse in the Black Country in the West Midlands.

Source: adapted from the *Express & Star*, 4.10.1999.

1. 'Poundland is a retailer.' Explain what this means.
2. (a) Suggest why Poundland owns two large warehouses. (b) Why might it need to build a third warehouse in the future?
3. Poundland could outsource its warehouse operations by hiring another business to own and run the warehousing needed for the chain of shops. Explain the possible advantages and disadvantages of this and suggest whether you think Poundland should adopt this strategy.

are factors like speed of delivery, reliability and safety. In general:

- the bulkier the product;
- the greater the quantities that have to be transported on a regular basis;
- the longer the distance that has to be travelled;

the more likely transport by rail, ship or pipeline will be cheaper. Road is most useful for fairly small loads taken over short distances.

Warehousing

Many goods cannot go straight from being produced to the final customer. Instead, they have to be stored, for instance in a yard, a tank or a WAREHOUSE. A warehouse is a building which is used to store products. Goods ranging from baked beans to car parts to furniture may be kept in a warehouse.

A business may have a warehouse to store the supplies it has bought from other businesses or the products it makes. For instance, supermarket companies have regional warehouses where goods are delivered from suppliers. The companies then deliver these goods to their supermarkets for sale.

Warehouses are used when it is impossible to deliver straight to the customer. They are also useful when it is cheaper to buy in bulk and store what is not needed immediately. However, in manufacturing there has been a trend towards **just-in-time** deliveries (☞ unit 62). Just-in-time is where goods are delivered straight to and from the production area. This is because warehouses are expensive to operate and it is costly to keep **stocks** (☞ unit 56) of goods.

Drinkfast.com is an e-commerce company based in the UK. It supplies alcoholic and soft drinks to consumers. Orders are placed on the company's web site. Deliveries are made from the company's warehouse in Banbury in Oxfordshire. The company does not own or operate any form of transport and uses outside contractors for deliveries.

Explaining your arguments carefully, suggest what type of transport would be suitable for:
(a) deliveries of drinks from the company to the customer;
(b) deliveries of drinks from manufacturers to the company;
(c) supply of gas to the warehouse;
(d) supply of wine from vineyards in California, USA to wine merchants in the UK;
(e) supply of wine from vineyards in Bordeaux in France to wine merchants in the UK.

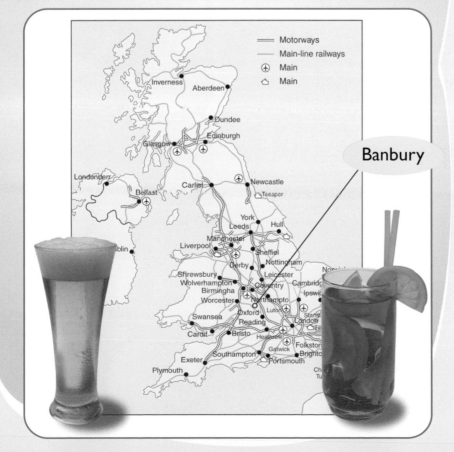

Banbury

key terms

Warehouse - a building dedicated to the storage of products.

✓ Checklist

1. What is meant by the 'channel of distribution' for a CD?
2. List SIX different types of transport.
3. Give ONE type of transport which would be suitable for transporting the following and ONE reason why it would be suitable: (a) water; (b) a car component from a factory in Birmingham to one in Coventry; (c) flowers from a grower in Holland to a wholesale market in London.
4. Why would bulky, low value products like bricks not be transported by aeroplane?
5. Why is reliability of transport important for a business?
6. Why do businesses use warehouses?

Production

Production and marketing

There is no point in producing something if it can't be sold. In the past, many businesses were PRODUCT ORIENTATED. This meant that they made a product and hoped that it would sell. Today, an increasing number of businesses are MARKET ORIENTATED. They realise that production and marketing must be linked. The business must find out what the customer wants before it produces anything. Products must be designed around the needs of the customer. **Market research** (☞ units 39-41) can help them identify those needs.

For instance, price is often a key factor for customers in deciding whether to buy. Market research might show that at £9.99 a product might sell well. At £14.99, it might be too expensive and sell badly. So a market orientated business will design the product around the **pricing point** of £9.99. It will look for ways in which it can cut costs to get down to this price. It might reduce the number of parts which need to be assembled. It might buy new labour saving machinery. It might reduce the quality of the product if this is acceptable to the customer.

Production which leads to a product which will sell profitably is therefore a key element of the **marketing mix** (☞ unit 38).

Product development

Research, development and planning are important before a new product is launched. In the planning stage, the business must decide:
- what is to be produced;
- how the product is to be made;
- where production is to take place;

- who will be the likely buyers of the product;
- how the product will be sold.

A manufacturer may carry out scientific or technological **research**. For instance, car and aeroplane manufacturers often have their own research centres. They test new materials which might be included in a new product. Or they might test a component for durability.

The potential new product then has to go through a process of **development**. This is where the original research idea is turned into a product which can be sold to the customer. The business may make prototypes to test the product, or they make produce sample products to **test market** (☞ unit 40).

RESEARCH AND DEVELOPMENT (R&D) is risky. A business can spend millions of pounds developing a product which is rejected before it goes on sale. In the pharmaceuticals industry, for instance, most drugs which reach the stage of being trialled on human beings have to be withdrawn. Some don't work.

Research and development are important before a product is launched

Others have severe side effects which can outweigh any benefits that the drug might give.

Assume that your mini-company is going to put designs on white T shirts or sweatshirts for children that have been bought in by the company.
(a) Make a list of all the things that you have to find out about before you even make a prototype shirt.
(b) Discuss THREE choices that you have made from your list in (a). For example, you would have to decide what designs to use. What factors would make you choose one design rather than another?

Patents, copyright and licences

Businesses can protect their developments through PATENTS and COPYRIGHT. A patent stops other businesses from using a process or making a product which has been invented or developed by the owner of the patent. Anyone who wishes to get this protection must file their invention at the **Patent Office**, run by government. If another business then copies that invention in one of its own products, it could be sued.

Copyright is similar to a patent. But it applies to the printed word, music and names or TRADE MARKS of products. For instance, a song or a novel will be protected by copyright. If an advertiser wanted to use a song in a commercial, it would have to get the agreement of the copyright owner. It may also have to negotiate a fee with the owner of the copyright. The owner would then receive a ROYALTY payment. Similarly, patents can be LICENSED. The owner of the patent gives someone else the right to use the invention, usually in return for a fee.

Patents and copyright give businesses a **monopoly** (☞ unit 16) on processes and products. It allows them to benefit from their exclusive use or to receive licence fees and royalties. Without patents and copyright, there would be little incentive for businesses to spend money on research and development. Instead, they would copy the products and processes of rivals.

GlaxoSmithKline (GSK) announced today that it is licensing a promising antidepressant drug from Merck KGaA, a German pharmaceuticals company. GSK will get the right to market the drug in the USA. Merck will retain some rights for European and other countries. The USA accounts for three-quarters of the worldwide antidepressant market.

GSK has been looking for a drug to replace its biggest selling product, the antidepressant Paxil/Seroxat. Last year, the drug made sales of 1.3 billion. But the patent on it runs out in 2006. After that, any drug company will be free to copy it.

Merck has little marketing presence in the USA. It would find it difficult to achieve large sales in the world's largest market. GSK, in contrast, has the second largest drugs sales force in this market. 7 000 sales reps cover the whole of the USA. GSK is recognised as having formidable marketing power to sell drugs in the USA.

Source: adapted from the *Financial Times*, 15.2.2001.

1. Explain what is meant by (a) 'licensing a ...drug' and (b) 'patent ... runs out in 2006'.
2. Suggest what are the benefits of licensing this drug for (a) GSK and (b) Merck.

✓Checklist

1. 'Management stated that the company needed to be far more market orientated.' What does this mean?
2. Why are production and marketing linked?
3. What is the difference between research and development?
4. 'R&D is a very risky activity for a business.' Why is this true?
5. Why are patents and copyrights important to businesses?

key terms

Copyright and patents - legal protection to prevent inventions or new products being copied by other businesses for their own use.
Licence - the legal right to use the copyright or patent of another business, usually in return for a royalty or fee.
Market orientated business - a business which develops products which have been researched and designed to meet the needs of customers.
Product orientated business - a business which develops products with little or no market research and which it hopes will prove successful in the market.
Research and development (R&D) - the process of scientific and technological research and then development of the findings of that research before a product is launched.
Royalty - payment for use of someone else's copyright.
Trade mark - unique name or other distinguishing feature of a product which is protected in law from being copied by rival businesses.

Purchasing and stocks

Stocks of finished goods are held in a warehouse

Purchasing

Businesses need to purchase goods and services to make their own products. For instance, a furniture maker will need timber. A food manufacturer will need ingredients. A manufacturer of televisions will need electrical parts. It will also need boxes for packaging.

In a large business, the **buying department** is in charge of buying the goods and services needed for production. The buying department will look at a number of factors when deciding what to buy from the **supplier**.

- It will be looking for the best possible **price** given the quality required.
- Buyers will know the minimum **quality** standard. This may be laid down in a **product specification**, a written document which describes exactly what is required. Only suppliers able to supply to the specification will be considered.
- Buyers will want a good **service**. They will be looking for suppliers which supply on time. They will also want suppliers to be flexible, accepting lower or higher orders if necessary. They want to make sure that the supplier is financially stable and will not go out of business before completing an order.

Production

In a small business, the owner may be in charge of production. The owner may supervise just a few workers employed by the firm. In a large manufacturing business, there is often a **production manager** responsible for deciding how goods should be produced. This manager will have a variety of goals. They may include:
- producing cost effectively;
- ensuring that the product meets strict quality specifications;
- meeting production targets and deadlines.

Stocks

Any business is likely to have STOCKS. These will include stocks of raw materials or ingredients waiting to be used in the production process. There may be stocks of **components** used to make other goods.

There are also likely to be stocks of **unfinished goods**. These are goods which are in the process of being made. Then there will be stocks of **finished goods**. These are goods waiting to be sent out to customers.

Stock management is very important to a business.

Cost Stocks cost money to hold. For instance, a business might hold £1 million worth of raw materials. It may have to borrow the money to

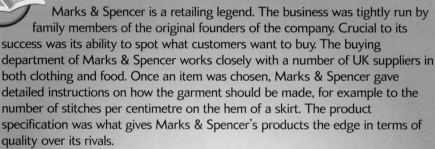

Marks & Spencer is a retailing legend. The business was tightly run by family members of the original founders of the company. Crucial to its success was its ability to spot what customers want to buy. The buying department of Marks & Spencer works closely with a number of UK suppliers in both clothing and food. Once an item was chosen, Marks & Spencer gave detailed instructions on how the garment should be made, for example to the number of stitches per centimetre on the hem of a skirt. The product specification was what gives Marks & Spencer's products the edge in terms of quality over its rivals.

In the late 1990s, however, Marks & Spencer faced a crisis. Sales and profits fell. One suggested reason was that the company's buyers misjudged changing market trends. In clothing, they failed to choose what customers wanted to buy. In food, the large supermarket chains caught up by offering high quality products, including ready meals. Marks & Spencer then lost its main competitive advantage.

Some also felt that Marks & Spencer had lost its quality edge in clothing. In the second half of the 1990s, the company moved away from buying nearly all its clothing products from British suppliers. Instead, it bought more cheaply from overseas businesses, including those in the Far East. But the quality overall was not as good as before. There was little to choose in terms of quality between Marks & Spencer and companies like Next or Gap. What's more, Marks & Spencer could not alter its product range as quickly. It now took more time to transport goods from abroad than it did when suppliers were in the UK.

Source: adapted from various sources 1999, 2000.

1. What is the role of the buying department at Marks & Spencer?
2. Explain why the following are important for buyers working at Marks & Spencer:
   (a) the price charged by suppliers; (b) product specifications; (c) quality of goods.
3. Discuss whether Marks & Spencer should change back to buying most of its clothing ranges from UK manufacturers.

Checklist

1. What does a purchasing manager do in a business?
2. Why is a product specification important for a purchasing manager?
3. What does a production manager do in a business?
4. What is the difference between overstocking and understocking?
5. Why is it important for a business not to carry excess stocks?

key terms

Stocks - materials that a business holds, waiting to be used in the production process, or finished stock waiting to be delivered to its customers.

pay for this stock. At a yearly rate of interest of 10 per cent, it will cost the company £100 000 per year or nearly £300 per day to keep the stock. The stock may have to be kept in a warehouse. This costs money to build or rent, insure and run. Stocks can also perish or deteriorate over time. Food in a supermarket, for instance, which passes its sell by date has to be thrown away. It is important therefore to keep stocks to a minimum and prevent **overstocking**.

Production needs Holding too little stock, **understocking**, could lead to loss of production and sales. If

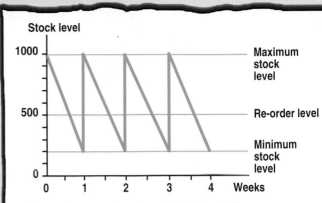

- 800 goods are used each week (1 000 - 200);
- Stock levels are not allowed to rise above 1 000 goods or fall below 200 goods;
- Stocks are re-ordered when they reach 500 goods;
- 800 goods are re-ordered and take around 3 days to arrive.

Figure 56.1

a car manufacturer, for instance, does not hold enough stocks, then its production lines could be brought to a halt. A shop which runs out of stock of a product could lose sales as customers go elsewhere.

Price Buying raw materials and components in large quantities may mean that a business can buy at competitive prices. Hence, holding more stock could reduce costs.

Stock control

Levels of stock can be shown on a chart, as in Figure 56.1. When stocks are received by the business, stock levels rise. This is shown by a vertical rise in the stock line. The **maximum stock level** on the chart shows the maximum amount of stock the business wants to keep at any one time. The **re-order level** shows the level of stock at which the business orders new stock. There is often a delay between ordering new stock and it arriving. So stock levels carry on falling before suddenly rising when the stock is delivered. If stock levels go below the **minimum stock level** shown on the chart, the business may have difficulty carrying on production.

Many businesses try to keep stocks to a minimum. They organise production so that stocks are delivered only when they are needed. This is called **'just-in-time' (JIT) production** (☞ unit 62).

Crenshaw Ltd is an engineering business. It makes a variety of metal parts and components. Many of the items are produced in batches of similar size. For example, bolts are made from stainless steel. Bearings are cast from high quality steel blocks. Demand can fluctuate. So the business purchases stock each week in the quantities required so that it does not hold large amounts of stock. The pattern of stock holding for the period June-July in shown in Figure 56.2.

1. Identify the (a) maximum stock level; (b) minimum stock level; (c) re-order level; (d) re-order quantity.
2. How many sheets did the business have In stock (a) at the end of June, (b) at the start of the second week in July; (c) at the start of the third week in July?
3. (a) What happened to stock levels in the first two weeks in July compared to the first week in June?
   (b) What might this indicate about sales in the first two weeks of July?
4. (a) What happened to stock in the last week of July?
   (b) Explain why this might have happened.

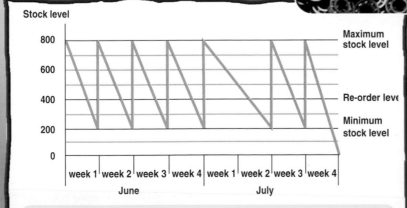

Figure 56.2

Providing defect free components and minimising emissions from motors are important aspects of quality

What is quality?

Some products have different **specifications** to others. A Rolls Royce may have different parts to a Ford Puma. One hi-fi may have more features than another. However, these products might all be seen as having QUALITY. A poor quality product is likely to be one that has faults or does not work correctly. Quality is about achieving a **standard** for a product or service which meets the needs of customers. Quality may also be about the **production process**. There may be poor quality if machines break down, supplies do not arrive on time and workers make errors.

Traditional quality control

In the past, quality control was seen as part of the chain of production. A **design** would be produced. This would include the specifications of the product and the materials to be used. The design would then be passed to the **production department** (☞ unit 54) It would decide how the product should be made. Once made, the product would be tested for quality by workers called **quality controllers** or **quality inspectors**. Only products that met the quality standards would be approved. Those that did not would be thrown away or sold as **seconds**. Quality inspectors would also test materials bought in from suppliers. They would make sure that supplies were of the right standard.

Total quality management (TQM)

More and more businesses are moving to TOTAL QUALITY MANAGEMENT (TQM). This has greatly changed the way in which quality is dealt with.

Quality as part of every process TQM makes quality part of every process. Quality is not tested just at certain stages of production. It is built into all stages of the production process.

Quality is everyone's job Before TQM, quality was the responsibility of the quality inspector. With TQM, every worker is responsible for quality. This may mean that a group of workers does the job of the quality inspector. It may also mean that quality is being tested at stages in the production process where it wasn't being tested before. If products or processes are not of the right quality, it is important that the workers involved identify the problem so it can be put right.

Customers and suppliers To help ensure quality, suppliers must satisfy

---

Hydropower Dynamics is a company which assembles and sells hydraulic hoses. These hoses are used to transfer fluids from one piece of machinery to another. It employs 60 workers. The company is dedicated to quality production. Its success can be judged from a number of major awards for quality it has gained. One major customer recently gave it a 'supplier quality' award for 100 per cent delivery on time and no rejects in a 12 month period.

The company expects every worker to accept that quality is their responsibility. There is a common sense approach to quality matters, which can be summarised in the Common Sense Quality (CSQ) technique:

- identify a problem;
- obtain the opinions of all those affected;
- utilise resources;
- provide a solution.

To push quality forward, the company has established 'Quality Bubbles'. These are workers and managers who form a group (or 'quality circle') to look at a specific quality issue. Using the CSQ technique, the group recommends solutions to problems. Ideally, a director of the company is part of the group. One advantage of this is that the director can argue the case at board level if financial assistance is needed for the quality improvement.

Source: adapted from Department for Trade and Industry, *From Quality to Excellence*, December 2000.

1. What does Hydropower Dynamics make?
2. Explain how the company builds quality into its manufacturing processes.
3. The company wants to increase sales from £4.5 million in 2000 to £10 million in 2005. Discuss the possible benefits and costs of its commitment to improving quality.

Purchasing · Stores · Despatch · Development · Quality Control · Accounts · Sales · Manufacturing

Figure 57.1 Quality bubbles at Hydropower Dynamics

the needs of customers. For example, workers in sales must make sure that customers who buy products are satisfied. But customers may also be workers within the business. So, for example, a manager must be satisfied by the work of an accountant. The manager is the customer and the accountant is the supplier. By recognising that their work affects customers, workers become responsible for what they do.

Just-in-time manufacturing

Just-in-time (JIT) manufacturing is a method of production where stocks are kept to minimum levels. Stocks are expensive to keep. So as soon as stocks are delivered to a business, they are used in production. Stocks of finished goods are immediately delivered to customers on the date they are promised. For this system to work, stocks coming in must be of the right quality. If they aren't, production may have to stop. Equally, if finished goods are only made just before they are due for delivery, there is no time to repair faults. Every good must be perfect.

Zero defects The aim of a business using TQM techniques is to have zero defects. This means that all work meets the required quality standards at every stage of the production process. To reach this, the business may set itself intermediate targets. For instance, it may aim to reduce defects to a certain level within the next year.

The role of management

Although every worker is responsible for quality, management must set up systems to ensure this quality. For instance, if a group of workers is producing faulty goods, there must be a system for identifying the nature of the problem. It could be they are working with inadequate machinery. They may not have been trained to do the job. There may be poor lighting where they work. Machines could be poorly spaced out on the factory floor. The system must then put this problem right.

Quality assurance When products or services are sold to customers a business gives its assurance that certain standards have been met. It will guarantee that legal requirements have been observed. It will also guarantee that quality has been maintained at all stages in the production process. It is impossible for every customer to check this. So **codes of practice** tell a customer that standards of quality have been achieved (☞ unit 58). The aim of quality assurance is to prevent production problems rather than finding them after they occur.

BAE Systems manufactures wing components for all Airbus aircraft. Aircraft wings are held together by 'fasteners' such as nuts, bolts and rivets. These fasteners would be delivered to BAE and placed in a 'store'. Having placed the fasteners on racks, they would be retrieved by staff at a later date when they were needed. Records were kept mainly on paper. The process of storing and retrieval was inefficient and there were frequent complaints about the service provided by the store staff to their 'customers', the production workers assembling the wings.

To tackle this, a project team was set up to analyse the problem and find a solution. The project team moved their office into the store to be able to understand how the store worked. It soon recognised the need to automate the operation with an ICT solution. This would incorporate lean supply chain principles and a bar code driven warehouse management system.

In practice, this meant that a computer system was installed. Each part was labelled with a bar code. The computer system showed staff on which rack to store the part and on which rack it could be retrieved when needed. Once established, the system was handling 250 000 transactions per annum and controlling 7 500 different parts from 70 suppliers.

The new system considerably improved the quality of the service provided. The computer could identify when parts needed reordering much better. The result was that shortages of parts at any one time fell from 700+ to less than 40. This was despite an 82 per cent reduction in stock held by BAE. The computer also told staff picking parts off the shelves the quickest route to take. Much of the paperwork was also eliminated. The result was that the time taken to pick stock fell by more than half. Stock was stored better and this led to a 10-20 per cent fall in wastage of stock.

Source: adapted from Department for Trade and Industry, *From Quality to Excellence*, December 2000.

1. Give THREE ways in which the quality of the service provided by the BAE store was poor before the new system was installed.
2. Explain why the new system improved quality of service.
3. Costs for BAE fell by enough for them to equal the spending on the new system within the first six months of operation. Explain why the new system could both improve quality and cost less to run.

Checklist

1. What is meant by 'quality' of a product?
2. How is quality maintained in a traditional business?
3. Why does everyone need to be involved in ensuring quality in a business?
4. Who are a worker's customers?
5. What is meant by 'zero defect' production?
6. Explain the role of management in TQM.

Products with quality standards

Bradley Mechanical is a business which manufactures valves for use in industries such as oil, chemicals and food products. It gained ISO 9001 standard in 2000. The process was not easy. The company found large gaps in its procedures which had to be rectified. For instance, it found that no systematic records were kept on the number of defects manufactured. So it had no idea whether defects were a problem. It also found that the company had no training policy. Some managers would take it upon themselves to approve a training grant for a worker. Other managers, for exactly the same training, would refer the application to the board of directors. Worse still, there were no criteria laid down as to whether training should be given or not.

Gaining ISO 9001 certification provided a foundation for quality assurance in the company. It helped retain orders from customers who were increasingly only dealing with companies with ISO 9001 certification. It also improved labour productivity and motivation, as well as raising quality levels.

But management found it was only the start. It embarked on the process of Total Quality Management (TQM). ISO 9001 meant that the company had procedures for dealing with quality. But it didn't necessarily mean that quality was good. For instance, ISO 9001 procedures showed that only 20 per cent of customers were 'very satisfied' with the service the company provided. One problem was that 35 per cent of all orders were delivered late. 10 per cent were delivered over a month late.

1. What problems with the company did Bradley Mechanical find in the process of gaining ISO 9001 accreditation?
2. What advantages did Bradley Mechanical gain from ISO 9001 accreditation?
3. Explain the difference between ISO 9001 and Total Quality Management (TQM).
4. Gaining ISO 9001 accreditation and adopting TQM cost Bradley Mechanical because thousands of worker hours were spent on them. Suggest whether it was worth it for the company. Justify your answer.

Product standards

Many products are made to **standards** (☞ unit 57) laid down by independent bodies. Perhaps the most well known in the UK is the **British Standards Institution**. It draws up standards for a wide range of products, from beds to nails to crash helmets. Some consumer products, like kettles or beds, are sold with **kite marks** on them. This shows that they have been made to a standard drawn up by the British Standards Institution.

There are other bodies which also set standards. For example, the British Electrotechnical Approvals Board tests and approves electrical products. The British Toy and Hobby Association grants a Lion Mark for approved toys.

System standards

Product standards are helpful in measuring quality. But they don't say anything about how that quality was achieved. A business might, for example, have to reject a quarter of

its production because it has not reached the right quality standard.

So there are also standards for **production systems**. These standards show that the way in which a product is made has quality. One such standard is ISO 9000. To get ISO 9000, a business has to prove that its production systems meet certain standards. If they don't, the business has to change them so that they conform.

ISO 9000 accreditation is available from quality assurance bodies like the British Standards Institution. There are standards available for different types of business. For instance, ISO 9001 is for manufacturing and service businesses with design. ISO 9002 is for manufacturing and services businesses without design. ISO 9003 is for suppliers only.

There are advantages to a business in meeting these standards. First, it is forced to review its quality procedures and make improvements to them. Second, because ISO 9000 is an international standard, it is widely recognised by potential customers. They know that they are buying from a business that is able to deliver quality products.

Benchmarking quality

Product and production standards may show that a business has a quality product or system. But it may still lag behind other businesses. For instance, a business making machine parts may have 5 000 faulty components in every 1 million produced. Another business making the same part may only have 500 faults per million.

BENCHMARKING is where one business compares itself with another. The other business is usually the 'best' in the industry. It might be a business which has:

* the lowest number of faults on its products;
* the shortest delivery time from the placing of an order;
* the highest output per worker;
* the shortest time to develop and produce a new product;
* the shortest call out time for after-sales service when a product develops a fault.

A business that benchmarks itself against another has to gather information not just on why the other business is better, but on how it achieves those results. The business must then change its own operations to reach the standards set by the other business. In this way, it will become a WORLD CLASS business. This means that it can compete with any similar business in the world.

Procedures are required for the following.
* Management responsibility, eg for creating a quality policy and quality systems, and appointing quality representatives.
* To review incoming orders.
* To control design planning, inputs, outputs, changes etc.
* To control documents and data, eg drawings, specifications.
* To control purchasing, eg lists and performance of suppliers.
* To control customer-supplied products, eg verify, store, handle.
* To identify and trace products.
* Controlling and planning of production, eg use of equipment, work instructions, monitoring and control of processes.
* Inspection and testing of a product at all stages of production.
* The control of inspection, measuring and test equipment.
* To check a product has or has not been tested.
* To identify products that do not meet standards.
* To take corrective or preventative action.
* Handling, storage, packaging, preservation and delivery.
* Control of quality records.
* Internal quality audits.
* Training.
* Servicing, eg site regulations.
* The use of statistical techniques, eg for sampling or testing.

Figure 58.1 *ISO 9001 requirements*

✓Checklist

1. (a) What does the British Standards Institution do?
   (b) What other organisations set standards in the UK?
2. How can ISO 9000 help a business achieve quality?
3. What are the advantages to a business of gaining ISO 9000 accreditation?
4. Why would a business want to benchmark its activities against world class companies?
5. Give FIVE ways in which a business might judge that it is lagging behind its competitors.

key terms

Benchmarking - **comparing the performance of one business or one factory with another and, in particular, with the best in the world.**
World class business - **a business which can compete successfully against the best businesses worldwide in the industry.**

Benchmarking helped Plastic Engineering (Leamington) improve its performance. The company makes parts for safety systems, such as seat belts, air bags, brakes and steering columns, for motor manufacturers.

It chose to use the Benchmark Index compiled and operated by the Small Business Service. The Small Business Service has collected data from a wide variety of companies and then uses this to compare the performance of a single company against this index. Plastic Engineering (Leamington) was compared to 200 other plastics companies on a wide range of indicators, such as delivery times, stock turnover, productivity per worker and wastage rates. It was also measured against a wide sample of companies in areas such as customer and staff satisfaction.

The company found that it was in the top 25 per cent of companies in areas such as product quality and customer satisfaction. However, it did less well in management/staff communication, stock turnover and productivity per worker.

It then made a fundamental reorganisation of the way it worked. For instance, the assembly line was scrapped and replaced by team working.

The results were excellent. The amount of stock kept in the factory has fallen from £240 000 to less than £200 000. There has been a 5 per cent cut in wastage. The on-time delivery rate to customers has improved from 60 per cent to 98 per cent. The output per machine and per worker has also increased.

Source: adapted from *The Sunday Times*, 15.10.2000.

1. What is the 'Benchmark Index'?
2. Give TWO examples of how Plastic Engineering (Leamington) improved its performance through benchmarking.
3. The large motor manufactures are putting pressure on their suppliers to cut their prices. For instance, a motor manufacturer might say that a supplier must, from now on, lower its prices by 4 per cent each year. Discuss how benchmarking might help a company like Plastic Engineering (Leamington) achieve these reductions in costs.

UNIT 59

Job and batch production

Building a new bridge is an example of job production

Production methods

The method of production for a mass produced car is different from that of a hand made glass bowl. This unit looks at two methods of production, job and batch production. In unit 60 another method of production, flow production, will be considered.

Job production

JOB PRODUCTION is where a single item is produced from start to finish. Each item produced is likely to be unique. For instance, a construction company may build a new office block in the centre of Manchester. This is a unique job with a unique design. It will not be one of many identical office blocks that the company could build.

Other examples of job production include bridges, new motorways, taxi rides, a high quality restaurant meal and a work of art. Each is produced specially. There are advantages and disadvantages to using job production methods.

Advantages The quality of work done with job production is usually high. Skilled workers are often needed to make unique products.

These workers tend to be well motivated because the work they do is never quite the same. Job production also allows customers to order exactly what they want. They do not have to accept something which is mass produced.

Disadvantages Job production is a relatively expensive way of producing a good or service. The skilled workers needed to make a one-off product may have to be paid high wages. The work may also be **labour intensive**, with fewer opportunities to automate parts of the process.

Batch production

BATCH PRODUCTION is where a business makes a number of the same product (a **batch**) at the same time. It will change production when it needs to make a batch of a different product or component. It will remake the original product when it is needed again. For instance, a ball bearing manufacturer might produce a million ball bearings of one size over three days. It will then change the settings on its machines to make ball bearings of another size. A bakery might make 2 000 tin loaves, followed by 500 cottage loaves, followed by 1 000 bread rolls.

Advantages Compared to job production, batch production allows

Virginia Webb opened her florist shop ten years ago. She has never had one moment of regret about giving up her job to run her own business.

What she most enjoys is the ability to create a unique product for customers. As the seasons change, so do the flowers which she uses. Weddings, funerals, birthdays and special occasions all provide opportunities to do something different. Fashions over the years change too. Floral decorations that she was making ten years ago are different from the ones she creates today.

One of the reasons why Virginia's shop is so successful is that she makes a point of consulting customers about what they want. Not only does this help keep customers happy, but it also encourages them to come back again.

1. What type of production is used to make floral bouquets and displays at Virginia's Shops?
2. Suggest why this is the best way to make these products.
3. The average amount spent on a bouquet of flowers for anniversary gift is £25. For flowers for a church wedding it would be £700. Suggest why it is so expensive to produce these products.

Food and construction products are often produced in batches

workers to **specialise** (☞ unit 2) and use specialist machinery more. Costs per unit produced should therefore be lower. It also means that different batches of slightly different products can be made.

Disadvantages Batch production leads to goods having to be stored. Keeping **stock** (☞ unit 56) increases costs. Specialist machinery may have to be cleaned or reset to produce a different batch of products. This can take time. Specialisation of workers may result in some workers doing the same repetitive job all day, which can be demotivating. The factory is also likely to be laid out in sections (called LAYOUT BY PROCESS). Each section will produce a particular batch of goods. In a car plant, for instance, one section might make the body panels. Parts will have to be moved from one section to another. This takes time and leads to higher costs.

Checklist

1. What is meant by job production?
2. Explain why (a) building a bridge across a motorway and (b) painting a house may be examples of job production.
3. What are (a) the advantages and (b) the disadvantages of job production?
4. What is the difference between job production and batch production?
5. What are (a) the advantages and (b) the disadvantages of batch production?

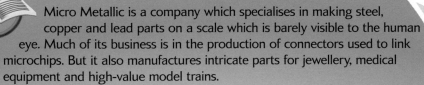

Micro Metallic is a company which specialises in making steel, copper and lead parts on a scale which is barely visible to the human eye. Much of its business is in the production of connectors used to link microchips. But it also manufactures intricate parts for jewellery, medical equipment and high-value model trains.

Typically, Micro Metallic makes its components in small batches of 50 000. This is well below the number that rival component makers would consider economic. Larger rivals generally use press machines to stamp out millions of copies of parts.

Many of the parts made by Micro Metallic are used by manufacturers when products are being developed. For example, manufacturers often want small quantities to use in prototypes of products or products at pre-production stage.

Because of the nature of Micro Metallic's work, it can charge premium prices for parts that customers often want in a hurry. These customers include industry giants like Nokia, the mobile phone company and Hewlett-Packard, the computer company. Explaining the success of the company, Bob Crutchley, the part-owner and founder of the company, said: 'there will always be a lot of work for businesses such as ourselves which fill a specific niche in the supply chain.'

Source: adapted from the *Financial Times*, 25.1.2000.

1. 'Typically, Micro Metallic makes its components in relatively small batches of 50 000.' Explain what this means.
2. Explain the likely (a) advantages and (b) 'disadvantages to Micro Metallic of using batch production.
3. Why do you think Micro Metallic can survive when its rivals and customers are such large companies?

key terms

Batch production - **a method of production where a product is made in stages, with a particular operation being carried out on all products in a group or batch.**
Job production - **a method of production where a product is made individually from start to finish like a bridge. Each product is likely to be different and unique.**
Layout by process - **where production facilities are laid out with different processes being performed in different parts of the building, and part finished goods are taken around the building to be worked on.**

Flow production

Investment in new rolling stock for railways has surged in recent years. Before privatisation, new investment had almost come to a halt. After privatisation, investment has been necessary for train operating companies to retain their franchises.

ALSTOM Transport is one of the world's three main makers of railway equipment. It has a factory in Birmingham where rolling stock has been made since 1845. In the past, a complete carriage or power unit (the engine part of the train) was gradually built up on a static 'stand'. Workers added components until the carriage was completed. A complete carriage is made up of about 3 000 parts.

In 2000, as a result of a £10 million investment, a start was made on changing the method of production. Four assembly lines will eventually be built. Each unit will have wheels put on close to the start of the manufacturing process. This will allow each unit to be moved from one production station to the next on a set of rails. Each of the four assembly lines will be capable of turning out one train unit a week. This is four times quicker than the 'static' method.

Source: adapted from the *Financial Times*, 25.10.2000.

1. Explain the difference between the two methods of production described in the data.
2. Suggest why the assembly line approach is 'four times quicker than the static method'.
3. What might be the disadvantages of introducing an assembly line to manufacture trains?

Flow production

FLOW PRODUCTION is a method of production used to make large numbers of identical or **standardised** products. The product is made continuously, often passing down an **assembly line**. A different task is carried out at each stage of production. For instance, in a car factory, a basic chassis is put onto an assembly line. As it moves down the line, components like wheels, engines, doors and windows are added. Workers on the assembly line perform the same task to the vehicle as it goes down the line. If 100 cars a day move down the line, then one worker will, for example, fit 100 bonnets. Another worker might fit 100 wheels. Flow production allows a business to gain the benefits of DIVISION OF LABOUR. This is the term used to describe the **specialisation** (☞ unit 2) of workers. Other products made in this way include MDF and pizzas. Wooden chips pass through various processes, such as forming, drying and pressing to make MDF. Dough is moulded, cut and baked to make pizzas.

Mass produced products are often made using repetitive flow production methods. This is where large quantities of the same product are manufactured. Complicated machinery is needed to carry out this repetitive work. The machines can sometimes run for 24 hours. Large blow moulding machines are used to make plastic containers which hold milk and oil, for example.

There are advantages and disadvantages to flow production.

Advantages Large numbers of products can be manufactured at very low cost. This is because so much capital machinery is used and so little time is lost in the production process. The cost of producing a new car on an assembly line, for example, is a fraction of the cost of a garage building a whole car from components as a one off job. Many of the workers on the assembly line may be unskilled. They only have to be taught to perform a few simple tasks which they repeat. Using unskilled workers cuts down the cost of labour. Also, very complex products can be manufactured using flow production methods. This is because many different types of worker and machine are used.

Disadvantages There may be problems with using assembly lines in production. They require a large amount of capital equipment. Once built, it is difficult, if not impossible, to adapt the assembly line to make

Flow production is typically used to make cars

other products. Jobs on an assembly line may be boring. A worker might perform the same operation several hundred times a day. This can demotivate workers and might result in poor quality. The product being assembled must be fairly standard. This is because both workers and machinery have been trained or designed to cope with only one type of operation. There are likely to be stocks of products waiting to used on the assembly line. These stocks cost money to hold. A breakdown of the assembly line at any point can also lead to a complete shut down. For instance, a strike by workers on one part of the assembly line can bring the whole line to a halt.

Process production

PROCESS PRODUCTION is a method of flow production where a product is made continuously by being passed through a production **plant** rather than an assembly line. For instance, at an oil refinery, crude oil is refined into petrol. An oil refinery is like a single huge machine (and hence is called a plant rather than a factory). The oil flows through pipes and tanks as it is chemically changed into petrol. Process production is used in the oil and chemical industries.

Process production has both advantages and disadvantages.

Advantages Process production is highly capital intensive. Using specialised machines or plant can reduce labour costs. It also allows products to be made to detailed specifications. Process production can lead to much higher levels of safety for workers compared to alternative methods.

Disadvantages The cost of installing machines or plant is often very high. If an accident happens, like part of a chemical plant blowing up, it can also cause major damage.

The chemicals industry in Europe is facing rapid change. Environmental concerns are one cause of this. Chemical companies are finding that they are having to work under ever increasing regulations. These are designed to limit pollution from chemical plants and reduce the risk of accidents. However, they are also pushing chemical companies to open new plants in the Third World where regulations are laxer.

The other cause of change is more positive. Chemical plants have traditionally been large and sprawling. They have been 'criss-crossed' by pipes taking gases and liquids from one piece of equipment like a reactor to another like a heat exchanger. The result is that three quarters of the cost of building a plant is made up of the pipes and structures and only one quarter by the essential pieces of equipment themselves. Today, there is increasing use of process intensification. This is where the same piece of equipment is made to perform two or more processes. This reduces the pipework, saves on land and lowers overall costs.

Source: adapted from the *Financial Times*, 3.7.2000.

1. Explain what method of production is used to produce chemicals in a chemical plant.
2. How are chemical companies lowering the cost of production according to the data?

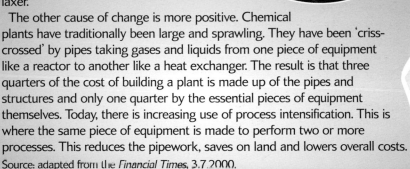

Checklist

1. Explain the difference between flow production, batch production and job production.
2. How are cars produced using a flow production method?
3. What are (a) the advantages and (b) the disadvantages of flow production?
4. What is the difference between production on an assembly line and process production?
5. What are (a) the advantages and (b) the disadvantages of process production?

3. (a) What is happening to the cost of production as a result of stricter environmental controls? (b) Discuss whether it would be in the best interests of (i) the chemical companies and (ii) society as a whole if environmental controls were relaxed.

Mass production and lean production

Motor vehicles are often mass produced

Automation

Technology is constantly changing. However, the rate of change of technology has been particularly fast over the past 200 years and is still increasing.

- **Mechanisation.** There was widespread mechanisation during the UK Industrial Revolution in the late 18th century and 19th century.

Machines driven by steam or water power replaced workers, but the workers still operated the machines.

- **Automation.** In the 20th century the process of automation meant that some workers no longer had to operate machines. Today workers often supervise machines as they work automatically. Automation has largely come about through the use of computers in the production process.

Mass production

Henry Ford founded the Ford motor car company in the USA in 1903. He revolutionised production techniques with his Model T Ford motor car. This was the first complex product to be MASS PRODUCED. Before, cars were built individually. Workers came to each car in a part of the factory and helped build the car. Ford built the first **production line** (☞ unit 60). On the production line, the workers and machines stayed at the same point in the factory. Cars were brought to the workers. Workers and machines could then **specialise** (☞ unit 2). Each worker only did one small operation. The tools and machines he used were specifically designed to help him with that one operation. Workers on the production line were often unskilled. They just needed to know how to complete their one operation.

Mass production reduced costs because the same product was being made a large number of times. 15 million Model T Fords, for instance, were made in the USA. They were made in just one colour, which was black.

The problems of mass production

Traditional mass production techniques had problems, however.

- Production lines and processes meant that the product was travelling long distances within the factory. This took time and meant that factory buildings and production lines were large. Both

Vincent Jarrott works in a factory producing machines for the textile industry. For the past four years, he has worked at a stamping machine.

He puts a flat piece of steel into the machine. Then he closes a gate to prevent his fingers getting trapped as he presses a button on the floor with his foot. The button brings the press down and makes a circular indent into the part. He then opens the gate, takes out the part and places it in a bin next to him. The whole operation should take 10 seconds.

Vincent is paid on a piece work basis. This means he is paid for every part stamped. He should produce six a minute, 360 an hour or 2 880 every eight hour shift. In practice, he can produce 4 000 a shift. But this means not using the guard. He jokes that he hangs up his brains when he hangs up his coat at the start of his shift. The work is boring. But if he wants to produce 4 000, he has to be alert all day. One slip bringing the press down too quickly and he could end up with no fingers or no hand.

If a part was stamped just 1 mm incorrectly, it has to be rejected. Quality is the responsibility of a quality inspector who visits twice a day. If the machine goes wrong just after the inspector has visited, half a day's work might be lost. Vincent isn't worried. He gets paid whether the part is perfect or faulty.

It is the responsibility of another worker to keep him supplied with unstamped parts which are bought from a warehouse on the factory site. The same worker takes the finished parts back to the warehouse or, if they are short of parts in the assembly section, to the building next door. Often, the worker will remove the finished parts before the quality inspector has inspected them.

1. 'The factory where Vincent works is both inefficient and dangerous.' Explain FIVE ways in which this is true.
2. Discuss TWO ways in which efficiency could be increased in the factory.

Circuit boards are mass produced but production may be customised for customers' needs

increased costs of production.

- Large volumes of **stocks** (☞ unit 56) were kept. If stocks of a particular part ran out, the production line could come to a halt. So large amounts of stock were kept to prevent this.
- **Communication** between workers was poor. They were scattered along the production line. There were also no systems designed to encourage workers to talk to each other about their work. Workers were seen more as robots than as people who could help improve production through their ideas.
- Workers had no responsibility for the **quality** (☞ unit 57) of their work. It was someone else's responsibility to make sure that products were of the right standard. The result was that quality was often poor and too many products coming off the production line had to be rejected.
- Production was inflexible. With poorly skilled workers and a rigid production line, it was difficult to change to produce different products quickly.

Lean production

Japanese businesses were the first to find solutions to the problems of mass production. Toyota, the car manufacturer, helped bring a second revolution in how products are manufactured. This system is called LEAN PRODUCTION. It is a system which attempts to reduce all inputs to the production process to a minimum. This includes everything from workers to raw materials to factory space. Techniques of lean production are dealt with in unit 62.

Mass customisation

One of the problems with **mass production** is that customers are forced to accept a standard product. Ford's Model T Ford, for instance, was only available in one colour, black. However, buyers often want products which are customised to their own needs. MASS CUSTOMISATION is the process of manufacturing a standard product in a large number of different variations to cater for the individual needs of customers.

Mass customisation has been made possible by the use of new technologies. For instance, machine tools can now be changed much more quickly than in the past due to computerisation. So a batch of one type of product can be made and this can be followed very quickly after retooling by another batch. In the past, it may not have been possible to change the tooling on a machine or it might have taken a long time. Increasing the speed of retooling a machine means that the cost of producing small **batches** (☞ unit 59) is much lower than it has been in the past.

✓Checklist

1. Give THREE features of mass production.
2. Explain FOUR problems with mass production.
3. How can lean production help a business?
4. Why might customers benefit from mass customisation?
5. What changes in technology have made mass customisation possible?

Hunter Douglas is a Dutch firm which is a leader in its market of supplying aluminium blinds. With sales of around £1 billion per year, it has customers all over the world. Only one third of sales are in Europe. Supplying aluminium blinds is complex because most blinds sold are made to measure. What's more, blinds come with different finishes, such as textiles or paints, and in a large number of different colours. There are 10 000 individual components from which a blind might be made and hundreds of thousands of different variants of the finished product which can be ordered.

To cope with this mass customisation, Hunter Douglas has to use extremely sophisticated production systems. It owns 20 assembly plants around the world to ensure quick local delivery. The time between an order being placed and delivered to the retailer is typically five days. To ensure that enough stock is kept at the assembly plant, sophisticated computer programs are used to predict demand for any single component. These programs also help the company maintain stocks at a minimum, since having too much stock is costly for the company. Computer systems and the internet are used to track orders as they go through the production and delivery system.

Source: adapted from the *Financial Times*, 25.10.2000.

1. Why does Hunter Douglas have to use 'mass customisation' production systems to satisfy its customers?
2. A computer failure at Hunter Douglas might be a problem for the company. Too little of one component might be ordered for stock and too much of another component might be ordered. Discuss how this might affect the company and its customers.

UNIT 62

Cell production, JIT and Kaizen

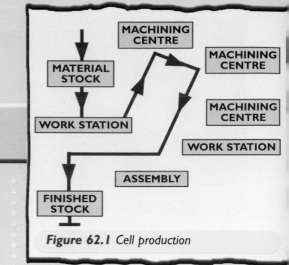

Figure 62.1 Cell production

Cell production

On a traditional production line, workers and materials are located at different points of the line. As the product moves down the line, it changes as components are added to it. On a car production line, for instance, the car may start as a chassis. Components such as the body shell, wheels, engines, doors and lights are added. When it rolls off the production line it is a complete car.

Lean production methods try to minimise the use of inputs such as raw materials, labour, machines or factory space (☞ unit 61). They suggest that CELL PRODUCTION may be a more efficient method of manufacturing. This is where production is broken down into various 'cells'. A cell has a number of tasks which make a product or complete a process. Cells are often U shaped or horse shoe shaped, as in Figure 62.1. Materials are brought to a point at the top of the cell. They are then worked on at different machines around the cell. The finished product ends up close to where it started.

Cell production is often more efficient than a traditional production line for a number of reasons.
- Machines in cells are placed much closer together. Cell production takes up less space on the factory floor as a result.
- Working more closely together, workers in the cell co-operate and sort out problems as a group. Cells are usually given production targets. This helps increase **productivity**.
- Quality improves. This is because of co-operation by workers in the cells. It is also easier to identify where faults in production are coming from.

Just-in-time (JIT) production

JUST-IN-TIME (JIT) production is where stocks are delivered only when they are needed for production. This means that stocks are kept to a minimum. In a large factory, stocks will be delivered by the supplier straight to the point on the production line or to the cell where they are required.

There are many advantages to JIT production.
- Holding stocks is costly. Money is tied up, which could be used elsewhere. Stocks have to be held in a warehouse or on a production line. This space costs the business money.
- Moving stock is costly too. It may have to be delivered to a warehouse and then taken out again to be put on the production line. This is far more costly than if the stock is delivered straight to the production line.
- Holding stock can affect quality. If workers know that large stocks are available, they won't be worried if

Yorkshire Fittings is owned by IMI (Imperial Metal Industries), a multinational company. It makes 130 million fairly simple copper fittings a year at its main plant in Leeds. These fittings are used by the plumbing trade, for instance in heating systems. About half of all buildings in the UK contain copper fittings made by the company.

In the 1990s, production was reorganised. Out went a system where products were moved from machine to machine across the factory to be finished. In came cell production, where each product is made from start to finish by a dedicated team of workers located in a small cell area of the factory. Each team is led by a qualified fitter, who has served a four year apprenticeship, and also by a manager who typically (though not always) has an engineering degree. Cell teams meet several times a week to discuss problems. Sometimes they go away from the factory for training sessions. 'We have worked hard to get rid of the boring, negative jobs as well as the view that you left your brain in the locker when you put your overalls on,' according to Peter Sutcliffe, managing director of operations.

Overall productivity is rising by about 10 per cent a year. Some of the cell teams, though, have increased production by up to ninefold in five years. Quality has considerably improved and customer complaints have dropped sharply.

Source: adapted from the *Financial Times*, 9.11.1999.

Cell production at IMI

1. What is meant by 'cell production'?
2. Suggest why cell production at Yorkshire Fittings has led to (a) rising productivity and (b) improved quality.
3. An outside consultant has suggested that having a manager with an engineering degree in charge of a cell is a waste of resources. He suggests that the company could save money by getting rid of this manager and letting the cell be led by the qualified fitter alone. Do you think this would benefit the company? Justify your answer.

some of their work is poor. Good components can always be taken out of stock and poor work thrown away. If there are no stocks, faulty materials can bring the whole production process to a halt.

Kaizen

Lean production is associated with KAIZEN. This is a Japanese word which means 'continuous improvement'. Kaizen implies that production can always be improved. Quality can be better, production times reduced and costs lowered.

In a traditional production line system, workers have no control over their work. It arrives on the production line, which has been designed by someone else. With Kaizen, workers have to be involved in the production process. In each cell, workers are part of a team. A problem faced by one worker in the cell is a problem for all the workers in the cell. The cell cannot produce anything if there is a problem with one part of it.

Kaizen also means that there must be ongoing training of the workforce. If workers are to be able to work flexibly, there must be MULTI-SKILLING. This is where workers are trained to do a variety of jobs which require more than one skill.

Workers are also involved in problem solving. For instance, there may be a company **suggestion scheme**. Workers may be invited to suggest ways in which the business could be improved. Most ideas are likely to be rejected. But a few can lead to important changes, which can save a business thousands of pounds.

QUALITY CIRCLES are another method of improving production. Workers are encouraged to meet, to discuss ways of improving work. Good ideas come from these discussions. But workers also become more aware of what is going on in the business and how their performance affects others.

These changes tend to lead to increases in productivity. Fewer workers are now needed to produce the same amount as before. Fewer machines are needed. Less factory space is required. This can then lead to a DOWNSIZING of a business. Factories are closed and workers made redundant. On the other hand, a business may find that by lowering its prices it is able to gain more orders. The same number of workers and factories now produce more.

In the past thirty years, the UK has seen a small increase in the output of manufacturing industry. But the number of workers employed and the number of factories has more than halved. There has also been a large increase in the imports of products from cheaper or better quality factories overseas. Unless UK firms adopt lean production techniques, they risk going out of business due to this competition.

Checklist

1. How is production organised (a) on a production line and (b) in a cell?
2. What is meant by just-in-time production techniques?
3. New production techniques often require fewer but better trained workers. Why is this?
4. What is the difference between a company suggestion scheme and a quality circle?
5. Why might greater efficiency in production lead to downsizing?

key terms

Cell production - a production system where a number of machines are grouped together, sometimes in a horse shoe shape, to perform a series of related operations.
Downsizing - reducing the number of inputs to the production process, such as the workforce or the number of factories, without necessarily reducing the output of the business.
Just-in-time (JIT) - a production system where stocks are only delivered when they are needed by the production system. This minimises stock levels in a business.
Kaizen - a production system which is designed to give continuous improvement in performance over a period of time.
Multi-skilling - where workers have more than one skill and are able to perform several tasks or jobs.
Quality circles - groups of workers who meet together to suggest ways in which production could be improved.

AB Electronics is owned by the TT Group. It owns three factories in Cardiff where 360 workers make car components, such as heater and air conditioner controls, switches and body electronics. In 1995, the company decided to implement kaizen. Workers were trained in how to use kaizen and formed into multi-level teams of five to six workers. The technique was explained to the whole workforce and the company guaranteed that no one would lose their jobs as a result of improvements made. One kaizen team has been made responsible for deciding what issues should be tackled. Once decided, a team is sent in, typically for a week. The teams are given the authority to make any changes they think are needed including buying new equipment.

For instance, one team looked at using labels on products. One member of the team suggested that it was unnecessary to use different sizes and materials for labels on different products. The team spent £438 on a new laser printer and saved £10 000 from the annual labelling cost of £23 000.

In another case, a kaizen team looked at a production cell making switches. Its productivity had already been considerably improved by a visit from the company's production engineers. However, the kaizen team saw a way to make further improvements. They changed the layout of the cell and moved the component stock system into the cell itself. They were able to produce exactly the same output with eight staff instead of twelve.

Source: adapted from *The Sunday Times*, 16.1.2000.

Production by the TT Group

1. What is kaizen?
2. Give ONE example of how AB Electronics was able to reduce costs by using kaizen.
3. Suggest why it was important for AB Electronics to reassure staff that no one would lose their jobs as a result of the use of kaizen.

New technologies in manufacturing

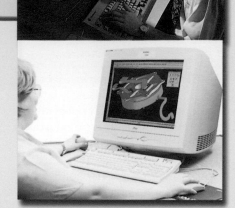

Producing 3D models using CAD

Old and new technologies

The computer and the microchip have revolutionised manufacturing. Machines now do much of the work that was done by workers in the past. This **mechanisation** (☞ unit 61) has taken place in many businesses. In some cases, there has been total **automation**. This is where machines operate automatically. Workers may simply be used to supervise production.

Computer aided design (CAD)

In the past, designs for products were developed on paper. Drawings would be made and calculations worked out by hand. Today, COMPUTER AIDED DESIGN (CAD) packages are often used for design work. Design is done on computer using CAD software. This allows the designer to:

- do style drawings, so that the end product looks good and is aesthetically pleasing;
- put in details of the structure of a product, like stress bars on a car body;
- make sure that the structure and the materials used are strong enough to do the job for which they are designed. The computer program does the calculations to work this out;
- produce two and three dimensional images of the structure, as well as drawings of individual parts of the design.

CAD speeds up the design process. It allows designs to be more sophisticated. Many alternative designs can be explored. Changes to designs can be made easily, at little cost. The computer program may be able to show the 'best' or optimal solution to a design problem. It may also remove the need for physical models or prototypes. Computer programs are good enough to clearly view designs and to test the strength of materials.

Computer Numerical Control (CNC) machines

In traditional manufacturing lathes and milling machines are used in production. A **milling machine**, for instance, is used to cut grooves, often into metal and plastic. A **lathe** cuts materials into cylinder shapes as they turn.

Today, these machines can be controlled by computer programs. They are called COMPUTER NUMERICAL CONTROLLED (CNC) machines. For instance, a CNC milling machine may be used to make a shape in a piece of metal. The operator would input the details of the shape to be cut from the metal. The computer would then choose the cutter that was needed from tools stored in the machine. The machine would mill out the shape quickly, using instructions from the computer. If a different shape was needed, the machine would be given instructions to select a suitable tool. This would save time and cost for a business. On a traditional milling machine, the cutter would have to be taken off by hand and replaced by a different one. CNC machines are also highly accurate. This cuts out the human error in traditional manufacturing.

Some CNC machines make use of **probes** and **co-ordinate measuring machines** (CMMs). These check that measurements are accurate.

Computer aided manufacturing (CAM)

Using computers in design and production means that the two processes can be linked. The computer

Philidas is part of the Haden MacLellan engineering group. It is a manufacturer of nuts, bolts and related fastener products. The businesses is located in Pontefract, Yorkshire. It concentrates on quality and high technology products. Philidas aims to solve very specific problems that face its customers. For instance, the company has devised a wheel nut for Ford vans that contains an in-built washer. This makes assembly easier, as well as making the vehicles safer.

Computer-aided-design is central to the company. Philidas's eight development engineers have worked to revamp its CAD system. Computers are now able to receive engineering drawings from car industry customers over the telephone network. In the past designs would have been sent on disk by courier.

Source: adapted from the *Financial Times*, 3.11.1999.

1. What does Philidas design and manufacture?
2. How might CAD help (a) improve quality and (b) reduce costs for the company?
3. Suggest what might be the effect on Philidas if fire destroyed its computer systems.

data generated in design can then be fed into the programs on CNC machines. This linkage of design and production is called COMPUTER AIDED MANUFACTURING (CAM) or CAD/CAM ENGINEERING. For instance, a manufacturer of metal components may design a part for a machine using a CAD package. This will be passed to CAM machines on the factory floor to produce the product

Robots

All the large motor manufacturing companies use robots on their production lines. A ROBOT, like a CNC machine, is controlled by a computer. The difference between a robot and a CNC machine is that a robot has some form of arm which moves materials. For instance, a robot might take a component from a rack and install it into a car engine. Like CNC machines, robots can be programmed as part of a CAM package, linking CAD design with the manufacturing process.

Automatically Guided Vehicles (AGVs)

Many manufacturing companies also use AUTOMATICALLY GUIDED

VEHICLES (AGVs). These are carriages on which components or parts can be put. They are then taken to another part of the factory. The AGV is guided by inductive wires which are put into the floor or on the ceiling along the route that the AGV will travel. The AGV has sensors which prevent it from crashing into objects if there is something in its path. The sensors are linked to the **programmable logic controller (plc)**. This is the microprocessor on board the AGV which has been programmed to control its movements.

Computer integrated manufacturing (CIM)

A few manufacturing plants around the world have COMPUTER INTEGRATED MANUFACTURING (CIM) systems. CIM is where the whole of the production process is controlled by computer technology. Workers in the factory supervise and check that the systems are operating properly. They also do maintenance work. CIM, for instance, means that parts are ordered by computer for the production line when they are

needed. An AGV may collect the parts from a store room. Or an outside supplier may be expected to deliver to the door of the factory from where it will be taken by an AGV to the production line. A robot may take the parts from the AGV and place them into components on the production line.

CIM is very complex and may be difficult to set up. It can also be very inflexible if, say, a production line needs to be used to manufacture a different product. For nearly all businesses, CAM is a more suitable solution to their production problems than CIM.

Orders for industrial robots were up by more than a third in the first half of 1999. This was mainly due to booming demand from motor manufacturers in the US and Europe. Car makers are some of the leading users of robots. They have the money to be able to afford expensive pieces of equipment. They also have standardised production for which robots are ideal. Finally, they have an incentive to replace workers by machines. This is not just because of better quality production, but also because much of the work that robots do would cause health and safety problems for workers.

The expense of robots at the moment prevents their more general use. In the future, though, as the price of robots falls, they are likely to perform many of the mundane jobs in the workplace. This could include cleaning the factory or office floor, or acting as a courier between workers.

Source: adapted from the *Financial Times*, 5.10.1999.

1. Explain why robots are often found in car manufacturing plants around the world.
2. Why might workers be likely to lose their jobs to robots in the future?
3. A taxi manufacturer is considering buying a robot for its assembly line. An engineering company is considering buying an AGV for its warehouse. What factors might these businesses take into account when making their decision?

Checklist

1. A manufacturer wants to design a new bicycle. How could CAD help it to do this?
2. What are the advantages of a CNC lathe over a traditional manual lathe operated by a worker?
3. How might a manufacturer of train carriage components use CAM to speed up production of a new design?
4. What is the difference between a robot and a CNC machine?
5. (a) How does an AGV know where to move and (b) what prevents it from bumping into an object in its path?
6. Why is CIM more complex than CAM?

UNIT 64

New technologies in service industries

Scanning bar codes has improved stock control

New technology

New technology, particularly ICT (INFORMATION AND COMMUNICATION TECHNOLOGIES), has transformed a number of service industries in recent decades. ICT is a group of technologies which make use of the microchip and computers. These technologies have allowed everything from satellite communication to emails and the internet, and from mobile telephones to the electronic storage of huge quantities of information.

> Barcodes have been around for 20 years . But they have become frozen in a time-warp. They are issued by an organisation called E-centre. Once a bar code has been allocated, E-centre has no control on the information that the bar code will contain.
>
> Wispa Bars provide a good example. All standard size Wispa Bars have the same bar code on their packaging. But when a company in the supply chain receives the product, it has to decide what information it wants each bar in the code to record. Take the name of the bar. Some companies key 'Wis' into their computer. Others 'Wispa'. A supermarket will key in a price for the product to be read at the check out. But it won't necessarily key in the maximum number of cartons of Wispas that can be stored on a pallet for transport. On the other hand, a haulage company handling distribution of Wispas will not key in a price, but the information about storage on pallets.
>
> This problem is important for two reasons. First, every time the Wispa bar is transferred between businesses, all the information about that product has to be keyed in to the company's computer for the bar code system to work. Second, it becomes difficult to interrogate the system. An internet shopper, for example, may want to know whether a food contains nuts. One supermarket may have keyed this information. Another might not.
>
> The solution is for the bar code to contain one set of information which gets transferred from business to business. Then, the bar code information at Tesco would be the same as at Asda or Sainsbury's. Tesco and Procter & Gamble have been testing a system developed by a company called Udex. Udex creates an internet entry for the product which is then downloaded by Procter & Gamble and Tesco. An internet library of information about products is thus created. Everyone has the same information. If the information needs updating, it can be done once by Udex. This just leaves information like the selling price to be keyed in by the individual business. The system is experimental but Tesco has been so impressed that it has asked all its suppliers to sign up to the system by the end of the financial year.
>
> Source: adapted from the *Financial Times*, 25.7.2000.

1. What is the bar code system for products?
2. What problems does the bar code system have (a) for businesses in the supply chain and (b) for an internet customer who wants to buy groceries from Sainsbury's?
3. What new technologies are used by the Udex system?
4. Discuss the advantages of the Udex system.

Financial services

The financial services sector, including banks, building societies, insurance companies and the stockbrokers, has been particularly affected by new technology. A hundred years ago, all transactions had to be recorded by hand. The telephone, the postal service and the typewriter helped increase efficiency within the sector. But financial services was an industry which relied upon paper records.

ICT has transformed this. Computers allow the storage and retrieval of information which is thousands of times the quantity of what was kept when everything was on paper. The number of customers in the UK has greatly increased. The number of transactions has grown even more. Examples include the following.

- A bank customer withdraws cash from a cash machine and the amount is electronically deducted from her account.
- Money is sent electronically from a bank account in the UK to an account with a different bank in Germany.
- An insurance salesperson is able to key in details of a customer to his laptop computer and give a quote immediately.

Distribution of goods

The distribution of goods from manufacturer to customer has also been greatly affected by new technology. Computer systems allow the distribution services to be much more efficient. They allow workers to know how much stock is in place or where it is in the distribution system.

The bar code system has proved particularly useful. Retailers, for example, use it to track the flow of stock from delivery through to sale at the checkout. EPOS (Electronic Point of Sale) systems, where bar codes are swiped at the checkout, can be used to automatically reorder stock. They also speed up the recording of prices, which would take longer if carried out manually.

If customers use a loyalty card, as in a supermarket, their purchases can be analysed. This can then be used for marketing. For example, a customer who buys a lot of wine can be invited to a wine tasting evening.

Leisure, tourism and travel

A major use of new technology in leisure, tourism and travel has been in booking systems. A hotel, for example, might have its booking and billing system on computer. An airline may go further and allow tickets to be bought through a remote computer system by a travel agent, or directly by the customer over the internet.

These industries are affected by new technology in other ways. For example, a guest in a hotel may be offered satellite television in her room. Railways use computers to control signalling. Air traffic control is dependent on computers too.

Communications industries

Communications industries, like the telephone industry, have been at the forefront of the technological revolution. Computers become much more efficient when they can talk to each other. This is what lies behind the internet and the World Wide Web (☞ unit 13). It is telephone connections that have mainly made this possible. Businesses can run **intranets** between different computers in the same business. The computers may all run off a single **computer server**, as for example in a school. However, the computers still need to be cabled together. Where businesses run several sites, this is most cheaply done across telephone wires.

Mobile phones are another example of the way new technology has changed how businesses work and

people live. For example, delivery companies can keep in contact with their vehicles by mobile phone. A manager can telephone a client whilst going to work on a train. As for consumers, can keep in contact with their friends and family wherever they are.

Other service industries

Other service industries have equally been affected by new technology. In health care, for example, computers are used to manage information, from paying staff wages to setting appointments to keeping patient records. New technology has allowed better care through scans and treatment such as laser surgery. In schools, accounts and record keeping have up till now been the main use of new technology. Students, though, have also benefited. Calculators are frequently used. Education may take place in the home via email. The laptop may one day replace exercise books for writing. Information retrieval over the internet is also likely to become more common.

✓Checklist

1. Give TWO examples of information technologies and TWO of communication technologies.
2. Explain briefly how ICT has changed the financial services sector of the economy.
3. How has EPOS changed retailing?
4. Explain how ICT has changed booking and reservations in the leisure and tourism industries.
5. Explain THREE ways in which computers have changed the way in which people work.

SMS (Short Message Service) wasn't intended to be a killer application. It was created by mobile phone operators to send maintenance messages to users. Because of this limited function, it was only given a maximum of 160 characters per message. Tapping out a message to send is also a fairly tedious exercise on a key pad customised for numbers rather than letters. But an estimated 200 billion SMS messages will be sent in 2001 worldwide with numbers continuing to rise after that. SMS messaging has been particularly taken up by young people anxious to gossip and keep in touch with their friends.

Source: adapted from *The Times*, 7.5.2001.

1. SMS is a way of sending a text message from one person to another. What new technology does it use?
2. What are the similarities and differences between email and a SMS text message?
3. Mobile phone companies have suggested that they might use SMS to beam adverts to mobile phone users. These adverts would appear as messages whether customers wanted them or not. Discuss what might be the advantages and disadvantages to mobile phone companies of doing this.

key terms

ICT (Information and Communication Technology) - the use of computers to store, handle, produce and retrieve information (information technology) whilst also allowing microchip based machines to talk to each other (communication technology).

UNIT 65

Technology and efficiency

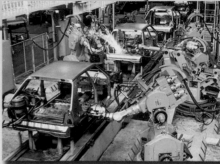

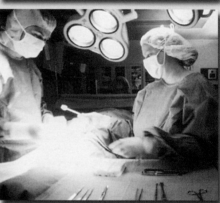

Competitiveness

Most businesses operate in **competitive markets** (☞ unit 18). They have to provide goods and services which are competitively priced. Goods must also satisfy technical standards, must be of high quality and must be delivered to customers on time. If they don't, they will lose customers. Ultimately, businesses which fail to remain efficient will be forced out of the market by more competitive businesses. Technology can play a key role in making any business efficient and competitive.

Lowering costs

Introducing new technology often leads to lower costs of production.
• New technology can reduce the

amount of labour needed in the production process. Installing a robot on a production line, for example, might replace many workers.
• Waste is reduced. For example, using CAD (Computer-Aided-Design) is likely to reduce the amount of waste in manufacturing compared to traditional hand drawn designs.
• The rate or speed of production may increase. Compared to the existing technology, the new technology may increase output using the same number of workers and factory space.

Quality

Quality is vital to any business. Technology allows businesses to produce to the necessary

Technology has improved the production of raw materials, the efficiency of manufacturing and the provision of services

Nearly all of today's television sets use a technology which is more than 100 years old. The cathode ray tube is the device which projects images onto the television screen. Since television sets were first produced, there have been a large number of refinements to the basic cathode ray tube technology. For example, in the 1950s, RCA, a US company, invented the shadowmask tube which made it practical to develop a colour television set. Since then, technologies have been invented to reduce flicker, improve colour, flatten the screen and allow for widescreen display. The move to digital technology is no threat to the cathode ray tube either since it can cope with both digital and analogue sources.

However, the cathode ray tube has one major drawback. Television sets become too heavy once screen sizes go above 37 inches. For this reason, the world's major electronics manufacturers have been working on alternatives to cathode ray tube projection. The goal is to produce a low cost television with a large screen, which is lightweight and has picture quality as good as if not better than with current cathode ray tube technology. For some years, companies such as Sony have been producing either liquid crystal display screen televisions or gas plasma televisions. But so far they have failed to break the cost and quality barriers. The company which does so could earn billions of pounds from its new technology.

Source: adapted from the *Financial Times* 4.5.2000.

1. Suggest why television manufacturers like Panasonic, JVC or Sony have spent large amounts of money over the years (a) improving existing cathode ray tube technology and (b) trying to develop alternative technologies.

specifications. The introduction of CNC (Computer Numerical Controlled) machines, for instance, has allowed manufacturing businesses to reduce the variance on work. Variance is the difference in size or weight between each component made. A 10mm bolt is unlikely to be exactly 10mm. It will be slightly longer or slightly shorter. CNC machines can reduce the differences between each bolt to, say, plus or minus 10/million mm.

Technology also allows businesses to check the quality of their output far more easily than before. This is essential in a business environment where buyers are expecting their suppliers to be working towards **zero defect** (☞ unit 57) deliveries.

Health and safety

Working conditions today in factories are much better than even 30 years ago. New technology is a major reason for this. Many dangerous and unpleasant jobs which used to be done by workers are now done by machines.

For instance, the use of lifting equipment prevents back injuries. Painting and spraying is another area where technology has transformed the workplace. Many coatings contain dangerous chemicals which, if breathed in or touched, can harm the worker. Use of fully automated spraying machines in sealed conditions means that workers do not need to be exposed to these dangers.

New products

New technology has always led to new innovative products. For example, steam technology in the 19th century led to the creation of railways. The invention of the petrol engine at the end of the 19th century led to the motor car. The microchip has led to computers, the internet, mobile phones and digital television.

New technology today has also enabled mass customisation of products (☞ unit 61). When Henry Ford set up the assembly line for the Model T Ford, customers were only offered black cars. Today, technology on a car assembly line can allow each car coming down the line to be different. In the future, offering a range of choices for a basic product is likely to be become more and more important. Customers will reward those businesses which offer them the greatest choice.

A Cannock laser cutting company has unveiled its latest piece of equipment which it hopes will continue to keep it at the forefront of the industry. Laser Process Ltd has installed a Trumpf twin headed high speed laser cutting system.

The system, the first of its kind in the UK, represents an investment of half a million pounds. The machine differs from standard machines in that it has two cutting heads which make it capable of high speed production. It also comes with a material handling system that allows for semi unmanned operation. These features mean that it will provide significant cost savings.

Lower costs will also allow the company to expand into new markets. Up till now, it was too expensive to make some cheap components using high cost laser cutting machines. The new facility will now enable the company to bid for work in these markets.

Source: adapted from the *Express & Star*, 11.9.2000.

1. Explain TWO ways in which the new laser machine will lead to lower production costs.
2. How will the new laser machine make Laser Process Ltd more competitive?
3. Discuss how other businesses in the industry might react to this investment by Laser Process Ltd.

✓Checklist

1. Why is it important for a business to be competitive?
2. Explain THREE ways in which introducing new technology could lower costs of production.
3. How can new technology help businesses approach zero defect targets?
4. How can new technologies improve health and safety in the workplace?
5. How can new technology lead to mass customisation in manufacturing?

Production and location

Industry on Merseyside - the availability of transport links and regional aid can influence location

Nearness to raw materials

Production influences the location of businesses. Businesses buy raw materials and other inputs from suppliers. In some industries, the cost of transporting these raw materials is very high. So businesses in these industries are sited near to the source of raw materials, to keep transport costs low.

In steel making, for instance, businesses use iron ore combined with energy, usually supplied by coal, to make the product. Both iron ore and coal are bulky, relatively low value products. Transport costs can be kept to a minimum if the steel works is located near to an iron ore and coal field. In Britain, the iron industry developed in the Ironbridge area of Shropshire in the 18th century because of this. Today, there are no large iron deposits left in the UK. Instead, the steel making industry is located on the coast, to take advantage of low cost, bulk delivery sea transport.

In **primary industries** (☞ unit 5), businesses have to locate their production facilities on sites where raw materials are available. A gold mine has to be located on top of gold deposits. An oil company has to put its oil rigs on top of oil fields.

Industries where costs of transporting raw materials are very small may be able to locate anywhere in the world. These industries are called FOOTLOOSE INDUSTRIES.

Nearness to markets

Some businesses have to be located near to their markets. One reason might be that the cost of transporting the finished good to the market is very high compared to the value of the good. Coca Cola, for instance, doesn't supply its drinks to other countries from one plant in the United States. To reduce costs, it has bottling plants in every country where it operates. 'Concentrated' Coca Cola is shipped to these plants, where it is changed into the finished drink and placed in cans or bottles.

Some businesses have to be near to their market because otherwise customers would not buy their products. Successful shops, for instance, tend to be sited near to places where customers drive to or walk by. Hairdressers have to be near their clients.

Closeness to the customer can also be vital for many business suppliers. Small businesses, for instance, will often buy from businesses in their local area. A small firm in Edinburgh won't, for instance, employ a Glasgow firm to do electrical repairs. Closeness is also usually essential if a business is supplying **just-in-time** (☞ unit 62) to a customer. There is a growing trend for suppliers of car parts to site themselves next to a car production plant. In some cases, the supplier is even located within the car plant to ensure instant delivery.

Industries which don't have to be located near their markets are more likely to be footloose industries.

Transport links

Transport **infrastructure**, ie motorways, airports, shipping routes, is vital to the success of any business (☞ unit 6). Transporting products quickly can reduce costs for a business. Being close to a motorway or port might reduce the time taken to transport goods over long distances. For instance, it might take a lorry two hours to travel 140 miles between two factories located just off a motorway, but four hours to travel 80 miles on congested narrow country roads. Equally, it might take weeks to send a container from London to Singapore by sea, but months for the same container to go

The Pilgrim Brewery is one of around 200 small breweries in the UK. It was set up in 1985 by David Roberts, who had previously worked for the government in the Civil Service. He started off the business in a small village called Woldingham in Sussex. His beers were sold locally because the sort of high quality beers he brewed could not be transported long distances. Three years later, he moved to Reigate, a town not far away from Woldingham. Reigate was attractive because it has particularly pure water supplies. Water is an essential ingredient of beer and pure water improves its taste.

Pilgrim Brewery's most serious problem has been getting its beers sold in pubs. Often pubs have been 'tied', which means they buy all their drinks from one large brewery. David Roberts would like to see the tax on beers from small breweries lowered. This would encourage more pubs to buy specialist beers.
Source: adapted from the *Financial Times*, 7.6.1999.

1. Explain why Pilgrim Brewery beers are sold mainly in the South East of England.
2. (a) Why did Pilgrim Brewery locate in Reigate? (b) Suggest why Pilgrim Brewery didn't transport water from Reigate to Woldingham.
3. Why might lowering the tax on beers from small breweries help Pilgrim Brewery sell more beer?

key terms

Footloose industries - industries where the costs of transporting raw materials and finished goods are relatively low, so they can be situated in a wide variety of locations.

✓Checklist

1. It costs more to transport clay to make bricks than to make the bricks themselves. Explain where a plant making bricks should be located.
2. 'Computer manufacturers are footloose.' What does this mean?
3. Give FIVE examples of businesses which need to be located near to their markets and explain why this is the case.
4. Why might being sited next to a motorway be an advantage for a manufacturer which delivers its products across the UK?
5. What types of industries tend to be sited away from large centres of population?
6. Why are businesses usually in favour of the building of better transport links?

from Moscow to Africa by road although the distance is shorter. Businesses trading with Europe may also gain an advantage over rivals by being located near to ports like Hull or Dover, or the Channel Tunnel in Folkestone.

Legal, social and environmental factors

Some businesses are forced to take legal, social and environmental factors into account when deciding where to locate production. Some production processes could cause major disasters if there was an accident. Nuclear power plants in the UK, for instance, are sited away from large centres of population because of this risk.

Local communities are increasingly unwilling to have any plant sited near them which could cause pollution. This means that it has become more difficult for firms in industries such as waste disposal or petrochemicals to find suitable sites.

The danger of pollution or accidents may even prevent a business from finding somewhere to locate. In the UK, it has been decided that the safest way to deal with nuclear waste is to store it in the ground. But the business responsible for the project has failed to find a site for this nuclear store, despite the jobs it would create in the local area.

The building of new transport infrastructure may also be a problem for industry. Because of objections from those living nearby and from environmentalists, motorway building in the UK has almost come to a halt. It is difficult to get planning permission to build extensions to major airports like Heathrow or Manchester. The result is longer journey times for goods and higher costs. Businesses may be forced to relocate if these costs become too high.

Government and location

The location of industry affects the prosperity of a region and of a

country. For example, the North East of England has had higher unemployment than the UK average for 50 years. This has led to lower than average incomes.

The UK government has tried to influence where businesses locate by giving grants and other forms of assistance. For example, a business setting up in the North East might be able to get a Regional Development Grant. Some of these grants are passed through local authorities. For example, they might be awarded a regeneration grant for part of their area. The local authority can then support schemes to attract businesses to locate in the area.

The European Union also gives funds to areas which have incomes below the European Union average. These funds are used for a variety of purposes, such as training and the building of infrastructure like new motorways. The money is given to governments, local authorities and regional organisations to distribute on its behalf.

Seabait is a company which grows ragworms. These worms are used as bait by anglers. The company packs the ragworms into cardboard boxes mixed with vermiculite to keep the worms in good condition. The dozen worms in each box are sold for £1.55 plus VAT to angling shops, which sell them on to anglers at £2.50 to £3.00. Boxes are dispatched from Seabait with guaranteed 24 hour delivery to shops because the worms will only keep for up to two weeks in best condition.

The company is located at Lynemouth, on the coast of Northumberland. The worms are grown in seawater in shallow tanks the size of football pitches. To get the ragworms to grow two to three times faster than normal, Seabait uses heated water. This comes cheaply from a power station next door. The business has strong links with Newcastle University, also in Northumberland. One of the co-founders of the company is a marine biologist at Newcastle University. He provides expert research advice on growing worms and how to deal with problems such as infection and breeding.

Since it was founded, Seabait has received government grants and loans worth £350 000. Government agencies, like British Coal Enterprise, have been willing to support the company because it is in an area of high unemployment where traditional industries like coal mining have been shrinking in size. Seabait hopes to expand in future. It wants to increase production of ragworms to reduce its average costs of production. It hopes to produce lugworms, also used in fishing. It also wants to develop worm-based feedstuffs for mainstream fish and prawn farming.

Source: adapted from the *Financial Times*, 30.1.1999.

1. (a) Where is Seabait located? (b) Explain THREE reasons why Seabait is located here.
2. Suggest the difficulties Seabait might face if it expanded its business.

Loan finance

Finance and small businesses

Jim O'Halloran has been travelling the world for the past twenty years. He has visited many countries, but his favourite was China. He found he was quite good at picking out rare or unusual gifts in the Far East. He would buy an item, such as a stone carving, and sell it on at a higher price to friends or family.

So he decided to make a business out of buying and selling. Part of the year, he would travel the world and buy whatever he thought was marketable. Then he would go back to the UK and sell the items to small gift shops or directly through fairs up and down the country.

Jim did well out of the business. But he never kept much in the way of financial reserves. He always relied on an overdraft which would see him through his foreign travels in the first half of the year. Then money would flow back in during the second half of the year as the Christmas buying season approached.

A friend suggested that Jim should cut back on his personal spending and use the money to clear his overdraft. The friend was worried about what would happen if the business did badly one year. There was a further problem that Jim had not thought about. What if he bought all these goods and then fell ill before he could start selling them in the UK?

1. Why did Jim O'Halloran need an overdraft?
2. 'Jim's overdraft limit today is £60 000.' Explain what this means.
3. Do you think that Jim's friend is giving good advice? Justify your answer by considering the advantages and disadvantages for Jim of running an overdraft.

Equity capital

Setting up in business costs money. For instance, setting up as a butcher involves buying or renting a shop, and buying stocks of meat to sell.

One source of finance for a new business is EQUITY or EQUITY CAPITAL. This is money which is put into the business by its owners. The butcher, for example, may have savings of £20 000 which are used to buy a lease on a shop and start a sole proprietorship. The butcher may go into **partnership** (☞ unit 25) with another person, with each putting in £10 000 of their own savings. Or the butcher may use the savings to set up a **private limited company** (☞ unit 27). Other people would then have to be

persuaded to invest in the company as shareholders.

It is often difficult for small and medium sized businesses to find individuals to become joint owners. When found, they are often:

- members of the family, like a parent or a relative;
- friends who can see a good business opportunity;
- people known through work;
- people who want to set up in business and also need to find someone prepared to invest in the business.

Retained profit

Once the business is running, it will hopefully make a profit. This profit is owned by the owners of the

business. Instead of being taken by the owners, profit may be kept back for use within the business. This RETAINED or UNDISTRIBUTED PROFIT could be used, for example, by the butcher to buy a second shop. Or it could be used to refit the existing shop. Or it could be used to increase the **working capital** (☞ unit 81) of the business. For instance, the business may buy more stock or have higher average balances of cash in the bank account.

Using retained profit has one advantage over borrowing or issuing new equity. The business doesn't have to make any payments on the money that is retained. It doesn't have to be repaid, so no interest or dividends are due on it.

Bank loans

Many new businesses borrow money in order to start. As they continue trading, they may need to borrow more money to survive or expand. Banks are the main source of LOANS for small businesses.

With a bank loan, the business usually borrows a fixed amount of money. It will then pay this back in regular fixed instalments. These repayments include the interest on the outstanding money owed. The bank may ask for SECURITY or COLLATERAL on the loan. This means that the business has to pledge assets to the bank. The bank can sell these assets if the business fails to repay the loan. The most common type of security is property. This could be a shop, factory or office which the business owns. For a sole trader, there is no distinction between the assets of the business and the personal assets of the owner because of unlimited liability (☞ unit 23). So owners may offer

key terms

Equity or equity capital - the monetary value of a business which belongs to the business owners. In a company this would be the value of their shares.

Loan - borrowing a sum of money which then has to be repaid with interest over a period of time, typically in fixed monthly instalments.

Mortgages - a loan where property is used as security.

Overdraft - borrowing money from a bank by drawing more money than is actually in a current account. Interest is charged on the amount overdrawn.

Retained or undistributed profit - profit which is kept back by a business and used to pay for investment in the business.

Security or collateral - assets owned by a business which are used to guarantee repayment of a loan. If the business fails to pay off the loan, the lender can sell what has been offered as security to get repayment.

Checklist

1. Why might capital be needed to start up and run a small business?
2. Who might be willing to put capital into a small business?
3. (a) What is undistributed profit?
   (b) What are the advantages to a business of using retained profit to finance investment?
4. Outline the difference between a bank loan, a mortgage and an overdraft.
5. What does it mean if a business has (a) a £20 000 overdraft limit and (b) its overdraft called in?

their own houses as security. Bank loans secured on property are called MORTGAGES.

Loans to small businesses may also be given by family relations or friends. If a business is starting up, a person may prefer to lend money rather than become a partner because of unlimited liability. If the business fails, the most a lender can lose is the value of the loan. As a part owner, they could be liable for debts of the business.

Bank overdrafts

Nearly all businesses have a current account at a bank. A business uses the cash in the account to pay its day to day bills using **cheques**. If a business has money in the account then it is said to be in the **black**. If a business spends more than it has in its account then it is said to be in the **red**.

Current accounts can be used to borrow money from a bank. There are times when a business needs to go into the red. For instance, it may need to make urgent payments. The bank can give the business an OVERDRAFT. This means that the bank will allow the business to draw out more money than it has in its

account. The maximum amount it can be overdrawn (i.e. borrow) is called its **overdraft limit**. For instance, a business might have an overdraft limit with its bank of £4 000. So long as the business stays within the £4 000 limit, the bank will pay its cheques. If it goes over the £4 000 limit, the bank could refuse to pay cheques that the business has issued. At worst, the bank could **call in** the overdraft. This means that it will demand immediate repayment of the money borrowed. Typically, this would lead to the failure of the business. It would not have the money to make the repayments.

The main advantage of an overdraft is that money is only borrowed when it is needed. This cuts down on the interest bill. Overdrafts, though, can be more expensive than they seem, particularly for a small business. Banks often charge an arrangement fee for the overdraft. They may charge a fee per quarter (three months) to maintain the overdraft limit. Banks may also make higher charges for cheques issued when the account is overdrawn.

Other sources of finance

Small businesses may also be able to obtain finance through **trade credit**, a type of borrowing. Equally they may be able to **lease** or purchase equipment using **hire purchase**. These are discussed in unit 69.

Sterling Knitwear is a business which designs and makes high-quality, hand-knitted cotton garments. Kirstie and Tom Sterling, the joint owners, design a new collection twice a year and then arrange for the garments to be made by outworkers mainly in Scotland.

An opportunity has come up for them to buy the business premises in Glasgow which they are currently renting. It is going to cost £300 000. Last year, the business made a profit of £40 000 which they intend to use for the purchase. They are also negotiating a mortgage from their bank. But the repayments on a £260 000 mortgage would put the survival of the business at risk. If sales fell sharply for whatever reason, they would be unable to keep up with the repayments.

However, their operations manager, Vishni, who deals with getting the garments made and distributed to customers, has said that she would like to take a stake in the business. Vishni is prepared to put up £100 000 in return for 20 per cent ownership of the business.

1. List the THREE ways mentioned in the article which could be used to finance the purchase of the building.
2. Why would their bank almost certainly demand collateral for its involvement in the purchase?
3. Should Kirstie and Tom accept Vishni's offer of £100 000 in return for 20 per cent of the business? In your answer argue the advantages and disadvantages of the proposal before coming to a conclusion.

Finance and large businesses

A stockbroker trading in shares of plcs

Retained profit

The most important source of finance for a large business in the UK is likely to be **retained profit** (☞ unit 67). An established business can build up profit over a number of years. If a public limited company (plc) has built up £20 million retained profit after 10 years of trading, it may not need to borrow to buy new machinery or factories.

Share capital for large businesses

Small and medium sized businesses often have difficulty raising **equity capital** (☞ unit 67).

Investors in the business tend to be friends and family. This is one of the main reasons why some medium sized businesses become **public limited companies** (☞ unit 28). A plc is able to offer shares for sale to individual investors and corporate investors like assurance companies.

When a business **goes public** (i.e. becomes a public limited company), it often offers shares in the company for sale. The money raised by the sale of these shares can then be used by the company for investment. Later, a plc may offer more shares for sale. Again, the money raised from this **share issue** is kept by the company. It may be used to finance investment.

The FLOTATION of a company is likely to be organised by a bank or a merchant bank. The bank will **place** or find buyers for the shares that are for sale. Banks are also likely to organise the sale of any further shares.

Investors may be more prepared to buy shares in a public limited company than a private limited company. This is because these shares can be sold on a **stock market**. A stock market is an organised market for the buying and selling of shares. All the shares which are bought and sold on stock markets, like the London Stock Exchange, are second hand shares. None of the money which changes hands would go to the company itself.

Types of share

Most shares issued by private and public limited companies are ORDINARY SHARES. The owners of the shares, the shareholders of the company, are entitled to receive a share of the profits. This share of the profits is called a **dividend** (☞ unit 21). The dividend can go up and down from year to year. This depends upon how much profit the company has made and how much it decides to give to its shareholders.

Limited companies can also issue PREFERENCE SHARES. These carry a fixed rate of dividend. So shareholders don't benefit from any increase in profits made by the company. However, they also don't suffer as much if the business has a bad year. In a poor trading year ordinary shareholders may receive

Big Yellow Group is a company which provides self-storage facilities. Individuals or businesses are able to rent space at one of their stores to store belongings or equipment. It floated on the Alternative Investment Market (AIM), a stock market which serves the needs of smaller public limited companies. It intended to use the money raised from the flotation to increase the number of its stores round the country.

Source: adapted from Big Yellow Group, *Share Prospectus 2000*.

1. What is the service that the Big Yellow Group offers its customers?
2. How much money did it hope to raise by floating on the Alternative Investment Market?
3. What might the money raised be used for?
4. In the prospectus, potential buyers are warned that the self-storage market could become more competitive. With more companies offering more storage space, there could be pressure on prices charged to customers to fall. If this happened, discuss what is likely to happen to (a) profits, (b) dividends and (c) the share price of the Big Yellow Group.

BIG YELLOW GROUP PLC
(Incorporated in England and Wales: Registered No. 3625199)

Admission to trading on the
ALTERNATIVE INVESTMENT MARKET
and
Placing and Offer of up to 45,470,000 Ordinary Shares
at 100p per share

Nominated Adviser and Broker
Cazenove & Co.

key terms

Debentures - a type of long term loan to a business where the loan can be bought and sold second hand on a stock exchange.

Flotation - when a business turns itself into a public limited company by selling some or all of its shares to buyers who can then trade these shares second hand on a stock exchange.

Ordinary shares - shares in a limited company where the company can vary the amount of dividend paid to shareholders depending upon the amount of profit made.

Preference shares - shares in a limited company where shareholders receive a fixed amount in £s in dividends each year. The company can choose not to pay a dividend in any one year it if feels it has not made enough profit. If dividends are paid, preference shareholders take priority over ordinary shareholders.

✓ Checklist

1. What is the most important source of finance for most large businesses?
2. What is meant if a company (a) goes public and (b) floats its shares on a stock exchange?
3. Explain the difference between an ordinary share and a preference share.
4. What is the difference between a debenture and a share?
5. Explain what is meant by a 'sale and lease back' agreement.

no dividend. But preference shareholders may be paid because they are entitled to the first share of any profits made by the company.

Borrowing money

Like small businesses, large businesses may borrow money from banks. **Loans** and **overdrafts** (☞ unit 67) are the most common way in which large businesses borrow money.

Large public limited companies can also borrow money through the City of London. They do this by issuing DEBENTURES (also called **stocks or bonds**). These are usually long term loans, normally for between 5 and 25 years. Interest has to be paid on the loan. A debenture where the money borrowed is in another currency is called a **Eurobond**. For instance, ICI, a UK company, might borrow German deutschmarks to finance the building of a chemical plant in Germany. Large private limited companies can also issue debentures. They are typically bought by banks.

Other sources of internal finance

Another way for a large business to raise money is to sell its assets. For instance, an expanding business might sell a factory and use the money to buy large premises. Large businesses might be able to negotiate a **sale and lease-back** scheme. Here, the business sells some or all of its property to another company, like a property company. At the same time, it signs an agreement to lease (i.e. rent) back the property for a fixed annual rent. The business receives a lump sum of money, which can be used to pay for expansion. The drawback is that the business now has to pay rent on the property.

Other sources of finance

Large businesses have other sources of finance available to them. These include **trade credit, factoring, leasing and hire purchase, and grants** (☞ unit 69).

Manganese Bronze is an engineering company with two core businesses. It makes the famous black London taxi cabs. It also has a components division. This produces bus doors and ramps, as well as metal powders and high quality cast parts for the motor and other industries.

In the financial year to 31 July 2000, Manganese Bronze retained profit of £1.14 million. Its net borrowings fell from £4 million to £2.9 million. The company's overdraft facility remained the same at £3 million, although it ended the year with £2.3 million in cash in its bank account.

During the year it continued to invest in new developments. It purchased property in London for £1.3 million which was used to sell taxis to taxi drivers. The property before had been leased (i.e. rented) from landlords. Research and development expenditure increased to £1.5 million. Research was concentrated on the components division and on developments to reduce exhaust emissions from taxis.

Source: adapted from Manganese Bronze Holdings plc, *Annual Report and Accounts*, 2000.

1. Suggest why Manganese Bronze (a) retained profit of £1.14 million rather than distributing it to its shareholders and (b) had an overdraft facility of £3 million when it had £2.3 million in the bank at the end of the year.
2. The company reduced its borrowings to £2.9 million. Discuss the advantages and disadvantages of this to the company and its shareholders.

Other sources of finance

Re Style GRANT

Grants may be available to help a company improve property

Trade credit

Businesses often get TRADE CREDIT from suppliers. Typically, a business does not have to pay for goods until one month after they have been delivered. Trade credit is a form of 'loan' from a supplier to a business buying goods. The advantage of trade credit to the business buying the goods is that this loan is free of interest charges. Also, the more a business buys, the more trade credit it is likely to get. So trade credit is a way of increasing the **working capital** (☞ unit 81) of the business.

There are disadvantages of trade credit to a business buying supplies. Suppliers may stop selling goods to a business if it owes too much money. They may be afraid that the business is in danger of going bankrupt or into liquidation, leaving unpaid debts. Also, there is no point in getting free credit for a month to order supplies if they are not going to be used. Further, a business getting trade credit is likely to be giving trade credit too. So a business will need to have the funds to offer credit to other businesses.

A problem for suppliers is that there may be costs involved in giving trade credit. For instance, some suppliers give discounts if their customers pay bills immediately.

Factoring

A business might use a FACTOR to reduce the amount of money it has to borrow on overdraft. A factor is a specialist finance company, often owned by a larger bank. It collects the money which is owed to a business on trade credit. The factor then charges a fee for its services.

The factor will advance (or pay) money to the business even if an invoice (a bill) hasn't been paid by a customer. The business is therefore guaranteed regular payment of its invoices. It also doesn't have to employ staff to chase and collect those bills. However, a factor will only give the business a percentage of the value of the invoice, usually 80 per cent, if it is unpaid. The other 20 per cent is given when its customers pay the factor. The advantage of using a factor is that it speeds up the **flow of cash** (☞ unit 74) through a business.

Leasing and hire purchase

If a business needs equipment, like a

Johnsons is a private limited company that manufactures plastic housings for videos and DVDs. It has grown rapidly in the last few years, but many of the businesses it supplies pay slowly or late. It is considering whether to use a factoring service to chase businesses that have not paid for deliveries.

1. How could RSB Commercial Services help Johnsons?

2. What might be the disadvantages to Johnsons of using RSB Commercial Services?

3. Johnsons could increase the amount of cash it has by increasing its bank overdraft. Do you think this would be better for the business than using the help of RSB Commercial Services?

Factoring

Bridge the cashflow gap and move your business forward

THE CLIENT RECEIVES
- An immediate injection of up to 90% of the value of approved trade debts unpaid on the date that the factoring agreement commences.
- The same level of finance on all approved invoices created during the life of the factoring agreement.
- A complete sales ledger service from RBS Commercial Services, who issue statements and reminder letters to customers and make telephone calls on overdue debts when appropriate.
- The FacFlow computer link which enables the client to see, on his/her own PC, the amount of finance available each day, to draw finance if required, and to see or print reports on individual customers and the whole sales ledger. It also enables the client to communicate with RBS Commercial Services by email.
- For a small extra charge RBS Commercial Services will provide credit advice on existing and new customers and bad debt protection on all approved accounts.

CRITERIA
The business must be creating suitable trade debts by selling goods or services to other businesses on credit terms of up to 120 days. Typically trade debts should not be concentrated in the hands of less than five current customers. It must be forecasting sales of over £300,000 in the next 12 months and be making adequate profits. Most manufacturing, service and distribution business are suitable.
Unsuitable businesses include the building and construction industry and its sub-contractors, most businesses involved in stage payments, retentions or advance payments.

CHARGES
RBS Commercial Services charge a service fee, which is typically between 1% and 2.5% of the value of every invoice. A discounting charge is made on all finance drawn by the client at a competitive rate and charged on a similar basis to that of a business overdraft.
Source: Royal Bank of Scotland.

key terms

Factor - a business which collects the debts of other businesses, for which it charges a fee.
Hire purchase - legally, renting equipment prior to buying it. In effect, it is a type of loan.
Leasing - renting equipment or premises.
Trade credit - where a supplier gives a customer of a period of time to pay a bill (or invoice) for goods once they have been sent.
Venture capital - money which is used by a venture capitalist to buy a share of what is hoped to be a growing business.

✔Checklist

1. Explain how a business can borrow money free of interest from other businesses.
2. How can a factor help a business increase the amount of cash it holds?
3. What are the differences between leasing and hire purchase?
4. How might a venture capitalist help a business?
5. Why might the government or the EU give a grant to a business?

photocopier or a company car, it could LEASE (i.e. rent) instead of buying outright. Leasing is therefore a way of financing investment in a business.

Many leasing contracts include maintenance contracts. This is where the leasing company maintains and repairs the machines as part of the price of the rental. Leasing equipment is usually more expensive over the lifetime of the machine than buying it outright. On the other hand, it could work out cheaper if the leasing firm can buy machines in bulk and pass on the discount to customers. There can also be tax advantages to renting equipment rather than buying outright.

Maintenance contracts included in a leasing deal can be expensive. But they may reduce the risk of sudden large bills if the machine breaks down.

HIRE PURCHASE is an alternative way of borrowing money. If a business bought a photocopier on hire purchase, it would pay a fixed number of instalments. Legally, each instalment is a rental payment. A **finance house**, a type of bank which specialises in hire purchase deals, would own the photocopier until the last instalment was made.

Venture capital

If a company is growing and its sales turnover is in millions of pounds, it might attract a venture capitalist to invest in the business. VENTURE CAPITAL companies specialise in buying shares of small but growing businesses, most of which are private limited companies. The venture capitalist hopes that in 3-5 years the business will have grown further and it will be able to sell its shareholding at a profit. For the business, the venture capitalist can provide much needed funds to invest in expansion. The original owners will own a smaller share of the business. But they hope that this smaller share will be much more valuable after a while because of the growth of the company.

Grants

Grants to businesses are given by a wide number of bodies. In the UK these include the UK government, through local Learning and Skills Councils, Princes Youth Business Trust and the European Union.

Grants are offered by Learning and Skills Councils to unemployed people who set up their own businesses. They also provide training and support. Other grants are available to businesses which operate in areas of low income and high unemployment.

Wayne Spooner had worked for a firm of metal finishers for ten years before he decided to set up in business on his own. The business specialised in metal polishing, chrome, nickel, stain and gold plating both for decorative and industrial finishing. Initially, he relied heavily on a bank loan he obtained, an overdraft and a Princes Youth Business Trust grant. When he approached suppliers, they were initially cautious. With no trading record, they were reluctant to give him any trade credit. They insisted on being paid before delivery of goods. But his gas and electricity suppliers, as well as BT, sent bills in arrears, which helped. Having survived for six months, he began to insist that his suppliers give him 30 days trade credit.

He was able to use the extra credit to buy in more supplies. It also helped reduce the pressure on his overdraft which had been threatening to go over his agreed limit with the bank. However, two years on, his most important customer went into receivership owing him £60 000 in trade credit that Wayne had given. He was told that he was unlikely to get any of the money back. His bank immediately put pressure on him to reduce his overdraft. Worse still, word got around his suppliers that he could be in serious financial trouble. Some suppliers began to insist that they would only sell him new supplies if he had paid all existing invoices owing to them.

1. How did obtaining trade credit help Wayne's business?
2. What problems did Wayne face because his most important customer went into receivership?
3. Discuss TWO ways in which Wayne could deal with the problems he now faces.

The choice of finance

External and internal sources of finance

EXTERNAL SOURCES OF FINANCE are those sources which are available from outside the business. They include borrowing from a bank, issuing shares and leasing. Typically, external sources of finance cost the business money. For instance, interest is charged on a loan. Dividends have to paid be on issued shares.

INTERNAL SOURCES OF FINANCE are those sources which are available from within the business. The main internal source of funds is retained profit. Keeping profit back for investment may lead to little extra cost for the business. It doesn't have to pay interest to lenders, for instance. But there is an opportunity cost (☞ unit 2) for the owners. If profit is retained, it means it cannot be paid out to them as owners. They have to give up a distribution of profits **now** for possible bigger gains **in future**. The risk for owners is that the retained profit will not help the business be more profitable in future. The money will then have been wasted.

When deciding whether to use internal or external funds, the owners of the business have to weigh up the costs and risks of each type of finance.

The use of finance

Different sources of finance are used for different types of investment in a business. In general, short term finance is used to pay for an increase in **cash** and **working capital** (☞ unit 81). Short term finance is money which often has to be repaid quickly. It includes overdrafts from banks and trade credit. A business may also raise **equity** (☞ unit 67) to increase its cash and working capital. For instance, when owners put money into a business, this may be used to increase the holdings of cash or the stocks of goods.

The purchase of **fixed capital** (☞ unit 79), such as equipment or buildings, is often financed using longer term methods. These might include bank loans, the issue of debentures, leasing, hire purchase and grants. Money raised through new equity could also be used for investment in equipment and buildings.

Cost

Different types of financing have different costs. Borrowing money means that interest has to be paid. Leasing a company car costs the hire of the lease. Issuing new shares means that extra dividends will have to be paid. Cost is a major factor which affects the type of finance a business will choose.

Risk

If a company had a loan from a bank it would have to pay interest. But a limited company can issue new shares and retain profit to increase its finance. Dividends to shareholders don't have to be given if profits fall or the company makes a loss. So borrowing is perhaps riskier than increasing the capital of the business.

One way of measuring this risk is

Table 70.1 shows how a sample of 189 small businesses in Essex and Hertfordshire financed new working and fixed capital. For instance, 151 out of the 189 businesses surveyed had an overdraft. 38.1 per cent of the businesses leased equipment.

1. What was the most popular way for firms to finance themselves?
2. What is the difference between leasing and hire purchase?
3. What 'other' methods of finance might there be which 11 of the businesses surveyed used?

Wordprocessing

4. The shareholders of a small furniture manufacturing business need money to finance expansion of their private limited company. They were thinking of issuing more shares in the business. Then they read the report in the *Business Banking Review* and saw the table. They noticed that very few businesses use share issues as a method of financing. Write a report, preferably word processed, (a) explaining why this might be the case and (b) arguing that share issues have many advantages over other methods of financing.

Type of finance	Number	Per cent
Overdraft	151	79.9
Loan	75	39.7
Leasing	72	38.1
Hire purchase	62	32.8
Share issues	11	5.8
Factoring	5	2.6
Other	11	5.8

Table 70.1 *Sources of finance*
Source: Survey of small companies in Essex and Hertfordshire, *Business Banking Review*.

to calculate the GEARING RATIO. This is the ratio of loans to the total capital of the business (loans + share capital). A company with more loans than share capital is said to be **high geared**. This is very risky. A business with loans of £1 million and share capital of £4 million is said to be **low geared**. This is relatively safe.

Availability of finance

Some types of finance are available to most businesses.

- Businesses, except those starting up, can use retained profit.
- Bank loans and overdrafts are frequently used. Smaller businesses, such as sole proprietorships, often complain that they are charged much higher rates of interest on loans and overdrafts than larger businesses. Banks justify this by arguing that smaller businesses are more likely to go bankrupt or into liquidation than larger businesses. Hence, lending to a smaller business is more risky. So banks have to charge higher rates of interest to make the same rate of profit overall compared to lending to larger businesses.
- Trade credit, hire purchase, leasing and factoring are also possibilities.
- Smaller businesses, like sole proprietors or partnerships, have difficulty finding people or businesses who might inject capital. So they tend to rely on borrowing money rather than raising equity.
- Private limited companies can issues shares, but they tend to be sold to a small number of people, often family or friends. Plcs can sell shares to the general public, often through stock exchanges. This puts them in contact with large numbers of potential investors.

✓Checklist

1. Explain what type of finance would be most suitable for (a) a new factory; (b) a company car; (c) an increase in purchases of components; (d) the takeover of another company; (e) an increase in the number of workers employed; (f) the setting up of a new subsidiary company.
2. Explain why the following might be considered poor business practice. (a) A small business buys a £50 000 new machine and finances it by increasing its overdraft. (b) A hotel business takes out a loan for £30 000 repayable over five years to pay for increased staff costs during very busy holiday months in July and August. (c) A business takes out a mortgage on its factory repayable over fifteen years to pay for a £30 000 company car for the chairperson.
3. Why wouldn't the following happen? (a) A sole proprietor issues shares in her company to finance an increase in working capital. (b) A partnership issues debentures on the Stock Exchange. (c) A public limited company negotiates a £400 loan from its bankers.
4. Explain why large businesses are likely to have a greater choice of finance than small businesses.

Watford Automotive Electricals (WAE) is a company which supplies electrical and electronic components, mainly to the motor industry. Its single largest customer in 2000 was MG Rover, which accounted for 30 per cent of its sales turnover.

The October 2000 announcement by MG Rover came as a blow to WAE. Suppliers were told that in future MG Rover would only pay its bills after 90 days instead of the current norm of 60 days. WAE, along with other suppliers, would be forced to give another 30 days trade credit to MG Rover.

WAE had already been hit by falling sales to MG Rover because the car company had cut production. For instance, MG Rover said that it would only be producing 1 000 a month of its Rover 75 cars in the three months to December 2000. This compared with 1 000 a week the previous year when the company was owned by BMW.

The finance director at WAE has put forward a number of alternative ways of dealing with this crisis. First, the company could accept the new trade credit terms. WAE would then have to raise finance of £3 million to cover this. Second, the company could accept the new terms but seek alternative customers as quickly as possible. This strategy would lead to MG Rover ceasing to be a customer of WAE. In the short term, however, there would still be a need to raise £3 million to cover the immediate loss of 30 days trade credit. Third, the company could refuse MG Rover's terms and insist on continued payment within 60 days. The risk is that MG Rover will cancel its contracts with WAE.

Source: adapted from the *Financial Times*, 3.10.2000.

1. Explain TWO ways in which WAE has been hit by the problems at MG Rover.
2. There are various ways in which the £3 million could be raised by WAE if the first alternative is accepted. They are to increase WAE's overdraft, to seek a bank loan and to issue new shares. Discuss which of these might be the best way of raising £3 million for the company.
3. Discuss which of the three alternatives presented in the data could be the best solution to the problems posed to WAE by MG Rover.

Profit and revenue

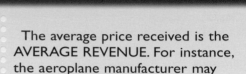
Revenue earned by selling goods

Profit

Businesses need to make a profit if they are to survive in the long term. Profit is the difference between the value of what the company sells and its costs of production. This is calculated over a period of time, like six months or a year.

Profit = sales revenue - costs

In practice, there are many types of **profit**. Businesses have gross profit, net profit, profit before tax and profit after tax (☞ unit 77). Each of these has a precise definition. But all of them are a measure of some type of revenue minus some type of cost.

Sales revenue or sales turnover

The value of the sales of a business can be given a number of different names. These include REVENUE or SALES REVENUE or TURNOVER or SALES TURNOVER. All of these terms mean the same thing. Sales revenue can be calculated in different ways.

Adding up the value of each sale An aircraft manufacturer may sell three aeroplanes in a month. The first may be sold for £12 million, the second for £10 million and the third for £8 million. Its sales revenue for the month would be £30 million (£12 million + £10 million + £8 million). This is its TOTAL REVENUE.

Multiplying the average price of a sale with the number sold The aircraft manufacturer might predict that it will sell 100 aeroplanes at an average price of £10 million each next year. The estimated sales revenue would then be £1 000 million (£10 million x 100).

The average price received is the AVERAGE REVENUE. For instance, the aeroplane manufacturer may

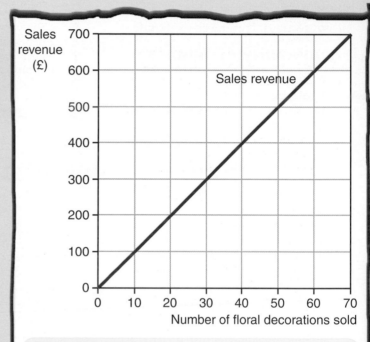

Figure 71.1 *Sales revenue*

Lincat Group plc is an engineering company which manufactures commercial catering and bar equipment. Europower plc is an engineering company which manufactures rubber and thermoplastic hose and couplings.

1. Calculate the profit for Lincat Group plc for each year between 1996 and 2000.
2. Calculate the costs for Europower plc for each year between 1996 and 2000.
3. Which company do you think performed best over the period 1996-2000 and why?
4. Between 1998 and 2000, the value of the pound was very high. This meant that it was difficult for companies to increase exports and many were forced to reduce their prices to remain competitive in overseas markets. Explain which of the two companies may have been most affected by this.

					£ million
	1996	1997	1998	1999	2000
Sales	24.6	24.1	24.4	24.2	25.8
Costs	22.7	21.5	19.5	19.0	20.3

Table 71.1 *Lincat Group plc, turnover and costs for each year to 30 June*
Source: adapted from Lincat Group plc, *Annual Report and Accounts.*

					£ million
	1996	1997	1998	1999	2000
Sales	40.0	38.6	38.6	30.1	30.9
Profit[2]	2.6	2.6	1.5	1.2	(0.3)

1. Brackets around a number in accounts mean that it is a minus number. So profit of (0.3) million means that the company has made a loss of 0.3 million.
2. Profit on ordinary activities before taxation.

Table 71.2 *Europower plc, turnover and profit[1] for each year to 29 June*
Source: adapted from Europower plc, *Annual Report and Accounts.*

Checklist

1. How is profit calculated?
2. A business increases its profit but costs also increase. What must have happened?
3. A business sells dresses at an average price of £10. What is the sales turnover of the business if its weekly sales are (a) 10 dresses, (b) 100 dresses and (c) 898 dresses?
4. The monthly turnover of a company is £2 million. The turnover of its tractor division was £1/2 million. What was the monthly turnover of the rest of the company?
5. A business has sent off a quote to a customer for a new contract. The quote was for £1 million. Explain why the marginal revenue of the company would be £1 million if it won the contract.
6. (a) A business has a customer which is currently buying 20 000 products a year for a total of £90 000. What is its average revenue for this customer? (b) (i) The customer has offered to increase its order to 25 000 products a year and is prepared to pay a total of £100 000. What is the marginal revenue to be received for the extra 5 000 products? (ii) Suggest whether the business should accept the increased order.

key terms

Average revenue - total revenue divided by the number of products sold.
Marginal revenue - the revenue gained from the sale of an extra product or unit of output.
Sales revenue or revenue or sales turnover or turnover - the money value of the sale of products by a business.
Total revenue - the sum of all the revenues from sales.

Beth Clarkstone runs a business selling pots of organic yoghurt to retailers and wholesalers. Last year, she sold 4 million pots and received £2 million.

1. (a) What was the sales revenue for Beth's business?
   (b) Calculate the average revenue per pot of the business.
   (c) If average revenue stayed unchanged, how many sales would she have to make in order to achieve sales revenues of (i) £4 million and (ii) £5 million?
2. A customer wants to increase its order from 10 000 pots a year to 15 000. The total revenue from the order will increase from £6 000 to £8 700.
   (a) What is the marginal revenue of the order? (b) Has the average revenue increased or fallen as a result of the new contract? Explain your answer.
   (c) Suggest, using the concept of economies of scale, why Beth may be prepared to accept the terms of the new contract.

only sell 50 aircraft in a year and receive total revenue of £1 000 million. Its average revenue received per aircraft would then be £20 million (£1 000 million ÷ 50).

Showing sales revenue on a graph

Sales revenue can be shown on a graph. A business might sell flower arrangements for £10 each. As the number of sales rises, so does sales revenue. In Figure 71.1, the sales revenue line rises from left to right.
- When the number of sales is zero, so is sales revenue.
- When the number of sales is 10, sales revenue is £100 (10 x £10).
- When the number of sales is 50, sales revenue is £500 (50 x £10).

Marginal revenue

The aircraft manufacturer might sell another aircraft to one of its customers for £15 million. This would be MARGINAL REVENUE for the business. Marginal revenue is the revenue gained from the last or extra sale.
- Marginal revenue can affect the

decisions made by businesses. For example, the aircraft manufacturer may have to decide whether to accept a new contract from a customer. The customer currently buys 10 aircraft a year from the business. If the price is £10 million per aircraft (the average revenue), the total revenue from the contract would be £100 million per year (£10 million x 10). The customer would like to increase its order to 12 aircraft per year. But it wants the aircraft manufacturer to reduce its price to £9 million per aircraft. Should it accept?

One way of deciding is to look at the marginal revenue from the order.
- The new contract would bring in a total revenue of £108 million (£9 million x 12).
- The old contract was worth £100 million.
- The extra or marginal revenue is just £8 million (£108 million - £100 million).

The aircraft manufacturer is almost certain to refuse. For supplying two extra aircraft, it will only receive an extra £8 million. This is unlikely to be profitable.

Costs

Wages of administration staff, excluding overtime and bonuses, are fixed costs. Materials used in production are variable costs

Business costs

Businesses have to pay out money for everything from wages to electricity bills to supplies. These costs can be split up in a number of different ways.

Fixed and variable costs

One way of classifying costs is into fixed costs and variable costs.

Fixed costs FIXED COSTS are costs which do not vary with the amount that the business produces (its **output**). For instance, a business may rent offices. The rent doesn't change if output goes up or down. Or a business may employ staff to deal with messages by phone, fax or email. Their wages will stay the same whatever the output of the business. Fixed costs may include:

- rent, mortgage repayments, business rates and insurance on premises;
- the wages, excluding overtime payments, and bonuses of permanent workers of a business;
- electricity, gas and telephone charges.

Fixed costs have to be paid even if nothing is produced. If a company closed down for six weeks over the Christmas period, it would still have to pay all its fixed costs during this period.

Fixed costs can be shown on a graph as in Figure 72.1. Costs are shown on the vertical axis and output on the horizontal axis. The fixed cost line is horizontal. This is because fixed costs stay the same however much is produced. Fixed costs for this business are £4 million if the business produces nothing, 2 million or 4 million units.

Variable costs VARIABLE COSTS are costs which change as output changes. For instance, a chocolate

manufacturer would use more cocoa beans if output of chocolate bars increased. Variable costs may include:

- raw materials and other inputs to the production process;
- overtime and bonus payments to staff which are linked to output and sales.

If a business produces nothing because it shuts down over the Christmas period then its variable cost for this period will be zero.

Variable costs can be shown on a graph as in Figure 72.2. Assume each unit costs £2. The variable cost line rises as output rises. If the business produces 2 million units, its variable costs will be £4 million (2 million x £2). If it produces 4 million units, its variable costs will be £8 million (4 million x £2).

Total costs TOTAL COSTS are the sum of these different types of cost. It is usual to assume that all costs are fixed or variable. So total costs equal fixed costs plus variable costs. A total cost line is shown in Figure 72.3. It is drawn by adding together the fixed and variable cost lines. If output is zero, total costs are

£4 million (the fixed costs). If output is 2 million units, total costs are £8 million (£4 million + £4 million). If output is 4 million units, total costs are £12 million (£4 million+ £8 million).

Direct and indirect costs

Some fixed costs are called OVERHEAD COSTS or INDIRECT COSTS. Other costs are then called DIRECT COSTS.

Direct costs are the direct costs of producing a good or service. For a steel manufacturer, the direct costs might be:

- raw materials like iron ore;
- the wages of production workers;
- the cost of plant and machinery like blast furnaces.

If output of goods or services rises, so do these direct costs.

Indirect costs are all the other costs of the business, which are not linked directly to production. For instance, for a steel manufacturer, these could include:

- all the office administration costs;
- sales costs like the cost of a sales

A cinema today offers a variety of services to its customers. What brings the customers into the cinema are the films being shown. But there will also be refreshments on offer, including popcorn and soft drinks. Then there is the merchandise area where film-associated products are sold.

1. Explain what you think the fixed costs of a cinema might be.
2. Explain what might be their variable costs.
3. (a) Suggest TWO ways in which a cinema could increase its revenues.
   (b) What are the likely effects of these suggestions on (i) fixed costs and (ii) variable costs?

key terms

Average costs - the total costs divided by the number of products made.
Capital expenditure - costs associated with the purchase of machines, equipment and buildings and other forms of capital.
Direct costs - costs associated with the production of a good or service such as raw materials and the wages of production workers.
Fixed costs - costs which remain the same whatever the level of output of the business.
Marginal cost - the cost of producing an additional unit of output.
Overhead or indirect costs - costs that are not associated directly with production. Examples include administration and marketing costs.
Revenue expenditure - costs associated with the day to day running of the business and its production.
Total costs - all the costs incurred by a business over a period of time. They are equal to fixed cost plus variable cost.
Variable costs - costs which vary directly with the output of the business.

force and advertising;

• the wage costs of managers and directors.

Even if output rises, these costs may not.

Direct costs are often the same as variable costs, but not always. For example, the wages of production workers (a direct cost) are often classified as fixed costs because businesses don't necessarily sack workers when output falls. Equally, indirect costs are often the same as

fixed costs but not always. For example, some firms spend a proportion of their sales revenue on advertising. This makes it into a variable cost. But advertising is an indirect cost of production.

Total, average and marginal costs

Total costs are all the costs of a business over a period of time. AVERAGE COSTS are the average costs of production. They are calculated by dividing total costs by the number of goods produced. So if a business had total costs of £12 million and produced 4 million units, the average cost of each unit would be £3 (£12 million ÷ 4 million).

MARGINAL COST is the cost of producing an extra unit. For instance, a small business may have total costs of £20 000 and be producing 20 units. If total costs were £22 000 when production rose to 21 units, then the marginal cost of the extra unit is £2 000.

Revenue and capital expenditure

Another way of dividing up costs is to distinguish between revenue and capital expenditure. REVENUE EXPENDITURE is the cost of the day to day running of the business and its production. CAPITAL EXPENDITURE is the cost of the

purchase of machines, equipment and buildings and other forms of **capital** (☞ unit 1).

The distinction between revenue expenditure and capital expenditure is important when a business draws up its **accounts** for the year.

Checklist

1. What is the difference between a fixed cost and a variable cost?
2. Identify (a) TWO fixed costs and (b) TWO variable costs which a music shop is likely to face.
3. Which of the following are likely to be (i) fixed costs and (ii) variable costs for a garden centre: (a) fertiliser; (b) a new car park; (c) ice creams; (d) plant pots; (e) the manager's salary; (f) a new potting shed; (g) new tables and chairs for the restaurant?
4. A new contract raises the total yearly sales of a business from £20 000 to £22 000. (a) What is the new total revenue? (b) What was the average revenue per unit if 10 units were produced when yearly sales were £20 000? (c) 11 units are produced when sales are £22 000. What is the marginal cost of this 11th unit?

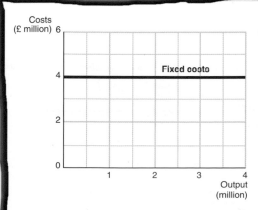

Figure 72.1 *Fixed costs: the fixed costs of a business are £4 million per year*

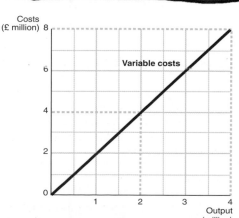

Figure 72.2 *Variable costs: the variable costs per year of a business are £2 per unit produced*

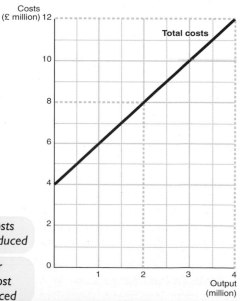

Figure 72.3 *Total costs: the total costs per year of a business are equal to the fixed cost plus the variable cost of £2 per unit produced*

UNIT 73

Break-even

Breaking even

A business can make a profit or a loss. A profit is when revenues are greater than costs. A loss is when revenues are less than costs. But there is another possibility. Revenues could exactly equal costs. If this happens, the business is at its BREAK-EVEN point.

For instance, look at Table 73.1. It shows the revenues and costs of a business which manufactures CDs.

Total revenue The business sells the CDs at £2 each. This £2 is the sales revenue per CD. So, if it sells 1 million CDs, its total revenue will be £2 million (£2 x 1 million). If it sells 6 million CDs, its total revenue will be £12 million (£2 x 6 million).

Total fixed costs These are costs which do not change as output changes (☞ unit 72). Whether the business produces 1 million or 6 million, fixed costs remain the same. Total fixed costs are £6 million.

Variable costs These are costs which change directly with output (☞ unit 72). The variable cost per CD is £0.50. So if output is 1 million, total variable cost is £0.5 million (£0.50 x 1 million). If output is 6 million, total variable cost is £3 million (£0.50 x 6 million).

Total costs These are fixed costs plus variable costs. When output is 2 million CDs, fixed costs are £6 million and variable costs are £1 million. So total costs are £7 million.

Break-even point Table 73.1 shows that the break-even level of output is 4 million CDs. At this level of output, total revenue equals total costs. Total revenue is £8 million (£2 x 4 million) and total costs are also £8 million (fixed cost of £6 million plus variable cost of £2 million).

Break-even charts

The information in Table 73.1 can be shown on a graph, as in Figure 73.1. This is called a BREAK-EVEN CHART. The shape of the total revenue and cost lines were explained in units 71 and 72.

Total revenue The total revenue line starts at 0. The business has no sales, so there is no revenue. The line rises as each sale brings in an extra £2 revenue. So if sales were 6 million, revenue would be £12 million.

Total costs The total cost line does not start at 0. Whatever the number of sales, there will always be fixed costs of £6 million. So the **total fixed cost** line is a straight horizontal line across the chart. The **total variable cost** line does increase as sales increase. It is equal to the distance between the total cost line and the total fixed cost line. In this case, it is equal to total cost minus £6 million. The **total cost line** is equal to the sum of total fixed cost and total variable cost. It starts at £6 million and then rises. If sales were 6 million, total costs would be £9 million.

Break-even, profit and loss The break-even point is where the total cost and total revenue lines cross. This is at a sales level of 4 million. Total costs and total revenue are both £8 million. To the right of the point, the business will make a profit. To the left it will make a loss.

Sales (million)	Total revenue (Average price, £2, x quantity sold	Total fixed cost	Total variable cost (£0.50 x quantity sold)	Totalcost (fixed cost + variable cost)	Profit/loss (Total revenue minus total cost)
					£ million
1	2.0	6.0	0.5	6.5	-4.5
2	4.0	6.0	1.0	7.0	-3.0
3	6.0	6.0	1.5	7.5	-1.5
4	**8.0**	**6.0**	**2.0**	**8.0**	**0.0**
5	10.0	6.0	2.5	8.5	1.5
6	12.0	6.0	3.0	9.0	3.0

Table 73.1 Break-even point

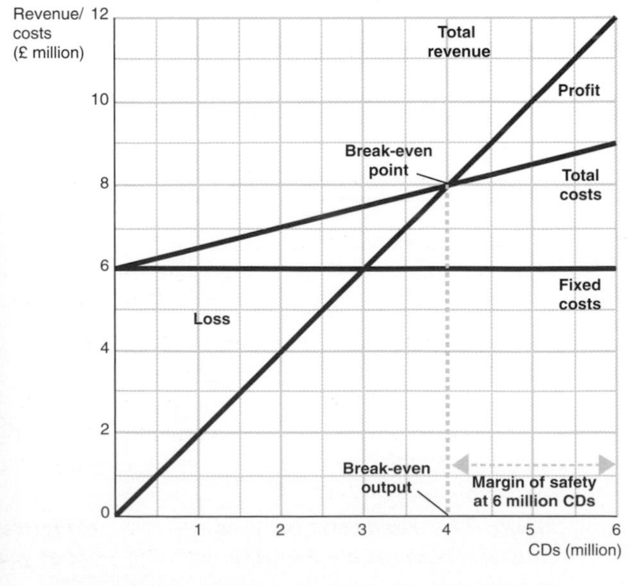

Figure 73.1 Break-even chart

If sales were 6 million, the business would make a profit of £3 million (£12 million - £9 million).

Margin of safety The number of sales above the break-even point is known as the MARGIN OF SAFETY. It is the range of output over which a profit can be made. If sales were 6 million CDs, the margin of safety would be 2 million CDs (6 million - 4 million).

Using break-even charts

Break-even charts can be used by a business to measure how well it has done in the past. For instance, a business might compare its margin of safety last year with the year before. However, break-even charts are mainly used to predict what might happen in the future. There are many examples of situations where this would helpful.

- A business may be making a loss. It would then be interested to know by how much sales would need to rise for it to break even. Or it may want to know by how much it needs to cut costs to break even.
- A business may want to launch a

new product. How many does it need to sell if it is to break even?
- A business may be starting up. It might apply for a loan from a bank. The bank might want to know when and at what level of sales the business thinks it will break even.

Problems of using break-even

Break-even charts appear easy to use. But they need to be treated with caution. It is not always possible to predict what will happen to revenues or costs as output increases. A business may predict that its costs will increase by 10 per cent if it increases output by 20 per cent. But there is not certain to happen.

They also take no account of sudden events. A sharp increase in wages or oil prices could make estimates of costs wrong. A further

Checklist

1. Explain the relationship between total variable cost, total fixed costs and total cost.
2. Three lines are normally drawn on a break-even chart. What are they?
3. Why is the fixed cost line on a break-even chart horizontal?
4. How much profit does a business make at its break-even point?
5. A business is currently producing 1 000 units per week and it is making a profit. Its break-even point is 600 units per week. (a) What is its margin of safety? (b) How would its margin of safety change if the break-even point (i) rose to 800 units and (ii) dropped to 300 units?
6. Why do businesses calculate break-even points?
7. What are the problems with using break-even charts to make decisions?

problem is that they assume everything produced is sold. But a business may build up stocks of goods to use at a later time.

Salma Chaudhry and Lisa Graham are web designers. They have come up with the idea of setting up a dot.com company which sells wacky birthday presents for teenagers and 'twentysomethings'. Their web site would be funny and show the presents 'in action' if they have moving parts. They advertise that it would be 'the place to hang out on the net'. They have done some quick calculations. The fixed costs of running the web site, hiring premises and wages for themselves would be £36 000 a year. The average spending per item bought by customers would be £12. Half of this, £6, would be the variable costs to the company of buying the stock and selling it.

Spreadsheet and graphics

1. Draw up a table of costs and revenues for the website similar to Table 73.2. Calculate figures for sales per year of 2 000, 4 000, 6 000, 8 000 and 10 000 items.
2. (a) From your table, draw a break-even chart.
   (b) Mark on it the break-even point.
3. Salma wants to know what would happen to the break-even point if the two founders of the company paid themselves an extra £6 000 a year each. (a) Show this by drawing a new break-even chart. (b) What is the new break-even point?
4. Salma and Lisa have drawn up a business plan to show their bank manager. They want to borrow £40 000 to start up the company. (a) If you were the bank manager looking at their proposal, what questions would you ask about their break-even calculations? (b) Do you think you would give them the loan? Justify your answer.

Number of customers	Total revenue	Total fixed cost	Total variable cost	Total cost	Profit £
2 000					
4 000					
6 000					
8 000					
10 000					

Table 73.2

Cash flow into and out of a business

How cash flows through a business

Cash flows through all businesses. It comes in and it goes out. Table 74.1 shows the flow of cash through a business during one month, July

Receipts The total flow of cash **into** the business, its RECEIPTS, was £11 000. Its main receipts for the month were for £10 000 worth of goods sold. It also sold a van owned by the company for £1 000.

Payments The total flow of cash **out** of the business, its PAYMENTS, was £12 000. It paid out £3 000 to suppliers, £4 000 in wages, £1 000 for VAT and £4 000 in other expenses such as rent.

Net cash flow The difference between the cash coming into the business and the cash flowing out is the NET CASH FLOW.

Net cash flow = receipts - payments

The business had a net cash flow

of -£1 000. This meant that £1 000 more flowed out than came in. This money had to come from somewhere. It came from the bank account of the business, where all its cash is kept. At the start of the month the business had £4 500 in the bank. This was the OPENING BALANCE. At the end of the month the CLOSING BALANCE was £1 000 less at £3 500.

Cash flow over a longer period

The flow of cash over a longer period is shown in Table 74.2.
* In July, August and September, net cash flow is negative. In each month more money is going out than is coming in (payments are more than receipts);
* In October, November and December, net cash flow is positive. In each month more money is coming into the business than is going out (receipts are more than payments).

At the end of the six months, the business has gained more cash than it has lost. This is because the closing balance in the last month is greater than the opening balance in the first month.

The closing balance in one month becomes the opening balance in the next. For example, the opening balance in August is £3 500. This is the same as the closing balance in July.

Receipts	
Sales	10 000
Disposal of assets	1 000
Total receipts	11 000
Payments	
Suppliers	3 000
Wages	4 000
VAT	1 000
Other expenses	4 000
Total	12 000
Net cash flow	- 1 000
Opening balance	4 500
Closing balance	3 500

Table 74.1 Cash flow statement, July (£)

Cash

The amount of CASH in a business at a point in time is not just notes and coins. It is also money deposited in bank or building society accounts which can be withdrawn immediately. The business is likely to pay out cash from its bank account using a **cheque**. Money will also be transferred into its account from other bank accounts. For instance, it may receive payments through cheques, **standing orders** or **direct debits** (☞ unit 16).

Receipts

Businesses can receive cash from a variety of sources.
* Receipts from sales.
* Loans from a bank.
* Interest on deposits in a bank or other financial assets.
* Rent on property leased to other businesses or individuals.

Rollason's is a family business which sells or rents out portable heating, de-humidifying and air-conditioning equipment. 80 per cent of its revenue comes from hiring out the equipment. In the last year:
* its wage bill will be £100 000;
* sales of equipment will be £200 000;
* the cost of buying new equipment for sale or rent will be £500 000;
* advertising and other marketing costs will be £50 000;
* revenue from the hire of equipment will be £800 000;
* all other costs will be £200 000.
1. (a) Which of these are receipts for the business? (b) What is the total value of receipts?
2. (a) Which of these are payments for the business? (b) What is the total value of payments?
3. What is the net cash flow of Rollason's?
4. If Rollason's had cash of £50 000 at the start of the year, how much would it have at the end of the year?

	July	August	September	October	November	December
Receipts	11 000	10 500	10 000	12 000	14 000	16 000
Payments	12 000	11 500	11 500	11 000	12 500	13 500
Net cash flow	- 1 000	- 1 000	- 1 500	1 000	1 500	2 500
Opening balance	4 500	3 500	2 500	1 000	2 000	3 500
Closing balance	3 500	2 500	1 000	2 000	3 500	6 000

Table 74.2 *Cash flow statement, July-December (£)*

✔Checklist

1. What is the difference between a receipt and a payment for a business?
2. (a) A newsagent receives cash from its customers. List FIVE different items which will lead to cash flowing into the business.
   (b) A newsagent pays out money. List FIVE different ways in which cash might flow out of the business.
3. What is the net cash flow of a business if (a) receipts are £500 and payments are £300; (b) receipts are £1 000 and payments are £1 200, (c) receipts are £3 million and payments are £2.8 million?
4. The opening balance for a business in June is £4 000 whilst its closing balance is £3 000. (a) What was its closing balance in May? (b) What was its net cash flow for June? (c) What is its opening balance in July?
5. A business has £300 in cash on its premises. It has £2 300 in its bank account and is owed £6 000 by its customers. If it were producing a cash flow statement, how much cash would it calculate it was holding?

key terms

Cash - notes, coins and balances in bank and building society accounts which can be withdrawn immediately.
Closing balance - the amount of cash that a business has at the end of a time period.
Net cash flow- the receipts of a business minus its payments.
Opening balance - the amount of cash that a business has at the start of a time period.
Payments - the cash flowing out of a business.

- Repayment of tax which has been overpaid, like VAT.
- The sale of assets like company cars, equipment or property.
- Financial capital introduced, such as the sale of new shares in a company, or an individual putting savings into a business.
- Grants from government.

Payments

Money flowing out of a business can be paid to a variety of sources.

- The purchase of stocks which are used in the production process or for resale.
- The wages of staff.
- Taxes on the wages of staff like employers' National Insurance contributions.
- VAT on sales.
- Marketing costs such as advertising.
- Administration costs.
- Rent on property.
- Repayments on loans.
- Hire purchase or leasing payments on equipment.
- Bank charges, including interest.
- For a company, corporation tax and dividends. For a sole trader or a partnership, drawings of owners.

Drape and Make is a curtain and upholstery business. It runs stalls at a number of markets in Cornwall. The stalls have different materials and styles of curtains and suite coverings on display. Customers can discuss their needs with the two partners of the business, who sell on the stalls. The curtains or coverings are then made to order by part time workers employed by the partners. Table 74.3 shows the cash flow statement for the business over three months last year.

1. Copy out Table 74.3. Fill in and calculate the net cash flow, opening balance and closing balance figures for May assuming sales of curtains are £3 000; sales of coverings are £2 500; wages of workers are £800; material costs are £1 500; van expenses are £800; stall hire is £400; a machine costs £500; other costs are £800; the partners pay themselves £1 500 (their drawings).
2. Fill in Table 74.3 for June assuming sales of curtains are £5 000; sales of coverings are £4 000; wages of workers are £2 100; material costs are £2 500; van expenses are £600; stall hire is £400; no machines are bought; other costs are £800; the partners pay themselves £2 000.

	April	May	June
Receipts			
Sales of curtains	4 000		
Sales of coverings	3 000		
Total	7 000		
Payments			
Wages of workers	1 000		
Material	2 000		
Van expenses	500		
Stall hire	300		
Machines	0		
Other costs	800		
Drawings of partners	2 000		
Total	6 600		
Net cash flow	400		
Opening balance	1 000		
Closing balance	1 400		

Table 74.3 *Cash flow statement of Drape and Make (£)*

	July	Aug	Sept	Oct	Nov	Dec
Receipts						
Sales	15 000	25 000	15 000	35 000	50 000	60 000
Capital from owners	5 000	0	0	0	0	5 000
Total receipts	20 000	25 000	15 000	35 000	50 000	65 000
Payments						
Production expenses	12 000	18 000	12 000	25 000	33 000	36 000
Administration costs	6 000	10 000	12 000	8 000	12 000	12 000
Machinery	0	0	0	0	0	2 000
Total payments	18 000	28 000	24 000	33 000	45 000	50 000
Net cash flow	2 000	- 3 000	- 9 000	2 000	5 000	15 000
Opening balance	6 000	8 000	5 000	- 4 000	- 2 000	3 000
Closing balance	8 000	5 000	- 4 000	- 2 000	3 000	18 000

Table 75.1 Cash flow forecast for the next sixth months (£)

It is important for managers to predict the future cash flow of a business

Cash flow forecasts

A CASH FLOW FORECAST is an estimate of what might happen to cash flow. It is a prediction of cash flow in the **future**.

Table 75.1 shows a cash flow forecast for the next six months of a business. It starts the period with £6 000 in cash (the opening balance).

- In July receipts are £20 000 and payments are £18 000. There is a net cash flow of £2 000. Added to the opening balance of £6 000, this gives a closing balance of £8 000. This becomes the opening balance next month.
- In August, net cash flow is negative, at -£3 000. But the opening balance is £8 000, so the business has enough money to cover this. The closing balance is £5 000.
- In September the business has a problem. There is negative net cash flow of -£9 000. The opening balance of £5 000 is not enough to cover this. So the closing balance is -£4 000. The business will have to find this money from somewhere. For example, it may borrow from a bank.
- There is also a problem in October. The opening balance is -£4 000. Positive net cash flow of

£2 000 only makes the closing balance -£2 000. The business may still have to borrow money.
- In November there is an opening balance of -£2 000. But the net cash flow of £5 000 is large enough to make the closing balance positive, at £3 000.
- In December net cash flow is £15 000. Added to the opening balance of £3 000, this gives a closing balance of £18 000.

The use of cash flow forecasts

Cash flow forecasts are used for a number of purposes.
- Businesses use them to plan future strategy. For example, a business may estimate that in a year's time its net cash flow will be negative by £1 million. It may not have the finance to cope with a net outflow of cash of this amount. So it will have to change its plans. It may try either to increase the amount of cash flowing into the business or reduce the amount of cash flowing out. It will then need to draw up a revised cash flow forecast.
- Businesses need to draw up cash flow forecasts if they want to borrow money. For example, banks often ask for a cash flow

forecast when a business applies for a loan. The bank wants to see that the business has thought carefully about its possible future survival and profitability. The bank will consider whether the cash flow forecasts are realistic. If they are, the bank will then need to consider whether the business can afford payments on the loan or overdraft.
- Any agency giving a grant will also want a cash flow forecast. A business often includes this as part of a **business plan** (☞ unit 110) when it applies for a grant. If the cash flow forecast is unrealistic, the grant is unlikely to be approved.

Cash flow statements

A CASH FLOW STATEMENT is a record of the cash inflows and outflows to a business in the **past** (☞ unit 74). It is a historical document. It can be used to monitor the performance of the business.
- It can be used to compare performance from month to month and from year to year. For instance, a business might find that its net cash flow was worse in June than the year before. This could tell a business that it is performing worse this year than last year.
- Past cash flow can be compared with predicted cash flow. For example, a small business might have forecast that it would have net cash flow in June of £10 000. But the actual net cash flow might have been only £2 000. The shortfall of £8 000 could be

serious for the business. It would then need to adopt strategies to cope with the problem.

Cash flow and profit

Profit and cash flow are different. For example, the business in Table 75.1 is profitable. Its total payments from July to December are £198 000. But it had total sales of £200 000. So it makes a profit of £2 000 over the six months. However, the business has cash flow problems. In September and October, it does not have enough money either within the business or coming in to cover payments. So in both of these months it has a negative closing balance. This means it has a **cash flow crisis**. Unless it can find the cash, for example by borrowing it from a bank, it will have to cease trading.

Improving cash flow

A business which doesn't have enough cash has a LIQUIDITY PROBLEM. There are various ways in which a business can improve its cash flow situation.

- It could seek more equity capital (☞ units 67 and 68). For a company, this might mean issuing new **shares**. For an unlimited business, it could mean the owners putting in some of their own money. Or the owners of the business could take less in profits out of the business, i.e. increase the level of **retained profit**.
- It could borrow money. For instance, it could take out a loan or increase its overdraft.
- It could delay paying its bills as long as possible. It could also put extra pressure on its customers to pay their bills earlier.
- It could use a **factor** (☞ unit 69) if the problem was that too many customers were paying their bills late. The factor would collect money from customers and keep a steady flow of cash coming into the business.
- It could reduce its stock levels. It might sell what it had in stock and avoid buying in new stock.

Gail Whittam owns a farm. She is looking at her cash flow statement for October to December last year compared with her forecast for the same period this year. Trading has been very difficult for the farming industry as prices have fallen. There is little sign that prices will rise in the near future.

Last year (actual outturn)	October	November	December
Receipts	100 000	90 000	80 000
Payments	80 000	85 000	80 000
Net cash flow	20 000	5 000	0
Opening balance	30 000	50 000	55 000
Closing balance	50 000	55 000	55 000

This year (forecast)	October	November	December
Receipts	80 000	70 000	60 000
Payments	82 000	85 000	80 000
Net cash flow	- 2 000	- 15 000	- 20 000
Opening balance	7 000	5 000	- 10 000
Closing balance	5 000	- 10 000	- 30 000

Table 75.2 Cash flow statement and forecast for Gail Whittam (£)

1. Compare actual
   (a) receipts,
   (b) payments and
   (c) net cash flow in October, November and December last year with her forecast for this year.
2. Gail has an overdraft facility at her bank of £15 000 which she isn't using at the moment.
   (a) Do you think that Gail will have a problem in October - December this year? Explain your answer.
   (b) Discuss TWO strategies which she could use to improve cash flow over the next 12 months.

For instance, a shop could increase its cash by holding a sale, but not replacing the stock sold.
- It could sell assets like buildings, vans and equipment.

Checklist

1. What is the difference between a cash flow statement and a cash flow forecast?
2. What use might the directors of a company make of a cash flow statement for the previous 12 months trading?
3. Why might a business draw up a cash flow forecast?
4. Explain why a business might turn down a highly profitable order because of cash flow problems.
5. How can a business solve a liquidity crisis?

Budgeting

Budgets

A BUDGET is a **plan** of what will happen. A teenager, for instance, might plan her spending over Christmas. The budget could include her income and spending in December.

- Income. She might decide to use £100 of her own savings. She might also get a £20 allowance from her parents and earn £40 from a part time job. This gives her a total income of £160 (£100 + £20 + £40).
- Spending. She might decide to spend £100 on presents and £60 on going out.

By breaking down total income and spending, it is much easier to manage her finances.

Budgets in business

It is important for businesses to have budgets. A small business might draw up a budget for its next year's trading. The budget shown in Table 76.1 is for a small restaurant. The owner plans to pay £50 000 for food and £45 000 for wages.

Other costs, including rent and heating, come to £45 000. In total, he plans for total costs of £140 000. If he plans for sales of £160 000, the business makes a profit of £20 000.

A larger company often has a **master budget**. This will be made up of information budgets from different parts of the business. For example, a business will have a **sales revenue budget**. This will show its planned sales revenue for a period. Table 76.2, for instance, shows a sales revenue budget of a furniture manufacturer over a year. A business will also have a **production budget**. This will show the planned costs of materials, labour and overheads, such as lighting.

Departments may also have their own budgets. So there might be a **marketing budget** and an **administration budget**, for instance.

Preparing a budget

Before preparing a budget, a

Revenue (£)		Costs (£)	
Sales	160 000	Food	50 000
		Wages	45 000
		Rent	5 000
		Gas, electricity and water	6 000
		Other costs	34 000
	160 000		140 000
		Profit	20 000
			160 000

Table 76.1 12 month budget for a restaurant

Products	Sales revenue (£)
Wardrobes	1 000 000
Dressers	500 000
Beds	300 000
Other items	200 000
Total sales	2 000 000

Table 76.2 12 month sales revenue budget for a furniture manufacturer

---

Michael Downing is drawing up a sales budget for his business for the next 12 months. The bakery business makes two main products, bread and cakes. This year, the business sold £500 000 worth of bread and £100 000 worth of cakes. Michael knows that the bread side of the business is currently making a loss. Sales over the past two years have fallen and the two bakery sites where production is located have large amounts of spare capacity. The cake side of the business, however, is profitable, although like bread sales, cake sales have been falling too.

Michael has decided that the way back to profitability is to improve sales. He is launching a marketing campaign promoting the benefits of buying from a small local baker. He has budgeted for a 20 per cent increase in bread sales compared to last year and a 10 per cent increase in cake sales. His budget is shown in Table 76.3.

1. How much, according to his budget, is Michael planning to sell over the next 12 months?
2. What are the objectives of the business?
3. Why has Michael decided to put bread sales of £600 000 into his budget?
4. Suggest TWO factors that could determine whether or not his sales revenue budget proves realistic.

	£ revenue
Bread	600 000
Cakes	110 000
	710 000

Table 76.3 Sales revenue budget, 12 months

business should have set its **objectives** (☞ unit 20). The budget is then prepared in the light of these objectives. For example, the owner of the restaurant may decide that it is not making enough profit. So, in the budget for the next 12 months, he may plan to reduce the costs of the business.

There are two main ways that a business might get the information to put into its budget.

- It might base the budget on historical data. Existing budgets might be used to construct new budgets.
- There may be forecasts about what might happen in future. For instance, economists might predict that the economy is going to go into recession. Recessions tend to hit the restaurant trade hard. Fewer people feel that they can afford to go out to eat and spending falls. Workers also find it more difficult to negotiate wage

rises. So a recession forecast might lead the owner of the restaurant to budget for lower sales and lower costs.

Using a budget

Budgets can benefit a business in a number of ways.

Planning A budget is a plan against which day to day decisions can be made. For example, a business may have prepared a budget in December for the next 12 months. It might include £50 000 a month for spending on wages. The following May the business might find that it is underspending or overspending on wages. This could affect whether it decides to take on extra workers or whether it cuts down on the amount of overtime being worked.

Control In a large business, budgets are an important way in which

management can control separate parts of the business. They can judge the performance of a section of the company by looking at how well it is keeping to its budget.

Costs In any business, budgets are one of the key ways of ensuring that costs do not get out of control. If costs are not controlled, they could rise to such an extent that they threaten the survival of the business. Equally, sales budgets allow managers to see whether sales targets are being met.

Changes Budgets must be flexible. For example, if there was a sudden increase in trade, a restaurant might be forced to increase spending on food. It might also consider taking on extra staff. If the business stuck to the budget, the quality of service could fall and drive customers away. So budgets must be flexible when unexpected circumstances arise.

Saria is in charge of the transport department of a business which manufactures ceramic products. The company has two lorries which make deliveries to regular customers. Use is also made of outside contractors for deliveries to areas of the country not covered by regular deliveries.

Saria has drawn up the transport budget for next year. The senior managers have given her a total of £380 000 to spend. She has been told that the volume of goods to be transported will remain the same. However, she has been given 5 per cent less money than last year because senior management expect her to achieve efficiency savings.

Her budget is shown in Table 76.4.

1. Explain TWO reasons why it is important for the transport department to have a budget.
2. Saria has drawn up her budget based on last year's spending. Discuss whether this is likely to provide an accurate forecast of next year's spending.

	Costs (£)
Wages	90 000
Fuel	150 000
Maintenance and repairs	15 000
Administration costs	10 000
Payment to outside contractors	105 000
Other costs	10 000
	380 000

Table 76.4 Transport budget

key terms

Budget - a plan, for example for expenditure, by a business over a period of time, like a year.

Checklist

1. 'Budgeted spending for the next 12 months is £4 000.' Explain what this means.
2. What information might be used to draw up a budget?.
3. How can a budget help managers control a business?
4. Sales for a business are up 20 per cent on the budgeted figure. But costs are up by 25 per cent on budget. Explain whether this could cause a problem for the business.
5. Why should budgets be flexible?

The profit and loss account (1)

	£000
Sales turnover	31 531
Cost of sales	(23 723)
Gross profit	7 808

1. Figures in brackets are minus mumbers.

Source: adapted from Chamberlin & Hill, *Annual Report and Accounts 2000.*

Table 77.2 *Trading account for Chamberlin & Hill plc, 2000[1]*

The use of profit and loss accounts

The PROFIT AND LOSS ACCOUNT is a record of revenues and costs of the business over a period, like a year. It shows how much profit the business has made and what has happened to the profit. It has a number of uses.

* It is a record of **past** costs and revenues. But it can also help a business to make decisions about

	£000
Sales turnover	31 531
Cost of sales	(23 723)
Gross profit	7 808
Operating costs	(4 500)
Other	(7)
Net profit[2]	3 301
Taxation	(1 017)
Dividends	(800)
Retained profit	1 484

1. Figures in brackets are minus numbers.
2. Profit on ordinary activities before taxation.

Source: adapted from Chamberlin & Hill, *Annual Report and Accounts 2000.*

Table 77.1 *Profit and loss account for Chamberlin & Hill plc, 2000[1]*

the future. Experience in the past may allow a business to plan its revenue and costs more accurately next year. Businesses, however, often find that cash flow forecasts (☞ unit 75) are more useful when making these decisions.

* It is a summary of recent events for owners and possible investors in the business. Shareholders in limited companies, for instance, are often interested in trends in profits. This is because they determine, in part, how valuable is their share of the business.
* It is used by the tax authorities to assess a company's tax.
* It may be used by other businesses to judge whether it is safe to give trade credit (☞ unit 69).

An example of a profit and loss account for a manufacturing company, Chamberlin & Hill plc, is shown in Table 77.1.

The profit and loss account can be split into two parts - the TRADING ACCOUNT and the profit and loss account. If the business is a company, there will be a third part - the **appropriation account** (☞ unit 78).

The trading account

The first part of the profit and loss account is the **trading account**. The trading account of Chamberlin & Hill plc, a company which manufactures castings for the electrical, construction and transport industries, is shown in Table 77.2. The trading account is a record of sales turnover and the cost of sales.

* **Sales turnover** is the value of the sales or the sales revenue of the business (☞ unit 71). It is the amount received from the sales of goods or services.
* COST OF SALES is the cost of production. For a manufacturing company, this would include buying raw materials, as well as employing workers to make products. For a supermarket, it would include the cost of buying in goods to sell, as well as the wages of store staff.

The trading account shows the GROSS PROFIT of the business. This is the profit made before the overheads of the business are taken

Tables 77.3 and 77.4 show the trading accounts for two companies which provide information and communication technology and e-business services to other businesses.

					£ million
	1996	1997	1998	1999	2000
Turnover	38.6	69.8	128.8	191.3	184.9
Cost of sales	31.1	56.8	104.9	156.5	153.5

Source: adapted from MSB International plc, *Annual Report and Accounts*, 2000.

Table 77.3 *MSB International plc, trading account, 1996-2000*

					£ million
	1996	1997	1998	1999	2000
Turnover	87.5	135.3	216.1	283.9	506.3
Cost of sales	69.5	107.0	174.1	232.5	425.1

Source: adapted from Morse Holdings plc, *Annual Report and Accounts,* 2000.

Table 77.4 *Morse Holdings plc, trading account, 1996-2000*

1. Calculate the gross profit of (a) MSB International and (b) Morse Holdings between 1996 and 2000.
2. Suggest which business, in your opinion, has performed best between 1996 and 2000. Justify your answer from the data.

	£000
Gross profit	7 808
Distribution costs	(818)
Administration and selling costs	(3 682)
Interest received	29
Interest paid	(36)
Net profit[2]	3 301

1. Figures in brackets are minus numbers.
2. Profit on ordinary activities before taxation.

Source: adapted from Chamberlin & Hill, *Annual Report and Accounts 2000*.

Table 77.5 *Calculating net profit, Chamberlin & Hill plc, 2000[1]*

into account. Gross profit is defined as sales turnover (one measure of revenue) minus cost of sales (one measure of costs):

Gross profit = sales turnover - cost of sales

1. Who might look at a profit and loss account of a business and why?
2. What is included in the trading account?
3. What costs are taken into account when calculating net profit?
4. Describe TWO types of operating cost.
5. Why would an increase in non-sales revenue increase net profit but not gross profit, assuming all other costs and revenues stayed the same?

key terms

Cost of sales - costs of production such as raw materials costs and the wages of those directly involved in production.
Gross profit - sales turnover minus cost of sales.
Net profit - the profit made after all costs and revenues have been taken into account. It is equal to sales revenue plus non-sales revenue minus costs of sales and operating costs.
Profit and loss account - a record of the revenues and costs of a business over a period such as six months or a year.
Trading account - part of the profit and loss account which shows sales turnover, and cost of sales.

The profit and loss account

The **second** part of the account is the actual profit and loss account. This involves calculating net profit. The profit and loss account of Chamberlin & Hill plc is shown in Table 77.5.

NET PROFIT is the profit made by a business after all its costs have been taken into account. So it is revenue minus both the cost of sales and all the other costs of the business, the overheads.

Not all the revenue of a business is sales revenue. For instance, a business may receive interest on money which was deposited in a bank. It might also receive cash from the sale of assets, like **subsidiary companies** (☞ unit 30), factories and land. These non-sales revenues need to be added to sales revenue in order to calculate net profit.

Equally, not all costs are costs of sales. **Operating expenses** or **overhead costs** or **indirect costs** (☞ unit 72) are the costs which are not directly related to production. Table 77.5 shows some of the operating expenses of Chamberlin & Hill.

Distribution costs These include the costs of getting products to the customer.

Administration expenses These include the costs of employees not directly employed in production. For instance, the salaries of the directors of the company would be an administration expense. It also includes all the other costs of administering the company, such as the cost of running its headquarters.

Selling costs These are the costs of **marketing** (☞ unit 38) and selling products. For instance, a business may have a sales team to market its services. It might also spend money on advertising. Often they are included in distribution costs, but Chamberlin & Hill has included them with administration costs.

Net profit can be calculated either as:

Net profit = gross profit + non-sales revenue - operating cost

or using the definition for gross profit:

Net profit = sales revenue + non-sales revenue - cost of sales - operating cost

Ballett's is a chain of retailers selling clothes and equipment for younger children.

1. Copy out the profit and loss accounts for 1999-2001 and fill in the missing figures.
2. What has happened to (a) sales turnover, (b) cost of sales, (c) gross profit and (d) net profit over the three years?
3. Suggest whether the company is doing well or badly. Justify your answer from the data.

	£ million		
	1999	2000	2001
Sales turnover	1.1	1.3	1.6
Cost of sales	0.3	0.4	?
Gross profit	?	?	1.0
Operating expenses			
Distribution	(0.2)	?	(0.4)
Administration	(0.3)	(0.5)	?
Net profit[2]	?	0.1	(0.1)

1. Figures in brackets are minus numbers.
2. Profit on ordinary activities before taxation.

Table 77.6 *Ballett's, trading and profit and loss account for year ending 31 March[1]*

The appropriation account

There are three parts to the profit and loss account for a **company**:
- the trading account described in unit 77;
- the profit and loss account also described in unit 77.
- the appropriation account.

The APPROPRIATION ACCOUNT shows what happens to the net profit of a company. It can be distributed in one of three ways.
- It may be used to pay taxes on profits made to government. The main tax in the UK on company profits is corporation tax.
- The company could distribute part of the profits to its shareholders in dividends. This is the reward to shareholders, the owners, for investing in the company.

- Profits may be retained (i.e. kept back) to increase the assets of the company. This **retained profit** is the main way in which businesses tend to pay for new investment in the UK (☞ units 67 and 68).

Table 78.1 shows the appropriation account for Chamberlin & Hill for 2000. It paid just over £1 million in taxes on profits and distributed £800 000 to its various shareholders. It paid out less in taxes and dividends than it earned in net profit. So it was able to retain nearly £1.5 million in the business for future years.

Sole traders and partnerships accounts do not have an appropriation account. All the net profits of the business are transferred to the **balance sheet** (☞ units 79 to 80).

	£000
Net profit[2]	3 301
Taxation	(1 017)
Dividends	(800)
Retained profit	1 484

1. Figures in brackets are minus numbers.
2. Profit on ordinary activities before taxation.

Source: adapted from Chamberlin & Hill, *Annual Report and Accounts 2000*.

Table 78.1 *Appropriation account for Chamberlin & Hill, 2000[1]*

Depreciation

Businesses own buildings, machines, cars and office equipment. These wear out over time and, as a result, fall in value. This fall in value is called DEPRECIATION. It is counted as a cost because the fall in value is what it is costing the business to own and operate these

---

? Billingstone Group is a business which manufactures soap. It employs two sales representatives who travel the country trying to win orders. This year, it bought the senior rep a £16, 000 company car and the junior rep a £12, 000 car. It is the company policy to keep cars for three years and then sell them second hand.

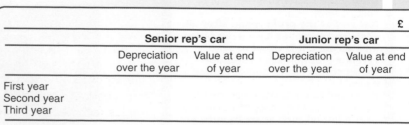

1. The finance director estimates that the senior rep's car will be worth £4,000 and the junior rep's car worth £3,000 at the end of the three years. Calculate (i) the depreciation and (ii) the value of each car at the end of each year and record your answer in Table 78.2. Use the straight line method of depreciation.
2. Now use the reducing balance method to depreciate the cars instead of the straight line method. The company depreciates its reps' cars at a rate of 35 per cent each year. Record your answers using Table 78.2 again. You will find this much easier if you use a calculator.
3. What is the difference between the values of cars using each method at the end of each year?

 Spreadsheet
4. Use a spreadsheet package to show the different amounts of depreciation and book values of a £20 000 car assuming a reducing balance method of depreciation is used. Calculate your answer for yearly rates of depreciation of 10 per cent, 20 per cent, 30 per cent and 40 per cent.

	Senior rep's car		Junior rep's car	£
	Depreciation over the year	Value at end of year	Depreciation over the year	Value at end of year
First year				
Second year				
Third year				

Table 78.2 *Depreciation*

The Range Cooker Company is one of the largest specialist suppliers of high quality range style domestic cookers in the UK. It also produces built in cooking appliances such as eye-level ovens. Growth for the company means that it is continually investing in new products and in premises. For the future, the company has submitted plans for a 16 000 square foot extension to its existing warehouse and office facilities.

	1999 £	2000 £
Net profit[2]	2 195 223	2 826 781
Taxation	(664 520)	(892 648)
Dividends	(675 750)	(1 590 000)
Retained profit	854 953	?

1. Figures in brackets are minus numbers.
2. Profit on ordinary activities before taxation.

Source: adapted from The Range Cooker Company plc, *Annual Report and Accounts 2000.*

Table 78.3 *Appropriation account for The Range Cooker Company plc, 1999 and 2000[1]*

1. What are the three ways in which the company has distributed its net profit?
2. Calculate the retained profit for The Range Cooker Company in 2000.
3. Suggest why over the period 1999 to 2000 (a) taxation rose for the company; (b) the company chose to increase its dividends to shareholders; (c) the company retained part of the profit instead of distributing it to shareholders.

assets. Some businesses include it in cost of sales in the trading account. But many include it as an overhead cost in the profit and loss account.

There are different ways of calculation depreciation. One way is called the **reducing balance method**. This is where a business simply takes off a percentage of the value of any asset, like a machine. For example, a business could take 10 per cent off the value of its machinery each year. A machine costing £100 000 and depreciated at 10 per cent per year would suffer depreciation of £10 000 (£100 000 × 10%) in its first year. Its value would therefore be £90 000.

Another method is called the **straight line method**. Say a machine was bought for £110 000 and would be sold for an estimated £10 000 in five years time. The business would therefore use up £100 000 worth of the machine over 5 years. Using this method, it would depreciate the machine at a fixed £20 000 each year for 5 years.

Costs of production and stock

Production costs or **cost of sales** in the trading account of the

profit and loss account (☞ unit 77) include the cost of materials used to make products. These costs are affected by CHANGES IN STOCK.

Stocks are materials, like threads used to make clothes. They are also finished products, like clothes themselves, which a business has in store. The materials are waiting to be made into products. The products are waiting to be sold to customers.

A business might start the year with opening stock of £6 000. It could end the year with closing stock of £2 000. Since stocks have fallen by £4 000, some of what was sold during the year must have been made using materials or products bought in previous years. Hence, the cost of sales must increase by the amount of stocks used (i.e. opening stock - closing stock) to calculate cost of sales for the year.

Alternatively, stocks might have risen during the year. This increase in stocks will not have contributed to production. Hence, the cost of sales for the year must fall by the amount of the extra stocks to calculate cost of sales.

The effect on cost of sales of

changes in stock can be calculated using the formula:

Cost of sales = cost of purchases + opening stock - closing stock

Checklist

1. How is net profit distributed in a company?
2. For what might retained profit be used?
3. Explain the difference between the reducing balance method of depreciation and the straight line method.
4. How might depreciation affect the profit and loss account?
5. How do changes in stocks affect (a) costs of sales and (b) gross profit?

Balance sheets - fixed and current assets

Machinery and stocks - fixed and current assets

The balance sheet

All businesses have ASSETS. These are what the business **owns**, such as buildings, offices, machinery, stocks and cash. Without assets, a business could not produce anything. To buy these assets, a business will need to raise funds from different **sources**. For example, a business might borrow money or it might **owe** money to other businesses for materials that it has received but not yet paid for. Money owed to others is called the LIABILITIES of a business.

The BALANCE SHEET is a record of the assets and liabilities of a business at a particular point in time. The balance sheet must balance. The assets of the business, what the business owns, **must** equal its liabilities, what it owes. Included in what it owes are the monies owed to the owners of the business, such as profit.

By law a limited company has to produce a balance sheet for its shareholders. This shows its assets and liabilities on the last day of its accounting year. Companies can choose any date on which to end their financial year. A company could, for instance, choose a financial year which runs from 1 February to 31 January or from 16 June one year to 15 June the next year.

Table 79.1 shows the balance sheet of Blacks Leisure Group plc, a sportswear and sports equipment retailer and wholesalers.

Fixed assets

The balance sheet starts with a record of the FIXED ASSETS of the business. There are three main types of fixed asset.

Tangible assets TANGIBLE ASSETS are physical assets which can be seen and touched. They include land as well as buildings such as factories, offices and plant. They also include all the machinery and equipment owned by a business, such as machine tools, computers, furniture, cars and trucks.

Intangible assets INTANGIBLE ASSETS are assets which can't physically be seen or touched. But they do have a value to the business. The most common type of intangible asset is GOODWILL. This is usually the value of the customer loyalty to the business and its reputation. For instance, if the business had to be set up from scratch, it might have to spend money on advertising to build up its customers. So one way of measuring goodwill is to estimate how much it would cost to set up the business with its customers.

	£000
Fixed assets	
Tangible assets	49 263
Intangible assets	42 823
Investments	4 304
	96 390
Current assets	
Stocks	45 165
Debtors	10 663
Cash at bank	3 480
	59 308
Current liabilities	
Creditors: amounts falling due within one year	(55 927)
Net current assets	3 381
Total assets less current liabilities	99 771
Long term liabilities	
Creditors: amounts falling due after more than one year	(36 237)
Provisions for liabilities and charges	(656)
Net assets	62 878
Capital and reserves	
Share capital	41 596
Retained profit and reserves	21 282
	62 878

Source: adapted from Blacks Leisure Group plc, *Annual Report and Accounts*, 2000.

1. Figures in brackets are minus numbers

***Table 79.1** Balance sheet, Blacks Leisure Group plc at 29 February 2000[1]*

Yordale Store is the only shop in the village of Melton. It enjoys steady trade during the week. Trade is helped by the fact that the village Post Office is next door. The store sells groceries. But it is also a newsagent, is licensed to sell alcoholic drinks and sells household and hardware items. The owner has just retired and sold the business for £185 000. Fixed assets were valued at £135 000. This included a £120 000 price estimate on the property itself. The value of the stock was £20 000. The goodwill, equal to 1¹/₂ times net profit, was £30 000.

1. Make a list of the fixed assets that such a shop might have.
2. The new owner paid £30 000 for the goodwill of the business. (a) Do you think you would have paid the same if you had bought the business? To answer this, make a list of the costs of attracting customers if you had to set up a new business in the area. Estimate or try to find out figures for those costs. (b) Suggest what might have happened to the goodwill value of the business if the village Post Office next door closed and the nearest Post Office was then five miles away in another village.

Investments These are investments (normally shareholdings) in other companies. They could also be loans to the government (called bonds) which earn interest for the company. Or they could be other types of long term financial investment by the company.

Current assets

CURRENT ASSETS are the assets of the business which can easily be turned into cash or are cash. They are known as the LIQUID ASSETS of the business. There are three main types of current asset.

Stocks Stocks are the raw materials and goods waiting to be processed, and finished goods awaiting sale. For a retailer like Blacks Leisure Group, stocks would be the goods bought and waiting for sale to customers.

Debtors DEBTORS are the people and businesses who owe the company money. In business, it is usual to deliver goods to other businesses and then give a minimum of 30 days to pay. For most businesses, nearly all debtors are other businesses.

Cash The most liquid asset is cash itself. Cash is notes and coins. It is also deposits in a bank or building society account where there is instant access to the money. This is usually through the use of a cheque book (☞ unit 74).

✓Checklist

1. What is the difference between the assets and liabilities of a business?
2. A shop is up for sale for £30 000. The tangible assets of the business are £20 000 and the rest of the price is goodwill. Why might a buyer be prepared to pay £10 000 for goodwill?
3. List FIVE fixed assets of a garage business.
4. What is the difference between the fixed assets of a business and its current assets?
5. What are the main types of liquid asset for a typical business?

Blacks Leisure Group is a retail and wholesale company which owns a number of major chains including AV, First Sport, Millets, Air, Free Spirit, Blacks Outdoor, O'Neill and Fila. The company specialises in sport and outdoor clothing and equipment, as well as sports fashion clothing, such as Pure Woman.

The financial year to 29 February 2000 was a very successful one for Blacks Leisure Group. Sales from existing chains increased from £147 million to £175 million. The Group also bought The Outdoor Group, the company which owned the Millets, Air and Free Spirit chains of shops. This added another £33 million to the sales of Blacks Leisure Group.

1. (a) Look at Table 79.2. What is the largest single type of current asset for Blacks Leisure Group? (b) Give FOUR examples of this current asset. (c) Why do you think this is likely to be the largest current asset for a sportswear and equipment retailer like Blacks Leisure Group?
2. (a) On 29 February 2000, how much did Blacks Leisure Group keep in cash at the bank and in hand ? (b) Why do you think Blacks Leisure Group needs to keep this type of current asset?
3. Debtors for Blacks Leisure Group is a relatively small proportion of current assets. Some debtors are banks and credit card companies which owe Blacks Leisure Group money from cheques and credit card transactions used by customers when paying at the till. Other debtors are retail businesses which buy from Blacks' two wholesale chains, O'Neill and Fila. Suggest why there has been a large change in the amount owing to Blacks by debtors.

	1999 £000	2000 £000
Stocks	21 250	45 165
Debtors	6 188	10 663
Cash at bank and in hand	2 557	3 480
Current assets	29 995	59 308

Source: adapted from Blacks Leisure Group plc, *Annual Report and Accounts*, 2000.

Table 79.2 *Blacks Leisure Group, current assets, 29 February 1999 and 2000*

Balance sheets - liabilities, capital and reserves

Blacks Leisure Group is a retail and wholesale company which owns a number of major chains including AV, First Sport, Millets, Air, Free Spirit, Blacks Outdoor, O'Neill and Fila. The company specialises in sport and outdoor clothing and equipment, as well as sports fashion clothing, such as Pure Woman.

The financial year to 29 February 2000 was a very successful one for Blacks Leisure Group. Sales from existing chains increased from £147 million to £175 million. The Group also bought The Outdoor Group, the company which owned the Millets, Air and Free Spirit chains of shops. This added another £33 million to the sales of Blacks Leisure Group.

1. Copy out Table 80.1, filling in the missing numbers shown by '?'.
2. Who might be the trade creditors of the company?
3. (a) What is a 'dividend'?
   (b) Why do you think that dividends appear as a current liability for Blacks Leisure Group?

Wordprocessing

4. Write a short report highlighting THREE important changes in Blacks Leisure Group's current liabilities between 1999 and 2000.

	£ million	
	1999	2000
Current assets	?	59 308
Current liabilities		
Repayments on loans due within one year	2 000	7 386
Bank overdrafts	2 879	6 927
Trade creditors	9 883	19 352
Tax on profits owed	6 658	9 105
Proposed dividend	1 341	1 729
Other creditors	4 413	11 428
Total	27 174	55 927
Net current assets	2 821	?

Source: adapted from Blacks Leisure Group plc, *Annual Report and Accounts*, 2000.

Table 80.1 *Current assets and liabilities, Blacks Leisure Group plc at 29 March 1999 and 2000[1]*

	£000
Fixed assets	
Tangible assets	49 263
Intangible assets	42 823
Investments	4 304
	96 390
Current assets	
Stocks	45 165
Debtors	10 663
Cash at bank	3 480
	59 308
Current liabilities	
Creditors: amounts falling due within one year	(55 927)
Net current assets	3 381
Total assets less current liabilities	99 771
Long term liabilities	
Creditors: amounts falling due after more than one year	(36 237)
Provisions for liabilities and charges	(656)
Net assets	62 878
Capital and reserves	
Share capital	41 596
Retained profit and reserves	21 282
	62 878

Source: adapted from Blacks Leisure Group plc, *Annual Report and Accounts*, 2000.
1. Figures in brackets are minus numbers.

Table 80.2 *Balance sheet, Blacks Leisure Group plc at 29 February 2000[1]*

The balance sheet

The first part of the balance sheet shown in Table 80.2 was explained in unit 79. The rest of the balance sheet will be explained in this unit.

Current liabilities

CURRENT LIABILITIES are what the business owes and will have to pay within the next 12 months.

- For most businesses, the most important current liability is the money it owes to its CREDITORS. Just as a business has to give trade credit to other businesses, so it can get trade credit. Typically, businesses have to give 30 days credit on goods or services they sell to other businesses.
- Many businesses also borrow money from the bank on **overdraft** (☞ unit 67). In theory, the bank can demand that the money be repaid immediately. So overdrafts are a current liability.
- Another important current liability is tax owed to the government. The company may have earned profit in the past on which it will have to pay corporation tax and advanced corporation tax in the future.
- A company may have promised to pay dividends to its shareholders, but have not yet actually paid them out. This is then a current liability because the dividends will have to be paid within 12 months.

Net current assets or working capital

Current assets minus current liabilities is called NET CURRENT ASSETS. Another name for this is **working capital**. The working capital of the business is very important as is explained in unit 81.

Long term liabilities

The LONG TERM LIABILITIES are what the business owes and will have to be paid back in more than

12 months time. This includes long term loans which, for instance, might be repaid over 5 years. It could also include **mortgages** (☞ unit 67). These are loans taken out where land or buildings are given as security. For smaller companies, there might be **hire purchase agreements** (☞ unit 69), which is another form of borrowing. Other liabilities might be taxation owed (or deferred) from previous years.

Capital and reserves

The final type of liability of a business is the money owed to its owners. For a company, its owners are its shareholders. The shareholders put money into the business when the shares were first sold. Hence, the business owes this money to its shareholders. This is known as its **share capital**.

The value of share capital has nothing to do with the current value of the shares on a stock market. The value of the share capital in a company reflects their value when they were first issued. The current value of the shares reflects what the business is currently worth.

Most businesses are also likely to keep back some of their profits each year. This is known as **retained profit**. The money is added to the **reserves** of the business. It is money which is owed to the owners of the business. It is therefore a liability for the business. Instead of distributing (i.e. giving) it to the owners, the business decides to set it aside for future investment or to cover possible problems.

Sole traders, partnerships and companies

The balance sheet of a sole proprietorship or partnership is different from that of a limited company. The **main** difference is that there would be no share capital because there are no shareholders. So the value of the money put into the business by the sole trader or the partners would be shown where the share capital is shown in Table 80.2.

The Oriental Restaurant Group is a plc which operates a number of Chinese and Thai restaurants in the London area. It also owns a wholesaling business, Chuanglee. In the financial year 1999-2000, it launched a chain of restaurants under the 'Yellow River Cafe' brand name. By the end of the year, three restaurants or cafes had been opened. It also launched The Central Production Kitchen, a business dedicated to supplying restaurants in the company with high quality products.

1. (a) What is a liability for a business? (b) Suggest why the liabilities, both current and long term, of the Oriental Restaurant Group increased between the financial years 1999 and 2000.
2. (a) What has happened to the retained profit and reserves between 1999 and 2000? (b) (i) What might retained profit be used for by a business? (ii) Suggest why the amount of retained profit owned by the company changed between 1999 and 2000.
3. (a) What has happened to the net assets of the business between 1999 and 2000? (b) Do you think the company is doing better in March 2000 than it was in March 1999? Justify your answer.

	£millions	£millions
	1999	**2000**
Fixed assets		
Tangible assets	5.6	6.1
Investments	0.2	0.2
	5.8	6.3
Current assets		
Stocks	0.1	0.2
Debtors	0.9	1.2
Cash at bank	1.2	0.1
	2.2	1.5
Current liabilities		
Creditors: amounts falling due within one year	(1.0)	(2.0)
Net current assets	1.2	(0.5)
Total assets less current liabilities	7.0	5.8
Long term liabilities		
Creditors: amounts falling due after more than one year	(0.2)	(1.3)
Provisions for liabilities and charges	(0.4)	(0.4)
Net assets	6.4	4.1
Capital and reserves		
Share capital	4.6	4.6
Retained profit and reserves	1.8	(0.5)
	6.4	4.1

Source: adapted from Oriental Restaurant Group plc, *Annual Report and Accounts*, 2000.
1. Figures in brackets are minus numbers.
2. Figures rounded to the nearest £0.1 million.

Table 80.3 *Balance sheet, Oriental Restaurant Group plc at 31 March 2000*[1,2]

Checklist

1. Who might be owed the money which appears as a current liability on the balance sheet of a business?
2. Why is a mortgage a long term liability for a business?
3. Why is share capital a liability for a business?
4. For what might a business use its retained profit and reserves?
5. What is the difference between the balance sheet of a company and a sole trader or partnership?

key terms

Creditors - people, other businesses or government to whom a business owes money.
Current liabilities - what the business owes and will have to pay within the next 12 months.
Long term liabilities - what the business owes and will have to pay in more than 12 months time.
Net current assets or working capital - current assets minus current liabilities.

Working capital

	£000
Current assets	
Stocks	15 309
Debtors	27 629
Cash at bank	39 667
	82 605
Current liabilities	
Trade creditors	6 052
Taxes	6 124
Other creditors	2 734
Proposed dividend	6 515
	21 425
Net current assets	
(working capital)	61 180

Source: adapted from Renishaw, *Annual Report and Accounts*, 2000.

Table 81.1 *Working capital, Renishaw, 28 July 2000*

Current assets and current liabilities

A business needs **fixed assets** to produce goods and services. Fixed assets are the machines, factories, offices, etc. which the business owns. But a business also needs WORKING CAPITAL to keep it running from day to day. Working capital is what the business owns which is cash or could easily be turned into cash **minus** what it owes and needs paying soon.

So working capital is **current assets**, which may be:
● the value of the **cash** owned by the business as notes and coins or deposits in the bank;
● the **stocks** of the business, such as raw materials or finished goods;
● the **debtors** (☞ unit 79) of the business, the businesses which have received goods from the business but have not yet paid for them;
minus
current liabilities which may be:
● money owed to the bank which might be repaid within the next 12 months;
● what it owes to other businesses for goods and services that it has received but not yet paid for (its **creditors** ☞ unit 79);
● other monies owed, such as to the government in tax, or for a company to its shareholders in dividends promised but not yet paid out.

The formula for calculating working capital is:

Current assets - current liabilities
or
(cash + debtors + stock) -
(bank overdraft or loan + creditors
+ other monies owed)

Working capital is the value of **net current assets**. This is the current assets of the business left over after the current liabilities have been taken away. The value of the working capital of a business is recorded on its **balance sheet** (☞ units 79 and 80). The working capital of Renishaw, a manufacturer of metrology (measurement) products, such as probes, is shown in Table 81.1.

The working capital cycle

Every business has a working capital cycle. Look at Figure 81.1. A business has to buy in materials and components. Then it can produce goods and services. These products are sold to customers who usually get 30 days to pay for them. So customers become debtors for the business. After 30 days, the customers then pay the business. From this cash, the company has to pay for the raw materials it originally bought. It also has to pay, for instance, for the wages of its workers, its overheads, taxes, repayments on loans, and dividends to shareholders. So current assets and liabilities, like cash, stocks, debtors, creditors and bank loan repayments, are constantly going around the financial system of the business. The sale of products produces the cash to pay the bills of the business.

The need for working capital

Businesses need working capital. They have to have enough current assets left over, after allowing for current liabilities, to pay day to day bills. A business with a lack of working capital may suffer problems.
● It may not be able to pay for stocks. Without enough stocks of materials or components the production of finished goods will be affected. If a business doesn't have stocks of finished goods it

Peter Mitchell's timber business is not as successful as he had hoped. He has found that his profit has been growing each year. But he has still found problems in making payments at various times of the year. This is often the case in summer when there is a rise in sales. He has thought about the reasons for the problems he is facing.

He feels that he needs to increase his working capital. To do this he has decided to get more cash into the business. He proposes to increase the overdraft with the bank and reduce stocks.

Wordprocessing
Write a letter to Peter explaining:
1. the difference between cash, working capital and profit;
2. the likely effects of a lack of working capital on (a) the production and (b) the profit of the business in future;
3. whether his proposals will increase (a) cash and (b) working capital.

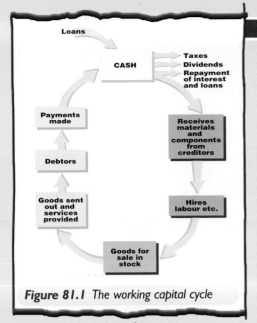

Figure 81.1 *The working capital cycle*

may lose orders from customers who want immediate delivery.

• Businesses that are unable to pay their current bills may not get trade credit from suppliers. They may not be allowed 30 days to pay their bills, for instance. Some suppliers may even refuse to supply orders. If a business is refused trade credit or supplies, it may not be able to produce enough goods to satisfy customers.

• It may lose an increase in orders for finished products because it can't afford to take on extra workers. It might even be forced to close if it misses a payment on a loan and the bank insists on the loan being repaid immediately.

There is a difference between **working capital problems** and **cash flow problems** (☞ unit 75). For instance, a business may have large amounts of stock and is owed money by other businesses, but has no cash. Current assets are greater than current liabilities and so it has working capital. But it has no cash. If it can't get the money it is owed or it can't sell its stocks, it has a cash flow problem.

Increasing cash may not mean an increase in working capital. For instance, a business may increase its overdraft to raise cash. But it will then owe money to a bank. So its liabilities will increase as well as its assets. The danger is that the bank may ask the business to reduce its overdraft in future. If it can't pay, it risks being driven out of business by the bank.

Working capital and profit

As with cash flow, a business can be profitable but have working capital problems. For example, a business may receive an order for £4 000 worth of goods on which it will make £1 000 in profit. But, its suppliers may refuse to give it any more trade credit. It may have already spent up to its overdraft limit at the bank. It may have no cash or stocks of materials. In these circumstances, it may have to turn away the order because it can't get the materials to make up the order. All businesses must have enough working capital if they are to survive profitably in the long term.

key terms

Working capital - current assets minus current liabilities, which in a typical business means cash plus debtors plus stock *minus* bank overdraft plus creditors plus other monies owed for payment within 12 months.

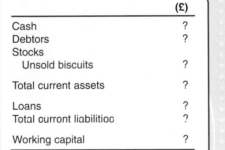

EITHER follow the working capital that flows around your business and draw up a table like Table 81.2 to show working capital at a point in time OR complete the following.

Your mini company activity makes biscuits to be sold in school. £5 cash has been put into the business to start it up. You have also borrowed another £10 cash from your parents to buy the ingredients and provide a float.

100 biscuits will be made on the first day. The ingredients bought and used are 500 gm of margarine at 70p; 500 gm of caster sugar at 40p; 6 eggs at 60p; 1 kg of plain flour at 40p.

Each biscuit will sell for 6p. On the first day you sell 75 out of 100 biscuits for cash. You also sell another 5 biscuits to customers who promise to pay you the next day.

1. Calculate the value of your working capital by filling in Table 81.2:
   (a) **before** you have bought any ingredients, but **after** you have received the cash to start up the business and the loan;
   (b) at the end of the first day of trading, after you have sold the biscuits;
   (c) at the end of the first week, after you have repaid the loan to parents and collected any money owing from biscuits bought on credit.
2. At the beginning of the second week, one of the company members says that the left over biscuits are stale and can't be sold. What will happen to your working capital if the biscuits are written off (in this case, thrown away)?
3. Does the business have a working capital problem? Explain your answer.

	(£)
Cash	?
Debtors	?
Stocks	
Unsold biscuits	?
Total current assets	?
Loans	?
Total current liabilities	?
Working capital	?

Table 81.2 *Working capital for biscuit company*

Checklist

1. What is the difference between the current assets of a business and its current liabilities?
2. Explain what will happen to the working capital of a business if (a) its cash increases; (b) its stocks rise; (c) its creditors rise; (d) its debtors fall; (e) it increases its bank overdraft by £1 000 and uses the money to buy extra stock; (f) it sells £1 000 of stock for cash; (g) it reduces its bank overdraft because it has increased the price of its products for sale.
3. Explain why a business might get into problems if (a) its suppliers stop giving it trade credit; (b) its overdraft is at the limit agreed with its bank.
4. (a) What is the difference between cash and working capital? (b) 'A cash flow crisis is one example of a working capital problem for a business.' Explain what this means.

Working capital ratios

	£m	£m
Stocks	11.0	
Debtors	29.0	
Cash at bank and in hand	46.3	
Current assets		**86.3**
Trade creditors	18.0	
Taxes	11.2	
Proposed dividend	1.1	
Other creditors	12.9	
Current liabilities		**43.2**
Working capital		**43.1**

1. Figures rounded to the nearest £0.1 million.

Source: adapted from Silent Night Holdings plc, *Annual Report and Accounts*, 2000.

Table 82.1 *Working capital at 29 January, Silentnight Holdings plc[1]*

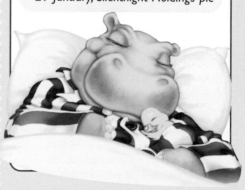

Jarvis Porter Group and Coral Products both manufacture packaging. Jarvis Porter makes speciality packaging for goods like perfume and drinks, print labels and dripmat board products such as beer mats. Coral Products manufactures injection moulded plastic products such as CD, DVD and video boxes and plastic food boxes for use in the kitchen.

1. Calculate from Table 82.2 (a) the total current assets, (b) the current ratio and (c) the acid test ratio for both companies in 1999 and 2000.
2. (a) Which company has (i) the highest current ratio and (ii) the highest acid test ratio? (b) There is a sudden downturn in the UK economy and the packaging industry is very badly affected through loss of orders. Discuss which of the two companies in Table 82.2 you think might find it easiest to survive this situation.

	Jarvis Porter Group plc[2]		Coral Products plc[3]	
	1999	**2000**	**1999**	**2000**
	£m[1]			
Current assets				
Stocks	16.2	11.5	1.3	2.5
Debtors	24.2	16.0	3.2	4.9
Cash	2.7	7.3	0.8	0.2
Current liabilities	35.9	20.6	4.3	6.7

1. Figures rounded to the nearest £0.1 million.
2. at 29 February.
3. at 30 April.

Source: adapted from Jarvis Porter Group plc and Coral Products plc, *Annual Report and Accounts*, 2000.

Table 82.2 *Working capital of two packaging companies*

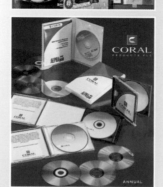

Enough working capital?

Working capital is important for a business. If it does not have enough working capital it may not be able to pay its day to day expenses (☞ unit 81). How can a business find out if it has enough working capital? Businesses often work out accounting ratios to help them make decisions. The CURRENT RATIO and the ACID TEST RATIO are two ratios that might help a business to decide if it has enough working capital.

Current ratio

One way for a business to decide if it has enough working capital is to compare its **current assets** with its **current liabilities** (☞ unit 79). If current assets are a lot greater than current liabilities a business may be able to cope with a sudden crisis. For instance, the bankers of a business might suddenly decide to 'call in' an overdraft (i.e. ask for it to be repaid). Or a major customer might go out of business leaving unpaid bills. Both of these will increase the current liabilities and reduce the working capital of a business. But if there are enough current assets compared to current liabilities, it will still be able to carry on paying its day to day bills.

The ratio of current assets to current liabilities is called the **current ratio**. It can be calculated as:

$$\text{Current ratio} = \frac{\text{current assets}}{\text{current liabilities}}$$

The higher the ratio of current assets to current liabilities, the higher the amount of working capital in the business. The higher the ratio, therefore, the safer is the business.

Accountants often advise that a **typical** business should have a current ratio of 1.5 to 1 to 2:1. If it is less than this, the business may not be able to pay its bills and may be forced to close down. If it is much more, the business is likely to have resources tied up in unproductive assets. Lowering stock levels or reducing the amount of cash could release funds to invest so the business grows or to earn interest in a bank account.

Table 82.1 shows the current assets and liabilities of Silentnight Holdings. The company is the market leader in two sectors of the UK domestic furniture market - beds and assembled cabinet furniture. In 2000,

key terms

Acid test ratio - the ratio of current assets minus stocks to current liabilities.
Current ratio - the ratio of current assets to current liabilities.

Checklist

1. What could happen to a business which does not have enough working capital?
2. A manufacturing business finds that its current ratio falls from 2.5:1 to 1:1. (a) Why does this suggest that the business is in trouble? (b) Suggest what might have caused this fall.
3. Calculate the current ratio and the acid test ratio of a business which has (a) current assets of £6 million, stocks of £4 million and current liabilities of £3 million; (b) current assets of £16 million, stocks of £9 million and current liabilities of £10 million.
4. A manufacturing business has a current ratio of 3:1 but an acid test ratio of only 0.5:1. (a) What must be its most important type of current asset? (b) Why might the business face problems in the future?

TEX Holdings is a UK manufacturing company which is split into three divisions - engineering, plastics and boards and panels. It makes a wide variety of products and provides services for other businesses.

1. (a) What is a 'current asset'?
   (b) Debtors of TEX Holdings include businesses both in the UK and overseas. What are debtors?
   (c) Calculate the value of current assets for (i) 1999 and (ii) 2000 from Table 82.3.
2. (a) What is a current liability?
   (b) If TEX Holdings had a loan which must be repaid in 6 months time and one which must be repaid in 5 years time, which of these is a current liability and why? (c) From Table 82.3, calculate the total value of current liabilities for (i) 1999 and (ii) 2000.
3. Calculate for (i) 1999 and (ii) 2000 the company's (a) working capital, (b) current ratio and (c) acid test ratio.
4. Explain whether you think TEX Holdings' current ratio and acid test ratio would suggest that the company is a safe company in which to invest and buy shares.

	£m[1]	
	1999	2000
Current assets		
Cash at bank and in hand	0.4	2.5
Debtors	5.6	5.8
Stocks	4.9	4.0
Current liabilities		
Bank loans and overdrafts	0.2	0.2
Trade creditors	3.0	3.3
Taxes	0.4	1.1
Proposed dividend	0.3	0.5
Other creditors	2.6	2.6

1. Figures rounded to the nearest £0.1 million.

Source: adapted from TEX Holdings plc, *Annual Report and Accounts*, 2000.

Table 82.3 *Current assets and liabilities at 31 March, TEX Holdings plc*

its current assets were £86.3 million, whilst its current liabilities were £43.2 million. This meant that its current ratio was nearly 2 to 1 (£86.3 million ÷ £43.2 million). So it was a safe business from the viewpoint of its current ratio.

Not all businesses are typical. Supermarkets, for example, often have current ratios of less than 1. This is because they are given trade credit of at least 30 days by their suppliers, but give little trade credit themselves. Their customers pay immediately as they go through the checkouts. The result is that current assets are small in relation to current liabilities.

The acid test ratio

Stock is part of the working capital of the business. However, it might be difficult to sell off stock quickly if a business needs cash.

So a better measure of whether a business has enough working capital might be the **acid test ratio**. This excludes stock from current assets when calculating the ratio of current assets to current liabilities. It can be calculated as:

$$\text{Acid test ratio} = \frac{\text{current assets - stock}}{\text{current liabilities}}$$

Like the current ratio, the higher the acid test ratio, the safer is the business and the less likely it is to become insolvent. A typical business should have an acid test ratio of between 0.5 to 1 and 1 to 1.

Table 82.1 shows that the value of currents assets minus stocks for Silent Night Holdings was £75.3 million (£86.3 million - £11.0 million). So its acid test ratio was 1.74 to 1 (£75.3 million ÷ £43.2 million). This is well above the suggested ratio for safety. It indicates that Silentnight Holdings is a very safe company. But is it keeping too much in current assets other than stocks? For example, should the company be holding so much cash? Or there might be a good reason why the company's acid test ratio is high which is not shown up by the figures in Table 82.1.

	£ million[1]	
	2000	2001
Sales turnover	15.0	20.0
Cost of sales	10.0	14.0
Gross profit	5.0	6.0
Ratio of gross profit to sales	33%	30%

1. Figures rounded to the nearest £0.1 million.

Table 83.1 *Yilnaz Ltd, trading account*

Gross profit margins

Gross profit is the difference between sales revenue and the cost of sales. Table 83.1 seems to show that Yilnaz Ltd, a chemicals business, is doing well. Over 12 months it has increased its sales. It has also increased its gross profits. But, in fact, there is cause for concern.

This is because the cost of sales has risen faster than sales turnover. Sales turnover went up by 33 per cent (from £15 to £20 million). But the cost of sales went up more, by 40 per cent (from £10 million to £14 million).

One way of looking at what is happening to the cost of sales in relation to sales turnover is to work out the RATIO OF GROSS PROFIT TO SALES TURNOVER. This is also known as the GROSS PROFIT MARGIN and can be calculated as:

Ratio of gross profit to sales or gross profit margin (as a %)

$$= \frac{\text{Gross profit}}{\text{Sales turnover}} \times 100$$

The gross profit margin for Yilnaz in 2000 was 33 per cent (£5 million ÷ £15 million x 100). In 2001 it was 30 per cent (£6 million ÷ £20 million x 100).

If the gross profit margin is increasing, sales costs must be falling in relation to the value of sales. This

	£ million[1]	
	2000	2001
Sales turnover	15.0	20.0
Cost of sales	10.0	14.0
Gross profit	5.0	6.0
Overheads[2]	2.0	2.5
Net profit[3]	3.0	3.5
Ratio of net profit to sales	20%	17.5%

1. Figures rounded to the nearest £0.1 million.
2. Distribution costs, administration costs and exceptional items.
3. Profit on ordinary activities before taxation.

Table 83.2 *Yilnaz Ltd, profit and loss account*

is usually a good indicator for the company. If the ratio is falling, as in Table 83.1, sales costs are rising in relation to the value of sales. This is often a worrying trend for a business. It could mean that the business is losing control of its costs as it expands.

Net profit

Gross profit is important, but it doesn't include overhead costs. For the owners of a business, the final net profit figure is possibly more important. Table 83.2 shows the overhead costs and net profit at Yilnaz between 2000 and 2001. Again, Yilnaz would seem to be doing well. Over 12 months it has increased its net profits. But there is cause for concern. Costs have risen faster than sales turnover. For Yilnaz, this is true both of cost of sales and overhead costs.

This can be measured using another indicator, the RATIO OF NET PROFIT TO SALES TURNOVER or NET PROFIT MARGIN.

Northern Recruitment Group plc is a company which specialises in providing employment services to other businesses and to individual workers. As a recruitment agency, it helps businesses find both permanent and temporary staff. It also provides advice on employment issues, as well as organising training.

1. Look at Table 83.3. Do sales revenue figures indicate that Northern Recruitment Group has been doing well or badly? Explain your answer.
2. Now look at the cost of sales as well as the revenue.
   (a) Calculate for each year (i) the gross profit and (ii) the gross profit margin.
   (b) Do you think the business has been doing well? Explain your answer.

focus

success

growth

	1996	1997	1998	1999	2000
				£ million[2]	
Sales revenue	7.3	10.4	14.0	25.3	27.1
Cost of sales	4.9	7.2	9.8	18.7	20.8

1. For the financial year to 30 June.
2. Rounded to the nearest £0.1 million.

Table 83.3 *Sales revenue and cost of sales[1]*
Source: adapted from Northern Recruitment Group Group PLC, *Annual Report and Accounts*, 2000.

✓Checklist

1. The sales turnover of a company importing cycle parts went up from £2 million to £5 million. The cost of sales increased from £1 million to £2 million. What has happened to (a) gross profit and (b) the gross profit margin?
2. What is the difference between gross profit and net profit?
3. The net profit of a plc went up from £2 million to £5 million. Sales turnover increased from £20 million to £100 million. (a) What has happened to the net profit margin? (b) Explain whether this is a good indicator for the business.
4. There is a worsening of profit margins for a business. (a) Is this likely to be good or bad for the business? (b) What might have caused it?

Monsoon is a high street fashion retailer which owns the Monsoon and Accessorize chains of stores.

1. Just looking at the sales turnover figures, do you think Monsoon performed well between 1996 and 2000?
2. (a) Describe how (i) gross profit and (ii) net profit has changed over the period. (b) How well is the business doing according to these figures?
3. (a) Calculate the net profit margin for Monsoon between 1996 and 2000. (b) What do these figures suggest about the performance of the company?
4. Suggest TWO ways in which the company could increase profitability in the next few years.

	1996	1997	1998	1999	2000
					£ million
Sales turnover	79.6	107.9	123.4	132.0	154.5
Gross profit	50.0	67.6	77.0	80.5	94.7
Overheads	31.4	42.2	49.3	60.1	71.7
Net profit before tax[2]	18.6	25.4	27.7	20.4	23.0

1. Figures rounded to the nearest £0.1 million.
2. Profit on ordinary activities before taxation.

Table 83.4 *Monsoon plc: profit and loss account[1]*
Source: adapted from Monsoon plc, *Annual Report and Accounts*, 2000.

key terms

Gross profit margin or ratio of gross profit to sales - gross profit divided by sales turnover expressed as a percentage.
Net profit margin or ratio of net profit to sales - net profit divided by sales turnover expressed as a percentage.

Ratio of net profit to sales or net profit margin (as a %)

$$= \frac{\text{Net profit}}{\text{Sales turnover}} \times 100$$

It shows how much net profit a business is making per £ of product sold. The higher the profit per £ and therefore the higher the ratio, the more profitable a business is likely to be. On the other hand, a lower ratio is often a sign that there is cause for concern.

For Yilnaz, the net profit margin in 2000 was 20 per cent (£3 million ÷ £15 million x 100). In 2001, it was 17.5 per cent (£3.5 million ÷ £20 million x 100).

Making comparisons

Yilnaz, in Tables 83.1 and 83.2, saw both its gross and net profit margins fall as sales increased. This is often a sign that the business has lost control of its costs. However, falling profit margins could also be caused by other factors.

- **Competition** in an industry could have increased. A business may have to cut its prices to maintain sales. Cutting prices will lower sales revenue and lead to a fall in profit margins.
- The economy could move into **recession**. With sales falling for many businesses, there will be pressure on them to cut prices. Again falls in prices lead to lower sales revenues and lower profit margins. For a business which exports products, a recession in an overseas market is likely to lead to lower profit margins for the same reasons.
- The **value of the pound** may increase. This makes the price of UK exports more expensive to foreigners and the price of imports less expensive for UK businesses (☞ unit 10). A response is to cut prices, but this could lead to lower profit margins
- A business may find that the only way to grow further is to take orders with lower profit margins. For example, a breakfast cereal producer may earn net profit margins of 20 per cent on **branded** products sold to supermarkets. A supermarket may ask it to produce an **own label** range (☞ unit 48). The supermarket may not be prepared to pay as much for this range as it would for branded products. The own label range may only earn net profit margins of 10 per cent. The breakfast cereal producer is likely to accept the order because it will increase overall profits. But its overall profit margins will fall.

Judging performance

Return on capital employed

Unit 83 explained how gross and net profit ratios can be used to measure business performance. Another ratio which is useful is the RATE OF RETURN ON CAPITAL EMPLOYED (ROCE). This looks at profit (or returns) in relation to capital.

Say you had £20 in a bank account (your **capital**). If you received £10 interest over a year, you would have made a 50 per cent **return** on your money (10 ÷ 20 × 100). You might think that this is a good rate of return. But if you had £1 million in the account the return would be less than 1 per cent. In this case you are likely to have done badly.

Similarly, a business can't say how well it has done until it compares its profit with the amount of capital in the business. This is what ROCE shows.

$$ROCE\ (\%) = \frac{Net\ profit}{Capital\ employed} \times 100$$

Capital employed is defined as the fixed assets and the net current assets, minus any amounts that must be repaid (including borrowing) in over a year's time on the balance sheet of a business.

Table 84.1 shows profit, capital employed and the ROCE for Fuller, Smith and Turner plc. The company both brews beers and owns pubs, bars and hotels. To calculate its ROCE for 1996, the net profit of £10.6 million was divided by the capital employed of £117.8 million. The number was then multiplied by 100 to make it into a percentage of 9.0 per cent. Between 1996 and 1999, the ROCE for Fuller Smith & Turner increased from 9.0 per cent to 10.4 per cent. This might suggest an improvement in performance of the company. In 2000, the ROCE fell back to 9.5 per cent. This was due to a fall in profits at a time when the value of the capital employed rose. This might indicate poorer performance by the business.

	1996	1997	1998	1999	£ million 2000
Net profit[1]	10.6	11.0	11.9	14.4	13.7
Capital employed	117.8	120.7	128.0	138.7	144.5
Rate of return on capital employed[2]	9.0%	9.1%	9.3%	10.4%	9.5%

1. Net profit before taxation.
2. Rounded to the nearest 0.1%.

Table 84.1 *Fuller Smith & Turner plc: ROCE*
Source: adapted from Fuller Smith & Turner, *Annual Report and Accounts*.

	House of Frazer to 29 Jan £m	James Beattie plc to 31 Jan £m	Austin Reed plc to 31 Jan £m
Sales turnover	815.7	106.6	113.6
Gross profit	274.9	35.0	57.5
Net profit[1]	17.8	10.3	1.2
Capital employed	246.6	43.7	46.4
Ratio of gross profit to sales turnover[2]	34%	33%	51%
Ratio of net profit to sales turnover[2]	2%	10%	1%
Return on capital employed[2]	7%	24%	3%

1. Net profit before taxation.
2. Rounded to the nearest 1%.

Table 84.2 *Business information*
Source: adapted from 2000 Annual Report and Accounts of House of Frazer plc, James Beattie plc and Austin Reed plc.

Hewden Stuart is the leader in the market for equipment rental and related services in the UK. Its customers include businesses in construction, engineering, petrochemicals, rail, utilities, leisure, environmental waste management and public works. It also hires out equipment to the general public. The equipment hired out ranges from cranes to power generators to electrical saws.

1. How did the company perform over the period 1996 to 2000 according to (a) its sales turnover figures and (b) net profit figures?
2. (a) Calculate the rate of return on capital employed (ROCE) for each year between 1996 and 2000. (b) How well did the company perform as measured by its ROCE over the period?
3. In the financial year to January 2000, the lifting hire operations of Hewden Stuart saw sales turnover fall by 4.9 per cent, whilst profits fell by 26.9 per cent according to the *Annual Report and Accounts*. This was mainly because of considerable competition in this sector of the market. Hewden Stuart was forced to cut rental prices to generate sales. (a) Suggest how this might explain company performance in the financial year to January 2000. (b) Discuss TWO strategies which the company could use to resolve this problem.

	1996	1997	1998	1999	£ million 2000
Sales turnover	160.3	167.2	194.7	240.4	256.0
Net profit[2]	36.3	29.4	38.6	41.3	40.5
Capital employed	165.3	177.2	182.2	203.0	222.4

1. Financial year to 31 January.
2. Profit on ordinary activities before taxation.

Table 84.3 *Hewden Stuart plc: profit and loss account[1]*
Source: adapted from Hewden Stuart plc, *Annual Report and Accounts*, 2000.

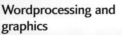

Matalan and Peacocks are both retailers selling clothes and homewares. They have been at the forefront, with companies like New Look, of 'value retailing'. This means setting low prices on goods whilst offering ranges of fashionable products. The success of companies like Matalan and Peacocks has been one of the factors which have led to difficulties for longer established retailers like Marks & Spencer and British Home Stores.

Wordprocessing and graphics

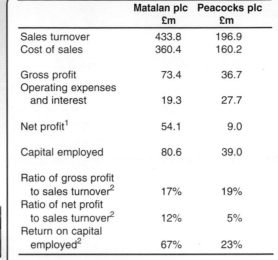

1. Write a report comparing Matalan and Peacocks. Illustrate some of the data about the companies using suitable charts and graphs. Explain which company you think, from the limited information, is doing better.

	Matalan plc £m	Peacocks plc £m
Sales turnover	433.8	196.9
Cost of sales	360.4	160.2
Gross profit	73.4	36.7
Operating expenses and interest	19.3	27.7
Net profit[1]	54.1	9.0
Capital employed	80.6	39.0
Ratio of gross profit to sales turnover[2]	17%	19%
Ratio of net profit to sales turnover[2]	12%	5%
Return on capital employed[2]	67%	23%

1. Net profit before taxation
2. Rounded to the nearest 1%.

Table 84.4 *Business information*
Source: adapted from Matalan plc and Peacocks plc, *Annual Report and Accounts*, 2000.

Because the three companies are plcs, stock market investors look at these statistics when deciding whether to buy or sell shares. House of Frazer's shares at the end of January 2000 were priced at 59p, compared to 91.5p for Austin Reed's and 156p for James Beattie's. This is despite House of Frazer being a much larger company based on sales and capital employed than the other two businesses. However, the share price reflects the ability of a business to make profit. The stock market perhaps felt that James Beattie was the best performing of the three companies at the end of January 2000.

Judging performance

Making comparisons over a number of years is helpful to a business. However, a business can also compare itself with similar businesses to see whether or not it is doing well. Look at Table 84.2. It shows the accounts for three retailers. House of Frazer and James Beattie are **department stores** (☞ unit 52). Austin Reed is a clothing retailer operating the Austin Reed, Country Casual and Chester Barrie chains of stores. How do these companies compare?

Turnover, gross profit and net profit House of Frazer sells between 7 and 8 times more than either James Beattie and Austin Reed. House of Frazer also makes more gross and net profit than the other two retailers.

Gross profit margin Austin Reed had the highest ratio of **gross profit to sales turnover** (☞ unit 83) of the three businesses at 51 per cent. House of Frazer and James Beattie, in contrast, achieved 33-34 per cent. One reason for this could be that Austin Reed was more efficient than the department stores in controlling its costs of sales. But it could be that gross profit margins on clothes are higher than on many other goods sold in department stores. Perhaps like is not being compared with like.

Net profit margin James Beattie's ratio of **net profit to sales turnover** is five times that of House of Frazer and ten times that of Austin Reed. This means that James Beattie is able to make more profit per £1 of sales after both costs of sales and overheads have been deducted. The higher net profit margin at James Beattie would suggest that overheads were relatively higher at House of Frazer and Austin Reed.

Return on capital employed The ROCE at James Beattie was 24 per cent, compared to 7 per cent for House of Frazer and just 3 per cent for Austin Reed.

Overall, these statistics would suggest that James Beattie performed best in 2000. Both its ratio of net profit to sales turnover and ROCE were much higher than the other two retailers.

key terms

Rate of return on capital employed - net profits divided by capital employed in the business.

Checklist

1. A business has produced its accounts for the past three years. Calculate its ROCE if (a) in 1999 net profit was £1 million and capital employed was £10 million; (b) in 2000 net profit was £1.5 million and capital employed was £9 million; (c) in 2001 net profit was £2 million and capital employed was £12 million.
2. Explain, using examples, what the rate of return on capital shows about a business.
3. Andrew's Ltd has a higher rate of return on capital than Maine's Ltd. Who might be interested to know this information?

Investment appraisal

Investment

INVESTMENT means devoting resources **today** to gain rewards **in the future**. Businesses invest in a number of ways. For example, they invest in workers by training them (☞ unit 99). A business might put money into a bank account or in the shares of another business to gain interest, dividends or capital gains. But business investment usually refers to the purchase of **capital goods** (☞ unit 1) such as machines, equipment, plant, offices and factories. This unit will consider the factors that affect how much a business invests.

The pay back method

One way in which a business can decide whether to invest is to calculate the PAY BACK PERIOD.

For example, a business owner might go to a trade fair to buy a new machine. The machine costs £60 000. The owner might work out that the machine will make £15 000 a year for the business after its running costs have been taken into account. In four years, then, the machine will have **paid for itself** (because £60 000 = 4 x £15 000). This is the pay back period.

An advantage of using the pay back method to make investment decisions is that it is easy to make the calculations. It also shows something about the risk of an investment. If the pay back period is one year, things are unlikely to change much. So there is less risk that the investment will not pay off. But if the pay back period is five years, the investment is riskier. Many things could happen to alter

Investment in mines and machinery is likely to pay back over different lengths of time

predictions over a longer period of time. For instance, the economy could go into recession or new products might make the investment obsolete.

A disadvantage of using the pay back method is that it doesn't take into account that machines wear out at different rates. For example, one machine may have a pay back period of two years, but it may be completely worn out. Another machine doing the same job may be more expensive and have a pay back period of three years. But it might last for another 17 years. The pay back method suggests that a business should buy the machine with the shortest pay back period. But the more expensive machine is likely to be more useful in the long term.

The rate of interest

The rate of interest is likely to have an effect on investment decisions. The higher the rate of interest charged by banks on loans, or offered on savings, the lower is likely to be the level of business investment.

One reason is that many businesses finance their investment by borrowing the money. The higher

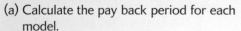

Steve Gorman, a production manager, is looking for a new machine. He is considering three models. Table 85.1 shows the price of each model. It also shows how much profit the model would make for the business after its running costs are taken into account.

(a) Calculate the pay back period for each model.
(b) The firm has a general rule that it will only invest if the pay back period is not more than three years. Which model(s) would it consider buying?
(c) Model A is expected to last for 20 years. Models B and C will have to be replaced after four years. How does this show the disadvantage of using the pay back method when deciding upon new investment?

Model	Purchase price of machine £	Profit £
A	40 000	10 000
B	50 000	25 000
C	100 000	40 000

Table 85.1

✓Checklist

1. A machine costs £80 000 to buy. What would be the pay back period if a business calculates that the machine makes (a) £10 000, (b) £20 000 and (c) £40 000 after taking into account its running costs?
2. What are (a) the advantages and (b) the disadvantages of using the pay back method as a way of evaluating an investment?
3. Explain why a rise in interest rates in the economy is likely to reduce the level of investment by businesses.
4. Explain how an organisation might use cost-benefit analysis to appraise an investment project.

key terms

Cost benefit analysis - **a method of evaluating an investment project which attempts to calculate all the benefits (the social benefits) and all the costs (the social costs) of an investment project and not just the private benefits and costs to an individual business.**
Investment - **using resources today that will gain rewards in future.**
Pay back period - **the length of time it takes for a business to pay for an investment from the money it makes less its running costs.**

Felkin Ltd is an electronics component manufacturer with factories both in the UK and in the USA. It provides components to a range of customers in industries such as mobile phones, computers and home entertainment equipment. It is considering making a £15 million investment in a new factory in the UK, financed through increased borrowing. The company has a policy that it will not undertake investment unless forecasts show that the investment will give a 15 per cent annual return on capital. In this case, the factory is projected to make a 16 per cent annual return on the assumption that UK interest rates are at 6 per cent.

The financial analysis for the new factory was completed in April when UK interest rates were at 5.75 per cent. By the time the board of directors of Felkin met to approve the investment two months later, UK interest rates had risen to 8 per cent.

1. What is meant by 'rate of return on capital'.
2. (a) If the board of directors had met in April, would they have given the go ahead for the investment project? Justify your answer. (b) Should they have approved the investment when, in fact, they met in June? Justify your answer.
3. Growth in demand for products such as computers and mobile phones over the past ten years has fluctuated. Suggest why Felkin insists that an investment should be predicted to have a rate of return of 15 per cent per year for it to go ahead when national interest rates are perhaps only a third of that figure.

the rate of interest, the greater the cost of the investment to a business. An investment might make a profit if money could be borrowed at 6 per cent. But it might make a loss if the rate of interest were 20 per cent.

Businesses often compare the rate of return on investment in physical capital to what they could earn if they put their money in the bank. The rate of return on capital (☞ unit 84) is the profit earned divided by the amount invested. If a new factory earned a business a profit of £5 million a year, but cost £100 million to build, then the rate of return would be 5 per cent (£5 million ÷ £100 million x 100).

But why bother investing in a new factory if the business could put the £100 million in the bank and earn 7 per cent interest a year?

This 7 per cent is the **opportunity cost** (☞ unit 2) of the investment decision - the next best alternative. If the next best alternative is better than the return on the investment, the business won't invest. Businesses in practice don't invest unless the rate of return is **much** higher than bank interest rates. This is because investing in new machines is much riskier than putting the money into a bank. Businesses need to be rewarded for taking that risk by earning much higher profits.

Cost benefit analysis

A private business will only look at its own costs, revenues and profits when making an investment decision. But sometimes the 'profit' to society from an investment is

much higher than just the profit a business makes. For example, a business helping to build a new railway line might make a profit by charging more than it costs to build the line. But the new line might encourage people to use trains, which might take cars off the road. This gives a benefit to society because there is likely to be less congestion and pollution.

Governments sometimes use COST BENEFIT ANALYSIS to decide whether to support an investment project. It looks at all the benefits, the **social benefits** (☞ unit 11), and all the costs, the **social costs**. If an investment makes a large social profit, the government often makes sure the investment goes ahead. Either it could undertake the investment itself, like building a new road. Or it could **subsidise** a private business to take on the investment, like building a new railway line.

Profit, success and ethics

Profit can allow research, innovation and improved efficiency

Business success

Units 21 and 22 showed that there are many ways of judging the success of a business. The level of profit or sales, the size of market share and the creation of jobs, wealth or benefits to society are some of these measures. But in a **market economy** (☞ unit 4) it could be argued that the main aim of a business is to make profit for its owners.

Comparing profit

How does a business know whether its profit is improving? A business has a number of measures of profit.

- **Gross profit** is sales revenue minus the cost of sales. **Net profit** is sales revenue minus the cost of sales and overheads (☞ unit 77).
- **Gross** and **net profit margins** are the the ratios of gross profit and net profit to sales turnover (☞ unit 83).

- **Rate of return on capital employed (ROCE)** is the ratio of net profit to the capital of the business (☞ unit 84).

A business can compare these measures to those in previous years to see if it is making more profit.

Businesses might also compare their profit margins and ROCE with those of other businesses. It is possible to compare figures with those of **limited companies** because their past accounts are available from Companies House (☞ unit 27). Small businesses can also use the Benchmark Index from the Small Business Service for comparison. **Benchmarking** (☞ unit 58) allows a business to compare its performance against the 'best' in the industry.

The role of profit

In market and mixed economies profit has a number of important roles.

Incentives Profit is an incentive for businesses to provide the goods and services that customers want. Businesses which make losses fail to provide customers with products they want to buy at a reasonable price. In the long term, they will cease trading. The workers, factories and offices they use will be bought by other businesses which make a profit. Businesses which make profits are those which do provide customers with products they want to buy.

Signals Profit acts as a **signal**. It shows businesses where to invest. For instance, businesses in an industry may be making high levels of profit. This will encourage them to invest in order to expand and make even more profit. New firms will enter the market and supply products, hoping to gain high profits.

Risks Profit rewards those who take **risks**. There is no point in investing money in a new factory if it earns the same amount of profit as in a bank account. Building and operating a new factory has high risks. What happens if customers no longer want what the factory produces? Putting money into a bank account, in contrast, has very little risk. So the rate of return on investment in a factory must be higher than the rate of return on money in a bank account.

The higher the risk of an investment, the higher the profit that needs to be earned. For example, the world's top drug companies make huge profits on a small number of successful drugs. But for every successful drug, there are hundreds which fail during development. It costs drugs companies billions of pounds each year for these failures which earn nothing for the businesses.

Wolverhampton residents have won the battle to shut down a pollution-plagued recycling plant. The ten-year-old plant, which recycled tyres, closed last June following a fire. The Environmental Agency, called in to investigate, ordered that the company, Sita, should reduce the number of tyres being burnt. A refurbishment, costing £4 million, was then announced by Sita. However, when the estimated cost spiralled to £6 million, the company announced that the refurbishment would not take place and that the plant would not reopen.

Local residents were jubilant. They claimed that fumes from the plant caused breathing problems, and noise and air pollution. The pollution made living in the local area unbearable.

Source: adapted from the *Express & Star* ,16 January 2001.

1, (a) How much did Sita originally estimate it would cost to refurbish the plant? (b) By how much did this estimate increase by January 2001? (c) Suggest why this change in cost led to Sita's decision to close the plant.
2. Local residents had been campaigning to close the plant for many years. (a) Suggest why the company kept the plant despite this campaign. (b) Discuss whether the plant should have been closed before June 2000.

Profit and ethics

Some argue that businesses should not be allowed to make profits. They suggest that profits are a sign of excessive market power. For example, a business may have a **monopoly** (☞ unit 18). This means that it is the only business supplying products in a market. Consumers can't choose to buy from another business. This gives the monopolist the power to influence the market and to exploit customers.

Another argument is that profits lead to higher prices. If a product is priced at £5, and £1 of that is profit, then it could be sold for £4 at cost price. So customers have to pay more for products for a business to make profits.

A third argument is that businesses do not pay for the **externalities** (☞ unit 11) they create. These are costs, like pollution, which are not included as a cost of production. But society still has to pay for them, for instance in the damage pollution causes to the environment.

Those in favour of profits would say that the government should prevent businesses from exploiting customers and harming the environment. Businesses with monopoly power should be broken

up into smaller competing companies or should be regulated (☞ units 8 and 18). The government should discourage damage to the environment by taxing harmful activities or placing limits on them by passing laws.

They also argue that profit leads to innovation and efficiency. In planned economies (☞ unit 4) businesses often are not expected to make a profit. Co-operative societies (☞ unit 31) in the UK don't aim to make profits for their owners. There are also some building societies and assurance companies in the UK which are non-profit making. All these businesses have been criticised for failing to innovate and provide products at the lowest prices. Co-operative societies, for example, have lost customers to profit making supermarket chains because they have failed to provide what the customer wants. The former Soviet Union has now adopted a mixed economy because its industries became inefficient with state planning. Profit adds to costs, but in a competitive market it leads to efficiency and innovation.

PowderJect Pharmaceuticals is a company which is developing a needle free alternative to deliveries of vaccines and medicines by needle. Traditionally, liquid vaccines have been injected into subjects using a needle. Many patients dislike needles and the pain they cause. Needle injections usually have to be administered by costly health care professionals like nurses. Liquid vaccines also sometimes need to be kept at specified refrigerated temperatures, which can increase costs of storage or transport. PowderJect Pharmaceuticals has developed an alternative.

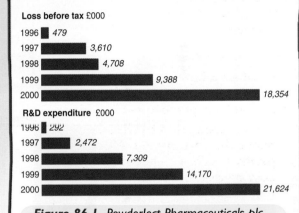

Figure 86.1 *PowderJect Pharmaceuticals plc, profit/loss and expenditure on R&D, 1996-2000*
Source: adapted from PowderJect Pharmaceuticals plc, *Annual Report and Accounts*, 2000.

Vaccines and medicines are produced as powders rather than liquids. They are then injected into patients using a PowderJect delivery device ®. This pushes the powder onto the outer layer of skin. The procedure is painless and simple enough for patients to self administer. The powder doesn't need to be refrigerated. The company has undertaken clinical trials of the system to show that the system is safe and effective. Much of the work shows that PowderJect makes vaccines more effective on patients than traditional injections.

Figure 86.1 shows how losses at the company have grown. The main reason has been the build up of spending on research and development (R&D). The company is not yet selling any powder injection products commercially, although it is receiving payments from drug companies which have signed collaborative deals. These deals give the drugs companies rights to develop and market certain PowderJect products once they have been approved for use.

Source: adapted from PowderJect Pharmaceuticals, *Annual Report and Accounts*, 2000.

1. Approximately how much money did PowderJect Pharmaceuticals lose between 1996 and 2000?
2. There are an estimated 8 to 12 billion individual injections using needles each year worldwide. Suggest why an investor would want to buy shares in a company which has lost so much money so far and whose products could fail to be approved for sale in the future.
3. PowderJect has taken out patents to protect other companies copying its work for the next 20 years. Discuss the possible costs and benefits to society of giving PowderJect a monopoly on its technology for such a long time.

✓Checklist

1. How can the success of a business be judged?
2. How might a business find out if its profit position is improving?
3. Explain how profits act as a signal in allocating resources in an economy.
4. Business X, a leisure company, is making very high profits. Business Y, a shipbuilder, is making a loss. Explain what is likely to happen in (a) the leisure industry and (b) the shipbuilding industry.
5. Give THREE reasons why business should not make excessive profits.
6. How can government prevent firms from exploiting customers or the environment?

Directors, managers and workers often have different roles in a business

Shareholders

Companies are owned by **shareholders** (☞ unit 27). In a large public limited company, most shareholders have little to do with the running of the company. There is a **divorce of ownership and control** (☞ unit 28). At the Annual General Meeting (AGM, ☞ unit 27), they have a chance to pass resolutions which affect the running of the company. They also have the power to elect new directors onto the board of the company. In practice, events at AGMs are run and controlled by the directors. The wishes of the board of directors are hardly ever overturned by a vote at the AGM.

Shareholders have two main ROLES. First, they provide new **equity capital** (☞ unit 67) for a company. If the company issues new shares, existing shareholders will often buy the new shares. They are therefore a source of finance for the business. Second, they decide who owns the business. If shareholders do not like the way the company is being run, they may sell their shares. This is important if the shares are sold to another company wanting to **take over** (☞ unit 33) the business. Takeovers often result in most of the top directors and managers being forced to leave the company.

Directors

Directors are appointed by shareholders to take strategic decisions about the running of the company. In law, their main duty is to act in the shareholders' interests.

Some of the directors are **non-executive directors** (☞ unit 27). They have no other job within the company apart from being directors. Some of the directors, though, are **executive directors**. They have major jobs within the company, such as chief executive or finance director. These are management jobs. So executive directors are both directors and managers.

The Board of Directors takes the major decisions to do with the company. It sets the strategy which it then tells the managers of the company to put into practice.

Abbey National, the high street bank, is experimenting with 'franchising'. Over 40 branches in four areas of the country have been given a certain amount of independence. At the moment, staff remain employees of the Abbey National. But they are given bonuses if their area generates higher profits.

Partly the change is about raising sales. Franchise areas have the power to override instructions from the main offices in Milton Keynes or London. For example, Alan Thomas, an area sales manager in South West Wales advised his Merthyr Tydfil branch to ignore a promotion for mortgages over £200 000. In an area where the average house costs only £33 000, he told the branch staff to concentrate on selling cheap home insurance instead. But it is also about lowering costs. There is increased awareness by managers and counter staff that switching computer screens off when not in use or controlling telephone bills can lower costs and raise profit.

At the moment, the scheme is not a true franchise. But if it proves successful, it could be that Abbey National will allow local managers to buy a local franchise. They will cease to be employees of Abbey National and will become the owners of their own business. Their workers would then also cease to work for Abbey National and would become employees of the franchise. The directors of Abbey National will have to decide whether franchising is the best way to maximise profits for Abbey National shareholders.

Source: adapted from *The Guardian*, 1.11.2000.

1. Explain the role of (a) a manager, (b) counter staff, (c) directors and (d) shareholders in Abbey National. Use examples from the passage to illustrate your answer.
2. Discuss how franchising would change the role of managers who bought an Abbey National franchise.

Managers

Managers are paid employees of the company. They have to run the business on a day to day business. Many managers will run a **department** (☞ unit 90). They will be responsible for a specific task within the organisation, like finance or sales.

The main role of a manager is to organise resources to complete a task. The more senior the manager, the less likely they are to do any direct production work. For example, the manager of a small shoe shop is likely to serve customers. But area managers for a shoe company may not have any sales contact with customers. The managing director of the company at head office is unlikely to have direct contact with customers.

Workers

Sometimes, a distinction is made between the **workers** of a company and those who are managers or directors. Workers complete the main day to day tasks of the company. For example, in a factory, the **shop floor workers** would be operating machines or transporting stock from place to place. The shop floor is where production takes place. There will also be **office workers**, like secretaries, who deal with administration.

However, sometimes managers are classed as workers because they are EMPLOYEES of the company. This means that they have a **contract of employment** (☞ unit 105). This says that the company has hired them and is responsible for paying them their wages.

Some employees will be FULL TIME WORKERS. Typically they will work for around 40 hours a week and have rights to paid annual holidays. Some employees will be PART TIME workers. They will only work a fraction of the full time hours. If an employee works for 10 hours a week when a full time worker works 40 hours, the part time worker may be paid one quarter of the pay (10 ÷ 40) of the full time worker.

Smaller businesses

The smaller the business, the more likely it is that the roles of owner, director, manager and worker will be shared. In a sole proprietorship, for example, the owner is likely to direct and manage the business as well as be a worker. In a private limited company with one hundred employees, the board of directors is likely to be made up completely of managers. Some of the managers are also likely to be the owners of the company.

Fillingham Mouldings is a company which manufactures polyurethane mouldings for the furniture and leisure industries.

Margaret Fillingham plays a number of roles within the company. She is the chairperson and chief executive. She also handles the company's accounts and deals with invoices and other financial work. When needed, she helps on the shop floor.

Margaret and Chris, her husband, own all the shares in the company. Chris is the marketing director and is responsible for gaining orders for the company's products. He also works on the shop floor when he has time or when an urgent order needs getting out.

There are eight shop floor workers who produce the mouldings. Between them, they also do any maintenance work on the machines. They also pack the products ready for delivery. One of the eight is a supervisor who is in charge of the shop floor. They employ two part time staff to handle administration and answer the phone.

1. Explain how many workers there are at Fillingham Mouldings.
2. Who might be classified as white collar workers?
3. Explain how many shop floor workers there are in the company.
4. Who are the employees of the company?
5. A customer rings up wanting a price quotation on some urgent work which needs to be delivered in five days time. Suggest what each person in the business might do to make this a successful contract both for Fillingham Mouldings and for the customer.

Checklist

1. What roles do shareholders play in a company?
2. What is the role of the director in a company?
3. What is the role of a manager?
4. In a small business, why might a worker be the manager and also the owner?

key terms

Employees - workers who are employed by a business.
Full time worker - a worker who works a normal working week.
Part time worker - a worker who works a fraction of a normal working week.
Role - the tasks which a person must do and the responsibilities they must take to fulfil a particular position within a business.

Organisation trees and the chain of command

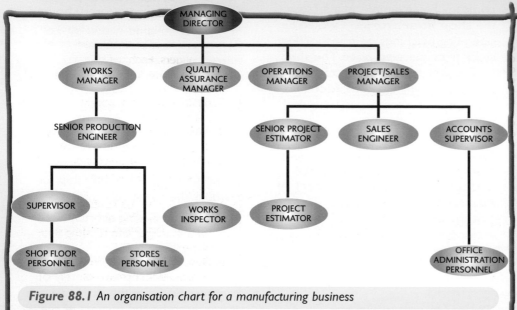

Figure 88.1 An organisation chart for a manufacturing business

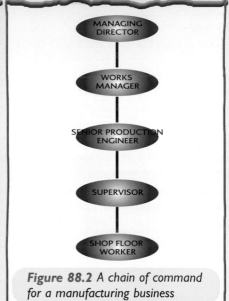

Figure 88.2 A chain of command for a manufacturing business

Organisation

In a large business, workers **specialise** (☞ unit 3). Each worker takes on a **role** and does a given job of work. For example, some workers are shop floor workers, some are clerical workers, whilst others are managers. Workers need to know:
- what jobs they are supposed to do;
- who is in charge of them;
- who they are in charge of ;
- how they relate to the wider ORGANISATION.

This can be shown on an ORGANISATION TREE or CHART.

Organisation trees

Figure 88.1 shows a simplified organisation tree for a manufacturing business. The business has a HIERARCHY, the series of layers in the organisation. At the top is the Managing Director (MD). Next in the hierarchy are managers, such as the Works Manager and Quality Assurance Manager. These are 'middle managers', between the senior management and the workers. At the bottom of the hierarchy are the shop floor workers.

Each worker, apart from the Managing Director, has a LINE MANAGER. This is someone immediately above the worker, to whom he or she reports. Because there tend to be more people lower down in the organisation, a hierarchy is often said to be a **pyramid**.

The chain of command

The person at the top of the organisational pyramid is in a position of AUTHORITY over workers lower down the pyramid. So the MD in Figure 88.1 is in authority over four managers. The MD can give orders to workers lower down the hierarchy, the SUBORDINATES. For instance, the MD could tell the Works Manager to increase production this week. In the organisational pyramid, there is therefore a CHAIN OF COMMAND from the top to the bottom.

The length of the chain of command

The **length** of the chain of command shown in Figure 88.2 is typical of manufacturing companies. Figure 88.2 shows that there are 5 layers in the hierarchy from the Group Managing Director through to the shop floor personnel.

The longer the chain of command, the more difficulties a business can face.

Draw an organisation chart for your school or college.
You will need to find out how the school or college is organised. The organisation chart is likely to be complicated because there is a number of different functions being fulfilled by different workers in the hierarchy. You might find that the same teacher or lecturer needs to be put into two separate places on the chart - as a subject teacher and as a tutor for instance.

- Messages can get lost or distorted as they go up and down the chain of command, as in a game of Chinese whispers.
- Managing change can also be problem. In a sole proprietorship (☞ unit 23), change is simple. The sole trader decides to change and acts on that decision. In a large organisation, the chairperson might decide on change, but it might be resisted further down the hierarchy. The longer the chain of command, the more groups there are to resist that change.

Delayering

Some large businesses try to resolve the problems of long chains of command by flattening it. This is called DELAYERING. They cut out large numbers of middle managers and push responsibility and decision making down the line. In a factory, for instance, it is possible to eliminate supervisors and quality control inspectors. Workers can be organised into groups and made responsible for their own work in terms of output and quality.

This EMPOWERMENT of workers can **motivate** (☞ units 96 and 97) them more. However, it usually means that workers have to be better trained to cope with the extra responsibilities. Workers might have to be paid more because they are doing a more responsible job. Delayering should lead to workers becoming more **productive**. Fewer workers are needed to do the same amount of work. Businesses can then downsize (☞ unit 62), making workers redundant whilst producing as much as before.

✓Checklist

1. Draw an organisational tree for a company with 32 workers, a board of directors, a managing director, four managers each of whom have two assistant managers. Each assistant manager controls the same number of workers.
2. Explain the term 'middle management'.
3. 'The chain of command is very long.' What does this mean?
4. What are the problems of having a long chain of command?
5. In a plc, who has control over (a) the managing director, (b) a manager and (c) shop floor workers?
6. How can delayering in an organisation increase its efficiency?

Figure 88.3 shows the chain of command for Lockley's, a chain which sells home furnishings. It aims to offer the best quality at affordable prices for products such as reproduction beds, dressers and tables.

1. Who is (a) at the top and (b) at the bottom of the chain of command at Lockley's?
2. A store manager issues orders. Who might he or she issue an order to?
3. Who would be subordinate to a supervisor?
4. Lockley's decides that it wishes to reduce the chain of command in the organisation by cutting out one of the layers of management. It decides to abolish the post of assistant manager. (a) Explain what might be advantages of this for the company. (b) What might be the disadvantages?

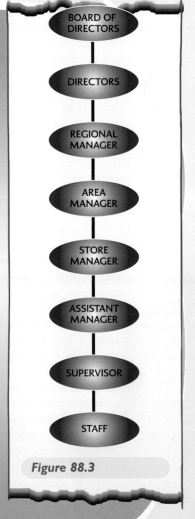

BOARD OF DIRECTORS

DIRECTORS

REGIONAL MANAGER

AREA MANAGER

STORE MANAGER

ASSISTANT MANAGER

SUPERVISOR

STAFF

Figure 88.3

key terms

Authority - the right to decide what to do in a situation and take command of it.
Chain of command - the path (or chain) down which orders (or commands) are passed. In a company, this goes from the board of directors down to shop floor workers.
Delayering - removing layers of management and workers in a hierarchy so that there are fewer workers in the chain of command.
Empowerment - giving more responsibility to workers further down the chain of command in a hierarchy.
Hierarchy - structure of different levels of authority in a business organisation, one on top of the other.
Line manager - an employee who is responsible for overseeing the work of others further down the hierarchy of an organisation.
Organisation - the way in which a business is structured for it to achieve its objectives.
Organisation tree or chart - a diagram which shows the internal structure of an organisation.
Subordinates - workers in the hierarchy who work under the control of a more senior worker.

UNIT 89

Formal meetings and informal discussions

Formal channels of communication

Information in a business passes along CHANNELS OF COMMUNICATION. Channels which are recognised and approved by the business and by employee representatives such as **trade unions** (☞ unit 101) are called

> Your school or college is likely to be a business organisation. It has formal channels of communication. Find out the formal channel(s) of communication for the following situations.
> 1. A pupil or student is persistently late for business studies lessons.
> 2. A pupil or student needs a bus pass.
> 3. A teacher or lecturer wants to order some business studies textbooks.
> 4. A teacher or lecturer wants a white board installed in the teaching room.
> 5. A pupil or student needs afternoon release to be able to appear in a show running for two weeks at a local theatre.
> 6. A student or pupil wants to book time to use a computer.

FORMAL CHANNELS OF COMMUNICATION. There are two main types.

- **Vertical communication** is communication up and down the **hierarchy** (☞ unit 88) of the business. For instance, a clerical assistant in an insurance company might ask a supervisor for authorisation to pay a claim. A chief executive might send a note to a member of the personnel department asking for a venue to be booked for a meeting of the board of directors.
- **Horizontal communication** occurs when workers at the same level in a business communicate with each other. For instance, one telesales worker might leave a note for another about problems with the equipment they are using.

Informal channels of communication

Often, communication doesn't get passed along official channels. INFORMAL COMMUNICATION is called communication through the GRAPEVINE. For instance, a manager in a finance department may have a friend who works in sales. If they chat after work about what is going on in the company, they are passing information through the grapevine.

Channels of communication should be clearly laid down by a business. If they are not, then information may be sent to the wrong people or get lost.

Communication through the grapevine can sometimes be a problem because messages may get distorted the

more people they go through. On the other hand, the grapevine can be very useful. Managers need as much information as possible to do their job properly. This might mean getting more information than they 'officially' receive.

Effective communication

The fewer the stages through which a communication passes (i.e the shorter the **chain of communication**), the less likely it is that a message will be misinterpreted. One of the advantages of a small business compared to a large company is that, with very few people employed, it may be easier to communicate effectively. Poor communication is one reason why a business may experience **diseconomies of scale** (☞ unit 34). Poor communication leads to the average cost of production rising as a company gets larger.

Span of control

A managing director cannot be expected to organise or supervise every single worker in a large company. This job would be too large. Instead, the managing director only controls the work of immediate subordinates. The number of people that a worker directly controls is called a SPAN OF CONTROL.

The span of control - how big?

The span of control varies depending upon circumstances.

- The more complex the supervision task, the smaller the span of control should be. The supervision task can be complex if checking work is difficult and time consuming. It can also be more complex if the workers which need supervising are not particularly good at their job.
- The span of control has to be small if communication with subordinates is time consuming.
- The better the supervisor, the more people that can be supervised.
- The more the supervisor DELEGATES work, the greater can be the span of control. Delegation means passing down responsibility to **subordinates** to complete tasks. Delegation frees up a supervisor's time to supervise the work of more workers. It also **empowers** subordinates. Workers further down the chain of command are likely to be more motivated. This is because they are being shown trust and can use their own talents and skills more.

Checklist

1. What is the difference between vertical and horizontal communication?
2. What are the advantages of organising work through formal groups?
3. Why is communication through a grapevine both useful and a possible problem for a business organisation?
4. 'The span of control of the managing director is very small.' What does this mean?
5. What factors determine the best number for a span of control of a manager?

Gary Roberts is one of 357 managers of a local chain of newsagents in London. The job is not easy. The main problem is that he has to work very long hours. He has asked his superiors to appoint an assistant manager, but they have always said that his newsagents was too small to justify this.

So he has to struggle alone with the task of running the shop and its 46 workers. There are thirty youngsters delivering newspapers, both in the morning and the evening. Then there are 16 adult staff. All but two of them are part-time. He barely gets to know some of the staff before they leave. This is because the turnover of staff is high. Many young people, when they find how hard the job is, only last one week. As for adult staff, they often complain about the low wages and how they would like to get a job somewhere else.

Gary would like to lead from the front, spending time in the shop. Instead, he finds himself alone in the back office doing all the paperwork. Maureen, who has been with the shop for 18 years, has often told him that he ought to let her do some of this. But Gary finds it difficult to trust anyone to get the paperwork done properly. When Gary does get into the shop, it is usually because one of the staff has phoned in sick and he can't find a replacement. Sickness is, in fact, a real problem. Even though most of the staff don't get sick pay, there still seems an unduly high level of staff absenteeism. There is also the problem that sometimes money goes 'missing'.

1. (a) What is meant by the 'span of control'? (b) How large Is Gary's span of control?
2. (a) List the problems that Gary faces as manager. (b) Discuss whether these problems are caused by Gary having too large a span of control.
3. To what extent would Gary's problems be solved if an assistant manager were appointed?

key terms

Channels of communication - the paths taken by messages, such as horizontal communication, vertical communication or grapevine communication.
Delegation - passing down of authority for work to another worker further down the hierarchy of the organisation.
Formal channels of communication - channels which are recognised and approved by the business and by employee representatives such as trade unions.
Informal communication or communication through the grapevine - communication through channels which are not formally recognised by the business.
Span of control - the number of people who report directly to another worker in a superior position.

UNIT 90

Departments and groups

An informal group - friends from different departments meeting at lunch time

Departments

Most businesses are organised by FUNCTION (☞ unit 35). This means that a business is organised according to what people do.

In a medium to large business, the whole organisation is likely to be split up into different DEPARTMENTS. Each department is responsible for a certain aspect of the work of a business. For example, in a manufacturing business, the production department will be responsible for making goods. The finance department will be responsible for dealing with accounts and paying invoices. The marketing department will be responsible for promotion.

Departments may be further subdivided into **sections**. These will include groups of workers within a department. For example, if there are 300 people working in a department, they may be divided further into smaller groups each with its own manager.

Each department or section can specialise in the work they do. This should lead to greater efficiency. However, all the departments are **interdependent**. They have to rely on each other to make the whole business work effectively.

Formal groups

Sections and departments are examples of FORMAL GROUPS. These are groups set up by the organisation to carry out tasks.

There are many advantages to organising work through formal groups.

- Each group and possibly even each worker within a group can specialise. This should lead to higher output and lower costs.
- The group will have a clear position within the structure of the business (☞ unit 88). This means that other groups know which group to ask when they need help. For instance, finance matters can be referred to the finance manager. Knowing who is doing what in a business saves time and ensures lower costs.
- Communication in the business is improved, again because there is a clear structure.
- Workers can act as a team, receive support from others in the group and have their work supervised.

A formal group - cinema staff

Kristie Mason works as a buyer for Grain's, a national chain of high street clothing retailers in its buying department. She spends at least one day a week on the road in the UK and also makes frequent trips abroad, visiting possible suppliers. For these visits, he has to liaise with the accounts department. It has arranged a contract with a travel agent to book flights and hotels. It also deals with claims for expenses.

Kristie has recently been promoted from assistant buyer. The personnel department issued her with a new contract and arranged for her to get a company car. She has regular interviews with a personnel manager to review her career and see what challenges she might want to take on next.

She likes to get into stores on a regular basis to discuss with staff how sales have been going. Store staff can also help with her ideas for what might be fashionable next season. Visits are arranged by the stores department. They are usually arranged for days when she is visiting a UK supplier and can pop into the nearest store.

1. List the four departments of Grain's mentioned in the article.
2. Briefly suggest what is the function of each of these departments.
3. Kristie is thinking of taking a leave of absence and returning to the business at a later date. How might each of the departments in the business be affected?

key terms

Department - a group of workers which is made responsible for a particular aspect of the work of a business, such as production, sales or finance.

Formal groups - groups created by an organisation to complete specific tasks.

Function - tasks or jobs. Organisation by function means that a business is organised according to tasks that have to be completed, such as production or finance.

Informal groups - groups of people who join together outside the formal structure of an organisation.

Checklist

1. What is the function of a department in a business?
2. Why are departments in a business interdependent?
3. What are the advantages of organising work through formal groups?
4. Why can informal groups be (a) an advantage and (b) a disadvantage for a business?

Informal groups

An INFORMAL GROUP is a group which is not set up by the organisation, but comes into existence by itself. A group of workers who play squash together would be an example.

Informal groups can be good for business. People who form a group tend to get on well together and may work better as a result. Informal groups can sometimes lead to information getting through which otherwise would get clogged up if there was poor communication in a business.

Informal groups can also be a problem for a business. Most medium to large businesses have groups of people who spend their time together moaning about other workers and poor decision making by their managers. The group may try to prevent change in the business because members of the group don't want to alter the way things are done.

Whether good or bad for the business, it is unlikely that a business can stop informal groups being formed. It therefore has to take these groups into account when managing change and making decisions.

The arrival of Michael Carson as head of the accounting department was not a good day for the seven staff in the department. Michael Carson was a man of limited abilities. However, he assumed that, because he was the head of the department, he knew more and was more able than any of his staff. It soon became obvious that any work passed to him could easily take weeks to complete and might not be accurate or correct.

Everyone adjusted their work patterns to get around him. Staff in the accounting department avoided consulting him on any serious issue. Instead, they would ask each other for advice or approach the managing director on an informal basis. Staff from outside the department would have a quiet word with one of the accounting staff when they needed a job doing. Because Michael Carson spent most of his day sitting at his desk in the open plan accounts office, the 'quiet word' was often spoken over a coffee at the coffee machine in the corridor or during a game of squash after work.

The managing director was always very caring of his staff and always assumed the best of his workers. However, after two years, even he had to accept that Michael Carson was causing problems to the smooth running of the business.

1. What is the difference between a formal group and an informal group in a business? Explain your answer using examples from the passage.
2. Why was Michael Carson 'causing problems to the smooth running of the business'?
3. Discuss what the managing director should do now that he has recognised there is a problem.

Job centres help unemployed workers find jobs

Why recruit and select?

Businesses need workers. How many workers they employ depends upon what tasks need to be done, the cost of the workers and how much businesses can afford to pay. A business might carry out **human resource planning** to find out how many workers and what types of worker are needed. Recruiting workers with the right skills, and paying them what the business can afford, is very important.

Internal recruitment

Businesses that want to recruit workers have a variety of ways in which they can find applicants. One is INTERNAL RECRUITMENT. This is when a business appoints someone to a post who is already working in the organisation. For example, the post of production manager might be filled by a machine operator with great experience. Or a senior sales assistant may be given the job as manager of a sales team.

An advantage of appointing from inside the business is that the person is already working in the organisation. They will know how it works and may even have had experience of the job. They are also likely to settle into the job quicker. On the other hand, a new employee may have a fresh approach and work harder.

External recruitment

EXTERNAL RECRUITMENT is when a business appoints someone from outside the organisation. There is a number of different channels through which a business can **communicate** with potential applicants.

Jobcentres A business may notify the local Jobcentre of the vacancy. Jobcentres are paid for by the government. They are responsible for helping workers, including the unemployed, to find jobs or to get training. They also provide a service to businesses which want to recruit workers. The services they provide are mostly free to workers and businesses. However, most of the

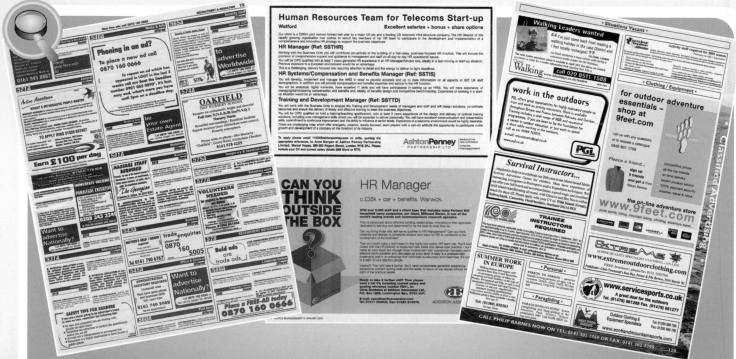

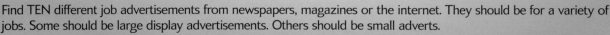

Find TEN different job advertisements from newspapers, magazines or the internet. They should be for a variety of jobs. Some should be large display advertisements. Others should be small adverts.

1. Compare the advertisements. Do they all give salary levels? Do they give an address and a telephone number? How much detail about jobs do they give? Do they state what experience and qualifications are needed?
2. Which advertisements do you think are going to get the most enquiries? Explain your reasons carefully.

jobs notified to Jobcentres tend to be manual jobs in manufacturing or lower level work in service industries.

Private employment agencies Private employment agencies, like Jobcentres, advertise jobs on behalf of businesses. Most private employment agencies specialise. For instance, there are agencies which deal mainly with temporary work. Others deal with nursing jobs or executive posts. This helps businesses looking for these types of workers to find them. Unlike Jobcentres, agencies charge for their services.

Advertising Businesses can advertise in a variety of media. **Newspapers** can reach a large number of people. Local newspapers are used to attract workers who live in the local area. The jobs advertised tend to be for workers up to middle management level. Businesses often use national newspapers for more senior jobs. For example, executive posts might be advertised in the *Financial Times* or *The Sunday Times*. In some industries jobs are advertised in **specialist magazines** or newspapers. For example, jobs in teaching tend to be advertised in *The Times Educational Supplement*. Accountancy jobs might be advertised in *Accountancy Age*. National advertising would be seen by a wide range of people across the country. So

a business would hope to have more applicants from which to choose. **Television advertising** is rarely used because it is so costly. However, the army has run recruitment campaigns on television. Businesses are increasingly advertising on the internet (☞ unit 13). A business may have its own site advertising vacancies. Or sites may advertise particular occupations or jobs in an industry.

Word of mouth Agencies and advertising are important ways of attracting recruits. However, the most important way in which people find out about jobs is through word of mouth, as Figure 91.1 shows. Someone may know that a job is vacant and tell the person who

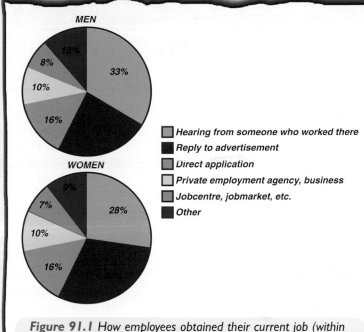

Figure 91.1 *How employees obtained their current job (within the last three months)*
Source: adapted from *Labour Market Statistics*, Office for National Statistics.

actually applies for the job. If a vacancy can be filled by word of mouth, it can save on advertising costs. Businesses will find it easiest to fill vacancies by word of mouth when there are plenty of suitable workers looking for a job. This could be, for instance, at a time of high unemployment.

MECHANICAL FITTER
West Bromwich

Due to internal promotion Robinson Brothers are seeking to recruit a Mechanical Fitter. The job entails the performance of a variety of general engineering tasks including pipe fitting, fabrication, installation and maintenance of pumps, gearboxes, seals and other process equipment.

Applicants should be apprentice served and/or possess C&G Part 3 in mechanical engineering or equivalent. Work in a process industry and particularly previous experience in the chemical industry will be advantageous. The ability to work at heights and in protective clothing is essential.

Remuneration will be dependent on experience. Other benefits include 25 days annual holiday, Company Sick pay and pension schemes. The hours of work are 0800-16.06 Monday-Friday, a 38 hour week.

If you think you can fill this engineering role send your CV to ED Wilson, Personnel Officer at Robinson Brothers Ltd., Phoenix Street, West Bromwich, West Midlands B70 0AH or E-mail E R Wilson@robinsonbrothers.ltd.uk. Alternatively, for an application form telephone 0121 553 2451

Closing date for applications is Friday, 6th April.

1. What does it mean when the advertisement says 'due to internal promotion'?
2. What are the advantages and disadvantages to Robinson Brothers Ltd of advertising in a local newspaper like the *Express & Star* rather than (a) using a Jobcentre or (b) advertising in a national newspaper or (c) using the internet?

Source: *Express & Star*, 22.3.2001.

Checklist

1. Why do businesses need to recruit workers?
2. Distinguish between internal and external recruitment.
3. Describe THREE different ways in which a business could recruit externally.
4. Look at Figure 91.1. Explain how workers get a job.

key terms

Internal recruitment - when a business looks to its own existing employees to fill a post.
External recruitment - when a business seeks to get someone from outside the organisation to fill a post.

The interveiw is an important part of the selection process

Application

Sometimes a business needs to fill a post quickly. If the job is unskilled, it may interview immediately anyone who rings or calls in. For many jobs, though, there is a formal procedure.

Applicants often ask for **particulars** of the job. These are a general description of the business, along with details of the job itself. These details may include a JOB DESCRIPTION. This sets out what the person appointed will have to do. A job description for a supervisor on a production line is shown in Figure 92.1.

The particulars will explain how the applicant should apply. For some jobs, the business will ask for a CURRICULUM VITAE (CV) and a letter of application. A CV is a document, often one or two sides of A4 paper, which gives details about the applicant. These might include his or her name, address, age, qualifications and employment history. The letter of application is a letter in which the applicant explains why he or she wants the job and is particularly suited to that job.

Alternatively, the applicant might be sent and asked to fill in a JOB APPLICATION FORM. This asks for the information which would typically be contained in a CV. It may also include space for the letter of application.

Selecting for interview

Having received CVs and letters of application, a business is in a position to start the **selection** process. CVs and

General statement of major contribution to position
Responsible for the efficient operation and performance of the production system on two shifts.

Regular duties
1. Review performance daily. Ensure corrective action is planned and carried out.
2. Liaise with manufacturer of equipment to ensure modifications are made to hardware and software.
3. Review daily scrap and take corrective action. Hold and organise quality meetings.
4. Liaise with management and other production managers to coordinate development of products.
5. Ensure supply and control of production orders.
6. Monitor performance of tools and equipment.
7. Ensure effective procedures for back up of data for computers.
8. Plan tool distribution on machines.
9. Liaise with maintenance department.
10. Maintain company health and safety regulations.
11. Monitor and maintain disciplinary and absence procedures.
12. Act as back up cover for both shifts.

Education requirements
Technical engineering qualifications, computer system training an advantage.

Previous experience
Active role in operation of similar production system preferred but not essential

Responsible to
Machine shop manager

Responsible for
System team leaders and operation teams

Figure 92.1 *Systems supervisor, job description*

B&Q, the do-it-yourself chain, is a company that makes use of psychometric testing. These are personality tests used by businesses when recruiting staff. The test used by B&Q was devised by Gallup, better known for its opinion polls. The Gallup test asks the applicant to agree or disagree with such questions as 'my appearance is very important to me' and 'my word is my bond'. B&Q uses these tests to filter out unsuitable applicants from the 40 000 job applications it receives each year.

A problem arose, however, following the appointment of Carl Filer at B&Q's Bournemouth store as a shop assistant. Within days Carl was promoted. However, the store manager failed to get the results of Carl's psychometric test before this. When they came through, the test allegedly showed that Carl was unsuitable for employment. The store manager then sacked him.

The TUC (Trades Union Congress) said that psychometric testing was only one part of the selection process.
'Employers should be careful about how they use it. In this case, it is someone who has demonstrated that they are more than capable of doing the job, having been offered

promotion, and that seems more relevant than the answers given to a survey.'

B&Q said it might rehire Carl and blamed the knee-jerk reaction on the store manager who had failed to contact head office. However, it said that the test was 'scientifically proven' to give accurate assessments of candidates.

Source: adapted from the *Financial Times*, 21.4.2001.

1. What is psychometric testing?
2. Why might B&Q want to know whether 'appearance' or 'my word is my bond' is important for a candidate?
3. Discuss whether B&Q should re-employ Carl Filer.

letters of application will be compared to the skills, qualities and experience needed for the job. For example, a business may be looking for a newly qualified graduate to fill a post. So people who have gained a degree in the last two years are likely to be interviewed. Or a business may be looking for an experienced secretary. The CV and the letter of application will say whether a candidate has worked as a secretary. They will also show what qualifications the candidate has for the post.

Having looked through the CVs and letters of application, the business is likely to **shortlist** candidates for **interview**. This means selecting a small number of candidates to be interviewed.

Interviewing

The interview is a very important part of the selection process. It allows the employer and the applicant to meet. The employer is trying to find out whether the person would make a suitable employee. The applicant is trying to decide whether the job and the business is right for him or her.

A number of techniques may be used at an interview.

- Almost certainly, there will be a face to face interview. Interviewers will ask the applicant a variety of question in a formal interview.
- There may be an informal meeting. This allows applicants to give more information about themselves.

A business may also **test** applicants at an interview.

- Applicants may be asked to take a written or physical test. For example, they may have to answer questions that relate to the job or they may be asked to take a maths or English test.
- Applicants may carry out simulations. For example, they may be given details of a business problem. They may then be asked to discuss a solution or carry out an activity to solve the problem.

Interviews try to match applicants' skills with the qualities the business is looking for. For example, a business may want to fill a post in sales. Sales people must deal with customers. So someone who can communicate clearly and 'get on' with people is more likely to be appointed.

There may be several rounds of interviews. A number of candidates will be 'knocked out' at each stage. The more senior the appointment, the longer the interview process is likely to take.

After the interview one person will be offered the job, subject to **references**. This is a report on the potential employee. It is often written by the applicant's current employer or someone who knows them. School leavers, for instance, might ask a teacher to write a reference. The reference is a final check that the information given by the candidate at the interview is correct.

Established over ten years, Stone Computers is a successful and dynamic company, dedicated to the manufacture of reliable and quality based personal computers. Our main customer base revolves around the public sector where we provide excellent service and value for money.

INTERNAL ACCOUNT EXECUTIVE

Due to our continuing success we are looking to recruit an Internal Account Executive who demonstrates the same passion, commitment and energy to the end user as us.

The individual we are seeking will have responsibility for developing their own close business relationships with new and existing customers, identifying and driving through opportunities into winning business.

Candidates should be able to demonstrate a track record in IT sales, be strong communicators and possess the commitment to succeed.

In return we offer an attractive basic salary of £15,000-£16,000 with OTE of £25,000 together with the prospect of exciting future career opportunities.

Please apply in writing enclosing current and concise CV to:
Jane Potts, Stone Computers, Emerald Way, Stone Business Park, Stone, Staffordshire ST15 OSR. e-mail: jane.potts@oegroup.co.uk

Source: *Express & Star*, 22.3.2001.

1. Describe briefly the job that is being offered in the advertisement.
2. To apply, you are asked to forward your CV. (a) What is a CV? (b) Describe THREE characteristics the company is looking for in suitable applicants which might be found on their CVs. (c) Having received CVs, how is Stone Computers likely to select a candidate?
3. Draw up a list of FIVE questions that might be asked of candidates who are interviewed for the job. For each one, explain why you think it is an important question.

key terms

Curriculum vitae - a brief listing of the main details about an applicant, including name, address, age, qualifications and experience.
Job application form - a form which a business issues to applicants to complete when applying for a job, which asks for relevant details about the applicant.
Job description - a document that describes the duties of a worker and his or her status in the organisation.

Checklist

1. An applicant for a transport lorry driver's job is sent a job description. What might be contained in this job description?
2. How might a business ask applicants to send in details about themselves and why they want the job?
3. What techniques might a business use when interviewing candidates?
4. Why do businesses usually ask for references for an applicant?

Factors affecting wages

Demand and supply

Different workers earn different amounts. The chief executive of a large company might earn a basic yearly salary of £1 million. There may even be bonuses and fringe benefits on top of this. On the other hand, the lowest paid adult workers in the UK earn the MINIMUM WAGE set by the government. There are reasons why workers earn different amounts. They can best be explained in terms of the **demand** for and **supply** of workers.

Demand for workers Large companies are often prepared to pay a high price to attract the right person to a senior job. If the right chief executive can raise profits by £300 million a year, the business could easily afford to pay a salary of £1 million a year. As for doctors, people are prepared to pay a high price to get the right medical advice and treatment. But there is a limited demand for cleaners. If cleaners were paid £30 an hour, businesses would reduce their need for cleaning services. They might invest in floor coverings which minimised the need

Well trained workers, in demand from businesses, tend to be paid higher wages

for cleaning. They might even ask staff to clean their own areas of work. This would mean that fewer cleaners would be needed.

Supply of workers There is a limited supply of highly skilled workers. Few people have the skills needed to be a successful chief executive. The number of doctors is limited because only those who have been through a long period of training can practice as doctors. So these workers are often paid higher wages. But many workers could work in sales for a business. Almost all workers could do a cleaning job.

In general, the greater the demand for workers and the less the supply, the higher will be the rate of pay.

Factors affecting demand and supply

Skills, training and education Most workers could do unskilled work, such as delivering packages to different departments in a large business. There are far fewer workers with skills and qualifications to become accountants or senior managers, for instance. So, as there are fewer skilled workers, they tend to be paid more than unskilled workers. That is why education and training is so important for any future career.

Official figures published today will show that unemployment has dropped below the million mark for the first time in 25 years. In the past, falling unemployment has led to rising inflation. Businesses have been forced to compete for a shrinking pool of workers either without a job or prepared to move jobs. They have responded to this falling supply of available workers by increasing the wages they offer. But higher wages mean higher costs for businesses. These higher costs are passed on to the customer in higher prices.

Today, there are signs of above average wage increases in some industries. In the fast growing 'new economy' sector of electrical and optical manufacturing, wages are up 6.1 per cent on the year before. This sector includes computer and mobile phone manufacturing. The highest growth, though, has been in real estate, renting and business services. This includes professions such as accountancy and architecture, as well as estate agents. Demand for these workers has grown as the economy and the housing market have boomed.

But, overall, there is little sign that wages are increasing at a faster rate than over the past five years. In many areas of the country, there is still a pool of unemployed to draw from. Through the New Deal and other programmes, the government has been helping the unemployed to acquire skills needed for the workplace. There are also still several million people at home who can be drawn into work if the jobs are offered. Many businesses might have fewer applicants for each job. But they can still appoint staff without offering large pay rises.

Source: adapted from the *Financial Times*, 14.3.2001.

1. Explain the meaning of (a) unemployment; (b) inflation; (c) boom in the economy.
2. Why might falling unemployment lead to businesses being forced to offer higher wages to recruit staff?
3. (a) In which industries were there particularly high wage increases in 2001?
   (b) Explain why wages were rising in these industries.
4. A supermarket in Newcastle-upon-Tyne wants to recruit 50 new shop workers. The area has above average unemployment for the UK. Suggest why it will not have to increase its current wage rates to attract the 50 new staff.

Experience Experienced workers are likely to know more about the job than someone new to the job. This tends to make them more **productive**. So they are in greater demand by employers. Businesses often recognise this by building age and length of service into some of their payment systems. In some payment systems (☞ unit 95), workers are given **increments** (or extra amounts) for each year of service completed. Each increment is worth £x more in salary.

Motivation and retention Pay is an important **motivator** for workers (☞ units 96 and 97). Businesses don't want their workers to feel underpaid because this will demotivate them. It will also lead to workers leaving the business to work for another employer paying higher wages. So, in the long term, businesses have to pay the **market rate**. This is the wage which is just high enough to retain existing staff and recruit new staff.

Conditions of work The more desirable the conditions of work, the lower the pay a business tends to offer its workers. For instance, managers of a hotel might be offered free accommodation. Without this perk, the hotel would have to pay more to find people to work as managers. Coal miners and North Sea oil rig workers tend to be paid more because their jobs are unpleasant and dangerous.

Trade unions Trade unions are organisations which exist to protect their members (☞ unit 101). They fight for higher pay on behalf of their members. Strong trade unions may be able to force a business to pay a higher rate than if workers had to negotiate individually.

The economic environment The state of the economy can affect wages. When the economy goes into **recession**, the rate of wage increases tends to fall. This is because unemployment tends to rise, but businesses want to recruit fewer workers. When the economy is in **boom**, the reverse happens. Unemployment falls, but businesses want to recruit many new workers. So the rate of wage increases tends to rise.

Another factor is the prosperity of a region within the economy. Average wages in Northern Ireland, for example, are below those of the South East of England. Much of this reflects differences in levels of unemployment. In Northern Ireland, unemployment rates have tended to be higher than those in the South East of England. So businesses have a larger supply of workers to draw from to fill vacancies.

Look at the photograph.

1. How much do you think that the workers in the photograph are likely to be paid?
2. Explain why they might be paid these amounts.

You might find it useful to look in local or national newspapers, company reports or the **internet** to see what similar jobs are being paid.

A mechanic in a garage

Journalist

Part time artist

Accountant

Research/ laboratory technician

Company executive

✓Checklist

1. 'Employers demand labour. Workers supply labour.' Explain what this means.
2. Use demand and supply to explain why (a) doctors tend to be highly paid but (b) doctors' receptionists tend to be lower paid.
3. Explain TWO factors which might affect the level of pay of (a) coal miners; (b) workers in the Third World; (c) a manager of a pub; (d) a production line worker in a factory making sandwiches.
4. Why might age affect a worker's pay?
5. Explain how the qualifications you gain at school, college and university will affect how much you are likely to earn when you get a job.

Free car parking is a fringe benefit for workers

Gross and net pay

The GROSS PAY or GROSS EARNINGS of workers is likely to be different from their NET PAY or NET EARNINGS. Gross earnings are earnings before any tax and other **deductions** have been taken away. Net earnings are earnings after deductions. This is often called **take-home pay** because it is what the worker has left to spend. There is a number of deductions that may be taken away from earnings.

Income tax Employers are responsible for keeping back some of their employees' pay and then sending it to the Inland Revenue, the government department responsible for collecting income tax. This system is known as the PAYE system (pay-as-you-earn).

National Insurance contributions Employees' National Insurance contributions (NICs) are another type of tax on earnings paid to the government. They entitle the worker to receive state benefits, such as unemployment benefit and the basic retirement pension.

Payments to a pension scheme These may include the pension scheme of the company for which the employee works, a personal pension, a stakeholder pension, or the additional state pension scheme (called SERPS - the State Earnings Related Pension Scheme).

Other deductions These might include payments for trade union membership or payments to a charity, such as through the Gift Aid scheme.

Details of these deductions are found on a pay slip. By law, information about deductions from pay must be given to every employee.

Other forms of payment

Workers can be paid in other ways than money. In the coal industry, for instance, it was traditional to give coal miners coal in addition to their

---

? Toni Greene works at The Excelsior Hotel. Figure 94.1 shows her pay slip.

1. What is Toni Greene's total gross pay?
2. What are her deductions? In your answer include the figure for the total level of deductions.
3. Calculate Toni's net pay which would appear on the pay slip in place of the '?' sign.
4. Toni gets a 10 per cent pay rise on basic pay. There is no change in her overtime payment. Copy out the pay slip and put in the new figures for (a) basic pay; (b) overtime; (c) PAYE tax; (d) National Insurance; (e) pension payments; (f) total gross pay; (g) net pay. When making your calculations you need to take into account that:
   - pension payments are 10 per cent of basic pay;
   - National Insurance is payable at 10 per cent of any increase in salary;
   - income tax is 22 per cent of any increase in earnings minus deductions for pension payments, e.g if extra earnings were £100, pension payments would then be £10, and so income tax would be 22% of £90 (£100 - £10).

DESCRIPTION	HOURS	RATE	AMOUNT	DESCRIPTION	AMOUNT	DESCRIPTION	AMOUNT
BASIC PAY			1300.00	PAYE Tax	185.21	Total Gross Pay TD	1420.0
OVERTIME	10.00	12.00	120.00	National Insurance	104.40	Tax paid TD	185.2
				Pension	130.00	National Insurance TD	104.4
						Pension TD	130.0
						===============	
						Total Gross Pay	1420.0

	DATE	DEPT.	PAY POINT	TAX CODE	EMPLOYEE NO	EMPLOYEE NAME	NET PAY
1	30/04/2001	0		453L	2	T Greene	?

Figure 94.1 *Pay slip for Toni Greene*
Note: TD = amount paid so far this year 'to date'.

key terms

Basic pay - pay earned for working the basic working week.
Fringe benefits - payment in kind over and above the wage or salary, such as a company car.
Gross pay or earnings - total earnings, including basic pay and overtime payments.
Net pay or earnings - earnings after deductions such as tax or pension contributions have been taken away.

✓ Checklist

1. What is the difference between gross and net pay?
2. What are the most common forms of deductions from a worker's pay?
3. List FIVE common fringe benefits given by businesses.
4. Why do businesses give fringe benefits to their employees?

Graeme Corcoran had a good job as a senior manager in a company which supplied and installed lighting for other businesses. He was paid £40 000 a year and enjoyed a number of other benefits. There was a company car, free contributions into the company pension scheme, free membership of BUPA for his family, and a range of life and sickness insurance.

But a new managing director was appointed whom he didn't really get on with very well. There were no promotion prospects within the company. He had also been thinking for some time that he would like to set up his own business. So he resigned and immediately went into business on his own. The first year was tough. He only managed to pay himself £15 000 and was forced to run a smaller car than before. He couldn't afford the £2 500 it would have cost for all the medical and life insurances he enjoyed before. As for his pension, that would have to wait too. Talking to a friend, though, he found out some worrying news. He would need to build up a £600 000 pot of pension savings if he wanted to retire at 60 with a pension of around £20 000 a year at today's prices.

1. What fringe benefits did Graeme enjoy when he was an employee of a lighting company?
2. (a) Explain what were the likely advantages to the lighting company of giving Graeme so many fringe benefits. (b) What were the likely advantages to Graeme of receiving these fringe benefits?
3. (a) Explain whether Graeme was better off in his first year after leaving his paid job. (b) Suggest what would have to happen to him and his business if he were to be better off at age (i) 50 and (ii) 65 than in his previous job.

wages. This is an example of a FRINGE BENEFIT. The more senior the position you hold in a company, the more fringe benefits you are likely to receive. One of the most important fringe benefits shown in Figure 94.2 for most workers is the subsidised company pension scheme. A company usually provides a proportion of payments into a scheme so that workers can get an occupational pension when they retire.

Fringe benefits are often given for tax reasons. The business pays less tax and other contributions in providing £1 000 worth of fringe benefits than it would if it paid an extra £1 000 in wages to a worker. Similarly, a worker may find there is a tax gain in receiving a fringe benefit rather than cash.

Fringe benefits are also used to motivate workers. The company car, for instance, is very important to many workers in senior positions.

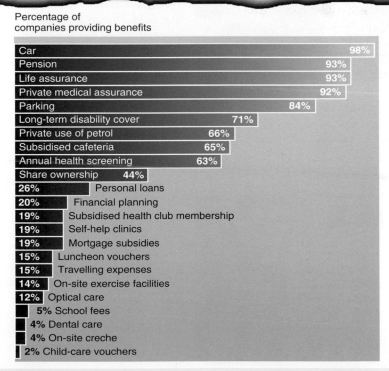

Percentage of companies providing benefits

Benefit	Percentage
Car	98%
Pension	93%
Life assurance	93%
Private medical assurance	92%
Parking	84%
Long-term disability cover	71%
Private use of petrol	66%
Subsidised cafeteria	65%
Annual health screening	63%
Share ownership	44%
Personal loans	26%
Financial planning	20%
Subsidised health club membership	19%
Self-help clinics	19%
Mortgage subsidies	19%
Luncheon vouchers	15%
Travelling expenses	15%
On-site exercise facilities	14%
Optical care	12%
School fees	5%
Dental care	4%
On-site creche	4%
Child-care vouchers	2%

Figure 94.2 *The main fringe benefits provided by companies (percentage providing fringe benefits)*
Source: adapted from CBI/Towers Perrin.

Manual employees are often paid wages and salespeople may be paid commission

1. List the THREE main types of payment system available to employers.
2. Which payment system do you think might be used by a business for each of the workers shown in the photographs? Give reasons for your choice.

Frank Stevenson is a casual worker in the building industry. He is hired on a job by job basis.

Maria Jimenez is a worker on a production line.

Liz Hartill is a primary school teacher.

John Osei is the managing director of a multinational company.

Payment systems

There is a variety of different ways in which a worker can be paid. Businesses differ in the PAYMENT SYSTEMS they use. A business may also use different payment systems for different groups of workers that it employs.

Time-based systems

MANUAL WORKERS or BLUE COLLAR WORKERS are workers who usually do physical work, like operating a machine in a factory. They have tended to be paid WAGES on a time based system. They are paid a certain amount for each hour worked. If they work longer than the agreed basic working week, such as 38 hours, they may get OVERTIME. This is often paid at a higher hourly rate, such as **time-and-a-quarter** or **double time**. This means that they are paid $1\frac{1}{4}$ or 2 times the basic pay per hour for every hour of overtime worked.

  For instance, a production worker may work a basic working week of 36 hours. He is paid £10 an hour. This means his basic pay is £360. He might then work 2 hours overtime at time-and-a-half. So he has earned an extra 2 hours at £15 an hour. This make his **gross earnings** £390 (£360 + £30).

Salaries

NON-MANUAL or WHITE COLLAR WORKERS are often paid SALARIES. A non-manual worker does non-physical work, like an office worker or a teacher. Salaries tend to be paid monthly rather than weekly. Salaried workers are paid to do a particular job. Overtime is not usually paid because salaried workers are expected to work for

as long as it takes to do their job. Salaried managers in business often work 40-60 hours a week.

Results-based systems

Some workers are paid according to how much they produce. Workers on PIECE RATES are paid for every item they make. If they produce nothing during the day, they get paid nothing. Sales staff may be paid on **commision** (☞ unit 51). For every sale they achieve, they get paid a certain amount. Some sales staff are paid totally on commission. So if they sell nothing, they get paid nothing. Others are paid commission as a BONUS. Bonuses are given as a reward for doing well. Non-sales staff may be given bonuses if, for instance, their department achieves a particular target for work. This is called a **group bonus**.

  Top managers in medium to large companies are increasingly being given **share options**. They may be given the chance in, say, five years time to buy a number of shares at today's prices. This is meant to motivate top managers and benefit shareholders. The higher the share price has risen, the more profit the manager will make from selling the shares in five years time. But equally, the higher the share price, the better it is for shareholders. Share options also help retain good managers. If they leave to get a job elsewhere before they can **exercise** (i.e. take) their share options, they lose them completely.

Which payment system?

A business has to make decisions about which payment systems to use for different groups of workers.

The payment system used depends partly on what is possible. A business would find it very difficult to use piece rates for a manager, for example, because it is difficult to measure output. A business paying its office staff on a commission basis wouldn't be possible either because they don't sell anything. Even sales staff might not be paid commission if sales are a team effort rather than the result of the work of one person.

Some payment systems are used because they reduce the tax bill of employers and employees. Fringe benefits are an example of this.

More importantly, payment systems reflect different views about what **motivates** workers (☞ unit 96-97). One view (the scientific management school) says that pay has an effect on workers' motivation. Linking pay directly with work done should ensure that workers work as hard as possible.

Other theories, however, suggest that pay is not the only factor affecting workers' motivation. Many businesses today stress how important it is for workers to feel part of the company. Workers also need their achievements to be recognised. Paying wages for working a fixed number of hours can lead to 'clock watching'. Workers can feel that **being at work** is more important than **what they do** when they are at work. Effort and the quality of what is produced can be poor. So an increasing number of workers are now paid a salary. Some are also allowed to buy shares in the

company or are paid a bonus as a reward. This partly reflects changing views about motivation. It also reflects the increase in **white collar** and **service** jobs in the economy (☞ unit 5).

In 2000, the government abandoned its existing pay structures in the Civil Service. This followed a damning report from the Treasury's public services productivity panel.

The Civil Service had been operating a bonus scheme based on individual achievement. Workers were set targets at the beginning of the year. At the end of the year they were judged on whether they had achieved each of those targets. This 'box marking' system had destroyed morale. One reason for this was that almost all of the individual workers worked in integrated teams. It was difficult, if not impossible, for the success or failure of the individual in achieving a target to be separated from the success or failure of the team. Another problem was that managers lacked the skills and experience to operate the scheme efficiently. Measurement of performance was often inaccurate. Too many targets were seen by staff as irrelevant and they were not clearly explained.

The report concluded that the bonus system 'failed to increase either the commitment of staff or the quality of their work'. They were 'ineffective and discredited'.

Source: adapted from *People Management*, 17.2.2000.

1. What is meant by a 'bonus scheme'?
2. On what basis were bonuses given in the Civil Service, according to the article?
3. What criticisms were made of the scheme?
4. Suggest why the scheme' failed to increase the commitment of staff or the quality of their work'. Justify your answer.

Checklist

1. What is the difference between a time-based payment system and a salary payment system?
2. How does a results-based system work?
3. What is the difference between piece rates and a bonus?
4. Why might a company give share options to its top managers?
5. What factors affect which type of payment system is used by a business?

key terms

Bonus - addition to the basic wage or salary, for example for achieving a production or sales target.
Manual or blue collar workers - workers who do mainly physical work like an assembly line worker.
Non-manual or white collar workers - workers who do non-physical work, like an office worker or a teacher.
Overtime - time worked over and above the basic working week.
Payment systems - methods of organising the payment of workers, such as piece rates or salaries.
Piece rates - a payment system where individual workers' wages are determined by how much they produce.
Salaries - pay, usually of non-manual workers, expressed as a yearly figure but paid monthly.
Wages - tend to be paid to manual workers for working a fixed number of hours per week plus overtime.

The importance of motivation

All businesses need to MOTIVATE their workers. A well motivated workforce is more likely to work hard. This will help a business improve the quality of its product, keep its costs down, make a profit and remain competitive. But what makes a workforce motivated?

One way of finding out is to consider the **needs** of workers. What do workers want from their job? The American researcher, A.H.Maslow, put the needs of workers in order of importance. This HIERARCHY OF NEEDS can be seen in Figure 96.1.

The hierarchy of needs

Physiological needs People's most basic need is a **physiological** need. A physiological need means satisfying the needs of the body, for example by eating food, having shelter and keeping warm (☞ unit 1). Without food and shelter, people could starve or freeze to death. So the most basic reason why people work is that they can earn the money to buy food and shelter. Physiological needs can also be satisfied by good working conditions. For example, heating in an office satisfies the need for warmth. Being allowed to take tea breaks or lunch breaks means that workers can satisfy their need for food and drink.

Safety needs People want to protect themselves against events which will damage their quality of life. At work, employees want to know that they will not suffer an accident which could injure them. They also want to know that they are safe from dismissal. This could reduce their income or take it away altogether.

Love and belonging This is a higher order need. People want to feel accepted as part of a group, such as a family or a club. They also want to be trusted and to be able to support others. Employees may satisfy this need in the workplace by working in teams. They are likely to cooperate and communicate with other workers. This should encourage a feeling of belonging. But if workers work alone and do not talk to others they may feel isolated and unwanted, and lack a sense of belonging. Also, if a manager bullies staff, subordinates are unlikely to feel loved.

Self-esteem needs People want to feel that others respect them for what they can do. They want to respect themselves too, feeling that they have achieved something and are good at a task. Having a successful career, where other workers look up to you and admire you will satisfy these needs. Being part of a successful company can also give workers the feeling that they are successful.

Self-actualisation This is the highest order need, according to Maslow. It is the ability to realise your

Workers' needs may include sa[...] or working with others in a tea[...]

Richer Sounds was started by Julian Richer in 1979. He specialised in selling end of line hi-fi equipment at a low price from a single shop. Today, his business has grown to include shops across the UK. It now sells standard hi-fi equipment at low prices.

Julian Richer's style of management towards his workforce is unusual by most standards. He places great emphasis on establishing a rapport with every new member of staff. He invites new employees to his house for three days where they 'work hard and play hard'. They undergo an intensive training course, but also enjoy tennis, badminton, snooker, swimming, dance and films.

Staff are encouraged to express their ideas. They are given £5 each, once a month, to visit the pub with other employees and talk about new ideas.

Each month one Richer Sounds store is picked out as having given the best customer service. Staff at that store are rewarded with the use of a luxury Mercedes limousine. The company also provides staff with the use of nine holiday homes which they can book free of charge.

Julian Richer wants to put the customer first. But to do that, he knows that he must also put his workforce first, creating amongst them a 'buzz' and a sense of excitement which they will then communicate to their customers.

Source: adapted from Richer Sounds company information.

1. Richer Sounds pays its workers a wage, satisfying their physiological needs.
   (a) What other needs, according to Maslow, might workers want satisfying?
   (b) How might Richer Sounds satisfy these needs, according to the article?
2. Staff at Richer Sounds on average take only 1-2 per cent of their working year off for sickness and other reasons. This is below the national average. Suggest why absenteeism is lower at Richer Sounds.

key terms

Hierarchy of needs - placing needs in order of importance, starting with basic human needs.
Job satisfaction - the amount of enjoyment, satisfaction or pleasure that a worker gets out of doing a particular job.
Motivation - in work, the desire to complete a task.

Checklist

1. Why is a motivated workforce important for a business?
2. What is the difference for a worker between (a) physiological and safety needs and (b) love and belonging needs and self esteem needs?
3. What is meant by 'self-actualisation'?
4. Why, according to Maslow's theory, are the following likely to be demotivated? (a) A worker whose pay has been cut from £150 a week to £100 a week. (b) A worker who is being bullied by his boss. (c) A worker who sits at a machine all day stamping out metal parts.

Jeff Simpson was employed as an accountant by Bearing and James Partners. Shortly after his appointment in January 2001 Jeff asked the partners on a number of occasions for a formal contract of employment. He also requested clarification of his duties and responsibilities. But he didn't receive either.

Then in September 2001 he was moved out of the office occupied by the main accounts team. He was given an office in another part of the building and rarely saw work colleagues in the day. This office was filthy. The windows were taped with PVC tape. The carpet was extremely dirty and dusty. The desk was full of dust. Paint was flaking from the ceilings and walls. The room was cold and damp. He had to ask for a portable heater. But he found he couldn't use it for most of the day because the fumes given off by the heater affected his chest and eyes.

What's more, in his old office, he had been working with new computers and new software. In his new office, he had an outdated computer with old software.

He complained about the move and his new working conditions. Shortly after, Jeff Simpson was sacked.

1. List the five needs in Maslow's hierarchy of needs.
2. 'Bearing and James Partners failed to satisfy almost every work need of Jeff Simpson.' Explain why this was the case, giving examples from the data.
3. In January 2001 Jeff Simpson arrived for his first day at work at the business keen and motivated to do well. Give FIVE examples of how Bearing and James Partners could have continued to motivate Jeff and explain why each would have been a motivator for him.

full potential. Being given a demanding job, where workers can use their creative talents, may satisfy the need for self-actualisation. Workers who have the ability to shape their working day in the way they want are more likely to satisfy this need than those who have to stick to a rigid timetable. Workers who are doing boring, repetitive jobs are unlikely to satisfy this need. They will have little scope to use their talent and flair at work.

Fulfilling needs

Businesses that use the hierarchy of needs to motivate workers must be aware of certain things.

- Workers are motivated by achieving the next level in the hierarchy of needs. When a worker is well paid, pay is no longer a motivator. In this case having job security, a safety need, is likely to be more motivating than more pay.
- If a need is not satisfied, it can demotivate workers. Workers will not be motivated, for instance, if they are poorly paid or if they do not feel accepted as part of a group.
- Lower level needs must be satisfied first. Poorly paid workers are likely to be demotivated even if their higher level needs are met. This is not always the case though. At times workers may work all night, with little food, in order to make a deadline that gives them self-esteem.

Workers in more senior positions in a business are more likely to have JOB SATISFACTION. In terms of Maslow's hierarchy of needs, these workers are likely to have more opportunities to meet higher level needs. They are likely to be the highest paid, have high self-esteem and have the greatest chance for self-actualisation. Manual workers, on the other hand, are least likely to have their needs met. They are likely to be the least well paid, have less job security and have little opportunity for self-actualisation.

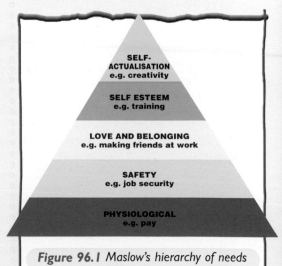

Figure 96.1 *Maslow's hierarchy of needs*

SELF-ACTUALISATION
e.g. creativity

SELF ESTEEM
e.g. training

LOVE AND BELONGING
e.g. making friends at work

SAFETY
e.g. job security

PHYSIOLOGICAL
e.g. pay

Workers may be motivated by pay or by other factors, such as good work facilities

Scientific management

Maslow's hierarchy of needs (☞ unit 96) is not the only theory of motivation. The first modern theory of motivation was put forward by Frederick Taylor in a book, *The Principles of Scientific Management*, published in 1911.

He argued that the workplace was usually badly organised. Each worker would approach a task in a different way. Some workers were highly efficient at what they did, but most were not. What's more, efficient workers had no incentive to work hard. Why should they produce twice as much as the next worker but get the same amount of pay? In fact, there was an incentive to work as little as possible because this made the job much easier. He also argued that workers needed to be closely supervised so that their work output could be measured. He judged that most workers didn't want to accept responsibility for the work they did.

To change this, Frederick Taylor proposed that managers should approach their task scientifically. They should find out what was the best way of doing a particular task. Then they should teach all the workers how to do it in this one way. Pay should be linked to the expected output of an efficient worker. They should also receive a 'fair day's pay for a fair day's work'. The easiest way to do this was to use a **piece rate** system (☞ unit 95). So workers who worked less hard would receive less pay. This would motivate them to work harder. A piece rate system would also mean that managers would be forced to supervise their workers in order to calculate their pay.

The human relations school of thought

A different view of motivation emerged from an experiment carried out between 1927 and 1932 at the Hawthorne Plant of the Western Electric company in Chicago. The researchers initially believed in Taylor's scientific management theories. Over a five year period, changes were made in lighting and heating, incentive schemes, rest periods and hours of work. Each time a change was made, output rose. This was true even when conditions of work were put back to how they were at the start of the experiment.

Elton Mayo reported on this experiment. He concluded that output was rising because of the attention that

Danny Holt worked at a credit card call centre for six months. There were fifty workers at the call centre. Forty two were on the bottom grade with five supervisors and three more senior managers. The average length of stay of basic grade workers in the job (the 'turnover rate') was just 7 months.

Staff were given targets for the number of calls per hour that they should deal with. For example, those dealing with customer queries were expected to deal with 12 calls an hour. Those who consistently failed to achieve this were advised that they should resign. Supervisors always let staff know whether they had achieved their target at the end of each shift.

The call centre was open 24 hours a day, seven days a week. Staff were rotated around each shift. However, the company expected staff to change shift at very short notice if other staff were away ill. Danny felt that he could never plan ahead for his family or social life because of this.

If basic grade staff wanted to go to the toilet when on duty, they had to put up their hands and wait for the supervisor to give permission. Supervisors were given instructions to allow a maximum of two workers to go to the toilet at any one time. The computer software which controlled the centre could also state how long a staff member had not been answering calls. Some staff were told that they were going to the toilet too often.

Every phone call could be overheard by supervisors if they chose to listen in. A random number of calls were also taped and were made available for replay by management. A particular staff member's calls could also be taped over a period of time, for training purposes or to monitor their performance. Danny found it very threatening to know that a supervisor might be listening in to any of his phone calls.

1. Explain how the management at the call centre controlled the work of basic grade employees.
2. Suggest why Danny might have found the working conditions demotivating.
3. Discuss what changes might be made at the call centre to reduce the poor motivation of staff.

Theory X	Theory Y
Workers are motivated by money	Workers are motivated by many needs
Workers are lazy and dislike work	Workers can enjoy work
Workers are selfish, ignore the needs of organisations, avoid responsibility and lack ambition	Workers can organise themselves and take responsibility
Workers need to be controlled and directed by management	It is up to management to allow workers to be creative and to apply their job knowledge

Table 97.1 McGregor's Theory X and Theory Y

Motivating factors	Demotivating or 'hygiene' factors
Sense of achievement	Pay
Chance of promotion	Working conditions
Responsibility	Company rules and policy
Nature of the job itself	Fear of redundancy
Recognition by management	Treatment at work
Personal development	Feelings of inadequacy

Table 97.2 Factors which motivate and demotivate workers

was being given to the workers. This motivated the workers to work more productively. The rising productivity due to the attention paid to workers came to be known as the **Hawthorne effect**.

Theory X and Theory Y

A later American researcher, Douglas McGregor, in *The Human Side of Enterprise*, published in 1960, contrasted the two main schools of motivation. The views of the Scientific Management school of thought were called Theory X. The alternative Human Relations school, building on the work of researchers like Mayo and Maslow, he called Theory Y. According to Theory Y, workers want both their basic and higher needs fulfilling when they go to work. Workers work best in conditions where they are trusted, and where they are given an opportunity to fulfil themselves. The contrasting views of Theory X and Theory Y are shown in Table 97.1.

Job satisfaction

Another American researcher, Frederick Herzberg, came to similar conclusions. He suggested that a number of factors in a job would motivate workers. They would then get **job satisfaction**. For example, workers who were given a sense of achievement or offered training would be more motivated. These factors are shown in Table 97.2.

He also put forward what he called **hygiene factors**. These could demotivate workers if they were not met. For example, not receiving a reasonable wage or poor working conditions could demotivate staff.

He suggested that once a hygiene factor was satisfied, adding more to it would not motivate workers. For example, if a worker feels that she is getting a fair wage already, increasing her pay will not motivate her to worker harder or better. According to Herzberg, hygiene factors can only demotivate workers but not motivate them.

Job enlargement and job enrichment

The work of researchers such as Maslow and Herzberg has led to ideas that workers' jobs could be made more satisfying through:

- **job enlargement** - instead of a worker doing one small task every day, they would be able to do a variety of tasks. This would make the work less monotonous and boring;
- **job enrichment** - where workers are given some opportunities to choose how to complete a particular job of work, usually working in a team.

Checklist

1. What, according to Frederick Taylor, motivates workers to work?
2. What is the role of management in motivating workers according to the scientific management school?
3. What is the Hawthorne Effect?
4. What is the difference between Theory X and Theory Y?
5. (a) What are 'hygiene factors'? (b) What, according to Herzberg, motivates workers?
6. How could an employer increase the amount of job satisfaction gained by its workers?

Karen Deacon worked on an assembly line at an engineering manufacturers making components. She found the work boring and repetitive. Some days, she also found that her right wrist felt very stiff and it was painful to move. She brought the matter to the attention of the supervisor who said that the workplace was going to be restructured. She hoped this would deal with the problem.

Within a week, the assembly line was dismantled and replaced by a manufacturing cell. There were six workers in the cell responsible for producing common components. Initially, she still did the same work as before. But all the members of the cell were given training so that they could do each other's jobs. They were then allowed to decide amongst themselves who did what job each day. They were also given responsibility for deciding when to take breaks during the day. The cell was given a target for production. Over the cell, hanging from the ceiling, was the weekly target with the production actually achieved for the previous week.

Karen's wrist problem disappeared. She also began looking forward to going to work.

1. 'Karen benefited from both job enlargement and job enrichment.' Explain, giving examples, what this means.
2. Discuss whether displaying production levels and targets would be motivating or demotivating for the workers in the cell.

UNIT 98

Leadership styles

Leadership

Managers and directors need to be LEADERS. Leadership is difficult to define precisely but it usually involves:
- setting targets or goals. For example, a business may set a target of a 10 per cent increas in sales. Or it might aim for a 5 per cent reduction in costs;
- organising work. Examples might be allocating a task to an individual or deciding on the resources needed to undertake a project;
- monitoring work to see whether goals are being achieved;
- motivating workers to achieve goals.

There are four main types of leader - autocratic, persuasive and democratic, consultative and democratic, and laissez-faire.

Richard Branson and Bill Gates - leaders of the Virgin and Microsoft businesses

? Leadership styles can be illustrated by diagrams which show how leaders communicate with the others.

1. Explain which style of leadership (autocratic, democratic or laissez-faire) is shown in Figures 98.1-98.3.
2. A medium sized company is facing a crisis. Sales have been falling and it needs a new approach to marketing quickly or it may go out of business. Which type of leadership style do you think would be best in this situation? Explain your answer carefully.

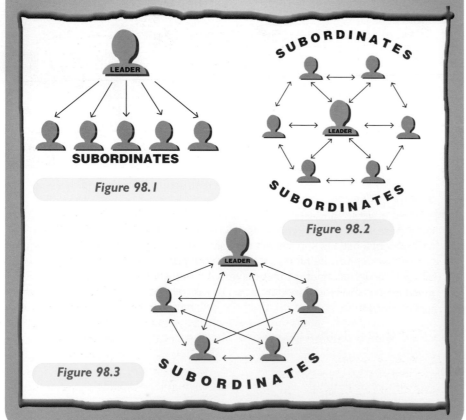

Figure 98.1

Figure 98.2

Figure 98.3

Autocratic leaders

An AUTOCRATIC LEADER is one who makes all the decisions. The leader then tells those working under him or her what to do. The role of workers lower in the hierarchy is to carry out the orders of the leader.

Communication (☞ units 106-108) flows from the leader to subordinates and back again. There is little need for subordinates to communicate with one another because they receive orders from above. If the leader is making the right decisions, this can be a very effective form of leadership. The leader is able to have a powerful influence on the business and its employees. However, it may mean that subordinates feel frustrated. They may also become demotivated because they can't fulfil their **higher order needs** (☞ unit 96).

Persuasive and democratic leaders

A DEMOCRATIC LEADER is one who shares some of the decision making with subordinates. Persuasive leaders, like autocratic leaders, make decisions alone. But then they 'persuade' workers under them to accept their decisions through discussion and reasoning.

Checklist

1. What is the role of a leader?
2. Explain why the head chef in a large restaurant could be described as a 'leader'.
3. What are the differences between an autocratic leader and a laissez-faire leader?
4. Compare TWO types of democratic leadership.
5. Explain what type of leadership you think might be most effective in (a) a rock band; (b) the army; (c) a school; (d) a car manufacturer; (e) a hairdressing salon.

William Critchlow was a legend in his lifetime. He built up Critchlow's from a sweet shop in Preston to a large multinational food company. Notoriously secretive, only one photograph taken of him years ago is available today. The company headquarters in Essex are surrounded by parkland and a mile long wall.

Within the company, William Critchlow expected his orders to be carried out to the letter. At board meetings, he would encourage his senior managers to put forward their points of view. John, his son, and Erica, his daughter, were two of these senior managers. He always listened with great respect. But having heard their advice, he would then make the decision about what to do.

Brand managers were vital to the success of the business. Each brand would have its own manager responsible for that product. Brand managers would have a budget for promotion. They were expected to use this budget to expand sales. Managers would be recruited straight from university and given training. Having proved themselves with small brands, they would be given larger and larger brands to manage. They might also be promoted into a different area of the business, such as personnel, if their skills were more suited. William Critchlow kept a close watch on all his managers and their development. Only he could approve a promotion. Sometimes he would recommend that the individual would have a better future outside the company.

1. What type of leader (autocratic, democratic or laissez-faire) was William Critchlow? Explain your answer.
2. Suggest why Critchlow's grew to be a successful company.
3. When William Critchlow died, he was succeeded as chief executive by his daughter, Erica. She was determined to assert her authority. She made more decisions without consulting the board. She also made brand managers consult her before making decisions. Discuss the possible advantages and disadvantages of this different style of leadership.

Workers are likely to be more motivated under this type of leadership. This is because they may feel more involved in decision making. However, decision making can take longer because the leader has to spend time persuading others.

Consultative and democratic leaders

This is a different type of democratic leader. Consultative leaders consult or ask for others' opinions before coming to a decision. The final decision will take account of what subordinates have said. More time may have to be spent making decisions than with a persuasive leader. But workers may feel even more involved and motivated with an effective consultative leader.

Laissez-faire leaders

A LAISSEZ-FAIRE LEADER makes very few decisions. These leaders allow workers under them to make many of their own decisions. Laissez-faire leadership allows **subordinates** (☞ unit 88) to be highly creative. But it can also lead to a feeling by subordinates that no one knows or cares about what is going on. Another unofficial or informal leader often then emerges who gives the business a greater sense of direction.

Effective leadership

What makes a leader a good leader? Effective leaders tend to possess some or all of the following qualities.
- They are experts in a particular field. They also have a good understanding of other areas in which they have to operate.
- They are creative and innovative. This often distinguishes them from their subordinates.
- They have a 'vision' for the business. For example, they might see that the business must move into a different market or be organised in a different way.
- They come up with practical solutions to problems. These might be major company problems. Or they might be day to day problems that occur unexpectedly.
- They can communicate their ideas and decisions to subordinates. They can also motivate subordinates. This is vital if subordinates are going to carry out the ideas and strategy of the leader.

Training can be on the job or off the job

The objectives of training

Training is a cost for a business. So it is important that the business gets 'value for money' from training programmes. There is a number of possible objectives of training for a business.

Induction INDUCTION training is given to new workers. The objective is to make them familiar with the workings of the business and the area in which they are going to work. New workers at a shoe shop may be trained, for example, to check stock, use a cash till and deal with customers.

Upgrading skills With technology and markets changing all the time, workers need to **upgrade** their existing skills. For example, a hotel receptionist may have to be trained to use a new computerised booking system. Equally, upgrading skills is often necessary for a worker to gain **promotion**. In some professions, like accountancy or banking, this may involve passing examinations.

Retraining Over time, jobs disappear or change. Workers with skills to do these jobs need retraining to do different jobs.

Creating flexibility Businesses increasingly want their workers to be flexible and have a number of skills. They can then do a variety of jobs rather than just one. In a factory, for example, management may want workers to cover the work of colleagues who are off sick or on holiday. This **multi-skilling** (☞ unit 62) can be achieved through training.

Increasing autonomy Many businesses today want to push

decision making down the **hierarchy** (☞ unit 88). For example, the decision about whether to call out the maintenance team to repair a machine might have been made by a production manager before. Now it might be made by the machine operator. Giving greater powers to staff, though, may involve giving them training in new skills.

Motivation Regular training can increase the **motivation** (☞ units 96 and 97) of workers. It gives confidence to workers so that they can tackle existing and new tasks. It is a way for **leaders** (☞ unit 98) to communicate their vision of change within an organisation. There is also a **Hawthorne effect** (☞ unit 97). This is where training makes workers feel that they are important to the organisation, so that they feel more motivated.

On and off the job training

There are two main methods of training. ON THE JOB training occurs when workers pick up skills by working alongside other workers. On the job training is cheap and often effective. However, it is unlikely to provide in depth training. It is also

Birds Eye Wall's has formed a strong partnership with its trade unions to offer learning at work. The company's Humberside, Lowestoft and Gloucester sites are all involved. The scheme starts off with 'springboard' days which run in worktime. During that day, workers find out about the scheme and the courses on offer. They are invited to put down their names for courses that interest them.

Workers attend these courses in their own time for which they have to pay. However, some of the cost of the courses is subsidised by the company and the trade unions. The courses are provided by local further education colleges. They cover a wide range from kick-boxing to scuba diving to motor mechanics to computer literacy.

These courses are not directly work related. However, both the company and the unions support them strongly because of their broad effect on training. Senior shop steward John Greenfields said: 'The view here is that if you are willing to learn new things, you are going to be more willing later on to learn things of benefit to the company and its work.' Management and unions also feel that the courses lead to greater motivation at work.

Source: adapted from Rural, Agricultural and Allied Workers, *Landworker*, March/April 2001.

1. What sort of courses are being offered through the Birds Eye Wall's scheme?
2. Discuss the advantages and disadvantages to Birds Eye Wall's of running the scheme.

unable to help whole groups of workers to change their skills.

To do this, OFF THE JOB training is often needed. Workers are taken away from the jobs to be trained. This may be done within a business. Either experts within the company may lead the course or an outside trainer may be brought in. Alternatively, employees may be sent on training courses provided by outside agencies. These include management colleges, further and higher education colleges and training consultancies.

Off the job training is more expensive than on the job training. Outside trainers have to be paid. Also, workers can't produce anything on the days when they are being trained. On the other hand, a wider rage of skills can be obtained. It can also provide workers with qualifications needed for their job.

Types of training

Businesses use a variety of types of training.

Induction training This has already been described above.

Apprenticeships, Youth Training and graduate training Young people straight out of school, college or university have specific training needs. They need short term induction training. They are also likely to need longer training to bring their skills up to the level required for a particular job. Some businesses offer Modern Apprenticeships (☞ unit 100). These give young people an extended period of training leading to qualification at NVQ levels 2 (GCSE level), 3 (equivalent to A level) or even 4 (approaching university degree standard). Some

businesses are also offering Youth Training (☞ unit 100). This is a scheme funded by the government where young people are given training and work experience. Young people coming from university also need training. So there may be a graduate training scheme.

Staff training Groups of workers may need to be trained together. Perhaps they need to learn the skills associated with new technology (skill training). They might need to learn about new health and safety procedures. A buying team might need to learn about new products now available from suppliers.

Staff development Individual workers have training needs too. Staff development programmes help staff who wish to gain skills and qualifications needed for promotion.

key terms

Induction - a period of training for workers new to a business when they find out about the business and the job they have to do.
Off the job training - training undertaken away from the the job either at the business or outside the business, for example at a college of further education.
On the job training - training in the workplace undertaken whilst doing a job.

✓Checklist

1. What might be the objectives of training for a business?
2. What might a worker gain from being trained?
3. What is the difference between on the job training and off the job training?
4. Where might a worker be trained off the job?
5. What types of training exist?

Ragland's is a ceramics company which makes electrical porcelain. This is typically used on transformers and capacitors for the power industry. It employs 150 workers.

- Peter has just joined the company. He will be working on the shop floor, initially in the ceramics section.
- Ela has also just joined the marketing department as a sales representative. She is ambitious and wants to gain promotion quickly.
- Tara works as an invoice clerk in the accounts department. Jennie, the accounts manager, thinks she is capable of filling a more important role in the accounts department, but she lacks the knowledge necessary for any promotion.
- Lee works soldering metal components together. However, the company has just patented a new design which gets rid of the need for soldering. His job will therefore disappear. He has been offered a new job in logistics, getting the product to the company's customers.

1. Explain why each of the four workers has training needs.
2. The company has a limited budget for training. It can only afford to spend money on formal training for two of these workers. Who do you think it should be? Explain your answer carefully.

RAGLAND'S

UNIT 100

Government and training

The need for government intervention

Six million British adults have no formal qualifications. One quarter of adults haven't undertaken any learning for three years. Nearly a third of companies don't offer their workers formal training. Many middle sized and small businesses rely on schools, colleges and other businesses to provide training. They then recruit (some would say 'poach' or 'headhunt') workers with the right skills and qualifications. This helps to explain why the government has to intervene in the training market.

Learning and Skills Councils

The Department for Education and Employment (DfEE) is the government department directly responsible for training. It supervises the work of Learning and Skills Councils. This is a national network of 47 Councils covering every part of the UK. It is controlled by the National Learning and Skill Council based in London. Learning and Skills Councils replaced Training and Enterprise Councils, TECs, in 2001.

Learnings and Skills Councils are led by a board made up of local business people, trade union representatives and government representatives. Their aims are:
* to increase the number of people over 16 actively engaged in learning;
* to raise the standard of post-16 education and training;
* to ensure that learning is relevant to the needs of individuals and business.

The Learning and Skills Councils have control of all post-16 education, including Further Education colleges and Sixth Form colleges.

Learning and Skills Councils have a large budget to promote training. This was £6.2 billion in 2002. They spend this money on a wide variety of schemes including the New Deal.

The New Deal

The New Deal was introduced in 1997. Initially, it was designed to provide jobs for unemployed 18-24 year olds. After assessment, unemployed young people are given help to find a job. This may include offering employers

Training motor mechanics

a subsidy to take them on. If they don't succeed then they will offered two options. They may be given up to 52 weeks of full time education and training to raise their level of skills

Wayne Treherne and Lee Broadbent have both secured full-time jobs after taking part in the New Deal 'Gateway to Work' programme. Wayne left school with almost no qualifications and then failed to hold down various warehouse jobs. The two-week Gateway to Work programme changed his life and his job prospects. He was offered a work trial at Jumpin' Jaks, a Swansea party venue. Within days he was taken on as a full-time employee. 'Working at Jumpin' Jaks is not just about pulling pints and collecting glasses - it's about meeting people from different backgrounds, cultures and age groups, developing excellent communication and customer service skills,' said Wayne.

After working for five years at BP Llandarcy, Lee lost his job when the plant closed. He was unemployed for a year before joining the scheme at Swansea College. After going through the Gateway to Work, he was employed for a trial period by Mono Equipment, manufacturers of bakery equipment, and was later taken on as a full-time fitter/assembler. Mono's personnel manager, Jan Bevan, said: 'Lee is a reliable employee and gets on well with people - he's good news.'

Source: adapted from DfEE, *Employment News*, May 2001.

1. The Gateway to Work programme is part of the New Deal. What is the New Deal?
2. How did the Gateway to Work programme (a) help Wayne and Lee and (b) help the businesses which employed them?
3. Businesses and workers pay taxes, some of which are used to pay for the New Deal. Discuss whether they would be better off paying lower taxes with schemes like the New Deal being scrapped.

and make them more employable. Or they may gain work experience on schemes designed to benefit the local community and the environment. The New Deal now also covers help and training for anyone who is unemployed in the long term.

Modern Apprenticeships

Modern Apprenticeships are designed to give young people traditional apprenticeship skills. Local Enterprise Councils subsidise young workers on these schemes. The rest of the cost is met by their employer. Young workers are trained to at least NVQ level 3 over a period of up to three years. NVQs are National Vocational Qualifications. These are qualifications like GCSEs or A levels, but are vocationally (i.e. work) orientated.

National Training Organisations

National Training Organisations cover training in specific industries. For example, the Construction Industry Training Board (CITB) is responsible for training of construction industry workers. In the case of the CITB, it is funded through a levy (or tax) on construction businesses. Training is particularly needed in the construction industry because so many construction businesses are

small and give little or no training to their workers. Accidents are also common in construction, This makes training even more essential.

Investors in People

Investors in People (IiP) is an initiative designed to make businesses think about their training needs. It is a **quality standard** (☞ unit 58).

To gain the IiP standard, a business has to consider its performance. It then needs to identify how that performance is not as good as it could be because of a lack of skills of workers. It must then commit itself to training staff to fill this skills gap. The process is ongoing. To keep IiP status, a business must agree to review its training needs on a regular basis.

The National Construction College East (NCCE) is run by the Construction Industry Training Board (CITB). The college is recognised as one of the world's leading residential training centres for people already working in, or looking to break into, a career in the construction industry.

The courses on offer have been designed to provide training at varied levels of competence. Most lead to National Vocational Qualifications (NVQ). For example, every year more than 400 youth trainees undertake NVQ level 2 courses. There are also more than 40 plant operation and maintenance courses available for both experienced and new plant operatives.

CITB colleges are funded by the industry levy. With this method of funding, companies that wish to train their 16-25 year old workforce can do so at any of the CITB colleges at no cost to the business by using a grant system.

As well as practical training, the college provides a recruitment service for companies looking for youth trainees. This service is in high demand. As a result more than 95 per cent of students enter permanent employment within the construction industry on completion of their training.

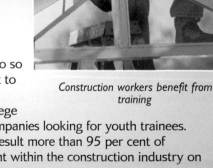

Construction workers benefit from training

Source: adapted from *Building, Trade and Industry*, April 2001.

1. What is the Construction Industry Training Board?
2. Suggest what are the advantages to businesses of (a) sending their employees for training at the National Construction College East and (b) for recruiting previously unemployed workers who have completed courses at the college.
3. The government allows the Construction Industry Training Board (CITB) to fund itself by raising a levy on all construction businesses. Discuss whether it would be better if the levy were removed and the CITB had to fund itself by charging for individual training courses.

✓Checklist

1. Why is there a need for governments to intervene to promote training?
2. How do Learning and Skills Councils encourage training?
3. What opportunities for training are offered under the New Deal?
4. What is a 'Modern Apprenticeship'?
5. What is the link between Investors in People and training?

Trade unions act as a pressure group to protect workers' interests

Communication

In some businesses, employees are members of a TRADE UNION. A trade union exists to protect the interests of its members in the workplace. Trade union representatives can negotiate with management on behalf of their members. This negotiation is called collective bargaining. It is 'collective' because many shareholders are represented by just a few managers. Equally, many workers are represented by just a few trade union officials. Collective bargaining provides a channel of communication (☞ unit 106) between workers and management.

Types of union

Trade unions may be placed in certain categories.

General unions Traditionally, general unions represented unskilled **blue collar workers** (☞ unit 95), such as factory workers and cleaners. Today's large general unions, such as the Transport and General Workers Union (T&G), recruit many different types of worker. Some general trade unions have been created in recent years by the merger of other types of union. For example, UNISON was formed by the merger of unions that represented public service workers.

Craft unions These unions represent workers with similar skills. In the past their members were mainly skilled blue collar workers, such as toolmakers and joiners. Craft unions today might still include the ceramic workers union, CATU.

Industrial unions These unions represent workers in a single industry. Examples are the National Union of Mineworkers (NUM) and the National Union of Railwayworkers (NUR). They only represent workers in the coal or rail industries.

Occupational unions These unions recruit workers from certain occupations. For example, the National Association of Teachers in Further and Higher Education (NATFHE) recruits lecturers and NAPO is the National Association of Probation Officers.

White collar unions These unions recruit non-manual workers. For example, the finance union UNIFI recruits members from the finance industry. These workers are mainly **white collar workers** (☞ unit 95).

Services to members

Workers belong to trade unions because they provide a range of services.

- They negotiate with employers and **employers' associations** (also known as trade associations, (☞ unit 14) over conditions of work, including pay, hours, holidays, equal opportunities and safety.
- They give legal protection to workers. They also offer advice about issues such as redundancy and unfair dismissal. If matters are serious enough, they will employ legal experts to defend members in court.
- They provide monetary

More than 200 poultry processing workers working for Moy Park gained a pay rise last month. It was the result of three years of negotiations between the T&G union and the management at Moy Park in Northern Ireland. The union had pressed for the work of some employees to be re-evaluated. Their jobs had changed. For example, computers were introduced into the duties of store workers at the company. Previously, the pay of store workers was assessed mainly on the physical side of the job. 70 workers will get their pay backdated.

The T&G union has also been working with the company to improve health and safety. Supervisors and shop stewards have undergone health and safety training. Forming health and safety committees will be the next step forward.

Source: adapted from Rural Agricultural and Allied Workers, *Landworker*, March/April 2001.

1. How have employees at Moy Park benefited from the work of the T&G?
2. Suggest who might sit on a 'health and safety committee'.

key terms

Joint consultative committee - **a committee of trade union and employer representatives which meets regularly to discuss issues of concern.**

Shop stewards or union representatives - **a trade union member elected by workers in a place of work to represent their interests to management.**

Trade union - **an organisation which represents the interests of the workers who are its members.**

✔Checklist

1. 'Collective bargaining provides a channel of communication.' What does this mean?
2. Describe the different types of trade union.
3. What services does a trade union provide for its members?
4. Explain the difference between a trade union member, a shop steward and a full time union official.
5. What is the TUC?

benefits. These vary from union to union. They can include strike pay, life insurance, mortgages and personal loans.

- They act as a **pressure group** (☞ unit 14). They try to pressure employers, trade associations and government to bring further benefits to workers. They also resist changes which are likely to harm the interests of workers.

Union organisation

Unions rely upon a mix of paid and unpaid workers and representatives to do the work of the union. At the bottom of the union hierarchy are the members themselves. They elect SHOP STEWARDS or UNION REPRESENTATIVES from amongst themselves in their place of work. Shop stewards are unpaid volunteers. They deal with problems of members directly or pass them on to someone else in the union better able to sort them out. Shop stewards may also negotiate with management over labour issues. They therefore act as the main channel of communication between workers and managers.

Negotiations with employers take place in a variety of ways. However, if the place of work is large enough, there may well be a JOINT CONSULTATIVE COMMITTEE. This is a committee made up of shop stewards and management representatives. The committee will meet regularly to discuss issues of concern.

Alongside the voluntary workers of the union, there are full time officials. These are paid by the union to give advice and help to members, shop stewards and branches.

Each year, a union holds an **annual conference**. This is the AGM of the union. Representatives are elected by members to go to the conference. The **motions** of the conference which are passed become policy for the union. The full time officials of the union then have to follow that policy.

Most unions belong to the TUC, the Trades Union Congress, in the same way that employers might belong to the CBI (☞ unit 14). The TUC acts as a pressure group for the trade union movement. It also helps individual trade unions to develop policy.

helping members
- Got a problem at work?
- Is your manager trying to change your office hours?
- Is it too hot or cold in your office?
- Are you having problems returning from maternity leave?
- Have you been selected for redundancy?
- Have you had an accident or been injured?

We can help with all these issues and more!

As well as negotiating pay and conditions, UNIFI provides a wide range of extra services for members

- We provide individual representation and legal support for members who need help.
- UNISERVICE Ltd brings you exclusive savings on such things as holidays, motoring and financial services.
- We have a Youth Network.
- There's a team of racial and sexual harassment counsellors and a Disability Advisory Committee. Full details can be found on the UNIFI Equality web site.
- UNIFI Education provides a range of courses free to all members, including training in assertiveness, computer skills and your rights at work, as well as how to get involved in UNIFI. We also run LearnDirect - a distance learning programme.
- To keep you in touch with what's new, we publish a bi-monthly magazine, FUSION.

Source: adapted from UNIFI Web site.

1. Jocelyn, Manu, Gail, Jai and Chloe are telesales workers in a call centre which sells insurance over the telephone. Explain what benefits they might gain by joining UNIFI.
2. How might their employer benefit because they are members of UNIFI?

UNIT 102

Industrial relations

Unions and workers may take industrial action in a dispute

Employee and worker objectives

Employers communicate with their workforce over a range of issues. These include pay, holidays, working conditions, contracts of employment, redundancies and staffing levels. INDUSTRIAL RELATIONS is the term used to describe the relationship between employers and workers.

Workers and employers in a business are likely to have different views about certain issues. As **stakeholders** (☞ unit 19) they will have their own objectives. Workers would like to earn more pay for less hours worked. But employers want to make profits. So they will want to keep costs, such as the wages of workers, down.

However, workers and employers may have some common objectives. Both workers and employers have an incentive to strive for quality in production. A quality product is likely to sell well. This should lead to profits for employers and higher wages and job security for workers. Workers also want to be motivated at work (☞ units 96 and 97). Many employers today recognise the need for a motivated workforce. If workers are motivated, they are likely to be more productive for the business. This should lead to greater profits.

Resolving disputes

Nearly all disputes between workers, trade unions and employers in the UK are resolved peacefully through negotiation. Occasionally, both sides find it useful to seek CONCILIATION. An outside body is brought in to listen to the arguments and suggest ways in which the two sides can come to an agreement.

More rarely, both sides will agree to go to ARBITRATION. This is where

an outside body listens to both sides and then delivers a recommended solution. The arbiter is acting like a judge, giving a verdict. Neither side is bound in law to accept the arbitration ruling. However, by agreeing to arbitration, both sides are saying that they will accept the verdict even if it goes against their interests.

The government funds ACAS, the Advisory, Conciliation and Arbitration Service, to provide conciliation and arbitration services. It also provides advice to businesses and unions on industrial relations issues.

Industrial action

If negotiations break down completely, either side may take

industrial action. Workers, for example, can:

- go on **strike** - perhaps a one day strike, or a strike where only key workers don't come in to work or, more serious, an all out strike by all workers;
- **ban overtime**;
- **boycott** work, such as refusing to work with new machinery.

Employers too can take action against workers. In particular, they can **lock out** their workers. They may either sack them all and employ new workers or state that only workers who are prepared to accept

Postal workers are likely to disrupt services in London, according to their union, the Communication Workers Union. The dispute is over a £400 million investment plan by the Post Office. It will introduce automatic sorting machines and other technological advances. However, automation is likely to see 2 000 postal workers' jobs disappear.

The Post Office says that the 2 000 jobs can be lost through normal staff turnover (workers resigning from their job and not being replaced) and voluntary transfers to different offices. The Post Office said: 'Royal Mail has a good track record of making such changes without the need for compulsory redundancy, and with the co-operation and flexibility of our employees will be able to carry on this success.'

Source: adapted from the *Financial Times*, 27.9.2000.

1. What is the cause of the dispute at the Post Office?
2. (a) How could postal workers 'disrupt services'? (b) What would they hope to achieve by such disruption?
3. What role could ACAS play in this dispute?
4. Discuss whether the Communications Union should take industrial action at this stage.

management terms will be allowed to work.

Union recognition

In the 1980s, trade union law was changed in a number of ways which reduced the power of trade unions. Many businesses decided to **de-recognise** unions altogether. This meant that their workers were still free to join a trade union. But employers would no longer recognise trade unions as the representatives of the workers. So they would not bargain with them any more.

Collective bargaining usually helped workers get better pay and conditions from their employers. By joining together, they were stronger in negotiation than if employees were alone and unrepresented. However, trade unions could be an advantage to employers, particularly in larger companies. This was because trade unions were a cost effective means of **communicating** with workers. Trade unions could channel the demands of workers to employers. The employers did not have to negotiate with every individual worker. At the same time, trade unions could help employers get acceptance from their workers for any deal negotiated.

In 1999, the **Employment Relations Act** (☞ unit 105) forced employers to **recognise** trade unions again if a majority of workers in a ballot voted in favour of recognition. This has given unions greater power with employers who don't want to negotiate with trade unions. Businesses and unions are also working together in partnership to improve health and safety and training, for example.

Single union agreements

In a few important cases, trade unions and employers have negotiated a **single union agreement**. This is where employers recognise only one union. This simplifies negotiations for employers. For the trade union which signs the deal, it gives greater power in the workplace.

Single union agreements are most common where a foreign firm has located a new factory in the UK. They have often been introduced alongside other industrial relations measures, such as **no-strike deals**. No strike deals are where workers agree not to strike in return for compulsory arbitration when employers and workers disagree.

Checklist

1. In what ways might the objectives of employers and workers be (a) different and (b) the same.
2. What is the difference between conciliation and arbitration?
3. Describe THREE types of industrial action that a trade union might take.
4. Why might a business want to de-recognise a trade union?
5. What might be the advantages to a business of (a) working with trade unions and (b) signing a single union agreement?

key terms

Arbitration - a method of settling a dispute which involves both parties agreeing to put their case to an independent outside arbitrator and accept his or her judgment as to how the dispute should be settled.
Conciliation - the process of helping two parties to a dispute to discuss and settle their dispute.
Industrial relations - the relationship between businesses and their workers.

The AEEU engineering trades union yesterday announced a recognition agreement with the UK Drilling Contractors Association.

The Association represents most of the active drilling companies in the North Sea who employ 90 per cent of North Sea drilling workers.

The initial agreement grants the AEEU collective bargaining rights over wages, hours and holidays, along with union facilities. A consultation committee will later discuss arrangements for negotiations over terms and conditions of work. The union expected to deliver 'major' improvements to these conditions.

Mr Richardson, speaking for the UK Drilling Contractors Association, said that he had been very impressed by AEEU's work on several cross-industry safety committees. He described the union as 'progressive and experienced'.

Source: adapted from the *Financial Times*, 10.6.2000.

1. What is meant by (a) collective bargaining and (b) union recognition?
2. What benefits might workers gain from union recognition?
3. Discuss whether it is in the best interests of employers to recognise trade unions.

UK and EU laws set out regulations to control safety at work

Health and safety

Employers, by law, have to provide workers with a healthy and safe environment in which to work. Work-related sickness and accidents at work are a problem for employees and businesses. Common problems are physical injuries, such as back problems, and psychological illness, such as stress. In the UK, over 1 million workers suffer an accident at work each year. Over 20 million working days are lost each year due to injuries at work.

The law

There are certain laws and regulations which affect health and safety in the workplace.

The Factories Act 1961 and The Offices, Shops and Railway Premises Act 1963

These two laws established minimum standards in a number of key work areas including temperature and ventilation, lighting, cleanliness, washing areas and toilets, space for people to work, clothing and first-aid facilities.

The Health and Safety at Work Act 1974

This is a law which puts an obligation on employers to protect workers and members of the public. Employers must have a written statement of their policy on health and safety. They must give training on health and safety issues. Managers and workers are personally responsible for ensuring safety in the workplace. The Act established the Health and Safety Executive, an organisation which enforces the law. Its inspectors can enter employers' premises to carry out checks on health and safety. Employers which fail to comply with the law can be taken to court and fined or even closed down. Individual managers and workers can be fined or imprisoned too for breaking the law.

The construction industry has one of the worst health and safety records in the UK. It accounts for one third of all health and safety prosecutions and one half of prohibition notices served on employers to stop work until an area of work is made safe. However, with only 128 safety inspectors employed to enforce the law over half a million construction sites and 160 000 building companies, it is impossible even to investigate all the deaths and major injuries reported.

Typical of the problem is the case of Michael and Carl Redgate, a father and son aged 49 and 18. They were employed with no previous training in demolition by a firm which itself had no experience of demolition work. Yet the firm accepted a job to demolish a brick kiln used to bake pottery. They sent the two workers out without any detailed instructions of how to take the kiln down safely. This was contrary to the Construction Design and Management (CDM) regulations issued under the Health and Safety Act 1974. Neither the pottery company nor the building company followed the other legal procedures required under these regulations, such as site inspection. The result was that the kiln collapsed on top of the two workers as they cut metalwork inside the kiln, killing them both.

Source: adapted from Labour Research, April 2001.

1. Explain, using the information from the article, why the construction industry has such a poor safety record.
2. Suggest what would be the costs and benefits (a) to building companies and (b) to construction workers if health and safety laws were enforced much more tightly in the industry.

The 1974 Act gave the government the power to introduce new regulations about health and safety when it felt they were necessary.

The Workplace (Health, Safety and Welfare) Regulations 1992

These made UK law conform to EU law. They set out a wide range of regulations to control safety at work. These included the safe use of equipment, the handling of heavy loads, the use of computers and screens and the use of protective clothing.

The Working Time Regulations 1998

Again this was UK implementation of EU law. The regulations laid down maximum working times for workers. For example, most workers cannot work more than 48 hours per week, or 13 hours in a day, or six days in a week. Workers must also be given rest breaks. These limits are designed to prevent excessive working which can cause accidents and health problems in the workplace.

The Control of Substances Hazardous to Health Regulations 1999

These are the latest regulations which protect workers from hazardous substances. These include nuclear fuels, chemicals, asbestos, bacteria and dust.

Problems

Workers may face problems if there is a poor record of health and safety.

- Workers may suffer pain or discomfort, both at work and outside.
- Workers may need to take time off. If they have a long term illness they may find that they receive sick pay. This is likely to be less than their usual pay.
- At worst, workers who are continually sick may lose their jobs.

Businesses also lose out.

- To prevent a fall in output, it may necessary for a business to hire temporary staff or pay workers overtime. This costs money.
- New or temporary staff may cause disruption to work.

- Workers may be distracted by illness, making them less productive.
- A poor health and safety record is likely to demotivate staff because their safety needs are not being met (☞ unit 96).
- The business may face court action if an employee sues the employer for damages.

Checklist

1. Why do (a) workers and (b) businesses lose from work-related illnesses?
2. What are the main issues covered by the Factory Act 1961 and the Offices, Shops and Railway Premises Act 1963?
3. What are the main provisions of the Health and Safety at Work Act 1974 and the regulations which have been issued under the Act?

The use of latex gloves is standard practice in the NHS. But an estimated 1 in 10 workers are allergic to latex. The material either gives them asthma, or they get dermatitis, a skin rash. Diane Chambers was a nurse at the Cardiff Royal Infirmary. She developed a widespread eczema on both her hands caused by contact dermatitis. Her condition deteriorated over time until, unable to work, she retired through ill health in November 1997. To start with, she didn't know what the cause of the problem was. However, she was eventually diagnosed as being allergic to latex and nickel. Diane Chambers said: 'I told my manager at the hospital, but they refused point blank to provide me with an alternative type of glove'. Alternative gloves are in fact easily available. Her union, UNISON, took the case up and won compensation of £100 000 for Diane Chambers.

Source: adapted from *Labour Research*, January 2001.

1. How did the employer fail to protect the health and safety of Diane Chambers?
2. A joint TUC and National Asthma Campaign report, *Latex: the gloves are off*, argued that the cost of having to replace one nurse can be three times the savings made from buying cheap latex gloves. Suggest why it might be cheaper for employers in the long run to provide more expensive protective clothes rather than lose staff.

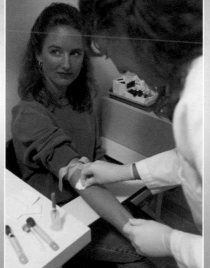
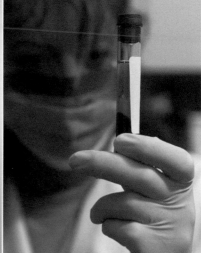

The use of latex gloves is common in the NHS

Advertisements must conform to codes of practice

Consumer protection

The **market** (☞ unit 3) cannot always prevent businesses from misleading their customers or supplying inadequate goods. So the government has to step in to protect the consumer. It does this by passing consumer protection laws. If a business breaks part of **criminal law**, it can be prosecuted and fined. The main consumer criminal laws are the following.

The Trades Description Act 1968

This states that it is illegal for products to be incorrectly described. If the label on a sweater says that it is machine washable at 40 degrees, then the colours in the sweater mustn't run at that temperature.

The Weights and Measures Acts

These acts make it illegal for a business to sell goods which are underweight or short measured.

The Food and Drugs Act 1955

This makes it illegal to sell food which is unfit for human consumption. The act also lays down minimum standards for what must be contained in food. For example, a meat sausage must contain at least 30 per cent meat.

The Consumer Credit Act 1974

This gives rights to consumers when taking out credit to buy products. For example, a consumer must be given a copy of any credit agreement signed.

Fining businesses doesn't help consumers get compensation. To do this, consumers have to use **civil law** to sue businesses. The two main Acts under civil law are the **Sale of Goods Act 1979** and the **Supply of Goods and Services Act 1982**. These acts allow consumers to sue a business if it sells them a product which:

- is not of merchantable quality. A sweater sold with a hole in it is not of merchantable quality for example;
- is not fit for the purpose. A tube of glue sold for glass which doesn't glue glass together is not fit for the purpose for example;
- doesn't meet the description applied. Socks labelled yellow in a presentation pack but which turn out to be blue do not meet the description applied for example.

The Sale and Supply of Goods Act 1994 amended these Acts so that customers could return part of a product. For example, a buyer might return one packet of crisps from a pack of six packets.

Codes of practice

The government has encouraged businesses to adopt codes of practice as an alternative to passing laws. Codes of practice are rules which businesses voluntarily agree to keep. But the codes have no legal status.

One important agency which enforces codes of practice is the **Advertising Standards Authority** (ASA). The British codes of advertising and sales promotion practice (BCAP) state that advertising must be legal, decent, honest and truthful and must not cause grave or widespread offence.

Mr Pierce bought a bedroom suite from Hollister Furniture Company for £1 950. The suite came with various pieces of furniture including a bed and a mattress. However, within days of using it, he noticed that it creaked and squeaked each time he moved in the night. Mr Pierce complained to Hollister's and, after investigation, the centre rail and slats were replaced. But this made no difference to the noise.

Mr Pierce complained again and Hollister's offered him a replacement bed. He accepted this but when the new bed arrived, it too squeaked. So he demanded that Hollister's take back all the furniture and give him a refund. He argued that if he bought a bed of a different make or design, it would not match the rest of the furniture. Hollister's refused and Mr Pierce consulted a solicitor. The solicitor sent a letter to Hollister's demanding repayment plus £200 in costs. Hollister's agreed and paid Mr Pierce £2 150.

1. What complaint did Mr Pierce make against the Hollister Furniture Company?
2. Mr Pierce's solicitor wrote in his letter that Hollister's were liable under the Sales of Goods Act. (a) How does this Act protect consumers? (b) Explain why Mr Pierce may have had a winning case under the Act.
3. Discuss whether it was in the best interests of Hollister's to refuse to give a full refund until a solicitor's letter arrived.

The ASA monitors all advertising except on television or radio. It is concerned with such things as alcohol and tobacco advertisements, and the portrayal of women and children. Large companies will often ask the ASA to check that their advertising campaign complies with the BCAP.

Consumers and business have a right to complain to the ASA about any advertisement. The ASA receives about 10 000 complaints each year. Many complaints do not merit formal investigation. Around one third are investigated. If the complaint is upheld, the ASA will ask the business to stop the advertisement. This was the case in 2000 when Virgin Energy withdrew a press advertisement for its new gas and electricity service. Powergen, Scottish Power, Yorkshire Electricity and Seeboard claimed the advertisement, which urged customers 'to take gas and electricity out of the hands of those institutions that for too long had grossly overcharged for basic needs' was misleading because it did not make clear which institutions it referred to. The companies also objected to the claim in the advertisement that customers would save money by switching to Virgin Energy. The ASA upheld both claims.

The ASA can't force businesses to withdraw advertisements. However it can make it uncomfortable for the businesses to ignore its request. It can also discourage misleading advertisements appearing in the first place. The ASA does have the legal sanction of referring a business to the Office of Fair Trading, which may take out an injunction to prevent certain claims in future advertisements.

Pressure groups

Pressure groups (☞ unit 14) are a further check on the activities of businesses. The Consumers Association, for example, is an organisation which defends consumers' rights by investigating and publishing reports on particular products. It also lobbies industry and government to promote consumers' interests.

There are also **trade associations**. These are organisations of businesses which defend their rights. They might take action, for example, to curb the power of large, powerful suppliers or customers.

✔Checklist

1. What is the difference between criminal law and civil law?
2. How does the Trade Descriptions Act 1968 help protect consumers?
3. What is the difference between the protection given to customers by the Food and Drugs Act 1955 and the Weights and Measures Acts?
4. What rights do the Sale of Goods Act and the Supply of Goods Act give to consumers?
5. Describe the work of the Advertising Standards Authority.
6. How does the Consumers' Association work to protect consumer rights?

The Advertising Standards Authority (ASA) has banned a press advertising campaign for British pork and bacon. The advert had been paid for by the Meat & Livestock Commission (MLC). This follows complaints by the Danish Bacon & Meat Council (DBMC), Vegetarian International Voice for Animals, Animal Aid and members of the public. The adverts were meant to encourage consumers to buy British pork by highlighting the good living standards that British pigs enjoyed compared with those in other countries. However, the ASA felt that they exaggerated a number of issues.

One advert showed a suckling sow with the caption 'After she's fed them, she could be fed to them.' This referred to the practice of putting meat and bonemeal into animal feed. However, the ASA ruled that there was almost no possibility of a piglet eating animal feed which contained remains of its own mother. This was especially true since the practice of using meat in animal feed had virtually ceased in European Union countries when the adverts starting running.

Another advert implied that pigs reared under the Assured British Pigs scheme led a relatively free life. However, the ASA thought that the advert exaggerated the amount of freedom enjoyed by British pigs under the scheme.

Source: adapted from *Marketing Week*, 15.2.2001.

1. What was the purpose of the adverts placed by the Meat & Livestock Commission?
2. Why did the ASA ban the adverts?
3. Suggest why (a) the Danish Bacon & Meat Council and (b) the Vegetarian International Voice for Animals objected to the adverts.
4. Discuss whether the government or a body like the ASA should have the power to control advertising.

The law

Businesses have to obey the law. If they fail to obey:

- they can be prosecuted by a number of government departments and agencies, such as the Health and Safety Inspectorate, and possibly fined;
- they can be sued by people or other businesses which have lost out as a result of their actions. Damages might then have to be paid.

Getting a job

In law, applicants for a job have rights. These rights try to give all applicants EQUAL OPPORTUNITIES when seeking work. Employers are not allowed to DISCRIMINATE against applicants because of their gender or racial origin, or on grounds of disability. A business, for instance, could not advertise for a 'female secretary' because this would be against the **Sex Discrimination Act 1975**. Equally, a business could not advertise for a 'secretary of European origin' because this would be against

the **Race Relations Act 1976**.

The **Disability Discrimination Act 1995** states that employers with 20 or more workers are not allowed to discriminate against disabled people in the process of recruitment or promotion. Not giving a job to a disabled applicant when he or she is the best person for the job is illegal. The only exception is if there is a substantial and relevant reason for not employing them. Such reasons might include having to move premises to employ just one disabled worker. But a reasonable adjustment might be building a ramp for a wheelchair or changing the lighting for a vision impaired worker.

At work

The law says that every employee must be given a CONTRACT OF EMPLOYMENT. This is an agreement between the employer and the employee. A written statement of the conditions of the contract must be given within 13 weeks. It will include

UK legislation makes it illegal to discriminate on grounds of gender, race or disability

rates of pay, hours of work, holidays and pension contributions. It will also include the amount of notice that must be given if the worker wants to leave or if the employer wants to make the worker redundant.

Under the **Equal Pay Act 1970**, female workers must be paid the same rate of pay as doing the same job, a similar job or a job with equal demands. Similarly, an employer can not discriminate against male workers.

Businesses must also be aware of **equal opportunities**. If a female worker applied for a more senior post in the company, the law says that she must have the same chance as any other employee. It would also be illegal for a business to discriminate against a worker on grounds of race, religion or disability because she was a woman, disabled or from an ethnic minority.

Adult workers in the UK must be paid at least the minimum wage according to the **Minimum Wage Act 1998**. Businesses which pay below this face prosecution. Businesses must also conform to the **Health and Safety at Work Act 1974** (☞ unit 103).

Employers cannot prevent a worker from joining a trade union. Under the **Employment Relations Act 1999**, an employer must also recognise the right of trade unions to negotiate with it on behalf of workers (☞ unit 102).

Leaving work

The law also affects workers when

The 105 UCATT trade union members who were made redundant last year when shopfitters Tim Tec International went out of business have finally won some recompense thanks to an employment tribunal ruling. Lawyers for the trade union UCATT persuaded the Nottingham employment tribunal that the company had failed to consult the workers properly, as it was required to do so by the 1992 Trade Union and Labour Relations Act. As a result the former employees will share £305 000 between them.

Source: adapted from UCATT, *Building Worker*, Spring 2001.

1. Suggest why the 105 shopfitters were made redundant.
2. What legal rights did they have in this situation, according to the article?
3. How did the workers gain compensation?
4. Many businesses complain that employment laws give too many rights to workers and too few rights to employers. (a) Suggest what costs employment laws might impose on businesses. (b) Discuss whether employment laws should be changed so that employers could make any worker redundant immediately and without having to give any reason.

they leave their job. Workers who have found new jobs have to **resign** from their posts. They then have to 'work out their notice'. Their contract of employment will state how much notice a worker needs to give his or employers when leaving.

Workers often pay into a pension scheme so that they can receive a pension when they **retire**. Many businesses run company pension schemes which provide a pension on top of the state retirement pension.

In law, a business can make workers **redundant** if their job 'no longer exists'. They then become entitled by law to redundancy pay. The amount paid out depends on the number of years the worker has been employed by the current employer and the salary at the time of the redundancy. Businesses are free to pay more than the minimum redundancy pay set down by law.

Trade unions, for example, may negotiate a redundancy package for their members.

In law, workers can be **dismissed** (i.e. sacked) if they are either unable to do the job or there is misconduct involved. In a serious case, such as behaviour which threatens the life of other workers, a worker may be dismissed immediately. In most cases, however, workers can only legally be dismissed if they have received a number of warnings from their employer. If the employer fails to go through the correct procedures, the sacked employee can take the business to an industrial tribunal on grounds of **unfair dismissal**. The **Employment Relations Bill 1999** states that a worker who has worked for a business for one year has a right not to be unfairly dismissed.

An INDUSTRIAL TRIBUNAL is a court of law which deals with issues

such as unfair dismissal, discrimination at work and sexual harassment. Lawyers don't have to be used. People can argue their own case in front of the tribunal. The tribunal is also informal, with members listening to presentations and asking questions to find out the truth about what happened. The idea is that the law is accessible to every worker. In practice, lawyers are often used. For example, a trade union member is likely to be represented by a lawyer hired by the union. The tribunal has the power to fine a business if it is breaking the law and can pay damages to workers.

key terms

Contract of employment - an agreement between the employer and employee about the conditions under which the employee will work, including rates of pay and holiday entitlements.
Discrimination - favouring one person rather than another. In the UK, it is illegal to discriminate in most jobs on grounds of gender, race or disability.
Equal opportunities - where everyone has the same chance.
Industrial tribunal - a court which deals with the law relating to employment.

Eurostar, the cross-Channel train company, was forced into a climbdown yesterday. The company had a skirts-only policy for female security staff. Last month, it sent home two workers for refusing to wear skirts. It claimed that its policy aimed to protect its 'corporate image' designed for a 'customer-facing organisation'.

Talks with the GBM, the trade union which represented the two workers, followed. The union threatened to take the case to an industrial tribunal if the women were dismissed.

Eurostar agreed to conduct a survey of customers and staff about the wearing of trousers. Only 12 per cent of female customers surveyed said they would prefer female security staff to wear skirts. 20 out of the 22 security staff said they wanted the choice of whether to wear skirts or trousers.

As a result, Eurostar yesterday reinstated the two workers and changed its policy to give female security employees the choice between skirts and trousers.

Source: adapted from the *Financial Times*, 18.11.1999.

1. Explain why Eurostar wanted its female security staff to wear skirts.
2. Suggest why Eurostar agreed to conduct a survey of customers and staff.
3. Discuss whether the GBM trade union would have won its case if it had taken it to an industrial tribunal.

Checklist

1. 'Businesses are not allowed to discriminate on grounds of gender or race.' Explain what this means.
2. What help does the law give to disabled people wanting to work?
3. What information does a contract of employment contain?
4. A man and a woman are paid different rates of pay for doing exactly the same job in a company. Is this legal? Explain your answer.
5. On what grounds can a business dismiss a worker?
6. Describe the work of an industrial tribunal.

Internal communication takes place during meetings

External communication - a message faxed to another business

Senders and receivers

There are always two parties to any COMMUNICATION.

The sender For example, an employee in the sales department of a business might send out a brochure to a potential customer. The head of the personnel department might give instructions to other heads of department about how to deal with a staff problem.

The receiver For example, a customer might receive a brochure from a business. Heads of department may receive instructions from the head of personnel. The receiver may give FEEDBACK. For example, the potential customer, having received a brochure, may enquire whether the sales department would give a discount for a bulk order, or whether there are delivery charges. Figure 106.1 shows this feedback.

Internal and external communication

Some communications are INTERNAL to the business. Examples of internal communication would be:

- one salesperson talking to another salesperson;
- the finance director sending a memo to sales staff;
- the head of the marketing department sending a message by email to other heads of department.

  Other communications are EXTERNAL, where a business communicates with people or organisations outside the business. Examples would be:

- a salesperson telephoning a customer;
- the head of production faxing a report to a health and safety inspector;
- a building company sending specifications for a building to a building inspector to be approved.

The importance of good communication

Good communication is essential to any business. For example:

- a clear instruction by a manager makes sure that a task gets done;
- an accurate memo from the accounts department might help clear up a misunderstanding.

  Poor external communication can lead to dissatisfied customers, a poor business image and problems with suppliers. Poor internal communications can lead to workers not understanding what they have to do, poor motivation of the workforce and duplication of effort. Overall, poor communication can lead to a loss of sales if customers are not satisfied. It also increases costs because work is not completed in the most efficient way. Mistakes are made and things get overlooked. All of these may lead to lower profits.

Communication skills

There is a number of key factors which make a communication effective.

Information What is communicated must be accurate. It must be **complete**, giving all the information necessary. It must also be **simple** and

129 London Road
Bricklington
Hamps
BR6 2EW

15.6.2001

Dear Sir

I am currently looking for a post in the field of finance and accounts. I enclose my CV and a letter explaining in more detail my past employment history and details of how I see my career progressing.

I would be grateful if you could consider me for any posts which you have vacant.

Yours faithfully

Carl Emmett

This letter has been sent to Glaxtec, a pharmaceuticals company in Bricklington.

1. Who is the sender of the communication?
2. What is the sender trying to communicate in the letter?.
3. Do you think the company should reply to the letter (a) if it has vacant posts and (ii) if it has no vacancies at present? Put arguments for and against.

Wordprocessing

4. Assume the company decides to reply. (a) As head of personnel, write a letter stating that the company has no vacancies at the moment, but will put the details on file for future reference. (b) When Carl receives this letter, discuss whether he should reply.

clear, so that the receiver can understand the information as quickly and easily as possible.

Sender and receiver The message must be sent from the right people to the right people.

Time and place Communication must take place at the right time and right place. A 2000 sales brochure is useless if it is sent out in 2001 because the product range may have changed. A notice about fire safety is in the wrong place if nobody can read it because it is pinned too high up. An urgent memo from London head office mustn't arrive at branches three weeks late.

Method The **method** of communication (☞ units 107 and 108), must be right. Methods include face to face communication, memos, telephone calls and the use of information and communication technology (ICT).

Barriers to communication

Not all communication is effective. There are various reasons why communication breaks down. The person sending the communication might not explain themselves very well. The receiver might not be capable of understanding the message because they lack understanding of technical **jargon**. The receiver might not hear the message because he or she is not paying attention. Or the receiver might choose to focus in on part of the message, but not all of it. Messages can get distorted if they go through too many people, like in a game of Chinese whispers. Equipment might break down or not be working very well.

Checklist

1. In communication, what is the difference between a sender and a receiver?
2. A company sends out a brochure to a customer. What feedback might it expect to receive?
3. What is the difference between internal and external communication?
4. List FOUR external communications which a local newsagent might send or receive.
5. Why is good communication important for a business?
6. What makes communication effective?

key terms

Communication - messages passed between a sender and receiver, through a medium such as a letter, fax, email or verbal message.
External communication - communication between the business and an outside individual or organisation like a customer, a supplier or a tax inspector.
Feedback - response to a message by its receiver to the sender.
Internal communication - communication within the business organisation.

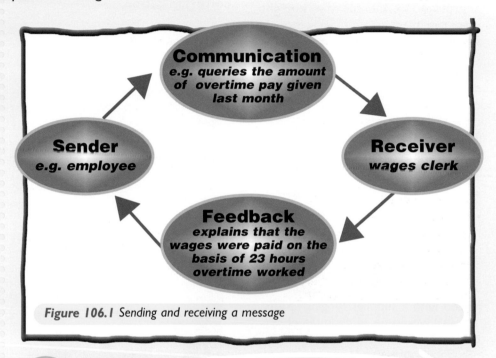

Communication
e.g. queries the amount of overtime pay given last month

Sender
e.g. employee

Receiver
wages clerk

Feedback
explains that the wages were paid on the basis of 23 hours overtime worked

Figure 106.1 Sending and receiving a message

Miranda Cohen owns a chain of four hairdressing salons in South Manchester. She employs 25 full time and part time hair stylists. Three of the salons are ladies hairdressing salons. The fourth is a unisex salon. The salons trade under the name of 'Miranda's'.

1. Give FIVE examples each of (a) external communications and (b) internal communications which might occur at Miranda's.
2. (a) State TWO ways in which Miranda's could communicate with potential customers who have not yet been to the salons. (b) Discuss what would make these communications effective for Miranda's.

Body language

When two or more people meet, messages are passed by the way they act and react physically. For instance, a manager interviewing a candidate for a job might laugh. This could be interpreted in different ways. It might relax the interviewee. Equally, it might signal to them that they have given a wrong answer.

The way we laugh, frown, walk and dress are all examples of **non-verbal** communication.

Verbal communication

Verbal or **oral** communication is when two or more people talk together. They may meet together informally. For instance, a manager might talk about a problem with an assistant over lunch. This is an example of **face-to-face** communication. The manager may want to find out about an order placed with a supplier. Ringing up the supplier would be an example of **telephone** communication.

Examples of more formal types of verbal communication include:

* a manager attending a **meeting** with other managers;
* a manager **interviewing** people for a job;
* a sales manager attending a **conference** to discuss future promotional events.

The manager can use the telephone and contact someone immediately. A letter may only get through 24 hours later. The conversation can be confidential and the two parties can exchange views. So receivers of the message can question anything that not understood. They can also give instant feedback.

The larger the number of people involved, the less likely there is to be feedback. In a staff meeting with 20 people, for example, the chances are that some people will not give any feedback at all.

Visual communication

Businesses can also use **visual communication**.

Verbal and visual communication

Look at the photographs.

1. What do you think is being communicated by the people in each photograph?
2. A manager is interviewing her deputy. The topic is her annual performance review. In this review, the manager is telling her how well she has performed over the past year given the performance targets set for her at the last review. The manager explains that she has missed her targets in two areas of performance. But in six other areas, she has exceeded her targets. As a consequence, she is to be given a performance related bonus for the year of £3 000.
(a) What non-verbal messages might the manager give in explaining (i) that two performance targets have been missed; (ii) that six performance targets have been achieved; (iii) that a bonus of £3 000 is to be given? (b) The deputy manager knows that three other deputy managers have been awarded pay rises of between £1 000 and £2 000. What non-verbal communication might she give when she is told she is to be awarded £3 000?

A business may have samples of its products on **display** for customers to look at in shops. A business may use **brochures** or **leaflets** which have visual images of its products for sale. **Posters** may be used to help sales. An advertising campaign may make use of both posters and displays, for example. A business may also have a **logo** which identifies its products.

Information and communication technology can also be used. A company **web site** (☞ unit 13) may have images of its products, for example. Television advertisements may also be used to show products and how they operate.

Visual communication can take place within and outside the organisation. A manager, for example, may be sent a **bar chart** or **graph** by head office showing trends in sales or costs. A manager may read a **newspaper article** which shows the market share of a rival business by means of a **pie chart**. The manager may also watch a BBC *Money Programme* **video** or a **CD Rom** about competition in the market. In its marketing, a business may use advertisements in newspapers and magazines to communicate with potential customers.

Visual images can improve communication for a business. Photographs, video or CD Rom may give a much clearer idea of a product than a written description. Most of the space in a mail order catalogue, for example, is devoted to pictures and not writing. Visual images are also much better at changing people's feelings and perceptions about a product or an issue than the written word. **Persuasive advertising** usually relies heavily on images for its effectiveness.

Checklist

1. Why might a manager use verbal communication to pass a message to another manager rather than write a memo?
2. What are the disadvantages of verbal communication?
3. List and then describe in words THREE pieces of visual communication in this book.
4. Why might a manager present sales figures over the past five years in the form of a graph rather than in words?

Gardener Blues Ltd is a manufacturer of tools and equipment. The fourth quarter (i.e. October -December) figures for 2001 have just come in. The head of marketing has sat down with the head of finance to review them.

1. What has happened to sales (a) in the fourth quarter and (b) for the whole calendar year over the past three years?
2. Discuss whether it is easier to spot the trends in the sales figures from the graph or from the table.

				£ million
	1st quarter	**2nd quarter**	**3rd quarter**	**4th quarter**
1999	4.4	3.7	5.6	6.2
2000	5.6	5.2	6.2	7.5
2001	7.9	6.1	8.6	9.8

Table 107.1 Gardener Blues Ltd, quarterly sales figures

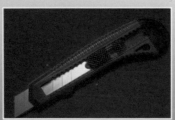

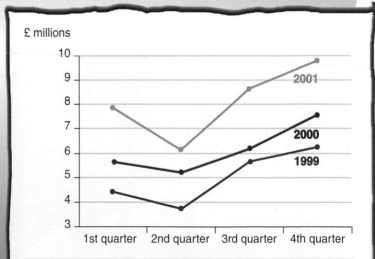

Figure 107.1 Gardener Blues Ltd, quarterly sales figures

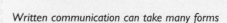

The Rank Group Plc

£2,041m Turnover

£307m Operating profit

Operating profit up 12%
Disposals totalling half a billion pounds
Proforma net debt down to £834m

36,000+ Employees

10,000,000+ Customers

Written communication

Written words are a useful means of communication.

- Because they can be stored, on paper or on a computer system for instance, they can give a permanent record of the communication. In contrast, there is unlikely to be a permanent record if a supervisor has an informal talk with her line manager.
- Written communication can reach large numbers of people. A company newsletter, for example, can be sent to all employees.
- Written communication can be very detailed. For example, a contract between two businesses may run to thousands of words.
- Written communication can often be used to explain product details

or to pass information to customers. For example, a brochure can show a product range and can list prices.

A disadvantage of written communication is that it rarely gives an opportunity for instant feedback. This means that it can be ignored. A notice on a noticeboard, for instance, might not be seen by an employee.

Types of written communication

There are many types of written communication.

Letters A letter is versatile and can convey plans, instructions, comment and analysis for instance. A **personal**

Petty Cash Voucher
For what required

Folio
Date
AMOUNT £ P

Signature
Passed by

Written communication can take many forms

letter is one which is sent with the understanding that it will only be read by the named receiver of the letter. An **open letter** is one where the sender wants anybody who is interested to read the letter. The

---

Esme Reid is the head of finance in Millers, a medium sized metal manufacturing company in Sheffield. Mike Alder is her personal secretary. Richard Fletcher is chairman of the company. Wakes is a company which buys 10 per cent by value of Millers' output. Below is an entry for Esme Reid's diary for Thursday 5 July.

1. For each entry in her diary, suggest what types of written communication might have been involved.
2. The buyers from Wakes explained during various meetings during the day that they wanted Millers to cut its prices by 10 per cent from October. Esme Reid has explained to the head of marketing at Millers that the maximum price cut the business could offer is 5 per cent. Discuss the advantages and disadvantages of trying to resolve this difference through written letters rather than face to face meetings.

5 July 2001
Thursday

8.30 Briefing meeting with Claire about the day

8.45 Look through incoming mail. Agree replies with Mike.

9.15 Continue writing financial report to Board of Directors.

10.00 Deal with emails.

10.15 Meeting with Richard Fletcher to discuss last month's financial statements.

12.15 Check and sign outgoing mail from Mike.

12.30 Lunch with buyers from Wakes.

2.00 Interview candidates for accounts clerk post.

4.00 Preparation for board meeting on 10 July.

18.00 Home.

letter might be **faxed** to the receiver rather than being sent by mail. This is when the letter is sent, via a fax (facsimile) machine, down the telephone wire to be printed out by a fax machine in the receiver's office.

Email Emails are letters which are sent over the internet. Typically they are written in a less formal style than a letter and are usually shorter. Files can also be attached to an email and sent with them. The files must already be on computer. Emails can provide instant communication because sending an email takes seconds. Email is widely used both for **internal** and **external** communication by businesses.

Memorandum or memo A memorandum (or 'memo') is a short letter. It usually gives instructions, such as a request for information. Memos are sometimes written on standard forms. They can also be sent out via email.

Circular or newsletter A circular is a communication which is sent to a number of people. For example, head office might sent out a circular to all managers with information

about new health and safety procedures.

Forms Forms are designed to make sure that all the information required is included in a communication. For example, an application form for a job typically asks applicants to give their name, address and age. It usually asks for details of work experience as well.

Minutes These are a written record of a meeting. Someone at the meeting makes a note of what was discussed and then writes this up. Minutes are important because they can be referred to. If there is a dispute about what was said at a meeting, the minutes might be able to clarify what really did happen. Because minutes are referred to, it is usual for the people attending the meeting to 'confirm' the minutes. This means that they agree that the written minutes do accurately reflect what was said at the meeting.

Reports A report is an extended piece of writing on a particular topic. Public limited companies have to produce an Annual Report for their shareholders. This gives details about how the company has performed

over the past 12 months. There are many other types of report. A director, for example, might have to present a report to the board about future staffing levels in the company. A report may contain graphs, charts and photographs as well as words and may be word processed on computer.

Databases Many businesses use databases. These are files of information kept, for example, on customer orders or on products. A salesperson could look at a database to find details of a customer's order if there was a query.

✓Checklist

1. What is the difference between a letter and a memo?
2. When might a business use a circular?
3. What are forms used for?
4. What is a report?
5. What makes an instruction manual effective?

INTERNAL MEMO

From **Peter Hughes**

Date **16/7/2001**

To **Anita Ray**

Ref **PH/20501**

Subject **Emails**

It has come to my attention that two members of your staff, Wayne Thuse and Gary Cherrill, have been sending internal emails to other members of staff which could be read as threatening or abusive. Could you get their employment files from personnel and contact Richard Turbot from the Technical Department to arrange to see the problem emails within the next 24 hours. Then arrange an appointment with my secretary to see me on Wednesday 18th to discuss where to go from here.

1. What is a memo?
2. Explain briefly why Peter Hughes is writing this memo to Anita Ray.
3. Discuss whether it would have been better for Peter Hughes to have rung Anita Ray with his message rather than send a memo.

New technology has created new products and h changed workers, work environment

Trafficmaster is a company which has developed traffic information systems. It has just added a new unique feature to Fleetstar, its fleet management suite. Live information about congestion can now be accessed on the control centre screen.

Trafficmaster has a network of sensors covering over 8 000 miles of the motorway and trunk road system in the UK. These sensors can detect the amount of congestion on a road. The information is then relayed to individual cars, vans or lorries, or to control centres for fleets of commercial vehicles. Control centres have the added facility that they can see where an individual vehicle is located through GPS. GPS is a tracking system which beams location information to and from a satellite orbiting the earth.

The new facility means that a system operator at a control centre can see whether a driver is heading towards a traffic jam. The operator then has the option of planning a new route or diverting the driver to another job. Instructions to the driver are usually given by mobile phone. The operator can also warn a customer that the driver will be late arriving because of traffic problems.

Source: adapted from the *Financial Times*, 30.4.2001.

1. How might the Trafficmaster technology change the work patterns of (a) a control centre manager and (b) a driver of a commercial vehicle?
2. Discuss whether the following stakeholders in a road haulage business are likely to benefit and lose out from the installation and use of Trafficmaster technology: (a) customers; (b) the owners; (c) other road users; (d) the owners of the business.

Control of emissions has improved the local environment

Stakeholders and owners

Modern technology has had an impact on many of the **stakeholders** (☞ unit 19) of businesses. Owners have been affected in a number of ways. For example, new technology has provided opportunities for owners to set up new businesses. The vast majority of UK businesses in the computer and internet field were set up after 1980. Equally, owners of traditional businesses, for instance in the textile industry, have seen their sales contract. Many have been forced to close. They have lost as others have gained from this transition.

Workers

Modern technology has also had an impact on workers. It has changed the way in which many people work. Traditional factories were noisy, dirty and often dangerous places. New technology, with new computer controlled machines (☞ unit 63), has considerably reduced noise, dirt and industrial accidents. At its most extreme, plants which manufacture microchips have to be completely clean environments. This is because dirt particles can damage the chips in the production process. In the office environment, typewriters have been

replaced by computers. Many workers are now expected to be able to use a computer to gather information and communicate with others.

The introduction of technology has meant that staff have had to develop new skills. Training and retraining has therefore been necessary. Workers have had to become more flexible in what they do. They need to recognise that the workplace will change as they become older.

New technology has also led to major changes in businesses and industries. Productivity (output per worker) has risen as new technology has been introduced. In the UK manufacturing industry, this has tended to result in a loss of jobs. This is part of the reason why half of all jobs in UK manufacturing were lost between 1970 and 2000. Workers has been made unemployed. To gain a new job, they have often had to retrain. Even within the service sector, where the number of jobs has risen, new technology can still cause a loss of jobs. Banking, for example, has been particularly affected by the introduction of new technology. Branches have closed and staff have been made redundant.

Managers

New technology has allowed managers to have much more information when making decisions. A company accountant, for example, is likely to use accounting software. This may be able to calculate performance ratios, such as gross and net profit margins (☞ units 82-84) from accounts data. A department store sales manager might have access to EPOS data. From this, he could read off today's sales for a product line across all department stores in the UK. He could compare sales in one store with another. He might use this to decide whether to reorder stock or in which stores to concentrate sales of a product.

Customers and suppliers

Customers have benefited from new technology in a number of ways. First, new technology has led to many new products coming onto the market. Mobile phones, CNC machines, and robots are just some of these. Second, many products are now of much better quality than before. A car, for example, is more comfortable and reliable than thirty years ago. Third, new technology tends to lead to lower prices for products because of

efficiency gains. Lastly, **e-commerce** (☞ unit 13) has provided a new way in which customers can buy products.

Suppliers have also benefited. Their customers expect new, better and cheaper products. Some suppliers now give quotes for products online to potential customers. In some industries, such as car manufacturing, there is a growing trend for suppliers to be part of the design process for new products. For example, a car manufacturer might share the specification for a new car with a supplier which makes electrical equipment such as headlights. The supplier is expected to design a headlight for a given price to fit the new car.

The local community

Local communities have been considerably affected by new technology. Industrial towns in the UK have been transformed as old, heavily polluting industries have been replaced by clean manufacturing plants and new service industries. The countryside has come under pressure, however, as cars have allowed people to commute to work.

The transition from old to new industries has led to some disruption. In the 1970s and 1980s, old manufacturing areas such as the West Midlands, Wales and the North West found it difficult to replace the jobs they lost. The result was unemployment. However, in the 1990s, unemployment fell in all regions as new industries expanded. This fall brought growing prosperity to these areas.

Crown House Engineering, a Wolverhampton building services firm, is helping construct one of the world's cleanest manufacturing centres. The Zetex plant in Oldham, Lancashire, will produce advanced semiconductors for use in hi-tech equipment and devices. These silicon wafers carry thousands of integrated circuits and discrete transistors with some of the elements just one thousandth of a millimetre wide. They are used in mobile electronic devices, such as cellular phones, computers, cars, Satellite TV, and industrial automation, as well as video and multimedia systems.

The Wolverhampton firm is providing the mechanical and electrical services for 'cleanrooms' where the semiconductors are manufactured. The slightest dust particle can damage the silicon wafers. The cleanrooms have to have less than ten dust particles per cubic foot of air, compared to a normal clean environment of around 1 000 dust particles per cubic foot. The £3.5 million contract is due to be finished shortly.

Source: adapted from the *Express & Star*, 7.5.2001.

1. Discuss what impact the new Zetex plant has and will have on the following stakeholders: (a) its customers; (b) its suppliers such as Crown House Engineering; (c) the local economy in Oldham; (d) its workers; (e) its owners.

✓Checklist

1. Who are the stakeholders in a business?
2. Give ONE way in which each has (a) benefited and (b) lost out from the introduction of modern technology.

Starting a business

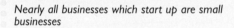

Identifying the opportunity

Nearly all businesses which start up are **small** businesses. Before setting up, the owners need to decide what they are going to produce. For most, it will be something with which they are familiar.

- Most likely, they will have worked in the industry already. For example, carpenters may have learnt skills working for building companies. They may then set up their own carpentry businesses.
- Some turn their hobby into a business. For example, a keen racing cyclist may set up a bicycle shop.
- Some use their general skills. For example, a manager of a factory may buy a franchise selling cleaning services. The skills needed to run a factory are similar to those needed to run a cleaning services company.

A few set themselves up with no business experience, but may have training. For example, people may train to be bricklayers and then become self-employed and so run their own businesses.

Anyone setting up in a business which they know little or nothing about risks failure. Running a business often requires experience and knowledge.

Researching the market

Businesses only survive if they can attract customers and at least make enough money to cover their costs. So it is important to research the market to find out whether there are likely to be enough customers. There are two main ways of **researching the market** (☞ units 40 and 41).

- **Desk research** involves finding existing information about the market. For instance, a person wanting to set up a hairdressing salon might look in *Yellow Pages* to find out the locations of all the salons in a local area in order to assess the likely competition.
- **Field researc**h involves finding information which is not available in books etc.

Researching the product

Some people who set up their own business know exactly what they are going to sell and how they are going to sell it. Most people, though, have to research their product. For example, someone setting up making wooden toys needs to know how to make the toys, where to buy supplies from and how to sell them.

Nearly all businesses which start up are small businesses

Finance

No business can be set up without finance. Most people who start their own business underestimate the amount of money they will

When Tariq Muhammad left university after gaining a pharmacy degree, he took a job in a chemists. The typical chemists today doesn't just dispense or sell medicines. It also sells everything from cosmetics to photo-developing to babies' nappies. But Tariq felt his talents were being wasted. So at age 25 he bought his own pharmacy and applied a new business formula to it. Out went the cosmetics and other consumer products. In came consulting rooms. His idea was to promote the pharmacy as a place where people could come for instant advice on minor ailments instead of waiting days for a doctor's appointment. The consultancy rooms give patients more privacy than discussing their bunions over a counter of perfumes. It also signals to patients that the pharmacist is someone who can give serious advice.

The formula proved a great success. Today he runs a chain of 18 pharmacies under the Pharmacy Plus brand name. When he buys a new pharmacy, he typically expects sales to rise 25 per cent within the first 18 months.

Source: adapted from *The Sunday Times*, 14.1.2001.

1. (a) What was Tariq's business idea? (b) How did he get the expertise to make that idea a success?
2. Suggest how Tariq might have raised the finance to buy his first pharmacy.
3. Discuss how likely it was that Tariq's first pharmacy might have been a financial failure.

need to set it up. They are often UNDERCAPITALISED. This causes problems as the business grows. Some businesses have the potential to be profitable. But they may fail because they run out of cash at a crucial early stage in the life of the business (☞ units 74 and 75). So it is important to work out how much money is needed to start the business.

It is also important to identify where the money will come from. It is likely that the owner will put some of his or her own money into the business. Friends and relatives may be persuaded to invest too. Otherwise, the most common source of finance is a loan or an overdraft from the bank. These need to be negotiated, preferably before the business is set up.

Identifying sources of help

Most new businesses don't survive for more than three years of trading. However, the chance of success for a new business is considerably increased if those setting up the business have received help from experts before the launch. Most new businesses receive some advice from their bank when they negotiate a loan or an overdraft. The bank is likely to insist on seeing a **business plan** (☞ unit 111) to help assess whether the business is likely to survive.

Many new small businesses turn to their local Learning and Skills Council or Business Links for help (☞ unit 14). They run courses for those thinking of setting up businesses. They can also identify any grants, loans or benefits that can be obtained from government.

The business plan

Drawing up a **business plan** is very important. The business plan sets out how the business is to be set up and run. Drawing up the business plan makes sure that all aspects of the new business have been considered. It helps people to be more realistic about the problems they are likely to face when the business starts trading. What is more, any applications for loans or grants will usually need to be supported by a business plan. So a business plan is crucial for financing the business.

You need to find a business opportunity for your mini-company.

1. Start by listing any experiences you have had which might be useful in a business. Do you have a part-time job? What hobbies could be turned into a business idea? Have you helped someone at home or with their business? Have you done anything at school or college that could be turned into a product or service that could be sold? Look for ideas on the **internet** which you might find interesting.
2. List any contacts you know that could help your business. People who may help could be a relation, a teacher or lecturer, a friend, a local business person or a neighbour.
3. List any resources which you could easily use in your business. Do you know someone who will drive you around? Is there somewhere to store products?
4. Compare the answers of all the people in your group. Are there any similarities? Does one person have a skill which could be supported by others? Do the answers suggest you will make a product or provide a service?
5. Most mini-companies find it difficult to come up with a business idea. Why does a lack of experience partly explain why this is so?

key terms

Undercapitalised - lacking the necessary financial resources to allow a business to trade without getting into financial difficulties.

Checklist

1. 'Businesses are most likely to succeed when they are started by people who have experience and training in the business area already.' Why might this be true?
2. Suggest and explain TWO ways in which someone wanting to set up a health and fitness club might research the market.
3. How might a new business research the product it is going to sell?
4. Give TWO ways in which a business might find the money to set up.
5. What help is available to businesses setting up?

A business plan may help businesses to obtain funds from banks

The purpose of the business plan

Many small businesses fail within a few years of setting up. One reason for failure is a lack of planning. The owners may not have thought clearly about the problems facing the business in future.

The chances of survival for a new business are greater if the owners draw up a BUSINESS PLAN. This is a document which includes information showing how a business might survive in a competitive world. It forces the owners to consider issues it may face. These may include the size of the market it needs, the skills it requires, its cash flow (☞ units 74 and 75), any collateral (☞ unit 67) and insurance.

The business plan is also important when raising funds. Without it, a business may not get external finance (☞ unit 70). For instance, a bank is unlikely to give a loan to a business unless it has seen its business plan. Banks use the plan to judge whether the business will be able to repay a loan. Government will not give grants to businesses without considering their business plans. A government agency will want to judge whether it is giving a grant to a business that is able to survive and create jobs.

The business plan

A typical business plan includes details about:
* the name of the business, a brief history, its location, its legal structure (whether it is a partnership for instance) and who would be the owners;
* the key personnel in the business including their position and salary;
* the product, whether it has been

test marketed and what market research had been carried out (☞ units 39-41);
* what equipment would be needed and its cost;
* what premises would be needed;
* who would be the suppliers to the business;
* what production methods (☞ units 59 and 60) would be used;

* what the total costs (☞ unit 72) of the business would be;
* What revenues (☞ unit 71) the business expected to receive;

Amanda (managing director), Miguel (production manager), Sarah (secretary) and Ruth (sales manager have decided to make leather and satin women's ties. Ten £5 shares in the company have been issued, one each to the four members of the board of the company and the remaining six to parents. Sample ties have been made. It took 40 minutes to make a satin tie and 50 minutes to make a leather tie. It is now early October and the company plans to sell its ties in school during 7 weeks in November and December.

The company has been able to borrow equipment such as scissors and tapes as well as premises for a fixed charge of £20. The raw material costs are £8.00 for a metre of satin. Six ties can be made from a metre of material. Leather is bought in pieces. It costs about £2.00 to buy the leather to make one tie. Presentation boxes can be bought for 50p each.

Wordprocessing and DTP
1. Using the example shown in Figure 111.1 and the description in the text EITHER draw up a business plan for your own mini-company OR draw up a business plan for Tieco.
2. What problems did you have in drawing up the business plan and what extra information would you have liked to have had?

- the break-even point (☞ unit 73), cash flow forecast for the first 12 months and the anticipated profit of the business;
- what financing the business would need and what assets it could use as security.

Part of a business plan is shown in Figure 111.1.

The business

a Name *DesignLine*
b Address *The Arcade, 120-121 Marks Lane*
  Bristol
c Limited Company/Partnership/Sole Trader *Limited company*
d What does your business do?
  Design a variety of publications, brochures and corporate identities.
  Printing of colour leaflets, advertising and short run publications
e Date you started trading *1.5.2001*
  (date you will start if you have a new business) *1.5.2001*
f What is your mission statement and what are your aims?
  To provide a quality design, reproduction and printing for the publishing industry.
g Capital structure

Limited Company Shareholders	Paid up value of shares held	% of total
Jenny Picton	£1000	50
Robson Gooding	£1000	50

Key staff

Name	Position	Date joined	Salary
Jenny Picton	*Director*	*1.5.2001*	£20,000
Robson Gooding	*Director*	*1.5.2001*	£20,000
Paul Charles	*Designer*	*1.5.2001*	£12,000
Diane Mitchell	*Designer*	*1.5.2001*	£12,000
Jo Torres	*Administrator*	*1.5.2001*	£10,000

Figure 111.1 *Part of a business plan for a design company*

Checklist

1. Why would a bank want to see a business plan before it loaned money to a new business?
2. Summarise what should be included in a business plan.
3. A business plan is a forecast.
   (a) What is being forecast in a business plan? (b) Why do you think it might be sensible to draw up a range of possible forecasts for a business?

Patrick O'Leary and Natalie Hogarth are the two managers of Venables Fruit Processing, a subsidiary of a large food company. In 2001, they got the chance to buy the subsidiary. The parent company had decided that fruit processing was not part of its main activities.

Venables Fruit Processing makes fruit fillings. About 60 tonnes a week are made and sold to high street bakeries and bakeries which make fruit products for supermarket chains. The factory is located in Tunbridge Wells and the company currently employs 17 people. Sales last year were £2 million with profits of £40 000.

Patrick and Natalie want to expand the company. There is still plenty of room for growth in the domestic market. They also see potential in the export market. They plan to employ a further five people in the technical and sales areas over the next 12 months aiming to expand sales by 20 per cent. They also plan to increase considerably the amount spent on advertising and other forms of promotion.

The parent company is asking £1 million for Venables Fruit Processing. Patrick and Natalie will each put in £50 000. The other £900 000 will come from a mixture of loans and equity capital (i.e. shares) from a venture capital company which specialises in helping finance small businesses.

1. Patrick and Natalie had to draw up a business plan before the venture capital company would provide finance. (a) Explain what would have been included in it. (b) Suggest why the venture capital company wanted to see a business plan.
2. At the end of their first year as an independent company, Venables Fruit Processing had succeeded in raising sales by 20 per cent. However, the company moved from making a profit of £40 000 to an annual loss of £20 000.
   (a) Why could the survival of the company be under threat? (b) Discuss TWO strategies that Patrick and Natalie could pursue to bring the company back into profit.

Business and change

Changing technology and changing markets have led to the development of new products

Change

All businesses have to change over time to survive. The environment in which they operate is constantly changing. So are methods of production and the products themselves.

Internal pressures

Some pressures for change come from within the business. These are called INTERNAL PRESSURES. Examples include the following.

- Changes in the cost of production may occur. For example, a business may have to give its workers a pay rise or material costs may rise. The business may react to this by putting up its prices. Or it may lower its costs by increasing the efficiency of production.
- New products may be developed by a business and put on the market. This will change what the business produces and has implications for investment, for instance.
- New processes or methods of production may be developed by a business. For example, new computer numerically controlled machines (CNCs ☞ unit 63) may be bought which could greatly reduce production costs.

External pressures

EXTERNAL PRESSURES for change are those that come from outside the business. There are many examples of external pressures.

Changing competition A business may see a change in the competition it faces in the market place. For example, a fish and chip shop on a parade of shops may face greater competition from the opening of a Chinese takeaway a few doors down. Or a rival company may be forced to close down, reducing competition in the market.

Changing technology Technology is constantly changing. New products might be introduced by a competitor, forcing a business to change its own product mix. Or a new type of production technology might come onto the market which the business is forced to buy because of savings in costs.

Changing markets The shape and size of markets never stays the same. For example, the introduction of cheap video tape recorders in the

The Money Channel, the financial broadcaster, has ceased trading. The company was launched in February 2000. It broadcast a mixture of programmes on themes such as stock market investments, borrowing and financial tax management. Audience figures grew to about 135 000 viewers per week. The channel was broadcast on digital television.

Revenues for the channel came from the sale of advertising. Key to the channel's success was interactive advertising. This is where viewers buy goods and services using their television remote control. The company said revenues from this source had not been enough to put it into profit.

Meanwhile, British Sky Broadcasting (BSkyB), the satellite television group, is to scale back coverage of business and finance on its Sky News channel. Programmes devoted solely to business news are no longer to be shown. Financial reports will be merged into the main news bulletins. Around 10 jobs at BSkyB will be lost as a result.

Source: adapted from the *Financial Times*, 2.5.2001 and 11.5.2001.

1. Explain why The Money Channel failed.
2. (a) Suggest TWO changes the company could have made which might have led to its survival. (b) Which of these do you think offered the best chance for survival?
3. Discuss whether BSkyB's decision to cut back broadcasting of programmes about business and finance could have been due to the failure of The Money Channel.

1980s opened up a new market for the hire of videos. DVD players in the early 21st century are likely to replace video recorders. The decline in the birth rate in the UK in the 1980s and 1990s led to a shrinkage in the number of teenagers buying clothes. On the other hand, rising incomes increased the demand for teenage clothes. These two opposing factors have meant that businesses in the marke have struggled to increase their sales.

Pressure groups Businesses today are coming under increased pressure from pressure groups. Whilst the power of trade unions has declined in the UK over the last 20 years, the power of environmental groups like Greenpeace has increased. Perhaps the most important ways in which pressure groups influence the decisions of businesses are through changes in the law or changes in the spending patterns of customers. A business can usually resist direct action by a pressure group like a picket outside a factory. But a business has to change if the law changes. Equally, environmental groups have achieved success in getting GM (genetically modified) food removed from supermarket shelves by persuading consumers not to buy it.

Takeovers and mergers
Takeovers and mergers can alter a business(☞ unit 33). If one business takes over another, it will increase its size and may allow it to enter new markets. For a business which is being taken over, it may lead to restructuring. Factories or offices may be closed to reduce costs. Parts of the business may be sold off. Employees, including senior management, may lose their jobs in the process.

Snackhouse announced yesterday its second profit warning in seven months. Snackhouse, formerly known as Benson Crisps, makes crisps and health snacks. Last October, the company warned it had lost a large contract with a major supermarket customer. In January of this year, it hinted that it was developing a new range of snacks. Yesterday, however, the company said that this had proved more complex than expected. Launch of the new range would be delayed several months. What is more, there were delays in starting a large new contract with another customer.

All this had left its factory at Kirkham in Lancashire underutilised. Snackhouse had tried to increase production by introducing promotions for its branded products. However, fierce competition from the supermarket's own-brand labels of crisps had made it difficult to increase sales.

Source: adapted from the *Financial Times*, 10.5.2001.

1. (a) Snackhouse suffered FOUR setbacks between October 2000 and May 2001. What were they? (b) Suggest the cause of each of these setbacks. (c) Discuss whether Snackhouse could have made different decisions which would have increased the profitability of the company over the 7 month period.

key terms

External pressures - factors outside the business that lead to change.
Internal pressures - factors within the business that lead to change.

Checklist

1. Explain THREE internal pressures which may force a business to change.
2. How might a business react to the following external pressures:
   (a) the government increases the minimum wage from £4.20 to £4.80 an hour;
   (b) a competitor cuts its prices by 10 per cent;
   (c) its main overseas market, accounting for 60 per cent of all sales, suffers a severe downturn, knocking one third off the income of the area?

The business environment

Cannel Haulage

Joe Cannel runs a live animal haulage business. He transports pigs, sheep and cattle to and from farms, livestock markets and abattoirs. He owns two lorries which he and his son, Andy, drive. The business is located in Staffordshire.

The fuel protests

It is September 2000. Farmers and hauliers start a blockade of Britain's fuel depots and refineries. Petrol tanker drivers refuse to take their lorries out on the road past the pickets on their gates. Jo Cannel is at an oil refinery at Stanlow on the river Mersey. He is protesting and demanding that the government slashes taxes on fuel.

Within one week, the whole country is running out of fuel. If the petrol tankers didn't start rolling again immediately, businesses would be forced to shut down, the shops would run out of food and hospitals and schools would close. In an economy where there is so much specialisation, every worker and every business is dependent on transport.

Joe is delighted. Surely the government would listen now by cutting taxes and giving far more help to farmers.

The farming community

The farming community was hit hard by falling prices in the second half of the 1990s. Beef prices had remained depressed since the start of the BSE crisis. Lamb prices were also very low, because British farmers were having to compete on world markets. As for pigs, prices began falling in 1998 and by 2000 many farmers were getting rid of their pig herds because they were making losses.

At the same time as all this was happening, farmers were hit further by rising animal welfare costs. New regulations for keeping pigs, for example, prevented pig farmers from keeping them tethered in sties. Instead, farmers had to give them more space, which increased costs of production.

Rising costs, coupled with falling prices, meant that many farmers were struggling to make any profit.

Competition

It seemed to Joe Cannel that everybody these days wanted to set up a haulage firm. Competition had increased greatly over the past ten years, driving down the prices haulage companies could charge. With the increases in taxes as well, it was difficult to make a profit these days.

Fuel prices and road tax

Between 1993 and 1999, the government increased the tax on petrol and diesel fuels by 4-6 per cent per year. The government justified this on environmental grounds, arguing that it wanted to see a fall in growth of journeys by polluting vehicles. In practice it meant rising fuel prices. In 1998 and 1999, the price of crude oil fell, which helped offset the increase in tax. But in 2000 crude oil prices nearly trebled and petrol prices shot up.

Over the same period, lorries also saw their road tax - the cost of the tax disk they have to carry - rise by far more than the rate of inflation.

Joe Cannel felt very angry about these tax increases. Road and fuel taxes had not gone up by nearly as much in continental countries like France.

Abattoirs

The BSE crisis, linked with more stringent EU regulations, led in the 1990s to the closure of many small local abattoirs. Conforming to new regulations involved hundreds of thousands of pounds of investment in new facilities, money small abattoirs owners could not afford. So this meant that animals had to be transported longer distances to be slaughtered.

At the same time, the supermarkets were taking an increasing share of the meat market. They wanted their slaughtered meat near their supermarkets. It was cheaper to move live animals from Yorkshire to an abattoir in Essex than to have the animals slaughtered in Yorkshire and move the meat to a distribution centre in Essex.

This was good news for businesses like Cannel Haulage. The longer the distance travelled, the more they could charge.

1. **Using your knowledge of Business Studies, explain the meaning of the following terms, giving examples. You may draw your examples from the Case Study or any other source.**
   (a) Competition. (b) Profit. (c) Taxes. (d) Business.
2. **(a) Explain how Joe Cannel (i) specialises and (ii) is interdependent with other businesses in the economy.**
   (b) What happens to the whole economy if a vital product like fuel is not available?
3. **Using a diagram, explain the chain of production from a beef farm in the UK to the dining table in a UK home.**
4. **(a) Write a letter to the Prime Minister from Joe Cannel. In the letter:**
   • **explain why farmers and hauliers are suffering economic difficulties;**
   • **put forward arguments to justify the government cutting taxes on fuel and giving financial aid to farmers.**
   (b) Write a letter back from the Prime Minister to Joe Cannel:
   • **thanking him for this letter;**
   • **explaining why his suggestions would have to lead to the raising of other taxes or cuts in public spending;**
   • **explaining why his suggestions could damage the environment.**

Business structure, control and organisation

Borewood shops

Borewood is a large village on the edge of Birmingham. It has a parade of shops and included in these is a hardware store and a hairdressers. The hardware store is owned by Jim and Patsy O'Brien. They are both in their late 60s and the lease on the store is up for sale. The hairdresser's next door, called Hair Today, is owned by another husband and wife team, Kate and Phil Thomas. They are both in their 30s.

Competition in the hairdressing market

Hair Today is a very successful business. Kate and Phil had adopted the business model of renting out space to individual hair stylists. Kate and Phil provided the premises, the receptionists and the cleaning staff. The hair stylists worked on their own account.

Hair Today was the only hairdressers on the parade of shops. The nearest competitor was half a mile away. Kate and Phil felt that the competition was fierce. After all, many people could have their hair done near where they worked rather than where they lived. But their business was doing very well. In fact, Kate and Phil were investigating setting up a second hairdressers in another affluent village a few miles away.

Competition in the hardware market

Jim and Patsy O'Brien are retiring after a long career in the hardware market. In their 20s, they established their first store. By their 40s, they owned a small chain of stores, each one a successful and profitable outlet. But then times began to get more difficult. Stores like B&Q, Do-It-All and Wickes were opened. These were large 'sheds' with a vast range of hardware products. Exploiting economies of scale, they could charge lower prices than those of the O'Briens. The presence of any such store near one of its outlets could take 50 per cent of its trade away in the first year. Inevitably, the O'Briens were forced to close these outlets. The last store at Borewood only survived because it was ten miles away from the nearest DIY superstore. Borewood was also an affluent village where customers were less sensitive to price and prepared to pay for the convenience of a local hardware store. Even so, sales were 25 per cent down on five years ago and the store was barely profitable.

Legal organisation

The O'Briens' business was a private limited company. When they had owned a chain of hardware stores, their accountant had pointed out the risk of having unlimited liability to them. So they changed from being a sole proprietorship, where Jim owned everything, to a company jointly owned by the husband and wife team.

Kate and Phil, however, had set up a partnership. Their solicitor had recommended that they draw up a formal Deed of Partnership. The Deed of Partnership made them equal partners in the business.

The large DIY outlets like B&Q were part of larger public limited companies. B&Q was part of the Kingfisher group, for example. Kingfisher itself is a multinational company. Amongst other assets, it owned a large DIY chain in France called Castorama. In 2001, Kingfisher announced that it was to demerge.

1. Using your knowledge of Business Studies, explain the meaning of the following terms, giving examples. You may draw your examples from the Case Study or any other source.
    (a) Multinational company. (b) Demerge.
    (c) Deed of Partnership. (d) Economies of scale.
2. (a) Outline the differences to the O'Briens when their business changed from being solely owned by Jim O'Brien to becoming a private limited company.
    (b) What would be the difference to Kate and Phil Thomas if they changed their business from a partnership to a private limited company?

3. What might be the business objectives of Kate and Phil Thomas?
4. (a) Discuss whether the O'Briens are running a successful business. In your answer, write about (i) the profitability of the business; (ii) its market share; (iii) its creation of wealth; (iv) its contribution to the local community.
    (b) Is the O'Briens' business more successful than that of Kate and Phil Thomas? Justify your answer.

Marketing

Chupa Chups

Chupa Chups might not be that familiar in the UK. But in 2000, 4 billion of its lollipops were sold in 168 countries around the world. Even in the UK, sales are now 150 million per year and growing fast.

Chupa Chups is a Spanish multinational confectionery company. It is the 25th largest confectionery company in the world with a market share of 0.9 per cent. If chocolate is excluded, it rises to the seventh largest company in the world behind Nestlé, Cadbury Schweppes, Haribo, Warner Lambert, Storck and Mars. In lollipops, it is the world's market leader with 34 per cent market share.

Expanding the brand

Chupa Chups has grown to have a very strong brand image in those countries where its products are on the market. Its strength can be seen from the fact that its lollipops sell for twice the price of local rivals in most countries.

Since the mid-1990s, it has been building on that strong brand image by diversifying. In key markets, it now sells a range of complementary life style products including toys, stationery, clothes, children's spectacles and sunglasses. In 1999, for example, it sold 50 000 pairs of Chupa Chups spectacles for children at a price of £50 a pair for the frames alone.

Chupa Chups does not manufacture or distribute these products. Instead, it gives licences to other companies, allowing them to use the Chupa Chups brand name. Licensing deals has the potential to raise Chupa Chups' profits considerably.

Marketing Chupa Chups

You would think that lollipops would be a children's product. Indeed, up until the 1990s, the management at Chupa Chups aimed its marketing at this traditional market, concentrating on rolling out the product to more countries.

But then Chupa Chups caught a new exciting wave which would see demand for its basic product expand to other age groups. In the mid-1990s, Johan Cruyff, then coach of Barcelona football club, quit smoking. Chupa Chups sent him a present of lollipops. It was a public relations dream when images of Mr Cruyff sucking a lollipop on the trainer's bench were shown on prime-time television. The company took this up by showing on its adverts 'celebrity suckers' - famous people consuming a Chupa Chups lollipop. The celebrities were picked as 'cool' icons for young people. The result was that consuming lollipops took off amongst younger people.

In the UK, Chupa Chups are on sale in clubs, bars and even second hand clothes shops. The core purchasers are now 12-14 year olds, but young adults account for between 15 and 20 per cent of sales. According to Sue McDermott, UK marketing manager: 'Our purchasers aren't aware that we market to them - we just seem to turn up in the cool places where they hang out.'

Source: adapted from the *Financial Times*, 31.5.2000.

1. **Using your knowledge of Business Studies, explain the meaning of the following terms, giving examples. You may draw your examples from the Case Study or any other source.**
   (a) Market share. (b) Market leader.
   (c) Demand. (d) Brand.
2. **Explain into which market segments Chupa Chups sells.**
3. **Discuss why public relations is so important to Chupa Chups.**
4. **In the Case Study, it is stated that Chupa Chups gave a licence for the manufacture of children's spectacles. Write a report discussing whether Chupa Chups benefited from this licensing deal. In your report:**
   • **assess the financial advantages of the deal to Chupa Chups;**
   • **discuss whether it helped promote the brand image of the company;**
   • **assess its possible impact on sales of Chupa Chups lollipops;**
   • **consider whether there might have been any disadvantages to the deal.**

Production

Windrush Appliances

Windrush Appliances is a medium sized company employing 700 workers. It manufactures appliances for larger companies which put their name on them and sell them to consumers. Windrush Appliances specialises in manufacturing tumble driers, barbecues and hostess trolleys.

Tumble drier manufacturing

Tumble driers are put together on an assembly line. The equipment is flexible and allows for batches of different models to be made. For example, a recent innovation has been 'fun' dryers which come in different colours rather than the standard white. The size of the batch made depends on the size of the order from the customer. The company keeps no stocks of finished tumble driers. Once made, they are immediately transported to the customer. Equally, the company keeps little in the way of stocks of parts. Components bought from outside will be ordered for the batch about to be made. Windrush Appliances will only buy from companies which guarantee to have components delivered on the date required.

Manufacturing

Manufacturing cells are used for the assembly of hostess trolleys and barbecues. Workers in the cells are allowed to decide which jobs each does. In some cells, workers prefer to keep to the same tasks from week to week. In others, jobs are rotated.

Each cell is responsible for its quality. All products are expected to have zero defects. Any problems with assembly quality can immediately be identified because every product carries a label with a code which identifies the date of manufacture and which cell was responsible for the assembly. The company prides itself that it has had no returns for faults on hostess trolleys or barbecues from retailers for the past three years.

The company is committed to kaizen. All workers are encouraged to make suggestions for improvement either through a suggestion box or directly to their immediate superior who must past the idea to a senior manager. When work is slacker in the summer, many employees also join quality circles. These look at specific aspects of work in the factory and suggest improvements.

Flexibility

Windrush Appliances, like a number of other small appliance manufacturers, does not have sufficient orders to make products all the year round. Demand for its products is seasonal. So in winter it manufactures far more tumble driers than in the summer. Equally, because of Ramadan and Christmas, it manufacturers hostess trolleys in the autumn. But barbecues are only made and bought in the spring and summer.

To cope with this seasonal demand, the company has to switch production from one product to the next. Workers have to be multiskilled as a result. Some of the machinery too is used to make parts for several different products. However, some of the equipment, such as the production line for tumble driers, has to be used less intensively in summer than in winter.

Research and design

Windrush Appliances has two designers who are responsible for developing new products. They use CAD packages in their design work. If components are to be bought from outside suppliers, the specifications are given using the CAD package. Equally, the CAD software can program the two CNC machines in the factory.

1. Using your knowledge of Business Studies, explain the meaning of the following terms, giving examples. You may draw your examples from the Case Study or any other source.
   (a) CAD package. (b) Zero defects. (c) Multiskilling. (d) Assembly line.
2. Explain how Windrush Appliances maintains quality in production.
3. Comment on the importance of just-in-time deliveries to (a) Windrush Appliances, (b) its customers and (c) its suppliers.
4. An existing customer approaches Windrush Appliances to ask whether it would consider supplying small upright freezers. Windrush Appliances has never made freezers or refrigerators. As the sales director of the company, write a report on whether or not to consider accepting this order. In your report:
   - consider the design and production challenges that this would bring;
   - consider the possible costs to the company if the customer was not satisfied with the product delivered;
   - consider the possible benefits to the company if the project was a success;
   - discuss the impact it would have on the finances of the company;
   - give a recommendation as to whether to go ahead, having considered all the arguments.

Accounting and finance

A fall in trade

The Jazz Place is a restaurant and bar. Up until last year it was a successful business, mainly because of passing trade. It was sited on Long Road which led into and out of town. But then the town council decided to make most of the town centre either a pedestrian area or a one way system. Long Road became a one way road out of town. The number of cars using it fell by 60 per cent. This helped cut congestion, but it ruined the trade of The Jazz Place. Within a year, sales turnover had halved.

Break-even

Patrick, the owner of The Jazz Place, has seen his profits falling over the past twelve months. He wants to know whether he can survive. He knows that his fixed costs, such as wages, rent, heating and lighting are £1 800 per week. He also knows that on average, customers spend £9 per person in the restaurant. Of that £9, one third (i.e. £3) represents the cost of the food and drink they consume. This £3 per customer is the only variable cost. He does a quick calculation and works out that he needs 300 customers per week to break even. Twelve months ago, he was getting 700 customers per week. Last week, this had fallen to 350.

Investigating the accounts

Patrick has just had a letter from the Inland Revenue saying that they intend to investigate his accounts. His accountant explains that they are suspicious because on the tax return he has just filed, there has been a big fall in profits. The accountant says there is nothing to worry about so long as he can satisfy them that trade has fallen sharply. The Inland Revenue have asked to see his profit and loss account and his balance sheet for the last tax year.

1. Using your knowledge of Business Studies, explain the meaning of the following terms, giving examples. You may draw your examples from the Case Study or any other source.
   (a) Sales turnover. (b) Profit.
   (c) Cash flow. (d) Repayments on a loan.
2. (a) Explain why the break-even point for The Jazz Place is 300 customers per week. To do this, draw a break-even chart showing on it (i) the fixed cost line; (ii) the total cost line; (iii) the total revenue line; (iv) the break-even point.
   (b) What was the margin of safety (i) a year ago; (ii) a week ago?
   (c) Patrick has not sacked any of his staff yet, even though the number of customers has fallen sharply. What would happen to the break-even point if he sacked some of the waiters?
3. (a) The Inland Revenue have asked to see last year's profit and loss account and balance sheet. What information is given in each of these?
   (b) Patrick took out a loan to refurbish the restaurant. This would have an impact on the profit and loss account and on the balance sheet. Explain what impact it might have.
4. Patrick needs to find the money to refurbish the restaurant.
   (a) List THREE ways in which he could raise this finance.
   (b) Discuss which of these three ways would be the best way for Patrick to raise the finance.

Reviving trade

Patrick has been considering various strategies to revive his trade. One strategy is to spend money on improving the decor of the restaurant. This would involve putting a new, larger and more colourful sign on the front of the restaurant and adding more lights. Inside, there would be new wall coverings, a new carpet, new tables and new crockery. He has had an estimate for this work and it comes to £30 000. It is a big investment. £10 000 could come from savings which he has made from past profits. The rest would probably have to be borrowed. Patrick is worried about the effect that the repayments would have on his cash flow, particularly if trade fell even more.

Calloway & Cardinal is a leather goods manufacturer based in Lancashire. It specialises in the production of goods related to the horse riding market, such as saddles. It employs 30 people.

Calloway & Cardinal needs to appoint a new secretary. The position requires the person to work at the reception area, taking all incoming telephone calls and dealing with visitors. It would also require the ability to write letters and handle a database using the Office Suite software. The salary is negotiable, but the company is looking to pay around £10 000 per year.

Calloway & Cardinal gained its Investors In People certification two years ago. The workforce is highly skilled because there is little opportunity for mechanisation of production. Customers are looking to buy a traditional hand made craft product.

   The company occasionally takes on an apprentice when another worker is coming up to retirement. The apprentice is taught all aspects of the leather trade before specialising in a particular craft. It is rare for an apprentice to leave the company once fully trained. Opportunities for working for other companies in the leather trade are not many and most, like Calloway & Cardinal, tend to train their own workers.

Calloway & Cardinal is a small company which prides itself on having good industrial relations. Four of the thirty workers belong to a trade union, but no union is officially recognised for bargaining purposes.

   Orders have been cut by 30 per cent because of the foot and mouth crisis. This has restricted movement of horses and people. Particularly important has been the cancellation of most horse trial events. These have traditionally been an important source of orders for the company. Jean Cardinal, one of the owners of the business, has assured staff that they will keep their jobs. However, all overtime has been cancelled. One of the craft workers who retired has not been replaced. Jean has also warned that she may not be able to afford to pay the normal £200 Christmas bonus to staff this year.

Jean Cardinal is frequently on the shop floor, talking to her staff. A couple of days a month, when she has no other important work to complete, she enjoys spending the day working alongside everyone else. She respects the traditional craft skills of her workers and discusses any changes in the product range or methods of manufacture with them. She employs a full time sales representative who is responsible for all aspects of marketing. Again, Jean consults this employee before making any decisions about marketing.

1. **Using your knowledge of Business Studies, explain the meaning of the following terms, giving examples. You may draw your examples from the Case Study or any other source.**
    (a) **Apprenticeship.** (b) **Investors in People.**
    (c) **Overtime.** (d) **Bonus.**
2. **Explain how Callow & Cardinal might (a) obtain applicants for the post of secretary and (b) select one of these applicants.**
3. **Discuss whether Jean Cardinal is an autocratic or democratic leader.**
4. (a) **What decisions has Jean Cardinal made because of the foot and mouth crisis?**
    (b) **Discuss whether these are likely to demotivate the staff.**

INDEX